Lansing

CAPITAL, CAMPUS, AND CARS

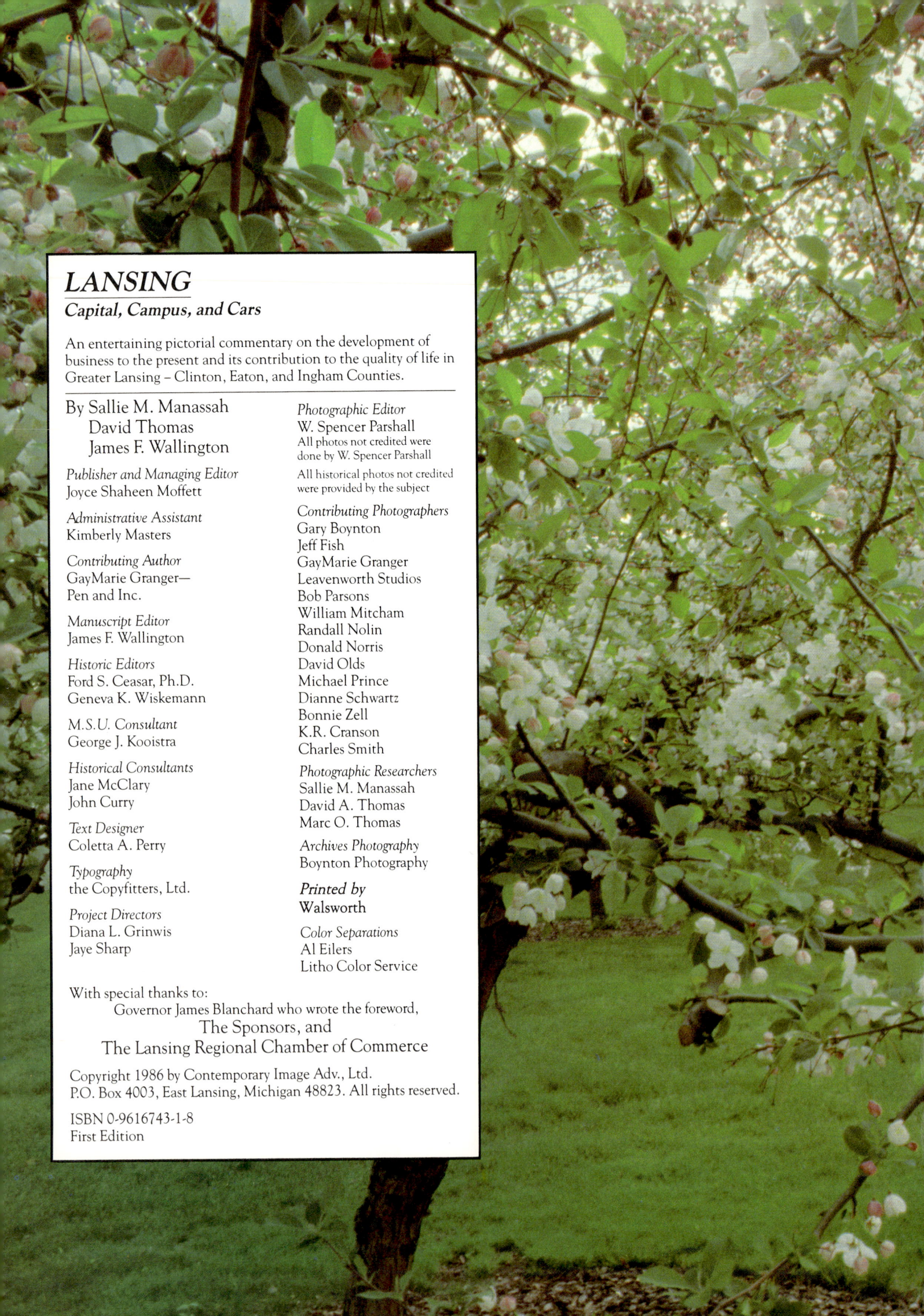

LANSING
Capital, Campus, and Cars

An entertaining pictorial commentary on the development of business to the present and its contribution to the quality of life in Greater Lansing – Clinton, Eaton, and Ingham Counties.

By Sallie M. Manassah
   David Thomas
   James F. Wallington

Publisher and Managing Editor
Joyce Shaheen Moffett

Administrative Assistant
Kimberly Masters

Contributing Author
GayMarie Granger—
Pen and Inc.

Manuscript Editor
James F. Wallington

Historic Editors
Ford S. Ceasar, Ph.D.
Geneva K. Wiskemann

M.S.U. Consultant
George J. Kooistra

Historical Consultants
Jane McClary
John Curry

Text Designer
Coletta A. Perry

Typography
the Copyfitters, Ltd.

Project Directors
Diana L. Grinwis
Jaye Sharp

Photographic Editor
W. Spencer Parshall
All photos not credited were
done by W. Spencer Parshall

All historical photos not credited
were provided by the subject

Contributing Photographers
Gary Boynton
Jeff Fish
GayMarie Granger
Leavenworth Studios
Bob Parsons
William Mitcham
Randall Nolin
Donald Norris
David Olds
Michael Prince
Dianne Schwartz
Bonnie Zell
K.R. Cranson
Charles Smith

Photographic Researchers
Sallie M. Manassah
David A. Thomas
Marc O. Thomas

Archives Photography
Boynton Photography

Printed by
Walsworth

Color Separations
Al Eilers
Litho Color Service

With special thanks to:
   Governor James Blanchard who wrote the foreword,
   The Sponsors, and
   The Lansing Regional Chamber of Commerce

Lansing

CAPITAL, CAMPUS, AND CARS

BY

SALLIE M. MANASSAH

DAVID A. THOMAS

JAMES F. WALLINGTON

PHOTOGRAPHY BY W. SPENCER PARSHALL

FOREWORD BY GOVERNOR JAMES BLANCHARD

JAMES J. BLANCHARD
GOVERNOR

Publication of an industrial and economic history of the Greater Lansing area could not come at a better time.

It comes as Michigan is aggressively seeking new businesses and new jobs. The story of our past, especially our recent dramatic economic comeback, can help focus on the strengths of this area and the opportunities it offers to present and future generations.

Equally important, Michigan is beginning to celebrate its Sesquicentennial, honoring the many achievements that have occurred in our state over the past 150 years. This book makes a valuable contribution to our celebration.

The Greater Lansing area plays an especially important role in shaping and projecting a positive image of Michigan. The capital of our state since 1847 and the home of many of our governmental agencies, Lansing is often the first city in Michigan seen by business leaders, politicians and educational leaders. Their perception of Michigan is often determined by their impressions of Lansing.

Lansing and its surrounding communities have much to offer, and they contribute greatly to Michigan's overall excellent quality of life. This is the home of Michigan State University, Lansing Community College and outstanding secondary school systems. This area has more than 300 industries, including the operations of world-leading corporations, excellent health care services and providers, thousands of acres of parks and playgrounds, more than 20 public golf courses, wildlife areas and a large, popular zoo. Cultural opportunities are enhanced by the Wharton Center, offering world class performances in the arts; the nationally known Impression 5 and R.E. Olds museums; and more than a dozen art galleries.

My wife Paula and I fell in love with this area while we were students at Michigan State. We feel fortunate indeed to be able to live in and enjoy Greater Lansing today. I hope that as you read this book and learn about this area's fascinating past, you will understand why so many people are working hard to make Lansing an even more outstanding place in which to live and work.

Sincerely,

James J. Blanchard
Governor

LANSING: CAPITAL, CAMPUS, AND CARS

SPONSORS AND BENEFACTORS

The Lansing community wishes to thank the following companies and individuals who contributed to the production of this book leaving behind a legacy — footsteps in the sand from the past — for the generations to come.

* Auto-Owners Insurance
* Blue Cross/Blue Shield
* Board of Water and Light
* Davenport College
* Delta Dental Insurance
* East Lansing, Michigan
* Estes Furniture
* Fairmont Builders
* Federal Mogul
* Fraser, Trebilcock, Davis & Foster
* Freeman & Smith, Architects
* General Motors
  Greater Lansing Board of Realtors

  Hager Fox Company
* Hannah Research & Technology
* Hasselbring-Clark
* Health Central
  Robert B. Hughes, CLU, ChFC
* Impression 5 Museum
* Ingham Medical Center
* Jackson National Life
  Koerts Glass & Paint Co.
* Lansing Community College
* Lansing General Hospital
* Lansing Public Schools
* Lansing Regional Chamber of Commerce

* Lee GMC Inc.
* Maner, Costerisan & Ellis
* Mayhood/Mertz Realtors
* Michigan Millers Insurance
* Michigan National Bank
* Michigan State University
* Michigan State University Clinical Center
  Mid-Michigan Rehabilitation
* Motor Wheel Corporation
* MST Freight Systems
* Oldsmobile
* Physician's Health Plan
* Roberts Corporation

* Saint Lawrence Hospital
* Sealed Power Corporation
  Senator William A. Sederburg
* Sheraton Hotel
* Sparrow Hospital
* Spartan Paper
  Representative Debbie Stabenow
* Story Inc.
  Union Federal Savings & Loan
  Universal Steel Company of Michigan
* WKAR-TV
* WLNS-TV
  Williams Auto-World

Denotes Corporate Sponsors who appear in a special "Partners in Lansing's Progress" Chapter that begins on page 165.

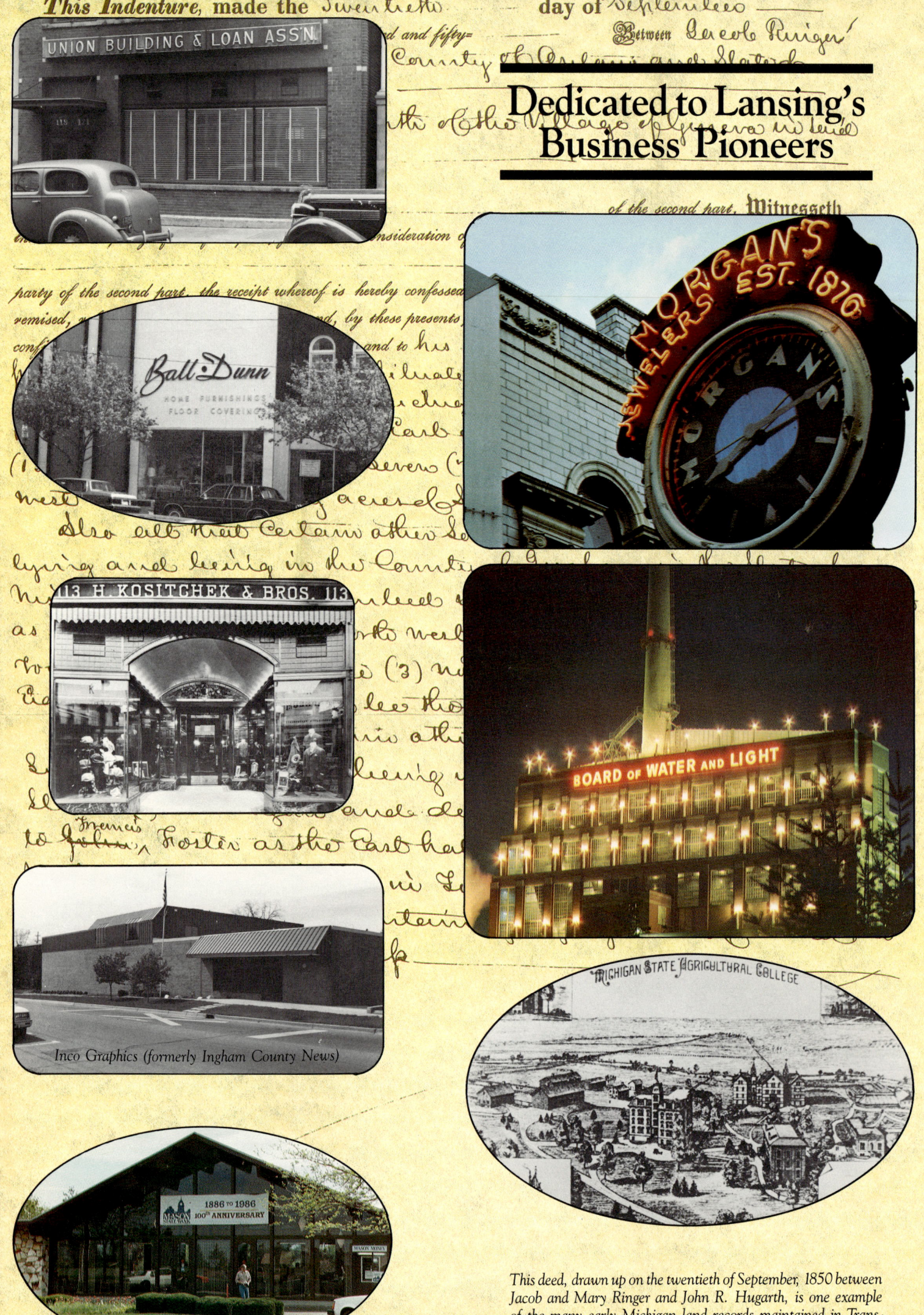

Dedicated to Lansing's Business Pioneers

This deed, drawn up on the twentieth of September, 1850 between Jacob and Mary Ringer and John R. Hugarth, is one example of the many early Michigan land records maintained in Transamerica Title Insurance Company title plants throughout Lansing.

Inco Graphics (formerly Ingham County News)

(originally the State Republican)

Clinton National Bank

Michigan Millers Insurance

THE STATE JOURNAL

Dancer's Fashions

Speaker, Hines & Thomas

INTERLAKE BUSINESS COLLEGE.

Now Davenport College

Consumers Power

Christman Company

Lansing School District

(formerly Simon Iron and Steel)

SUMMIT STEEL

Class at Cherry St. School

Photo B. Zell

Photo B. Zell

Photo B. Zell

X

Photo B. Zell

Historic Homes & Buildings

Photo B. Zell

Photo B. Zell

xi

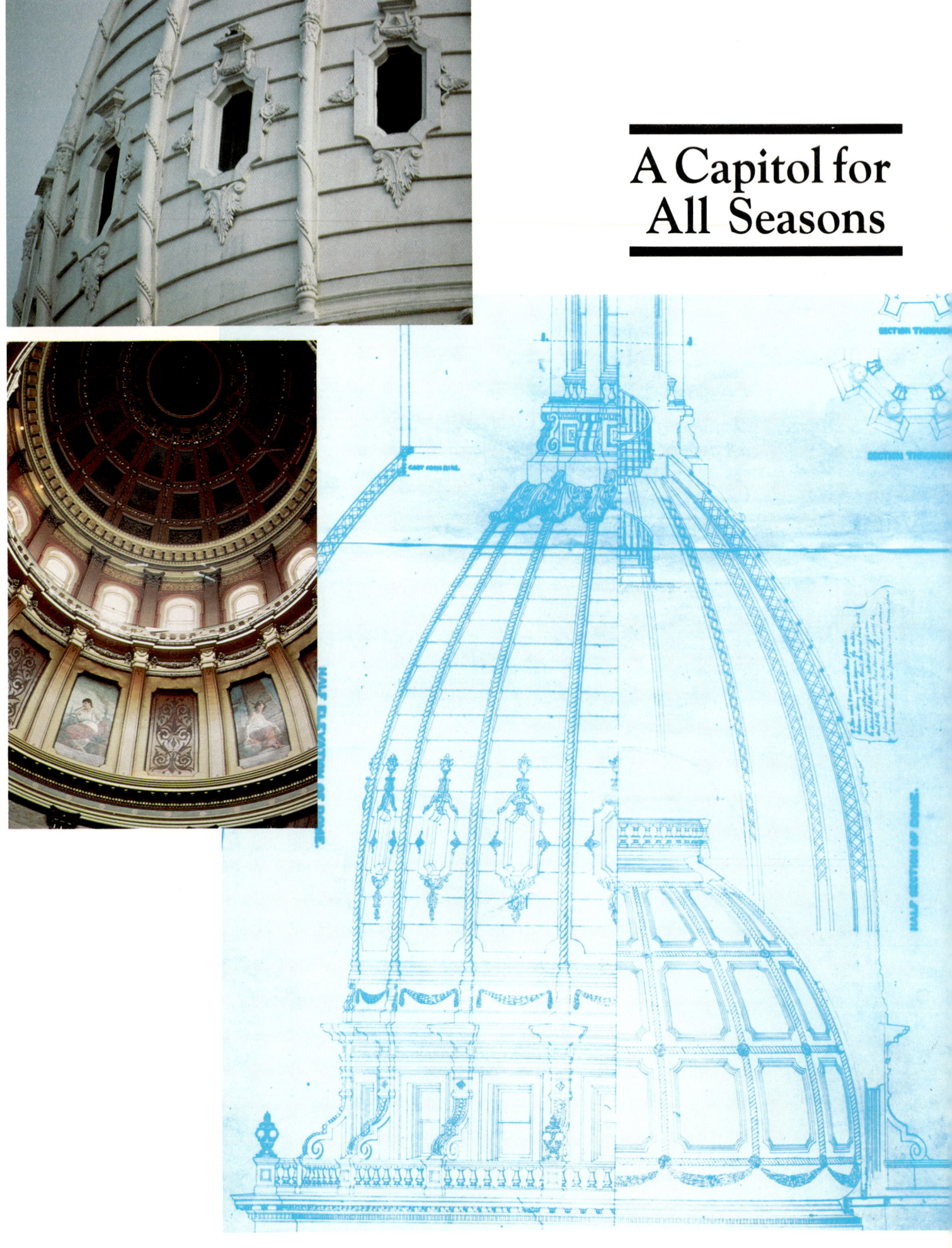

A Capitol for All Seasons

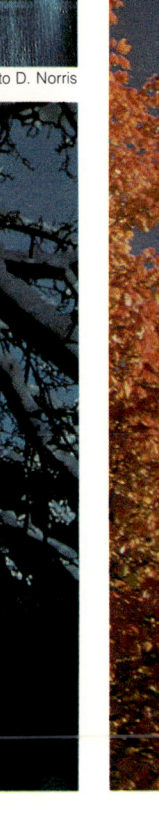

CONTENTS

William Harnden Foster. 10

Copyright 1910 Olds Motor Works.

Part I

Prologue

A Capital Decision

by James F. Wallington

Clark Sesquicentennial Farm Eagle, Clinton County

Deep-toned diesel trucks today roar overhead, carrying tons of auto parts to the nearby Olds plant. A few hundred yards away, other diesel monsters click along railroad tracks, hauling millions of dollars worth of Lansing-made automobiles to the Eastern seaboard and other markets.

Amidst this hubbub near Lansing's Main and River streets behind modern apartment buildings and aging homes and warehouses, two canoeists silently guide their craft out of the Red Cedar River into the Grand River.

These modern-day explorers are repeating a centuries-old ritual performed by countless Indians and scores of fur-seeking Frenchmen as well as other European settlers following the smoothest path to the big lake to the west. The Michigan State students paddle their canoe past the concrete towers that support the expressway carrying the powerful diesel giants of commerce. The thunder of the trucks and automobiles rumbling overhead persuades them to paddle quickly down the sluggish stream that never quite lived up to its grand name.

They barely glance at the land they pass in their modern-day explorations, thus joining other canoeists and boatmen in overlooking the territory beyond the river banks over the centuries. This land at the confluence of the Grand and the smaller river once named simply the Cedar was just a passing forest scene for Indians, explorers, fur trappers, surveyors and early pioneers. Except for an occasional, insignificant native encampment, Indian or white man did not stop to set up homes, farms or shops in the area of the Big Bend until the mid-1830s.

Historians described the area as forbidding because of its thick forest and marshlands. Ironically, it was this slight that led to the Big Bend area's election as the capital in the forest in 1847. (The Big Bend is the stretch of the Grand River that enters Ingham County on the southwest side of the city, flowing as far east as its confluence with the Red Cedar where it twists north for about two miles, passing through downtown Lansing two and half blocks from the Capitol to north Lansing where it makes a hard turn west and flows back into Eaton County on its way to Lake Michigan.)

While the wilderness that was to become Lansing was not disturbed, much of the surrounding territory was explored and developed. The Hopewell and Point Peninsula Indians, the Potawatomi, the Sauks and the Mascoutens traveled the two rivers and roamed the area for centuries. French explorers did not set foot in the Lower Peninsula until the mid-1660s after reaching the Upper Peninsula in 1622. The French, seeking the elusive passage to Asia, reached the U.P. through a series of rivers, lakes and portages from the St. Lawrence River to the Ottawa River, Lake Nipissing and Georgian Bay.

There is no record when the first French explorers or trappers traveled the Grand River past Lansing. According to respected Lansing historian Birt Darling, the Grand was first recorded on the "Map of Canada" in 1703. It would be another century-plus before settlers considered the area. Meanwhile, the French, British and the Americans as well as the Indians struggled for control of the Northwest Territory.

As the French influence ebbed in favor of the British and eventually the Americans through the French-Indian Wars and the Revolutionary War, the land near the confluence of the Grand and Cedar escaped unscathed. There were no white settlers to challenge the tribes whose warriors ventured hundreds of miles to support the French and their conquerors, the British. While European and Indian blood flowed at battles in Detroit, Monroe and Mackinaw, the Grand and Cedar flowed untainted.

Darling notes in his history of Lansing, *City in the Forest*, the first known description of what was to become Lansing was in 1790 by Hugh Heward paddling the Grand looking for trade, furs and the elusive Northwest Passage for British interests. He spotted two Indian families encamped on the east side of the river between Main and Michigan streets near the confluence of the Grand and the Cedar.

Central Michigan was open to American traders by the treaty of Greenville (Ohio) in 1795. In a seemingly rapid series of moves, the area evolved as a political entity – split off from the Northwest Territory as part of the Indiana Territory in 1803 and Michigan Territory in 1805. An 1807 treaty opened the Eastern Michigan interior to settlement. To the south and toward Detroit the movement of white settlers stirred the tribes to confront the Americans as allies to the British in the War of 1812 under a new leader, Tecumseh of the Shawnees of northern Indiana.

Darling pointed out the significance: *"One of Tecumseh's aides who frequently made the trip down the Grand River Trail (not the river but an early Indian path that became the early plank road and Grand River Avenue) to Canadian soil was stocky little Okemos, one of the chiefs of the mixed bands of Ottawas, Chippewas and Potawatomies. Legend had it that he was a nephew of Pontiac. Legend or not, he held power by virtue of his own audacity, and when Tecumseh's couriers brought the war belts to his villages, his warriors were in the vanguard.*

"For the redmen of interior valley it was the last stand. . . Tecumseh was killed and Okemos seriously wounded. The little chief (who had a home in the area named after him) vowed he and his people would fight no more. . .

"The War of 1812 opened the gates to Michigan Territory. Kentuckians, Ohioans and Pennsylvlanians who fought here returned with tales of good lands free for the asking. . . A trickle of settlers began to come into southeastern Michigan."

This trickle still had not disturbed the trees towering over Lansing, but it led to ambitious pioneering of the lower counties along the Indiana-Ohio border between Detroit and Chicago and into the Saginaw Valley. Near both the source and the mouth of the Grand River, there was settlement as the foundations of modern-day Jackson and Grand Rapids were being formed. Other sites on the Grand, such as Eaton Rapids and Ionia, were attracting settlers.

Eaton and Clinton counties abutting Lansing were being settled while nary a soul roamed the Lansing bush and swamp. Eaton attracted settlers diverting from the roads between Detroit and Chicago while DeWitt and the rest of Clinton attracted pioneers by the way of already-established Shiawassee County. Those headed for and beyond Clinton used a road from Detroit to Shiawassee and then the Saginaw River watershed to portage to the Looking Glass and Maple rivers which carried them toward Ionia and Grand Rapids, completely missing Ingham County.

This settling of farms and communities encircling Lansing through the rest of the decade following the War of 1812, the 1820s and 1830s was the spinoff of a seemingly endless migration of settlers from the northern portion of the original 13 states, particularly New York and Vermont. Their trek was eased by the opening in 1825 of the Erie Canal which fed ships sailing Lake Erie bound for Toledo, Monroe and Detroit.

The lands were opened by the Treaty of Saginaw signed with the Chippewas in 1819. Chief Okemos was one of the concurring chiefs who ceded land running west of the state's prinicipal meridian (where Meridian

Chief Okemos by John DeMartelly
Commissioned by Capitol Federal Savings & Loan

Courtesy Leavenworth Studios

Road was built in Ingham County about halfway between Okemos and Williamston). The ceded territory was inside the meridian generally from Alpena to Jackson, west to Kalamazoo and then north through Ionia to Higgins Lake.

William Webber, marveling at the lack of settlers in the heart of Michigan, wrote in an article on the Treaty of Saginaw that "it is difficult to imagine that the entire Saginaw Valley, with the present site of Lansing,. . . were, until 1819, the property of the Indians, with no right on the part of the white man to settle within it."

While the Americans were clearing the land for farming and settling at Charlotte, Howell, Middleville, Ionia, Lyons, Portland, Owosso and DeWitt, further political actions were shaping what would become Lansing. The territorial legislature created the borders of Ingham County in October of 1829 and the land was put on sale in 1830. But these were surveyor projections on a map; still no people in Ingham. The county would not become officially operative until it had sufficient population in another nine years.

Meanwhile, the traditional Indian and French-trader paths were evolving into crude and often-impassable roads consisting of, for the most part, two deep ruts. They were not surveyed and set out in any fashion; they went where the Indians wanted to go. Even the surveyors had difficulty moving along them.

ORIGINS

Birthplaces of Heads of Family in Lansing According to the 1860 Census

State (or country)	1st Ward	2nd Ward	3rd Ward	Total
New York	109	104	74	287
Germany	42	30	16	88
Ohio	8	7	21	36
Vermont	12	8	6	26
Ireland	10	8	8	26
England	5	6	13	24
Pennsylvania	3	5	14	22
Canada	6	2	8	16
Massachusetts	8	2	6	16
Connecticut	8	3	2	13
Michigan	4	1	6	11
Other*	13	13	8	34
Total	228	189	182	599

Other includes New Hampshire, New Jersey, Maine, Rhode Island, France, Belgium, Maryland, Nova Scotia, Virginia, Kentucky and Scotland.

The struggle of a trek in the fall of 1833 by DeWitt pioneer David Scott was described in a 1895 publication: ". . . he, with his wife and two sons. . . began their pilgrimage (from Ann Arbor) toward their new home (DeWitt) in big wagons drawn by oxen. They took one horse and 17 head of cattle. . . and were several days on the road. They forded rivers, drove into swamps, were often mired and were obliged to pitch their tents wherever night overtook them."

Often the pioneers hacked out their own paths, as the daughter of Ingham pioneer Joab Page described: "We were obliged to cut our road ahead of our teams."

Despite the hardships, the pioneers pushed on, as Page's daughter reported on one of the more heavily traveled trails near Jackson: "We counted in one day over 60 covered wagons. It was almost a continual string of teams, each carrying a family and their entire possessions."

But these wagons were not heading toward northern Ingham County. There were no clear trails feeding Lansing until after it was declared the capital in the 1840s. The major trails skirted the Big Bend area. The Shiawassee Trail was forged from Grand Blanc in 1831 into what is now the Corunna-Owosso area, opening DeWitt and the rest of Clinton County (it possibly was

followed by the Scott family). One of two Grand River trails was forged through Byron and "meandered through the woods, broad in spots, lost in others." Alfred and Benjamin Williams hacked out a road along the north shore of the Looking Glass river to the Maple where it joined the Grand in the Lyons area west of Lansing. There were roads to Marshall and Chicago with branches to Bellevue, Middleville, Ionia, Portland and Charlotte.

Three other crude trails slowly developed that became important to the establishment of Lansing. The Dexter trail (which still exists) from Ann Arbor was used by some of the county's earliest settlers in the late 1830s; many settlers used the southern Grand River trail that ran north through what became North Lansing (this road became important to the settlement of Lansing when the capital was established). A trail north from Jackson was ordered by Congress in 1839 to become a road, not to reach Lansing, but already established Clinton County.

The roads not only opened crude paths to new settlements, but fostered commerce. David Scott, after settling in the DeWitt area, soon built an inn or public house "because of the influx of land-lookers and settlers, who followed so rapidly. . ." "Scott's Place" is regarded as the beginning of DeWitt and one of the first commercial enterprises in what is now Greater Lansing.

Settlers found both the traveling and day-to-day living arduous. More trials of the Scotts were related in a pioneer historical journal: "Their nearest neighbors. . . were 40 miles away. They were obliged to go to Ann Arbor for their milling, blacksmithing and groceries. David went to Dexter, a distance of 80 miles on foot for a doctor, who came on horseback, stayed two days, put a $50 bill in his pocket and returned home. . . there was no hay here for fodder for the cattle, and trees were felled to supply this deficiency. . . At one time the cattle strayed away and were gone several days. When found they were on the grounds now occupied by the State Capitol."

Mrs. Allen Lounsberry, a pioneer who helped found Rochester Colony near St. Johns, faced "drawing supplies from Pontiac or Detroit through a still unbroken wilderness; losing the year's supplies as the result of depredations of wild animals; no neighbors except the forest peopled by beasts and red men; no schools. . ."

The Addison Cook family related that "brush and trees had to be cut before a house could be erected. Wild animals were numerous and troublesome. Mr. Cook had to get up many times in the night and drive Bruin from his pig pen. The old Dutch fire place with its stick chimney, crane, hooks, kettle, with an occasional tin baker, were the cooking utensils."

Another pioneer family wrote to their relatives in New York state in early spring that "Farmers (if such that may be called, who live in log huts with a garden spot cleared) are generally out of hay, fodder, or grain to feed their cattle, and some families lack a sufficient quantity for themselves.

"Potatoes are very scarce. After riding two whole days and making inquiry for two weeks, I have been able to buy 25 bushels, though money would not buy them. I was obliged to exchange the oats I had saved for seed to get them. . ."

But not all pioneer families were deprived. Mrs. Adelaide Aldrich Jones wrote of pioneering in Delhi Township: "When the family came from New York, they only brought their clothing, bedding and dishes. . . they soon had a homemade bedstead, a trundle bed, table and four benches. . . My mother said they were never pinched for food, everything planted grew so profusely and my father was a good workman. They soon had a cow or two, and. . . there were pigs in a pen. But money, real money, was a scarce article."

The flow of settlers along the path from Lake Erie to Lake Michigan and Chicago spawned spin-offs into the lower Ingham County wilderness in the early 1830s. Stockbridge Township, in southern Ingham, gets credit for many of Ingham's firsts by Ford S. Ceasar in his *Bicentennial History of Ingham County.* It was the site of the county's first settler, a David Rogers in 1835. That's the same year Rachel Lowe and Hiram Stocking are credited as having the first marriage in the county. Later in the year, a son was born to the couple, the county's first birth (the child died shortly afterwards).

Activity around Lansing quickened with current suburbs settled earlier than Lansing. In 1832, Okemos was the site of the first land purchase recorded in Ingham County; in 1834, Delta Mills was settled and became the site of a dam and a mill; in 1836, a mill was established in the center of the county on Sycamore Creek at what was named Mason in 1838 and which became the county seat in 1840.

But Lansing would *not* languish for long. By 1836 there was some rustling in the underbrush of Lansing Township. Frederick Bushnell came across the falls on the Grand River in North Lansing and visualized supplying waterpower to a community; after buying a plot of land, he died a year later in Louisiana. A surveyor, J.T. Durand, reached the area stretching south of the Big Bend to what is now Mt. Hope Avenue. He mapped out lots for a development called Biddle City

for Jackson brothers William and Jerry Ford who sold plots to speculators. Hurt by the panic of 1837, the project collapsed before nary a settler set foot on the land.

However, the chopping of axes and the pounding of hammers echoed in the thick forest just two miles west of the ill-fated Biddle City. Jacob Frederick Cooley, who earlier moved back to New York after settling in Leslie, became Lansing Township's first permanent resident in 1837. Despite an unhappy experience in Leslie, the tailor from New York State first inspected Biddle City with one of the Ford brothers. Instead he

Recreation of 1847 Store Window   Courtesy of Smith Floral

entered a deed for land between Jolly Road and the Grand River along Waverly Road near the present Waverly Road bridge, outside the Big Bend area.

So Lansing got its genesis from unsuccessful land developers and a previously unsuccessful settler who was a tailor, not a farmer or woodsman.

Meanwhile, Michigan was admitted to the union in 1837 and Ingham attracted sufficient numbers of settlers (822 inhabitants in 1837) to become a formal county in 1838. The county was named after a member of President Jackson's cabinet, Secretary of the Treasury Samuel D. Ingham, who never set foot in the county.

Plenty of obstacles confronted Cooley: he had no shelter that first winter except for a felled tree, branches, leaves and dirt. He nearly drowned near

Stevens T. Mason,
first Michigan governor

Courtesy State of Michigan Archives

Dimondale when his raft broke while he returned from Jackson with winter provisions; he would have frozen to death after the incident except for the kindness of an Indian couple. Cooley's family arrived in early summer of 1838 after a trek during which their hired horses and wagons were confiscated, forcing them to walk. They became lost and Lucy Cooley, leaving her sons Jacob and Lansing sitting on a stump, went looking for help; she luckily stumbled across one of the few settlers in the area between Jackson and Lansing. After celebrating the first Fourth of July in Lansing Township, the family ran out of provisions and Jacob Cooley nearly died from an illness. After he recovered, he left the family in the care of Indians and returned to Jackson to work as a tailor.

The turning point came for the Cooleys during the separation of 14 months when Jacob's tailoring earned money for survival. Lansing Township's first birth of a non-native child, Nathan Cooley, came January 6, 1840, while the father was away. Before returning from Jackson, Jacob Cooley promoted his new home, starting a trickle of settlers toward Lansing Township.

Another family attracted by Biddle City settled two miles southeast of the Cooleys in 1837. Believing he was swindled by the Fords' project, Joseph North settled near the Lansing-Delhi township line and challenged the Cooleys' claim as first in the township, including first settlers and the naming of the township. The township (thus, eventually the cities) was named by North after the New York State communities of Lansing and East Lansing, those after a New York patriot, John Lansing. The township was officially created in February, 1842, and was actually the seat of state government when it was first moved out of Detroit in 1848.

Besides Bushnell, the Fords, Cooleys and the Norths, others from New York were buying property in the Big Bend area. (The New York State invasion would continue unabated. By 1860, 48 per cent of the 599 households in Lansing would be headed by persons who migrated from New York State.) In 1835, speculators James Seymour and William H. Townsend bought sections north of the Fords' Biddle City in what is now the heart of downtown Lansing.

Absentee-owner Seymour grew impatient waiting for development, according to historian Darling, and sold 109 acres to John W. Burchard, also of Rochester, N.Y., in 1841. This was the land in North Lansing bought by Bushnell and purchased from his heirs by Seymour.

Boarding his family in Mason, Burchard set out to build a cabin for the family, a dam and a mill, which he completed in 1843 and moved his family north. This location which saw dreams die in the untimely death of Bushnell, was again ill-fated. When the Grand flooded with the spring thaw of 1844, a portion of the

Samuel D. Ingham

Courtesy Lansing Public Library

dam gave way and Burchard set out to inspect and possibly repair the break; Burchard's canoe overturned in the turbulent water and he drowned.

The property reverted to Seymour who was not about to give up; he was referred to Joab Page who was doing excellent work at the Rolfe Settlement prospering in Aurelius Township. Page, another New Yorker, agreed for the unheard of wage of $2.50 a week to take 11 members of the settlement, including the Rolfe clan and other able-bodied workers in the area, to finish the dam. They were to harness the flow of the Grand to supply power to the sawmill also under construction in the area that would be called Seymour Settlement, Lower Town, and North Lansing.

The project was marked with the birth of the first white child within what would become the city limits of Lansing: W. Marshall Pease was born July 4, 1845, to worker George Pease and his wife Orselia. The symbolism of this birth on Fourth of July and the successful completion of Lansing's first commercial venture set the stage for the establishment of the state capital.

However, the story of the capital moving from Detroit is one of commercial and political opportunism: Commercial because Seymour wanted a return on his land investments; political because out-state legislators did not want the capital in Wayne County and couldn't decide on an established outstate settlement. It was easier to follow the dictum of the constitution of 1835 to select a permanent site by 1847 by choosing a "non-place" in the middle of a wilderness than to pick one of the numerous established sites, including DeWitt, Lyons, Caledonia Township in Shiawassee Township and Eaton Rapids. However, Ann Arbor,

Jackson (then named Jacksonburgh) and Marshall, all served by a railroad, held the upper hand through much of the legislative haggling in 1846 and 1847 for a new site.

The 1847 legislature became hopelessly embroiled over such arguments as that Detroit, the capital since 1805, was open to foreign (English) attack across the Detroit River and that Ann Arbor, Jackson and Marshall were not central to the interior of the state. So land speculator Seymour and Ingham County Rep. Joseph K. Kilbourne entered the stalemate. Kilbourne, who fled the Patriot's War in Canada, was lobbying for a county of 5,268 inhabitants and a township of eight registered voters when he presented Seymour's offer of free land to build the Capitol in Lansing Township.

Maps he distributed showing the distances from different spots in the state helped stem the howl of laughter that greeted Kilbourne's proposal. The maps, which ignored the fact that there were no railroads or other good roads to the area of the Big Bend in the Grand, strengthened the so-called Northern Rangers, who were legislators who backed locating the capital north of the railroad from Detroit through Ann Arbor, Jackson and Marshall.

Historians generally agree that the Seymour's map indicating the advantages and the motion to place the Capitol in Lansing Township were greeted as a "huge joke" and was "received by a general laugh." But the growing trend around the country was to place the capitols in central, uncrowded areas e.g. Washington and Springfield, Illinois.

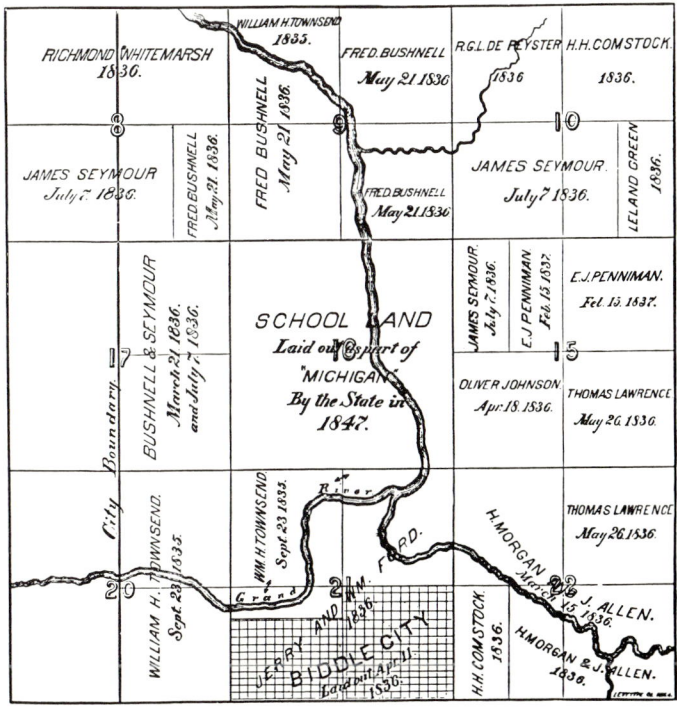

And, according to Rep. Enos Goodrich, a member of the legislature in 1847, it was no joke. The "map and red lines did more in attracting attention to Lansing than any or all speeches in the halls of legislation," he told the Michigan Pioneer Society in 1885.

Astute political journalist Willard Baird agreed in 1955 when he wrote in the *State Journal's Centennial Edition*:

"By now the hilarity of the house action was fading as other towns sensed that the Lansing location indeed presented a serious threat to their own plans for winning the capital. . . The members from Wayne County, who voted for the joke, now hung their heads in sorrow and mortification, while nothing could arrest the onward march of legislation. . . On March 9 (1847), after every device for delay and amendment had been exhausted, the final senate vote was taken. The Lansing Township location was approved 12-8."

Of course, newspapers in the southern counties opposed the action. *The Niles Republican* wrote on March 13, 1847, that it was "astonished," also remarking that Lansing "is an out of the way place and it is years before it can be approached with any convenience. We hope the governor will stick (use) his veto. . ."

The *Coldwater Republican* pointed out the following advantage three days later: "In case of invasion by a foreign foe, the Capitol of Michigan would be safe from attack. No enemy could ever prudently go as far into the interior for the purpose of destruction. . . The archives of the state are more safe and secure at Lansing than they would be at Detroit."

The legislature created a three-man commission to find an exact site for the Capitol and provided $10,000 for construction of temporary buildings by Christmas Day, nine months away, and in time for the 1848 session.

The commission, greeted by Seymour agent Joab Page who guided them to the site offered by Seymour, added irony in shunning Seymour's free land in favor of the federally-designated school section 16 (bounded by South Washington, West Allegan, South Capitol and West Washtenaw).

However, Seymour saw the Capitol placed adjacent to his and Townsend's lands. And most importantly, Lansing finally had a reason to exist.

The State Capitol in Detroit before relocation to Lansing

Chapter 1

The Road to Growth

by James F. Wallington

Everett House

The centuries old tranquility at the confluence of the Grand and Cedar was about to end forever as Lansing's meager population set out to build the home of a state government. But it was not going to be easy. Save for Joab Page's sawmill and lodge for a small collection of people near what is now called North Lansing, the area was bereft of the needs of building a new Capitol.

After selecting the site by May 22, 1847, the three-man commission had until the end of the year to meet the Michigan Legislature's dictum of preparing a place suitable for conducting the business of the state. They faced this task in the middle of a wilderness that lacked roads and a work force. There wasn't a hotel to lodge the workers and eventually the legislators.

One opponent of the Lansing site was not far from the truth when he said: "Shall we take the capital from (Detroit) and stick it down in the woods and mud of Grand River, amid choking miasma – where even the woodsman's axe has never awaken its echoes, where the howl of wolves, where the hissing of massasaugas and the groans of bullfrogs resound to the hammer of the woodpecker and the solitary notes of the nightingale?" In answer, another legislator suggested an appropriation for signposts "to direct the members of the next legislature to the seat of government. . . "

The site found a defender in the editor of the *Expounder* in Marshall which fought to become the new capital. He wrote on July 6, 1847:

"We had the pleasure. . . of visiting the new Capitol and we must say that in the location and general appearance, we were happily disappointed. Whatever doubt there may have been, and perhaps still is, about the policy of selecting a spot off from the present main thoroughfares of the state, there can be no dispute about the fact that commissioners have made a beautiful location. The school section upon the center of which the Capitol is to be built, is the handsomest body of heavily timbered land we have ever seen. The whole town as laid out is covered with majestic elm, beech, maple, oak, walnut and sycamore trees in great abundance."

The next eight months saw a minor miracle take place in the Big Bend of the Grand River. Men thirsty for work emerged from the wilderness to clear the forest from the Capitol site; settlers and entrepeneurs appeared to create the first businesses or to stake out sites for later sale; and the Grand River became a highway for rafts or flatboats carrying people, food, materials and other supplies from Jackson and Eaton Rapids. (Lansing's first railroad was still 13 years in the future.)

The *Niles Republican*, an early critic, took a milder approach on July 24, 1847: "On Thursday, last week we had a flying visit from Col. J.L. Glenn, Superintendent of the public buildings at the new capital. He speaks favorably of the location, and informs us that about 30 buildings are now in process of erection, and

Above: *Oldest known photograph of Lansing*
Right: *Hotels Wentworth and Kerns*

THE LANSING HOUSE

Gen. Lafayette C. Baker should have received more than $17,000 for the capture of President Abraham Lincoln's assassin, John Wilkes Booth. Congress, however, according to its records, awarded him only $3,750. Congress, perhaps, felt he had made a fortune since "he was building a big hotel in Lansing." The hotel was the Lansing House, completed in 1867, which was reportedly constructed from funds Baker got for the capture of Booth.

The Lansing House cost about $100,000 to construct, so Baker obviously came up with more than just his share of the reward money for the project. Funding for the hotel more than likely came from what the detective had stashed away from earnings by capturing bounty jumpers and traitors, and possibly from Lansing investors. Baker was the chief of the United States Secret Service, and mastermind behind the plan to capture Booth. His cousin, Lt. Luther B. Baker, received $4,000 for the part he played in the actual pursuit and capture.

The Bakers, determined to make their fortune, did come to Lansing to start work on the hotel, erected on the corner of Washington Avenue and Washtenaw Street, where the Knapp's Office Center now stands. The architect chosen for the project was Israel Gillett, who also designed Lansing's first capitol building and Central High School.

Newspaper reports boasted the Lansing House was "not inferior to any other in the State." The Lansing State Republican outlined each floor of the hotel as the project neared completion in November of 1866. The paper described the fourth-floor rooms as "among the

Lafayette and Luther Baker

finest in the whole house, so that the guests of this hotel need have no fears of the 'attic,' with its usual concomitant evils and vexations."

For years, the Lansing House, just a few blocks from the Capitol Building, was a favorite spot for legislators.

"It was a place to relax and discuss cultural aspects of the day in art and music, yes, and in state politics," historian Birt Darling said of the Lansing House. "And many a governor was made or unmade in the quiet corners of that lobby, or, more likely, in the hotel bar on the south end of the structure."

Lafayette Baker died in 1868, and the rest of the Bakers soon sold their interests in the hotel. Henry Downey took over the hotel in 1887, and it then became known as the "Downey." In all, the brick building experienced three major fires, and stayed in business until 1936 when it was razed to make way for the new J.W. Knapp store.

After the legacy of the Booth capture and the Lansing House, the Bakers kept making names for themselves. One of Lt. Baker's sons, Luther H. Baker, became mayor of East Lansing. Another son, Arthur D. Baker, was one of several family members connected with the Michigan Miller's Insurance Company, serving as company president. Arthur's son, Stannard L. Baker, later also became president of the company.

Lt. L.B. Baker and Buckskin

—Marc Thomas

that at present they have four stores, two good taverns and a large number of mechanics."

The travails of the capital commissioners in reaching Lansing were typical of the trek faced by others, as described in Justin Kestenbaum's Lansing history, *Out of a Wilderness:*

". . . it took three days to travel through the woods from Jackson, the nearest rail terminal, to Lansing Township. At Mason, they found that the swollen Sycamore Creek had washed out the bridges. A log was felled across the stream but commissioner David Smart refused to cross in that manner, and a raft had to be built. Between Mason and Lansing, the road was 'simply terrible.' The last 10 miles 'were nearly impassable by reason of the overflow of the streams', in low-lying places, the logs of the corduroy roads were afloat."

The early arrivals were welcomed to lodge at the Page settlement in Lower Town, but some entrepeneurs met the needs of housing by building hotels or rooming houses. The earliest hotel was erected in 1847 by James Seymour in Lower Town, so called because it was down stream on the Grand (also referred to as Dam town; the other areas of the Village of Michigan were Middle Town near the Capitol and Upper Town, up stream near the confluence of the Grand and Cedar rivers). A rooming house and dining hall was built by Smith Tooker, who became a prominent bridge builder.

Three hotels were concentrated at Upper Town on Main Street between Washington Avenue and River and Cedar streets (a wooden bridge spanned the Grand River in this area). The National House was built east of the river; west of the river the Michigan House was built on the corner of River and Main streets and Benton House on Washington Avenue at Main Street. A fifth hotel, the Lansing House, eventually was built of rough cut boards nearer the Capitol at Washington Avenue and Washtenaw Street.

The placid setting in the Big Bend area of the Grand River was disturbed nearly 24 hours a day by cutting, building and burning. Historian Darling describes the scene: "By day the smudge of burning brush and timber clouded the summer skies. By night the huge bonfires lighted the heavens, winking through the thinning forests as the workers sweated and strained to carve out streets and put up the Capitol by Christmas Day."

Willard Baird wrote that *"Board shanties and tents sprang up like mushrooms to house the workers and their families. There was neither time nor opportunity for observing the social niceties. Proper housing accommodations were practically unknown, and it was not uncommon*

Old and New Capitol Buildings

for as many as 30 persons to find themselves crowded at night in a field bed in a board shanty."

Sarah Dart, the daughter of Christopher Darling (who helped strengthen Burchard's dam and opened a store and bakery), recalled boarding house living conditions in the fall of 1847: *"It had a gabled roof, with just sufficient attic room for beds for the male members of the house. The ground floor was used for dining and sitting rooms, with possibly the kitchen partitioned off from one end. . . The other end of the room was partitioned off with bed-quilts for two sleeping rooms. One of these contained two beds separated only by a few inches of space, one occupied by my father and brother; the other by my aunt and myself."*

The two-story, white wood-framed Capitol capped with a belfry was completed in time for the 1848 session in the block now bounded by Washington and Capitol avenues and Allegan and Washtenaw streets southeast of the present Capitol. That was about all that was ready, except for scattered stores and four hotels. However, it was not enough. Stark realization hit the 88 legislators as they reached the raw community for the first session scheduled on Jan. 1, 1848.

Dart describes some of their problems: *"During the first few sessions of the legislature the members found much difficulty in securing board and rooms, the Benton, Lansing and Seymour hotels being about the only available places, these being usually well filled with transients. As they laboriously wended their way through mud and mire, around stumps, over logs and through brush, many an invective was hurled against the instigators of the removal of the State Capitol into this wilderness."*

Reporting to the Michigan State Pioneer Society in 1878, O.A. Jenison recalled that *"Bedrooms with the necessary appendages were out of the question.. . . the first three weeks I was here I do not remember of seeing a bed but once, and the pleasure of sleeping on one during this time was totally denied me. So I did the next best thing I could under the circumstances; I sat in a chair in the barroom every night,"* he continued *"and in the morning a number of us would go out doors, build a fire and turn round, like a turkey on a spit, to keep warm. But I do not speak of this complainingly; being young, healthy and hearty, and I rather enjoyed the fun."*

Jenison recounted that he found an office and "got a bedstead and a bedtick, gave a man a dollar for straw enough to fill the tick, and thought myself about as well off as any of my neighbors." One legislator reported he was able to board at a private home with some of the top state officials and lawmakers, but he was forced to put a bed in his Capitol office for lodging.

The *Pioneer History of Ingham County* reports that prominent Lansing men, fearing legislators would opt to return to Detroit, "made a house to house canvas to have citizens who had large comfortable homes take in the members of the legislature to room and board."

While the first sessions in the Capitol were filled with debate over the construction of plank roads and the changing the name of the capital from Michigan to Lansing (with Aloda, Onekama and Algoma some of the other contending names), the rest of the community of the less than 1,000 souls set out to perform the business of servicing the capital, the legislators, the civil servants, their families, and other settlers.

Indeed, the building of the capitol had a snowball

effect. By 1850 the federal census showed 1,029 residents in Lansing, compared to less than 100 estimated in 1845. Alvin Rolfe, son-in-law of Joab Page, told an historical group in 1895 that the Benton was the first brick building in the city: "The brick was manufactured at lower town by a man named Beal in 1847. The first grist mill was built in 1848. . . Joab Page and his sons-in-law helped build it."

Much of the early Lansing industry was built to take advantage of the Grand River waterpower, thus concentrating toward Lower Town where Joab Page built Seymour's sawmill, according to historian Samuel W. Durant who published his *History of Ingham and Eaton Counties* in 1880. A flour and grist mill was built in 1848 by A.N. Hart, E.B. Danforth and H.H. Smith, followed by the Pearl Mills in 1855, Pepper Mill in 1856, and Oriental Mills in 1857.

Heavier industry got its start in 1848 when an iron works was built; Fred Alton & Son started a barrel factory on River Street; and D.W. Buck started making chairs and other furniture. The Standard Castings Corp. had its start in 1850 and was still going in 1920, according to Dr. F.N. Turner's report in the *Pioneer History of Ingham County*. John W. Butler established a marble works in 1852; Lansing had a pottery by 1853, and a tannery by 1856. In 1857 James, Richard and George Turner started a foundry and machine shop.

The *Pioneer History* reported that saw mills "were

*Scofield & Parmalee Mills approximately 1870*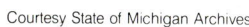

busy with great amounts of wood hauled into Lansing by ox teams the bells around the necks of which could be heard clanging through the streets. . . ."

The commissioners who platted the capital intended for the city's commercial center to be located several blocks south of the Capitol near the Grand and Cedar rivers, which explains how Main Street got its name although it is mainly a residential street today. "They apparently intended the residence section should be in (the) central part of town around the Capitol square," unofficial city historian J.P. Edmonds wrote. "For a few years this proved to be true."

"The first mercantile venture to be opened was the general store of Charles Bush, John Thomas and Daniel Lee located on the northeast corner of Main and Cedar streets," Edmonds wrote in 1944. The area was reachable by a bridge built over the Grand River at the foot of Main Street. Bush, Thomas and Lee also built the Benton House a few blocks east on Main Street and Washington Avenue, where it stood until 1900 when it was razed to make way for the R.E. Olds mansion.

Besides the general store, the Benton House, the National Hotel and the Michigan House, the Upper Town area had several other shops as well as a bowling alley, according to Durant. This area competed with the more established Lower Town, where Seymour built a plank walk between Franklin Street (now Grand River Avenue) to the Capitol so the legislators and other visitors could avoid the muddy paths and streets. Upper Town prospered two years before business started moving toward the center of town near the Capitol.

As Kestenbaum wrote: "The new capital grew feverishly in 1847, in the manner of a booming frontier town.. . . But the initial boom was short-lived. Cautious investors and settlers delayed coming to the new capital," either because they feared it would be moved or because "There was no settled country nearby to create business and the roads to the outer world were nearly impassable." The historian pointed out that the first newspaper, the *Lansing Republican*, wrote that "It became apparent that something more than a state house was necessary to support the village."

Life was becoming easier and more pleasant for some settlers. Sarah Chatterton wrote friends in Vermont on August 3, 1851, on her life on the corner of Hagadorn Road and Grand River Avenue in East Lansing:

"The Cedar River on the south side of our farm is an excellent spring of water pure and cold, as good as that in Vermont which we left. There is a beautiful flower garden in front of our house. The stage goes by here twice a day.

People say that this is the handsomest place in the county. The folks say it is not near as much work to clear up land as in Vermont. The roads do not go winding round hills and mountains but straight. We had a very pleasant journey coming here."

The decade of the fifties saw the establishment of what would join automaking and the capital as the area's largest employers, higher education institutions. The short-lived Michigan Female College was established in 1855 and Michigan Agricultural College in 1855 in what would become East Lansing.

Lansing grew as Ingham County grew, but the real spur to Lansing becoming the area's commercial center was assured in the completion of the plank road from Howell in 1853, finally connecting with the established plank road from Detroit. Almost overnight, arduous circuitous treks counted in days transformed into one-day trips between Detroit and the capital. Early settler Eben Dart remembered that in 1854 he left Detroit at 7 a.m. and reached Lansing at 9 p.m., the same day!

Huge stage coaches drawn by four horses carried 20 passengers plus express freight. Despite stopping every 12 or 16 miles to change teams, the stages averaged 8.5 miles an hour for the 80 some miles between Detroit and the Lansing terminus, initially at the Seymour House on Center and Franklin streets. Using much wood from trees cleared from fields for cultivation by farmers, the road opened beween Lansing and Okemos in June of 1851 and to Howell in December of 1852.

Grand Trunk Railroad

Grand Trunk carrying sugar beets

Railroad Photos Courtesy
of R. Nolin

Speakers at the formal opening hailed the new road for ending the control of "king mud" and providing Lansing's "first outlet to civilization."

"The arrival of the old fashioned stage coach in the early evening was the event of the day to the Lansingites," according to an account in the *Pioneer History of Ingham County.* "The stage could be heard a number of miles out on the plank road. . . In these old fashioned stage coaches the passengers soon became well acquainted as the roads were often so full of ruts and deep holes they would all be in a heap in the bottom of the coach."

Another account from the *Pioneer History:* "The rates are a cent a mile for one horse and two cents per mile for two horses, etc. If we are with private conveyance and going some distance, we pay for the whole distance and the gate keeper gives us tickets to pass us through the other gates, as we will have to pass one of these gates every four or five miles."

The road also carried freight destined for western Michigan, continuing over a rough road to Ionia and Grand Rapids. It remained a plank road until 1866 when the legislature approved the conversion to gravel and a toll road until early in 20th century.

The Lansing influence was heavy on the plank road. James Seymour and Hiram H. Smith, who became Lansing's first mayor, were among the incorporators and were among the contractors with Charles Seymour, son of James Seymour, and James Turner, who was treasurer and superintendent from 1851 until his death in 1869.

Although Lansing became a recognized city in February 1859, it waited for a railroad to be built. And it wasn't even a direct line when it came. The 28 miles of track were built from Owosso where it connected with the Detroit-Grand Rapids line. Direct rail connections to Jackson, Detroit, Flint, Battle Creek, Albion and Grand Rapids would come later.

Formed in 1847 to stretch through Lansing to the Ohio border, the Amboy, Lansing & Traverse Bay Railroad was completed between Owosso and Laingsburg by November 1860 and to Bath by Christmas of the same year. It took another two years until November of 1862 to reach North Lansing and another 10 months until August of 1863 to reach Michigan Avenue.

Apparently the marshy conditions between Bath and Lansing delayed completion. The *Lansing Republican* reported slow progress on a "sink hole" on May 21, 1862, and on August 6 that "the contractors have surrendered the job of filling the 'sink hole' to the enterprise of the city." The city apparently solved the "sink hole" in less than a month with the "iron laid into the city" on Nov. 5, 1862.

The slow progress led to derisement of the rail line nicknamed the "Ram's Horn" because "the road was just as crooked as that," according to one wag. Writing a tongue-in-cheek history of Lansing in 1870 under the name M. Dash, John Longyear said the trains were so slow it was necessary to mark chalk on the track to determine the direction of the train. Other wags said the line's initials of A.L. & T.B. meant "Awfully Long and Terribly Bumpy".

Two accounts in the *Pioneer History* also poked fun: Eben Dart said the "Ram's Horn" train ran so slowly that "people could get off the train and pick berries, then run and catch the train again;" and John Whiteley, an early agitator for the building of the railroad, said when trains "came to one of the high sand hills, all the people had to get off and walk so the locomotive could pull the empty cars up."

The arrival of the "Ram's Horn" gave travelers the choice of a daily train to Owosso for $1.25 to make connections to Pontiac, Detroit or Grand Rapids; or daily stage coaches to St. Johns, Jackson, Mason or Eaton Rapids for fares ranging from 75 cents to $2; a

DeWitt Station

tri-weekly stage to Detroit via Howell for $4; and a semi-weekly stage to Marshall through Charlotte for $2.

In the next decade, Lansing was put on the railroad map with four more lines, the next being the Lansing and Jackson Railroad which later added Saginaw to its title. Incorporated in 1864, the line was built through Mason to Lansing by June 1866. Taking control of the "Ram's Horn" to Owosso for the price of $1, the railroad reached Saginaw in 1867 and was extended to Otsego Lake and finally Mackinaw City later in the century. Legislators, lobbyists, state employees and the traveling public gained access to destinations on the lines built across the state in the 1840s and 50s. (The Lansing-Jackson portion still was in service in 1985 as part of Conrail; the "Ram's Horn" was abandoned in the 1970s, more than 100 years after construction.)

Two lines opened in 1869, the Ionia and Lansing Railroad to Grand Ledge, Portland and Ionia and the Peninsular Railroad to Battle Creek. The Ionia and Lansing consolidated with another line to reach Detroit, Greenville and Howard City in 1871 (Much of this line is part of the Chessie System, with the Grand Ledge to Portland, Ionia and Howard City portion abandoned). The Peninsular Railroad became a through line in 1877 when it was built to Flint and connected to Port Huron and Chicago (it is an important main line of the Grand Trunk- Canadian National U.S.-Canada system).

Another late arrival on the Lansing rail scene was the Northern Central Michigan Railroad which received permission in 1866 to build from Jonesville in Hillsdale County. But it didn't get to Albion until January 1872, Eaton Rapids September 1872 and Lansing January 1873 (later operating under Lake Shore & Michigan Southern, this line is abandoned except for a few miles inside Lansing to serve the *State Journal* newsprint warehouse. Its rail bed along the east bank of the Grand River was transformed into the Rollin Stebbins river walk-bike path in the 1970s-80s). In Eaton Rapids it crossed the Lansing area's only other major rail line, the Grand River Valley Road built from Jackson to Charlotte and Grand Rapids in 1870 (later part of the New York Central, this line is abandoned save for a few miles in Charlotte and Grand Rapids).

Except for a direct Grand Ledge-Grand Rapids line now operated by Chessie, a local industrial railroad operated by Conrail, and a shortlived, light rail interurban network built and abandoned in the early 20th century, Lansing had its rail network in place in 15 years. Dreams of a true northerly rail line through St.

Johns and Ithaca never materialized, although grading was done to St. Johns in 1880. The Lansing, St. Johns and St. Louis Electric Railroad Company eventually built an interurban line between Lansing and St. Johns. It operated from 1904 to 1929, but never reached St. Louis.

What did the rail lines mean to Lansing? Everything, especially progress, if you listened to the promoters and historians of the era. Pundit M. Dash seriously predicted the city would become a "great railway center" and pointed out "There are persons. . . who have passed over the same ground on horseback along an Indian trail, in a wagon on the new roads, and now. . . use the iron horse to perform the same journey."

Citing the railroads, the 1873 *Brown's City Directory of Lansing* said "The problem of Lansing's future is solved. The capital of the state and a common railroad center she must be a thriving and active city like Columbus, Indianapolis, Des Moines, Madison and Springfield. With an abundance of railroad competition, fine water power, coal near at hand, and wood of all kinds. . . there is no reason why Lansing should not become a thriving manufacturing city."

Even historian Durant was excited about Lansing's prospects: "Its central location and the subsequent construction of important lines of railway contributed in no small degree to its steady advancement, while its excellent water power and consequent manufacturing facilities have been important factors in its favor; but perhaps the most important consideration has been the rapid development of (the) natural, rich agricultural region which surrounds it."

The accessibility the railroads created was boasted in an advertisement in Brown's city directory: "Now opened and in operation to Otsego Lake. Most direct route to Northern Michigan, the great lumber and salt regions, to the Saginaw Valley, and to Magnetic Medicinal Springs of St. Louis (Michigan); the road is completed to within one county of the Straits of Mackinac." The same advertisement touts a connection in Mason with a daily stage line to and from Dansville.

The residents and business community were convinced of the importance of rail. "When the first railroad came into Lansing money and labor were freely given," early settler Mrs. D. L. Case told the Pioneer Society in 1884. "The work not progressing fast enough to satisfy our active businessmen, they left their places of business and worked with their own hands to carry forward the laying of the track which they had before paid for by their liberal subscriptions."

Novo Engine Foundry

Through the public subscriptions, local government contributed $40,000 to help build the "Ram's Horn," $66,400 to build the line from Jackson, $31,600 for the line to Ionia, $22,400 for the line to Battle Creek and several thousand dollars for the line from Jonesville in addition to $4,000 for a local roundhouse and shops. These funds were in addition to federal land grants offered as inducements to build rail lines.

Local backers of the rail lines were prominent, some involved in several enterprises, including James Turner who showed up early as a general store operator with Hiram H. Smith in Mason in the early 1840s. It was Turner who convinced Seymour to hire Joab Page, who became Lansing's first justice of the peace, to take over the Grand River mill and dam project after John Burchard drowned repairing the dam. With the Capitol being constructed, Turner and Smith liked the opportunities and moved from Mason to Lower Town in 1847 to operate their store and to establish a base for future endeavors: Turner as a land agent and the developer operator of plank and rail roads and Smith as a banker and the city's first mayor.

Turner, who built the first frame house in Lansing and was known as an acquaintance of Chief Okemos, actively promoted the "Ram's Horn" and Jackson lines although he was treasurer and superintendent of the plank road. But his main rail interest came in developing the Ionia and Lansing railroad. He became treasurer and his son, "Young Jim," was named paymaster. This started a long rail career for the son who became involved in the construction of the line between Lansing and Flint, a stretch heavily sought by American and Canadian rail barons because it created a major east-west competitor to the New York Central-Vanderbilt interests. Young Turner, who was mayor twice (1889 and 1896) and who went on to develop northern mineral interests, was credited with helping forge the combined rail lines between Detroit, Howell, Lansing and Lake Michigan in direct competition to the plank road.

Industrialist Orlando Mack Barnes, who arrived in Ingham County from New York in 1837, and lumber baron Charles J. Davis, mayor from 1897 to 1899, were instrumental in getting the line from Jackson built and taking over the "Ram's Horn." Barnes, an attorney for the railroad, spearheaded the effort to turn over the Jackson line to the Michigan Central which still owns the line under lease to Conrail. Barnes through the years was a state representative, Lansing mayor in 1877, a county prosecutor, a banker, lumber baron and historian who made and lost several fortunes and built one of the city's stateliest homes.

With the arrival of the railroad, Lansing was ready for growth. Its population was 3,085 in 1860, only 3,573 in 1864, and 5,243 in 1870. In the 1860s, the industrial output was $500,000 for all of Ingham County. The *Michigan State Gazeteer* for 1863 indicates Lansing boasts five hotels, two flour mills, three tanneries, two sash-blind factories, three iron foundaries, two printing offices, several brick yards and a large number of machine shops, several elegant private residences, coal in the vicinity, two weekly newspapers (the *Lansing*

Republican and the Michigan State Journal), a state reform school and a state agricultural college.

Two buildings that survived the 124 years and still standing in Lansing are the 1861 House on Grand Avenue and the Cherry Street School. Built in 1861 for Squire Haven, the 1861 house has recently been used as a restaurant and the home of the City Club. Also built in 1861, the Cherry Street School is now used for offices and considered one of Lansing's finest examples of adaptive reuse.

The aforementioned Hiram Smith was vice president and later a director of the new bank. The Lansing National Bank was started in 1872 and the Central Michigan Savings Bank in 1875, both located on the corner of Washington and Michigan.

A Lansing boom was at hand and Brown's city directory foresaw it in explaining the lack of growth for the city: "Much of the land about the city had been taken up by speculators from other states who refused to sell at reasonable prices. But the strongest element against

Lansing State Savings (Washington & Michigan)

Among industry Lansing added in the late 1860s and early 1870s were artificial stone manufacturers, a maker of staves, headings and barrels, two breweries, a chair factory, several more mills including the Lansing Woolen Mills, a builder of portable farm engines, an iron works, two carriage works, and a gas light company boasting five miles of gas mains, 61 street lamps and 200 private customers in 1872. The mills took special advantage of the rail lines by shipping their products to distant out-of-state markets that could not be reached previously.

Full-fledged banking did not start until 1864, following exchange offices and small private banks. An attempt to start the First National Bank was aborted before it even opened its doors when it was purchased by a group organizing the Second National Bank in 1864. Lansing never really had a First National Bank.

the growth of Lansing was the constant fear among many of its inhabitants of the removal of the capital to some other site.. . . it was not until the Legislature of 1871 voted $1,200,000 to be raised by taxation in six years for the purpose of building a state house that the question of Lansing retaining that position permanently was regarded as finally settled."

The business community responded robustly, according to Durant: "About 80 buildings costing from $300 upward were erected in 1871; from September 1871 to September 1872, more than 100 substantial buildings were erected at total cost of $372,400," including the opera house block at $40,000, and the Odd Fellows Institute at North Lansing at $30,000.

"In 1875 there was a great revival in building operations, about 250 new structures. . . of these 223 were dwellings and the remainder business buildings. . .

Bement Workers — Courtesy of Bob Bouck

A.O. Bement

Courtesy Lansing Public Library

among them the high school at $60,000, the Lansing Iron Works $9,000, Meads Flour Mill $33,000, a chair factory $20,000, Hart's Flour Mill $14,000, the Lake Shore and Southern Michigan elevator at $3,000, and 16 stores.

Three important events in the 1870s offered prosperous days for the capital:

1 - The laying of the cornerstone for a new Capitol on Oct. 3, 1873, attended by the largest crowd in Lansing's short history. Another huge crowd of 2,000 gathered five years later on Jan. 1, 1879, for the dedication of the imposing $1.2 million structure. The old Capitol, occupied by a manufacturer of handles, was destroyed by fire in December 16, 1882.

2 - The fascination of a young man named Olds in the combustible engine and its ability to power horseless carriages. (More on that in the next chapter.)

3 - The growth of the Bement Company which sparked Lansing's industrial growth. Edwin Bement, who moved in 1869 from Ohio where he operated a successful foundry, was credited in a *State Journal* headline for founding the "first industry of major proportions" in Lansing. Basically a plow works and casting foundry, Bement's firm relied on the railroad to bring in metals to go along with the Ingham wood and to ship out farm implements in great demand from New York to the Dakotas.

Sales growth from $4,000 in 1870 to $125,000 a decade later showed the strength of the firm operated by Bement and three sons, including Arthur who became mayor in 1892-93. When the implement market softened, the firm turned to stoves and became the nation's leading manufacturer of bobsleds.

By 1881 the Lansing Wagon Works, the Lansing Wheelbarrow Company headed by prominent civic leaders Edward W. Sparrow and A.C. Stebbins, and

the Clark & Co., another carriage works, helped make manufacturing as important to Lansing as the capital it was created to support.

At least two Lansing men were relying upon the Michigan forests to make their fortunes. James Moores moved from Ohio to become first a lumber magnate and then an industrialist who helped start the wheelbarrow firm. Historian Darling said Moores "hit the west coast of Michigan in 1873, and it is recorded that in 1880, he and his crews sent six million board feet of timber down the Muskegon River to set a record. They

Lansing Wheelbarrow Team — Courtesy Lansing Public Library

call Moores 'the man who rebuilt Chicago," with his wood after it was ravaged by fire in 1871.

Another lumber magnate James W. Potter moved the family's furniture business to Lansing from Potterville in 1889 to take advantage of the city's strong market. (Potterville was named after his father who was present at the raising of the first Capitol.)

Both Moores and Potter left their names in the city by donating major-sized park areas from their land holdings. Potter feared his park on Pennsylvania Avenue along the Red Cedar River was too far from the city center and persuaded the city's trolley operators to extend their tracks.

Two offbeat industries Lansing supported for short times were a health resort on the banks of the Grand River and cigar manufacturing. The resort was the Mineral Well House located east of the Grand River near the Red Cedar River on the site of a well drilled in 1867 to seek brine to produce salt. According to Edmonds, the well gushed 1,600 gallons an hour of "mineral water strongly impregnated with salt, lime, iron and other minerals supposed to have medicinal qualities."

So many people carried the water away in jugs and barrels, that the owners were inspired to build a hotel in 1870 to give people access to the water in 25 small bath rooms and a large bath. The baths proved popular enough to prompt the operation of two 50-passenger steam boats on the Grand River between the spa and the North Lansing dam, a trip of 2 1/2 miles for 10 cents. The 1873 Brown's directory told readers that "passengers on the Northern Central Michigan Railroad can reach the springs without change of cars because trains on this road stop at the hotel." The Mineral Well House survived to 1879 when on a February afternoon fire destroyed the building.

Another industry that regularly went up in smoke was cigar manufacturing which was operated as early as 1873 with the Brown directory carrying an advertisement for the Valley Cigar Factory. The advertisement read: "Oldest Established Factory in Central Michigan. Manufacturer of Havana and domestic cigars. Orders promptly attended to from old patrons, who have our thanks, and new ones solicited."

The impact of this industry could be found at the state-operated Michigan Reformatory where children manufactured cigars until 1875 and in an 1878 city directory which showed Gustave Berger, Henry Firth and A.A. Smith as cigar manufacturers. In an article in 1939, the *State Journal* reported that Lansing was a center of cigar making in 1892 with more than 20 factories.

A year later the city's most prominent cigar manufacturer, Hammell Cigar Co., moved from Ionia into a three-story brick building to have 100 employees make 3,000,000 cigars a year. Hammell was shortly followed into the city by Norton & Depue, a maker of 5,000 cigar boxes a week.

James Hammell, president of the cigar firm, became active in local politics and was elected an alderman and mayor from 1900 to 1903. It was during his tenure as mayor that the *State Journal* noted that cigar manufacturing hit hard times locally: in 1901, the cigar makers union asked the Lansing city council to back homemade or hand made cigars vs. machine made cigars that threatened to put 95 percent of the cigar makers out of business. Automation struck early as the *State Republican* noted on May 27, 1903, that the Hammell firm ceased making cigars.

The Headlight Flashes of 1895, a publication by the Michigan Central Railroad assessing major cities on its routes, reported Lansing population had hit 20,000. It listed several long-time local institutions and businesses already in existence, including the still-functioning Michigan School for the Blind and the Industrial School for Boys which operated until a decade ago in the area northwest of Eastern High School.

Businesses familiar today are listed in the *Headlight Flashes*, including the Silver Lead Paint Co.; C.J. Rouser, druggist; J.J. Heath, watchmaker and jeweler; H. Kositchek & Bros., clothiers and gents' furnishers, established six years; Olds & Son, Engine Works, established in 1880 ("They manufacture gasoline engines and in them have dispensed as nearly as possible with all complicated parts."); Lansing Business College (now Davenport College); the Michigan Wheel Co., established in 1891 (a forerunner of Motor Wheel); and J.M. LeClear and H.W. LeClear, photographers.

A survey of advertisements in the 1955 *State Journal Centennial Edition* found several other firms that boast a long existence, with six in existence more than a century in 1985. They include Morgan's Jewelers, 1876; Michigan Millers Mutual insurance 1881; Simon Iron & Steel, 1884 (now Summit Steel); and Union Building & Loan, 1886. Beach Manufacturing of Charlotte boasted to have started in 1895 and the Lansing Insurance Agency in 1898.

Lansing was ready for the turn of the century, riding the wheels of the "Merry Oldsmobile."

Chapter 2

The Engine Sparks a Flame

Lansing Wheelbarrow Co.   *Michigan State Archives*

by David A. Thomas

James M. Turner

In May of 1892, the *Scientific American* announced the invention of a steam carriage by Ransom E. Olds of Lansing, Mich., and accompanied the article with an engraving of the carriage. Declaring the new vehicle a success, the article concluded by reprinting Olds' tongue-in-cheek remarks about its advantages:

"The vehicle as a whole includes many new merits. Mr. Olds states that its great advantages are that it never kicks or bites, never tires out on long runs, and during hot weather he can ride fast enough to make a breeze without sweating the horse. It does not require care in the stable, and only eats while it is on the road, which is no more than at the rate of 1 cent per mile. Weight 1,200 pounds."

Olds' efforts during the next decade to produce a mass-selling, motor-driven vehicle were undoubtedly a crucial contribution to Lansing's growing reputation as a major Midwestern industrial city. The production of Olds' first automobile, however, did not mark the beginning of industrial production in Michigan's capital. Turn-of-the-century Lansing already had a number of large plants, employing thousands of workers and producing goods that were sold throughout the world.

Several of Lansing's largest companies by the late 1890s were veterans that had achieved commercial success long before Olds ever proposed building automobiles. The Clark Carriage Company, for example, started around 1865 as a horseshoer's shop. By 1900, it was producing a wide range of carriages, buggies and cutters, employing more than 100 workers and sending out five traveling salesmen.

The Lansing Wheelbarrow Company was even bigger. Founded in 1881, by 1899 the firm employed 400 workers and produced large numbers of wheelbarrows, hand carts, baggage carts, wooden rakes, fruit presses and horse pokes each year. The company claimed to be the largest manufacturer of wheelbarrows in the country, having a capacity to turn out between 400 to 500 a day.

Lansing's largest firm by the beginning of the 20th century, however, was Bement & Sons. Makers of farm implements and cooking stoves, it employed as many as 800 workers and had branches in Texas, Minnesota, Wisconsin, and Iowa.

While many of the city's old-time companies were doing a brisk business as the 20th century approached, the Lansing community was projecting a definite pro-business look to entrepreneurs looking for a location to launch their commercial ventures. Such successful businessmen as Daniel Buck (furniture), John Crotty (books and office supplies), James Turner (railroads), Frank B. Johnson (originally groceries and later telephones), A.O. Bement (agricultural implements), Charles J. Davis (railroads and lumber), and James Hammell (cigars) all served as mayor between 1886 and 1900, while the city council and the school board were well represented by the business community.

The city's two newspapers, the *State Republican* and the *Lansing Journal*, gave considerable space in their pages to business news and generally applauded city leaders when new firms decided to make Lansing their home. Even the building of a new store in town frequently received major press attention.

Under the headline, "The Finest In Michigan," the *Lansing Journal* described a hardware store opened in 1888: "Undoubtedly the finest hardware store in central Michigan is that recently erected by Jacob Stahl at 211 Washington Avenue."

Possibly with the idea of retaining an advertising account as well as promoting a local businessman, the paper went on to say:

Mr. Stahl's reputation as one of Lansing's most reliable and enterprising merchants is so thoroughly established that it is unnecessary for the Journal *to dilate upon the extensive business which he has built up. He came to Lansing 10 years ago, and opened a hardware store in the opera house block. From the first he demonstrated his ability to achieve success, and he has done it. His elegant new block is one of the finest in the State, and his faith in the capital city's future, which he has exhibited in erecting it cannot be too highly commended.*

In addition, the Lansing Improvement Company, founded in 1873 by such prominent city leaders as Edward Sparrow, J.J. Bush, J. S. Tooker and A. E. Cowles, aggressively promoted Lansing as a business mecca, and was credited with inducing such firms as the Lansing Chair Factory, the Lansing Pants and Overalls Company, and the Hammell Cigar Company to operate in the city.

Lansing's pro-business climate was probably a major factor in the opening of dozens of new businesses in Lansing during the 1890s. The Maud S. Wind Mill and Pump Company (1892), Jarvis Engine & Machine Works (1893), the Alexander Furnace and Manufacturing Co.(1894), the Collver Custom Shirt Factory (1895), the American Cut Glass Company (1896), and the Lansing Brewing Company (1898) were just a few of the newcomers during the 1890s.

All news, however, was not good. A nationwide depression between 1893 and 1898 affected Michigan and, on April 18, 1893, Lansing's Central Michigan Savings Bank closed its doors. Two more bank failures followed and Lansing was part of a nation-wide depression.

The *State Republican* reflected in 1899:

"Six years ago there was no city throughout the length and breadth of Michigan in a more prosperous and promising condition than Lansing. From 1877 to 1892 she had leaped forward like a young giantess and her ultimate destiny no one could foretell. But a check came. April 18, 1893, the beginning came when the Central Michigan Savings Bank closed its doors. It is not necessary to enter into details here. Suffice it to say that three quarters of a million dollars of the people's money was thus taken from the legitimate channels of trade and tied up in litigation where it was worth to the city not as much as the paper upon which it was printed."

While the *Republican* admitted that some city businesses "that were supposed to possess the strength of Gibralter toppled and sank into the abyss of financial ruin," it assured its readers that " Lansing is recovering her commercial strength, and the blood of trade once more circulates freely in her veins."

Lansing businessmen seemed to agree that better times had arrived and claimed that there was more demand for Lansing property than at any time during recent years.

"I saw something today I haven't seen for five years," real estate broker J. E. Carroll told the *Republican* in April of 1899. "A man was in here with $10,000 which he wanted to invest in property in Lansing."

Despite the poor economic times, many of Lansing's plants survived, producing for local, national and sometimes international markets. The Maud S. Wind Mill and Pump company, named after a famous harness horse of the 1880s, produced windmills as well as wood and steel tanks, and even maintained an export office in New York City. The Lansing Iron and Engine Works in 1897 had completed a new boiler system for the Industrial School, as well as supplying engines and boilers for the Lansing Wheelbarrow Company, Battle Creek Sanitarium and the Reading Robe & Canning Co. of Reading, Mich. That same year, the company also shipped a device to generate acetylene gas to Mexico City for use in gas generators that were planned for lighting systems that would eliminate Mexico's dependence on candles for illumination in its hotels and public buildings.

Other Lansing firms producing products that were shipped outside the mid- Michigan area included the Lansing Brewing Co.'s "Amber Cream" and "Export" beer; women's and children's mittens by the Michigan Knitting Company; the "Alexander" furnace by the Alexander Furnace & Manufacturing Co.; Bement's "Peerless Plow"; and the "Fox Flyer" bicycle by W.S. Holmes & Son.

One turn-of-the-century story that made its rounds in Lansing's business community told of a former Lansing man who entered a store in Sydney, Australia, to shop. Much to the man's surprise he found an article for sale made by Lansing's Hugh Lyons & Co. – a firm that specialized in products needed for store displays.

Lansing's efforts in attracting new business was not, of course, always successful. In the late 1880s, for example,

Bement Baseball Team

*Bement
Parade
Float*

23

the Gale Manufacturing Company of Albion let out the word that it was interested in moving. Several Michigan cities, including Lansing, expressed interest with offers to attract the company.

"There is strong suspicion extant that if Lansing desires to secure the Gale Manufacturing Works it will be necessary to give the thrifty company the entire city, with possibly two or three of the State Institutions thrown in," the *Lansing Journal* warned. "The frantic efforts of Flint, Bay City, Pontiac, and other towns to secure the works at any cash outlay has apparently temporarily obscured Lansing's vastly superior shipping and other advantages." Gale's tactics were apparently successful and the *Journal* concluded the episode on March 3, 1888, in a short story with a headline that read, "The Gale People Succeed in Squeezing Albion and Will Remain."

In another incident, in 1897, the Lansing Improvement Company attempted to induce an Ohio shoe company to locate in Lansing. The Ohio firm asked for a free building and $10,000 in cash. "This the Improvement Company thought they could not do on the showing made but made the gentlemen an offer of a site and a building." the *State Republican* reported. "This offer was refused and the gentlemen left town this afternoon."

By the mid-1890s, Lansing's business and industrial community was changing. Until that time, much of the city's industrial activity was spent in manufacturing wooden products from timber supplied by the surrounding forests. Such items as wagon spokes and wheels, carriages, carts, sleds, cigar boxes, and barrels were produced in great quantities.

In North Lansing, the grain mills attracted lines of farmers' wagons waiting to have loads of wheat ground. Near the mills on Franklin and Turner streets, hardware stores, harness shops, and blacksmith shops catered to the farmer's needs.

The invention of the gasoline engine, however, saw the emergence of such firms as P. F. Olds & Son, Bates and Edmonds and the Jarvis Engine & Machine Works as important members of Lansing's industrial community.

As Lansing moved its industrial base from wood and agricultural to machinery, the Michigan Agricultural College was establishing an engineering/mechanical arts department, hiring its first professor of mechanics in 1885. During the next 20 years teachers with a wide range of mechanical expertise taught at the college. Professor Rolla Carpenter, for example, had a background in heating, ventilating and gasoline engines; Professor Herman Vedder lectured on bridge construction, plumbing systems and water power; Professor Charles Weil, a graduate of the Massachusetts Institute of Technology, was an authority on heating plants; and Professor Arthur Sawyer combined knowledge of physics and electrical engineering in his lectures. Several of Lansing's machinery and engine companies employed graduates from MAC's mechanical department and contributed machinery to the department's workshops.

It wasn't, however, just the graduates of MAC's mechanical department who were beginning to make an impact on Lansing business. Lansing's pioneer merchants and factory owners were largely self-educated men, frequently serving an apprenticeship in a skilled trade before eventually starting their own company. The 1890s began seeing more and more men getting a college education before entering the business world.

Arthur Davis Baker, for example, earned a bachelor's degree at MAC before eventually becoming president of Michigan Miller's Insurance Company. Jason Elmer Hammond, who became president of the Hammond Publishing Company, also was an MAC graduate, while industrialist M. Ralph Carrier spent three years at Albion College, Lansing businessman C.C. Ludwig attended Ferris State, and Lansing Company president Harry Moore took classes at the University of Michigan and MAC. Several others attended Lansing Business College.

While the city's production plants were seeing better times by the late 1890s, the downtown retail merchants also were optimistic. One reason was Lansing's emergence as a popular convention site. In early 1897, for example, the Michigan Engineering Society, the Michigan State Miller's Association, the Michigan State Veterinary Association, the Michigan Horseshoers and the Michigan Republican Newspaper Association spon-

Dunham Hardware

Early photo of Lansing's Washington Avenue

sored Lansing conventions. In August, 1,000 veterans attended a reunion of the Wilcox Division of the Ninth Army Corps, while October saw 1,000 Oddfellows trek to Lansing for their annual convention – even though the *State Republican* reported that the group had been offered $5,000 to go to Detroit.

The Michigan Grange reported in its souvenir program for its 1902 Lansing convention that Lansing "has been for many years the favorite convention town in the state." Convention attendees filled up the city's hotels, especially the Downey which advertised such luxuries as a bath, elevator, steam heat, and both gas and electric light. Rooms in 1900 ranged from $3.50 for the most expensive suite at the Downey to a low of $1 at the Cooper House, the Franklin House, the Hotel Butler, the Hotel Maltby, the Van Dyne, and the Yerkes Hotel. Conventioneers flocked to such downtown stores as the Crotty's City Book Store, Louis Beck's clothing store, Parmelee and Jessop's shoe store, and the jewelry store of Gillett and Kirby for gifts for families left back home.

"The principal business street, Washington Avenue, is 2-1/2 miles long and 7 rods wide, and being level as a floor, makes one of the finest streets in America," the *Michigan Gazetteer and Business Directory* stated in 1895.

Downtown merchants were delighted when the street car line was completed at the Agricultural College in late 1897, and strongly supported the extension of the electric railway in all directions. Making it easy for mid-Michigan's rural population to get to Lansing, they knew, was good for business.

"Lansing is after every dollar's worth of trade that can be steered this way and her businessmen are alive to the fact that electric roads, in any direction, will bring more or less of it," the *State Republican* commented in October of 1898.

Lansing, of course, was not exclusively a town of large factories and retail establishments. Many people in turn-of-the-century Lansing operated small businesses in rooms above the bigger retail stores or, in many cases, out of their homes. Elva Ashley, for example, taught music, while C.E. Brownson built stairs, Edward Beecher was an artist, Allie Allen was a dressmaker, and Daniel Boess made a living sweeping chimneys.

While Lansing might very well have developed into a significant 20th-century manufacturing center without the help of Ransom E. Olds, his dream of a horseless carriage propelled Michigan's capital city to a commercial success that would have astounded the early pioneers who only 70 years earlier had first begun carving out a life in the vast wilderness of Ingham County.

Olds was born on June 3, 1864, in Geneva, Ohio, to Pliny and Sarah Whipple Olds. Pliny, who owned a blacksmith and machine shop in Geneva, also farmed and worked in the Cleveland iron foundries before moving to Lansing in 1880. There he established a machine shop on River Street under the name of P. F. Olds and Son (the "son" in those early years was not Ransom, but his older brother, Wallace). The venture was begun in an 18-by-26-foot building with "one iron planer, one engine lathe and an old drill," according to a 1901 report in the *State Republican*.

As a young man, R. E. Olds spent many hours assisting his father in the family business, gaining considerable experience as a mechanic. In 1885, he bought out his brother's interest in P. F. Olds and Son and became his father's sole partner. The shop originally concentrated on repairing machines that were used in Lansing-area industries and at nearby farms. The Olds firm, however, soon began producing steam engines, and, in an 1883 advertisement, brought attention to its "vertical steam engines of 3, 5 and 10 horsepower." The steam engines were moderate sellers at best and it wasn't until the development of a "one-horse-power gasoline engine" in the latter part of the 1880s that Ransom and Pliny Olds began to see their business achieve significant financial success. The new gasoline engine, actually a steam engine in which a gasoline burner was used to heat the water, was a hit and as many as 2,000 were produced between 1887 and 1892.

Even though most of the nation was in a severe depression between 1893 and 1897, the Olds firm continued strong as sales reached $29,000 in 1896. In early 1897, the *State Republican* reported that "P. F. Olds & Son are obliged to run their factory day and night because of a press of orders received since January 1."

Despite the immense amount of time Olds spent in overseeing the manufacturing and selling of the company's steam and gasoline engines (his father retired in 1894), he was fascinated with the concept of developing self-propelled vehicles that could replace the horse as a means of transportation. As a boy, Olds had been impressed by the train trip he had taken when his family moved to Lansing and by a boat trip he had taken on Lake Erie. If mechanical power could work for trains and boats, why couldn't it work for the family carriage?

Sometime around 1886, despite considerable apprehension from his father and his friends, Olds began developing a three-wheeled carriage, powered by an Olds steam engine. Then, in the summer of 1887 (historians do not agree on the exact date) Olds drove his horseless carriage through the streets of Lansing.

"I mounted to the seat and pulled the lever," Olds remembered in a paper presented to the Michigan Engineering Society in 1897. "She moved slowly, but speed was increased as it went down the platform out of the shop; there was a slight raise, however, before crossing the sidewalk and she refused to ascend the grade, so I at once dismounted, and going behind, gave it a push to be remembered which did the business, and it reached the sidewalk in safety."

Even though Olds reportedly reached speeds of up to 10 miles an hour, after about a block, "the efforts of the engine were exhausted" and he needed help to push the carriage back into the shop.

Olds didn't give up and pursued his horseless-carriage dream over the next few years. His second attempt occurred in 1892. In order to solve the power-shortage problems of his earlier vehicle, Olds used two steam engines mounted on a four-wheeled carriage. While more promising than his initial effort, the machine suffered from two deficiencies – an inability to climb hills and the lack of a reverse gear.

Looking northwest from just east of Michigan Avenue Bridge on Michigan Avenue about 1895. Shows Lake Shore and Michigan Southern Railroad Depot.

Michigan State Archives

The visiting *Scientific American* reporter was impressed when Olds gave him a special demonstration. "It carries two passengers besides the operator and it is the intention to couple on another vehicle behind if wishing to carry more passengers," he wrote. "The steam from the engines is entirely done away with by an ingenious contrivance of the inventor, and there is no smoke. The engines couple on direct, so there is no gearing whatever, and the rig runs as quietly as an ordinary carriage."

The resulting publicity attracted the attention of an English patent medicine firm, the Francis Times Company, which offered to buy the vehicle. After agreeing on a price of $400 it was shipped to the company's branch office in Bombay, India, probably making it the first Michigan-made, self-propelled automobile to be purchased anywhere and possibly the first sale of an American horseless carriage outside of the country.

When P. F. Olds & Son began making internal-combustion engines in the mid-1890s, Olds abandoned steam power in favor of internal combustion for his vehicles. In the summer of 1896, he produced his first true gasoline-powered carriage with the help of Frank G. Clark of Lansing's Clark & Co. Reporters from both the *Lansing Journal* and the *State Republican* were given a chance to ride in the new vehicle.

"Probably the most successful horseless carriage ever invented is the product of a Lansing man's ingenuity and now is in practical use in this city," the *Journal* writer reported. "Ransom E. Olds is the inventor and the manufacturer and he takes great pleasure in exhibiting the invention.

"[The body] is of the regular manufacture of A. Clark & Co., and Mr. F. G. Clark is part owner of the machine. The wheels are equipped with cushion tires, and except for the machinery underneath, the vehicle is to all appearance a fashionable trap . . . A short ride in the carriage this morning convinced the writer that it is a success and in time the horseless carriage will displace the horse for pleasure driving."

Olds knew, however, that successfully operating a single motorized vehicle was quite different from manufacturing it in large numbers. He knew that thousands of additional dollars were needed and that he could not raise the money by himself.

Help was close at hand, though, as some of Lansing's leading citizens had noticed Olds' success with his new car and were interested in investing. In the summer of 1897, Olds went to the office of businessman E.W. Sparrow to discuss the possibility of starting a company to produce horseless carriages. Years later, Olds described

the scene for writer Duane Yarnell.

"Olds, you guided your company through a pretty serious business panic," Sparrow reportedly said. "We've been considerably impressed by your judgement, and we're convinced that you're going to do much better. You've answered our questions honestly and if you believe your vehicle has a future, we're certainly willing to go along with you. Now, once again – are you willing to form a company to produce horseless carriages?" Olds replied, "Yes, I'm willing."

On August 23, 1897, under the headline, "Horseless Carriage," the *State Republican* reported the organization of the Olds Motor Vehicle Company that would soon begin building the "Olds' Horseless Carriage." Sparrow was elected president, E.F. Cooley was elected vice-president and A.C. Stebbins was made treasurer. Olds was given the title of "manager."

"Lansing citizens may congratulate themselves that the manufacture of the Olds' carriage is to be commenced in this city," the *Republican* wrote. "Had not local capitalists become interested, the factory would have been taken to some other city. Mr. Olds has had several offers from parties in Detroit and Chicago, who were anxious to put money into a company for the man-

nearby towns. On one occasion, the *State Republican* reported the Olds "made the run between Hastings and Charlotte, a distance of 30 miles, on one and one-half gallons of gasoline and while the roads were very poor and no end of hills and sand, he covered the distance in three and one-half hours."

It is uncertain how many vehicles Olds was able to

Mr. & Mrs.
Ransom E. Olds

ufacture of the carriage, but preferred to remain in Lansing."

The leader of the local investors was E.W. Sparrow. A land speculator and real estate developer, he also served as president of the Lansing Wheelbarrow Company. In addition, former Lansing resident and close associate of Sparrow, Samuel L. Smith of Detroit, invested. A past member of the Michigan House of Representatives, Smith had multiple business interests throughout the state and, before long, would play a crucial role in the career of R. E. Olds.

Olds began spending much of his time attempting to organize the automobile company, leaving management of the gasoline works to his brother, Wallace. Even in those days, however, he had a penchant for promotion and the local papers frequently covered his drives to

produce and sell during those early days in Lansing, but records indicate that selling gasoline engines was a much more profitable venture than selling horseless carriages. In 1898 the capitalization of the Olds Gasoline Engine Works was raised to $150,000, permitting expansions for producing more gasoline engines and for constructing gasoline carriages. Still, few vehicles were produced and energies continued to be focused on the production of gasoline engines.

Automotive historian George S. May contends: *"Lack of money, equipment and manpower does not appear to be the main cause of the delays that kept Olds vehicles off the market for so long. Olds' own uncertainty about the kind of automobile to produce and the best way of going about it was certainly part of the problem. However, it seems plausible that the delays in 1898 and 1899 were also due to a strug-*

gle between the Lansing-based backers of the Olds enter-prises and groups elsewhere to gain financial dominance over the operations – plus the maneuvering of Olds to secure the most advantageous terms from these competing groups."

In the spring of 1899, the stock of the Olds Gasoline Engine Works and the Olds Motor Vehicle Company were acquired by an investment group headed by Samuel L. Smith, and it was announced that a plant would be built in Detroit and that the size of the Lansing plant would be increased. The *State Republican* commented that "One object for which the deal was consummated was to take care of the increased demand for the Olds gas and gasoline engines. They have acquired a world wide reputation and are in great demand. The main purpose, however, is to manufacture the motor vehicles under the Olds patents, and also motor trucks, for which the patents are now pending."

The articles of association of the new company, the Olds Motor Works, stated that the corporate headquarters and the main manufacturing facilities were to be located in Detroit. Lansing was to have only a manufacturing branch.

Consequently, by the end of 1899, the Olds family had moved to Detroit and a new plant, designed by Lansing's Fred Thoman Jr., was under construction. The production of gasoline engines continued to be the main activity and money maker in the Detroit and Lansing factories as Olds spent much of 1900 experimenting with a variety of automotive models, including electric-powered vehicles. Finally by the fall, he had decided to concentrate on the building of a low cost ($650), no-frills runabout – soon to be known throughout the country as the "curved-dash Oldsmobile."

Production of the new runabout was reportedly underway by early 1901 and began receiving favorable mention shortly afterward in the nation's press. On March 9, however, a major fire struck the Detroit plant, crucially influencing the future of the Olds Motor Works and greatly impacting Lansing's destiny as a major automobile-producing capital.

"Fire which broke about 1:30 p.m. this afternoon at the rear of the Olds Motor Works, destroyed the big building, razing the walls and burning out the floors and fixtures within a short time," the *State Republican* reported. " Three men were badly injured and are now in the hospital. All the rest of the 150 to 200 employees who were in the building escaped in safety."

One of the most significant survivors of the fire was a single curved-dash Oldsmobile that was saved by time-keeper Jimmy Brady, who later became the mayor of Detroit.

Although obviously disappointed, Olds didn't let the fire stop his plans and continued to produce curved-dash vehicles in the Lansing plant and in temporary facilities in Detroit. Advertising was increased, changing from an emphasis on gasoline engines to automobiles.

One important marketing innovation was the 1901 Detroit-to-New York trip taken by Lansing's Roy D. Chapin. Chapin, an Olds' test driver and future head of the Hudson Motor Car Company, made the trip in seven and one-half days despite bad weather and poor roads. He arrived at New York's Waldorf Astoria during the fall New York Automobile Show, receiving considerable attention in the local and Eastern press. Olds later claimed the trip played a major role in the sale of 750 curved-dash Oldsmobiles to New York residents in 1902.

The curved-dash Oldsmobile was the best-selling car of its day with sales increasing from approximately 400 automobiles in 1901 to 4,000 two years later. Olds Motor Works had dealers in most major cities and its advertising campaigns probably were the most effective of any of the early 20th-century auto companies.

Meanwhile, the newly formed Lansing Business Men's Association, the forerunner of the Greater Lansing Chamber of Commerce, decided to invite R.E. Olds to return his auto plant to his hometown. Association president Harris E. Thomas offered Olds a 52-acre site in southwest Lansing on the old fairgrounds of the Central Michigan Fair Association. With more expansion opportunities than alternatives in Detroit, Olds and the company's stockholders decided to accept. While Oldsmobiles were produced in both Lansing and Detroit during 1902, all auto production had been shifted to the Lansing plant by 1905.

Although the success of the curved-dash runabout continued, disagreement over the direction of the Olds

Curved-Dash Olds

Motor Works were beginning to appear in the upper echelons of the company. Some say that Olds' staunch defense of continuing production of the curved-dash Oldsmobile directly conflicted with Fred Smith's (son of company president Samuel Smith and manager of the Detroit plant) view that the company's future lay in the building of bigger and more luxurious cars.

Personality conflicts and competition for control of the company, however, may have been as responsible for the Smith-Olds rift than any one specific issue. On January 11, 1904, the company's board selected Fred Smith to Olds' old position as vice president and general manager, while Olds' only official company position was as a member of the board of directors. Historian May writes that it seems likely "that long before his defeat in the board meeting of January 1904, Olds, finding it impossible to work with Fred Smith, was beginning to ease himself out of the firm."

By June, 1904, Olds resigned from the Olds Motor Works. Already having disposed of all his remaining stock, the action cut all official ties from the company that he had given his name.

Olds didn't stay out of the automobile business for long. On August 17, 1904, in headlines usually reserved for the ending of wars or electing of presidents, the *State Republican* announced, "R.E. OLDS CO., CAPITAL A MILLION, TO ERECT BIG AUTO FACTORY IN LANSING."

The story proudly pointed out that the new company "will be known as the R. E. Olds, Co., and all its stockholders are Lansing men, Mr. Olds having the controlling interest. A site for the factory has not yet been selected, but one will be decided upon speedily, and work on buildings, which will contain several acres of floor space, will be rushed. By the first of the year, Mr. Olds expects to have from 900 to 1,000 men at work constructing new models of automobiles that he has designed and which will embody his latest ideas as to the popular vehicles."

With two major automobile companies now located in Lansing, most observers (including the *Detroit Free Press* which ran the story under the headline "Lucky Lansing") agreed that Michigan's capital city was on the brink of something very exciting.

Trying out a Curved-Dash Olds

Chapter 3

The Iron Age

Almost everyone who lived in Lansing in 1906 was optimistic about the city. Interest in the city's economic health was so high that more than 500 people attended the January meeting of the Lansing Businessmen's Association.

"The price of a good, live energetic town is eternal vigilance," Association president A.A. Piatt told the gathering. "One beaver can't do much, but 500 beavers can build a big dam. If everyone here tonight will boost a little, what a big boost there will be."

Association secretary O.A. Jenison talked about the many good things that had happened to Lansing's economy during the past year. He told about the Olds Motor Works moving its Detroit plant back to Lansing. He pointed out that both the W.K. Prudden Co. and the New Way Motor Co. had built new plants, while the Auto Body Company in North Lansing had doubled the size of its facilities. He announced that the Lansing Sugar Company had its best year, and he congratulated the association for its role in convincing the Cronk Brothers gum factory to move its plant from Dowagiac to Lansing.

The *Lansing Journal* echoed Jenison's enthusiasm in a special business supplement entitled "Greater Lansing." It pointed out to companies considering Lansing as a home that the Lansing Fuel & Gas Light Company was able to generate 300,000 cubic feet of gas daily; that the fine street car system operated 85 cars on 151 miles of track; that the Michigan Central, Grand Trunk, Lake Shore & Michigan Southern and Pere Marquette railroads all serviced the city; and that Lansing's two telephone companies had 3,600 individual and business phone customers. Without a doubt, the *Journal* argued, Lansing was a fine place to do business.

Much of the optimism, of course, was generated by the knowledge that Lansing had two of the world's largest and most successful automobile companies in its city limits, and other businesses were being formed each month (or so it seemed) to manufacture needed auto parts.

Ransom E. Olds' new venture, the Reo Motor Car Company, was in the process of marketing a touring car (a less popular runabout was also manufactured), that at 1,500 pounds and $1,250 doubled the curved-dash Oldsmobile in both price and weight. Under the direction of plant manager Richard H. Scott and chief engineer Horace T. Thomas, Reo increased its first-year production of 864 vehicles in 1905 to an impressive 2,458 autos in 1906.

Reo promoted its automobiles with enthusiasm and originality. The Baby Reo, for example, was introduced to the public in early 1906 and billed as the "smallest auto in the world" – 1/8 the size of a regular car. The baby Reo, usually photographed filled with children to suggest the ease with which a Reo could be operated, was a hit at auto shows and was even featured in the Barnum and Bailey Circus. "The Reo Car Co. is negotiating to secure the services of the smallest person in the world to demonstrate the Baby at the shows," the *State Republican* reported.

Another attention getter was the 32-horsepower racing car called "Reo Bird," driven by Reo employee Daniel J. Wurgess. Wurgess won races in New York, New Jersey and Grosse Pointe during 1905. In September, Wurgess and the "Reo Bird" set a world record in the mile for middle-weight cars in Syracuse, N.Y.

While many of Reo's promotional campaigns were geared toward the national market, Olds also took advantage of opportunities to promote his automobile locally. In the fall of 1906, Olds led a parade of 25 Reos (it was later reported that several more autos joined the procession along the way) to Ionia and back, going through Grand Ledge, Portland, Muir, Pewamo, Fowler and St. Johns. Lumber company owner H. W. Rikard, drug store owner C.J. Rouser and *Lansing Journal* company manager Ira Clark drove their personal cars in what was billed as the "Reo Run."

While Reo was making a major impact on the

Photos this page:
Promotional Tours to Market Automobiles MSU Archives

national automotive scene, the Olds Motor Works was not content to play the bridesmaid role. In late 1905, 100 Olds agents from around the country were invited to Lansing to view the company's new models. The first day's activities started with breakfast at the Hotel Downey, then an all-day session at the factory learning about the new cars and, finally, an evening banquet with an orchestra and a Chicago vaudeville group. On Saturday, a seat at the Michigan-Wisconsin football

Sometimes the competition between Reo and the Olds Motor Works took on somewhat dramatic proportions. It was especially apparent in 1907 when President Theodore Roosevelt came to town to participate in the 50th anniversary of the Michigan Agricultural College. Both auto companies fought over the honor of chauffeuring the president to and from the ceremonies. A compromise was finally reached – a Reo, driven by R. E. Olds, picked up the president at the depot and

President Roosevelt rides to MAC

game in Ann Arbor was reserved for each participant.

"The entertainment was both generous and unique," Grand Rapids automobile agent George W. Hart told the *State Republican.* "We were immensely pleased. The new models of the Olds Motor Works are what we have been looking for. We have made large contracts and expect to do a big business."

The Olds Motor Works' 1905 model had been a slightly-changed version of the traditional curved-dash model. Selling for $750, it was advertised as "just as good" as previous models, "but with more style thrown in." In 1906, however, the new Oldsmobile sold for $2250 and featured a wheelbase increased from 66 to 106 1/2 inches and horsepower increased from seven to thirty-six. Even though the curved-dash would remain in the company's catalogue through 1907, the day of the bigger, more expensive car had arrived.

took him to the college campus. That night, an Oldsmobile took him back.

In the early days of America's automobile industry, auto companies produced only a portion of the total vehicle. Such parts as bodies, wheels and spark plugs were purchased from supplier companies. As the Olds Motor Works and Reo both established themselves in Lansing, suppliers began to form. In North Lansing, for example, Harris E. Thomas created one of the first automobile supply companies in 1901 – The Auto Body Company. There, between the Grand River and Turner Street, general manager H. E. Bradner supervised the production of bodies for the Olds Motor Works and carriages for the horse and buggy trade. Another firm, the Prudden Company, was a major supplier of wheels to the Olds Motor Works.

When Ransom E. Olds established Reo, he was com-

Early photo of Turner Street in North Lansing

mitted to getting as many parts as possible from local sources. Consequently, in 1906, Olds was instrumental in the establishment of the National Coil company (jump spark coils), the Michigan Screw Company (screws and nuts), and the Atlas Drop Forge Company (forgings) in Lansing. All supplied parts to both the local and national auto companies.

Other companies (some not connected to the auto industry) announced intentions to settle in Lansing during late 1906 and early 1907. The new firms included Detroit's Gusting A. Mops & Co. (cigars), the Hales Manufacturing Co. (enameling plant), the Michigan Wood Work company, and Barrette & Scully (also cigars). The *State Republican* reported in late 1906 that with negotiations underway by Atlas Drop Forge to purchase the old buildings of the Central Implement Co., there is "not a vacant factory in all of Lansing."

Reo and Oldsmobile were not the only two mid-Michigan companies that attempted to produce motorized vehicles in the early 1900s. Short-lived attempts at auto production were made by Madison Bates, Frank G. Clark and, in Charlotte, John L. Dolson. Clark, who produced the body for Olds' 1896 horseless carriage, joined Arthur C. Stebbins and Harris E. Thomas in 1902 to form the Clarkmobile Company. A 1903 catalogue in the Local History Room of the Lansing Public Library describes the Clarkmobile:

"After two years of experimenting, developing, and actual road test, we take pleasure in announcing the Clarkmobile ready for the market. Our policy will be to build only vehicles of the highest possible grade, using the best and latest devices and employing only the finest workmanship."

The Clarkmobile was advertised as a "$2,000 automobile at a $750 price," weighing 1,100 pounds and featuring a 7-horsepower engine with a jump-spark ignition. A machine-buffed leather top cost an extra $50 and $25 would purchase a plainer rubber top. Probably no more than 1,000 Clarkmobiles, however, were produced.

While the auto industry was thriving in Michigan's capital, motorized vehicles were presenting problems that were somewhat new to Lansing. In November of 1905, for example, former United States Deputy Marshal W.S. Abels was attempting to cross Michigan Avenue near Driscoll's Cigar Store when he was run down by a Reo. Ironically, the Reo's driver was in the process of attempting to get the car's horn fixed and was unable to warn Abels.

In another incident, Lansing attorney O.L. Matthews, left his touring car running when he entered the post office. "Apparently the brake of the machine failed to hold as Mr. Matthews came out of the post office to see his auto well started down the street without any driver," the *State Republican* reported. The auto then veered in the direction of the Capitol lawn, ran half on the curb and half on the pavement toward a telephone pole, and headed for almost certain disaster. Luckily, Matthews was quick on his feet, caught up to his vehicle and "climbed into the machine while it was in motion and throwing the steering wheel around turned the auto off the curb to the pavement again."

Lansing's emerging automobile industry did not immediately wipe out the city's dependence on the horse. City directories of the time listed 6 automobile parts manufacturers, 6 auto repair shops and 5 auto dealers. They also listed, however, 15 blacksmiths, 4 carriage and wagon dealers, 4 harness shops and 7 livery barns.

Times were changing, though, and slowly Lansing was realizing that its future lay in the automobile. One of the best examples of the ability to adapt to change was Rudolph Grammel. Taking over his father's harness business on Turner Street in 1892, the 16-year-old Grammel quickly became one of North Lansing's most respected businessmen and was credited by the local press at the time of his death as being the founder of the Turner Street Farmer's Market, the forerunner of the present-day City Market. Eventually, apparently realizing that the automobile had replaced the horse as Lansing's major form of transportation, Grammel closed his shop (now Two Doors Down Gallery at 1219 Turner) and accepted a job as "welfare director" at Reo.

While the automobile industry was attracting most of the attention in 1906, Lansing still had a reputation as one of the Midwest's top producers of gas and gasoline engines for farm, marine and industrial use. The Olds Gas Power Company (no longer owned by the Olds family) was still an industry leader and employed 200 people. Other Lansing plants producing gasoline engines included the Peerless Motor Company (40 employees), the New Way Motor Company (75 employees), the Bates & Edmunds Co. (120 employees), the Hildreth Motor and Pump Co. (50 employees), and the Beilfuss Motor Co. (10 employees).

Lansing-built engines frequently received attention in the industry's trade journals. On December 1, 1906, the *Cycle and Auto Trade Journal* featured a 2-horsepower marine engine made by Lansing's Lockwood-Ash Marine Motor Company.

The article, in the magazine's motor boat section, reported that the engine had been "designed by Fred Lockwood, who has been in the gas engine industry for the greater part of the last 18 years. The first motor of this design has been under test for two years and has proved entirely satisfactory . . . The motor, stripped, lists at $42.50 and for $12.50 extra is furnished with carburetor, spark coil, spark plug, battery, secondary and primary wires, cylinder oiler, grease cups, pet cock, propeller wheel, stuffing box and propeller shaft coupling."

Even though the automobile was not instantly replacing the horse, it was having a tremendous impact on Lansing's building industry. Houses needed to be built for the new auto workers, new plants had to be erected and old plants needed renovation. Lansing's major brickmaker, Clippert & Spaulding and Co., was an excellent testimonial to the city's building boom. On December 12, 1905, the *State Republican* reported that 10,000,000 bricks had been made by Clippert & Spaulding during the past year – 2,000,000 more than in any previous year.

City expansion was so great that local contractors

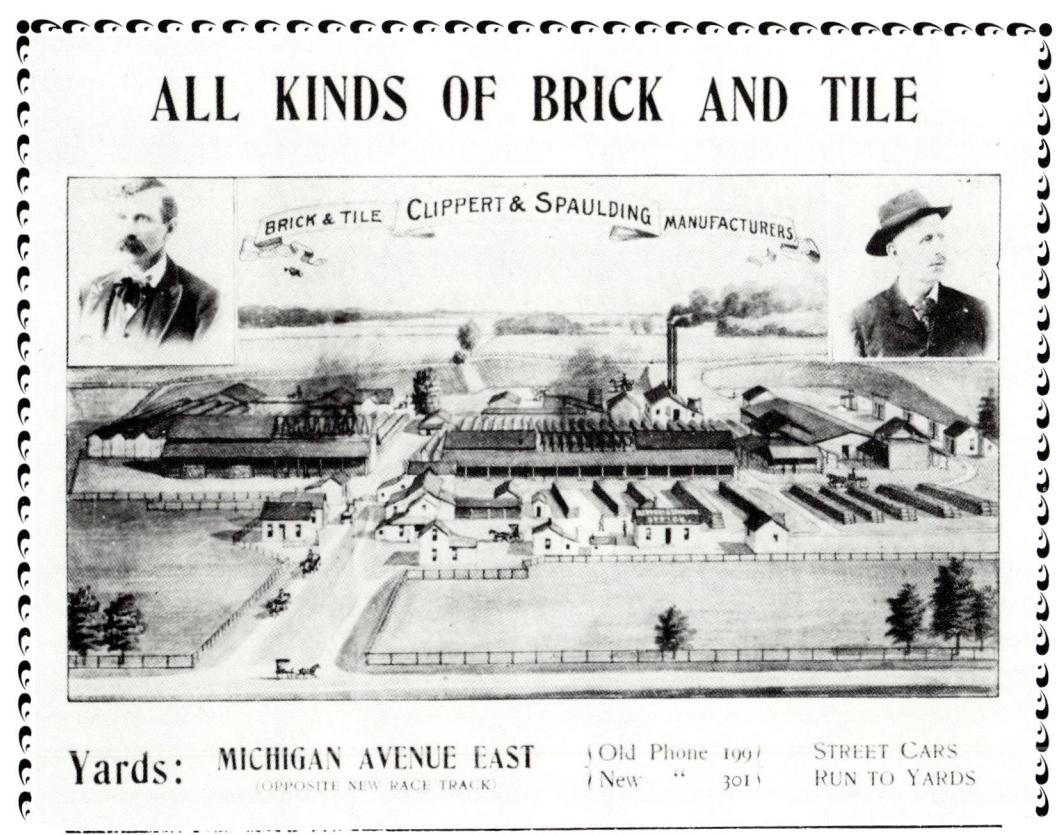

ALL KINDS OF BRICK AND TILE

BRICK & TILE CLIPPERT & SPAULDING MANUFACTURERS

Yards: MICHIGAN AVENUE EAST
(OPPOSITE NEW RACE TRACK)

Old Phone 1991
New " 301

STREET CARS
RUN TO YARDS

were having difficulty finding the labor to complete all their construction orders.

"Secretary O.A. Jenison of the Lansing Business Men's association stated this morning that there were over 300 dwellings under construction or in contemplation of erection in this city during the coming summer and that many of the contractors were experiencing great difficulty in securing the number of carpenters to perform the work," the *State Republican* reported. "It was reported today by one man identified with the building trades that there would be 100 more houses in process of construction at the present time if

Farmhouse designed by Darius Moon (Lansing architect) in Clinton County

the carpenters could be had."

There were also labor shortages in the manufacturing plants, not just in Lansing, but throughout the state. The local papers reported from time to time that representatives from other cities were in town in hopes of hiring Lansing's skilled workers.

The *Republican*, reflecting the positive attitude of the times, observed in 1906 that "Apparently the only men who have been influenced by the arguments (to leave Lansing for other jobs) have been the element which contracts "spring fever" every year about April 1. The more substantial element has appreciated the fact that there is not in the state a better town than Lansing for the working man or one which offers more chances for steady employment."

Supporting Lansing's claim to good working conditions was a 1905 state labor report that indicated the average daily wage for the 4,000 Lansing workers employed in manufacturing plants was $1.92 a day (the average wage for foremen was around $3 a day) and that

only four girls and 42 boys under the age of 16 were found to be working. A year later, it was reported that 600 additional workers were being employed in Lansing and the average wage had increased 13 cents a day.

Employment was also good for the area's architects. Darius B. Moon, one of Lansing's busiest architects prior to 1900, lists 31 projects in his personal records during the 1890s. For the first 10 years of the 20th century, however, 82 projects appear on his list. During the early 1900s Moon designed or remodeled houses for Chester D. Woodbury, R.E. Olds, Arthur Stebbins, Dr. J.W. Hagadorn, Henry Kositchek, Madison Bates, Jason Nichols, Benjamin Davis, and Hugh Lyons. He worked on industrial buildings for the Olds Motor Works, the Lansing Company, Lewis Beck (clothing store), Lewis Driscoll, Atlas Drop Forge, the Michigan Screw company, and Lansing's Fleming Hotel. And he played major roles in the design of Sparrow Hospital, Lansing's Liederkranz Hall, the Lutheran Church School (Chestnut Street) and the Foster Street School.

Just as busy during the early 20th century was Edwyn A. Bowd. Best known for his design of the Ingham County Courthouse (1903), the Carnegie Library (1903), and the Reo buildings (1904), much of his career was spent on the Michigan Agricultural College campus. Appointed MAC's official architect in early 1902, Bowd (and later the firm of Bowd and Munson) was responsible for the design of much of the campus during the next 40 years. In many cases, Bowd designed the building and Lansing's Christman Company did the construction. The Bowd/Christman Co. team was responsible for the Agricultural Building (1908), the Horticulture Building (1924), the present MSU Museum (1927), Giltner Hall (1931), the judging pavilion (1938) and Jenison Field House (1940).

Many of the building projects in the early 1900s were a combination of both the charitable and profit-making interests of members of the Lansing's business community. Lumberman and founder of the Lansing Wheelbarrow Company, James H. Moores, for example, constructed a road (Moores River Drive) along the Grand River. The effort was frequently lauded by the local press and Moores was congratulated for giving Lansing residents a scenic route to explore on Sunday afternoons. The new road also provided access to the subdivisions (28 houses had been built during 1905) that were being constructed near the new road on land owned by Moores.

Theodore E. Potter was not in the least secretive about his motives in offering to donate 2 1/2 acres of land to the Lansing Business Association to help

The depot and REO plant

attract a new factory to the area. "Mr. Potter wants it understood," the *Lansing Republican* reported, "that he is not acting wholly as a philanthropist as he has fifteen more acres in the same location."

While Lansing was going through a definite building boom, its rich were looking at Michigan's north country as a potential escape from the stress and pressures of city life. The community of Roaring Brook, located near Harbor Springs, became a special favorite. Around 1902, for example, Moon designed summer cottages for Arthur Stebbins and C.D. Woodbury at the summer resort.

But the most active architect for Lansing's rich was Earl Mead. Originally located in Lansing, Mead designed apartment houses at MAC for the "subfaculty" (1891), combined with Bowd to draft the plans for the First Baptist Church on Capitol Avenue (1889) and designed the New Church of Our Father at the corner of Capitol Avenue and Ottawa Street (1897). By the turn-of-the-century, however, he had moved to Harbor Springs and was working almost exclusively as a resort architect.

"People from the same town or church established resort associations on land purchased cheaply, donated by the adjacent town, or financed by the railroad," Kathryn Eckert of the Michigan History Division wrote in 1979. "For example, the Harbor Point Resort, originally named the Lansing Resort, was organized in 1878 when a group from Lansing, who had camped out on the site, formed a stock company, sold shares to 19 members, and purchased the point of land from Father Weicamp of Cross Village."

The land was cleared, walks and drives were constructed and a hotel, dock and a boathouse built. "Between 1896 and 1936 Earl Mead drafted plans for the original design and alterations of some thirty cot-

tages of this association," Eckert wrote.

As Lansing approached the end of the first decade of the 20th century, its industrial base was without a doubt dominated by the manufacturing of automobiles and gasoline engines. Lansing automobile pioneer James P. Edmunds wrote in 1942 that by the early 1900s Lansing had become "a gas engine center and the minds of a good share of the population were fixed on the business. "Gasoline" was literally "in the air."

In the spring of 1908, the *Lansing Republican* reported that the Lansing Cooperage Company was the city's only manufacturing concern that used no metal in making its products. Founded by early Lansing mayor, Jacob F. Schultz, the firm was once part of an industry that employed as many as 150 coopers and other workers in the 19th century. By 1908, it was Lansing's only barrel maker, producing pork and apple barrels.

"The trade of a cooper was once eagerly learned by young men, for the wages were large and the demand for their services great," the *Republican* commented. "However, like the colonial shoemaker and the timber hewer, the cooper is a man whose trade has been killed

Agriculture Hall on MSU campus

Gasoline was literally in the air   MSU Archives

kept pace with the rest of the industry with regard to model design and mechanical improvements. The 1911 models were basically the same ones Olds and his staff had developed in 1904."

Olds tried various approaches to boost sales, including hiring advertising genius Claude Hopkins and exploring merger possibilities with people such as Durant and John Willys. More important, however, was the announcement in June of 1910 that Reo had purchased the old Bement plant and planned to begin the manufacture of trucks. A few days later the *State*

by the changes of time and by the conditions of the present iron age."

Even though Lansing's "iron age" revolved around the Olds Motor Works and Reo, the two companies were beginning to experience difficult times and about to make changes that would determine their destinies. The first move was made by the Olds Motor Works. An industry giant in the early 1900s, the company sold only 1,600 cars in 1906 and 1,200 in 1907. Facing significant financial losses and with no obvious solution in sight, Fred Smith negotiated the sale of the Olds Motor Works to Billy Durant and his General Motors Company in 1908.

Official Oldsmobile histories tell the story of how Durant designed his first 1909 Oldsmobile model – the four-cylinder, $1250 Model 20: "So legend has it, he simply drove a Buick to the Olds plant, ordered it cut apart lengthwise and crosswise, had the pieces laid on the ground a few inches from each other and proudly announced the Oldsmobile Model 20."

Whatever Durant did to create the Model 20 he apparently did it right. Of the 6,575 Oldsmobiles sold that year, 5,325 were Model 20s, and employment at the Olds plant doubled to more than 1,000 workers.

Reo was struggling. In 1907, Reo had captured nine percent of the automobile market and ranked third behind Ford and Buick. By 1911, however, the company was in 10th place.

"The reasons for the decline are not difficult to spot," auto historian George May writes. "Reo had simply not

Ex-President Roosevelt enjoying a REO ride   President Taft in a REO

The plant of the REO Motor Car Co.

First "horseless carriage" invented   R. E. Olds first four-wheeled
by R. E. Olds in 1886   machine

1909 REO Touring Car

THERE ARE THREE RELIABLE REOS

Five-Passenger Touring Car	-	$1,000
Two or Four-Passenger Roadster	-	1,000
Two-Passenger Runabout,	-	500

Write for catalog, secure demonstration, and be convinced the REO is the car for you

REO MOTOR CAR COMPANY, Lansing, Michigan

CAPITAL AUTO COMPANY, Lansing, Michigan. - REO distributors for Central Michigan

Republican reported that the new Reo trucks had passed their first performance tests.

"A practical demonstration of the value of the automobile in commercial work has been given since the new Reo 1,500 pound delivery wagon was put into operation a week or so ago," the paper stated. "To try the car out, R.E. Olds used it in hauling rough castings from the plant of the Hildreth manufacturing company in North Lansing to the Reo works in the south end. Heretofore, this work has been done by teams, but now it is found that a great saving can be effected by using the new car."

In October, 1910, a new company, the Reo Motor Truck Company, was formed to manufacture the trucks, paying the Reo Motor Car Company $100,000 for the Bement property. A year later, 1,000 trucks were produced under the name "Speed Wagon."

In 1910 and again in 1914 (in 1912 the "wets" prevailed) Lansing residents voted to prohibit the sale of liquor in the city. While it was no longer legal to stop by a saloon for a drink after work, there were plenty of other "masculine diversions" to attract the factory worker after a hard day at the plant. Angel Priggooris's Majestic at 111 E. Michigan Ave. provided both bowling alleys and billiard tables to a largely male clientel. The fancy interior featured expensive hanging lamps over each table and large ferns in the corner. Priggooris also carried one of the city's largest selections of cigars. In addition to the Majestic, Lansing boasted another bowling alley, a shooting gallery and, at 129 W. Michigan Ave., Ernest Sayers' Turkish bath.

By 1917, however, Lansing's workingmen were generally more concerned about the possibility of war than

finding suitable after-work entertainment. When the United States officially entered the war on April 6, Lansing's laborers were in a patriotic frame of mind. Five days later, the *State Journal* reported that the armed services' need for men was "creating a drain especially on the Reo factories where a half dozen expert tool makers in one department left this week to enlist in the Navy."

An insufficient work force was to be a problem throughout the war and nowhere was it more visible than on the farms. Farmers, encouraged to grow more food as part of the war effort, simply could not find the manpower to harvest their crops. While pressure was applied to local factory owners to release some of their men for the harvests, little help was forthcoming.

"The Olds plant is the busiest it has ever been," said Edward Ver Linden, factory manager of the Olds Motor Works. "We are rushed to meet the demand for automobiles. If the farmer knows a man in our plant who is worth more on the farm than he is in our factory, and will help us find another man to take his place, we will release the farmer's man."

A partial solution to the farm labor problem was the Farm Help Bureau established by the *State Journal*. "Farmers who need men, and men who want farm work, are in many instances meeting at the counter in the *State Journal* office and going away together," the paper reported. "Others are leaving applications which are being filled almost within the hour of their receipt."

While factory owners were reluctant to give up their employees for farm labor, they were eager to assist the war effort in other ways. Men such as W.K. Prudden, Richard H. Scott, and C.E. Bement gave much of their

Farm at the corner of Grand River Avenue and Hagadorn Road around 1915

Cornerstone Setting Ceremony for Prudden Auditorium

time to war-related activities. One of their first projects was the organization of the Manufacturers Garden Committee. Under its plan, businessmen would obtain suitable gardening land and give their employees time off to garden, while the employees would do the planting, weeding and harvesting.

Lansing's factory employees also were strong supporters of the war effort and did not take kindly to fellow workers who were less enthusiastic. The failure of an employee to buy liberty bonds especially seemed to spark the wrath of co-workers. In one instance, a Novo Engine Company worker was loaded on a truck and hauled down to police headquarters "for investigation" because he refused to buy bonds.

"I have an invalid mother to support and have been saving my money for a surgical operation that I need to restore my health," the man told the police chief. While gaining the sympathy of almost everyone who heard the story, the man still was not forgiven until he agreed to buy $200 worth of bonds.

Women played a major role in Lansing's war labor force, and as many as 1,000 took over the jobs of men who had gone into the service. At the J.W. Knapp Company, Bertha Schultz was assigned the task of driving the store's delivery truck, apparently becoming the city's first woman truck driver.

"Shop superintendents as a whole have taken particular pains to place women where there is the least element of danger," the *State Journal* reported in 1918. "In many shops the women have their own rest rooms; their own lockers, mirrors and wash places and these are supervised by matrons. The shop uniform is now appearing and nearly all women are taking kindly to them."

Because of Lansing's many years of experience with building automobiles and gasoline engines, its factories were logical suppliers of goods needed for war use. One of the first contracts was secured by Dail Steel Products for production of its Wolverine Chemical closet – better known as an outhouse. "The U.S. Army is placing orders with the company after having experimented with the speciality for army uses," the *State Journal* reported. "The device has just been approved in rather an enthusiastic manner by army officials."

On December 19, 1917, Reo General Manager Richard Scott announced that his company had received an order to manufacture 3,000 five-ton caterpiller tractors for army use. In order to fill the order and continue its regular production of passenger cars and trucks, Scott said the company's current force of 5,000 men would be worked full time and a night crew added. Reo, in fact, became so busy making tractors during the summer of 1918 that the company had to cancel its summer baseball league.

On Dec. 28, 1917, Lansing companies received another major government contract – $3 million worth of wheels to be produced by the Prudden Wheel and the Auto Wheel companies. Prudden manager Harry F. Harper and Auto Wheel manager D.L. Porter announced the new contract would necessitate hiring 800 additional employees to meet the government's completion date of Jan. 1, 1919.

Other products being produced in Lansing for the war effort included kitchen trailers by the Olds Motor Works, trucks by the Duplex Truck Company, cement barrows by the Lansing Company, gasoline engines by the New Way Motor Company, airplane parts by Gier Pressed Steel, and motor parts by Michigan Crank Shaft. Lansing's Capital

Motion Pictures had a government contract to produce films promoting patriotic projects.

Shortages of coal were causing problems for Lansing businesses and residences, and area merchants were asked for assistance in solving the problem. In late 1917, the city's clothing stores agreed to open their shops at 8 a.m. instead of the usual 7 a.m. In early 1918, fuel administrator W.K. Prudden ordered that fruit and candy stores, restaurants, pool rooms, bowling alleys, cigar stores, and drug stores could open only between 8 a.m. and 5 p.m.

Sugar was also in short supply and its use was severely regulated by the government. While the sugar shortage tended to effect the housewife more than local industries, the True Blue Gum Company was virtually paralyzed.

"War has taught the British a new habit and the habit has made business for a Lansing firm," the *State Journal* reported. "Now Uncle Sam, in curtailing the amount

concentrated on producing goods for the military. Businessmen, trying to make a living, still had to market their goods and services to local shoppers and one of their favorite promotional campaigns was "Dollar Days." Held in September, Dollar Days, according to downtown promoters, was "not essentially a money making occasion for capital city merchants as much as it is an exhibition of what Lansing has. It is the one day in the year that Central Michigan has a chance to look the town over and get real bargains in the latest styles of all merchandise."

On Dollar Day in 1917, for example, $1 would buy a men's dress shirt at Simons Dry Goods, a leather handbag at Dancer-Brogan's, a men's sweater at Kositchek's, a carpet sweeper at Arbaugh's, 14 pounds of rice at the J. W. Knapp Company, and an air rifle at VanDervoort Hardware.

Despite the war, several buildings were being constructed near downtown. One of the most impressive

Auto Body Plant in North Lansing

of sugar gum manufacturers may use, has hit the Lansing concern a genuinely hard blow."

True Blue manager Sherd Wall explained that American and Canadian soldiers had apparently introduced chewing gum to the English who had "gone crazy" over it. True Blue had already sent thousands of pounds of chewing gum to England for the British army. When Wall cabled London merchants that he could no longer supply the gum because of a shortage of sugar, the merchants wired back to "make it without sugar." Unfortunately, according to Wall, the sugar was "absolutely necessary to harden the chicle and glucose."

Not all business activities during the war years were

was the $150,000 Reo clubhouse which was completed in early 1917. Designed exclusively for "recreational and social purposes," the clubhouse was opened for public inspection on May 13 with a special performance by the Reo orchestra. Using the motto "The greatest good to the greatest number," the clubhouse was to provide Reo employees with a place to enjoy lectures, concerts, movies, plays and dances.

A year later, architect E.A. Bowd announced plans for a six-story state office building on Walnut Street (later to be named the Lewis Cass Building). The building, according to Bowd, would be as fire-proof as possible and feature private corridors for employees, toilets on each floor, steam heat and bronze hardware. The new structure would bring together many different state departments which were then scattered throughout the Lansing business district.

On the MAC campus, officials were trying to decide how to replace the engineering complex that had been destroyed by fire in March of 1916. President Frank Kedzie decided to ask R.E. Olds for help and wired Olds who was vacationing in Florida.

"The Lansing auto manufacturer thought it over, recalling that Kedzie had previously proposed that he give a building to the college, and remembering, too, the money that his father had borrowed from Dr. R.C. Kedzie when Oldsmobile and Reo were less than dreams," MSU historian Madison Kuhn wrote. "Olds' gift of $100,000, supplemented by the accumulated surplus from the one- fifth mill tax, financed a replica of the destroyed building with three flanking shops."

The R.E. Olds Engineering building was formally dedicated on June 1, 1917. "The cost," points out Olds' biographer Duane Yarnell, "was $121,422 – more than 121 times the amount R.E. had once borrowed from Dr. Kedzie's father."

While Lansingites celebrated the war's conclusion in late 1918, the city's business community faced the problems of moving from a war to a peace-time economy. One of the most difficult tasks was faced by the management of the Auto Body Company. Auto Body had suffered substantially when the government had severely limited the production of pleasure cars during the war years. In addition, the company had not secured the war contracts that many Lansing firms had received and had been forced to make substantial reductions in its work force. In an effort to get the firm back on its feet, Lansing Company President A.C. Stebbins was temporarily named manager and the Chamber of Commerce pledged support.

"We believe that on general principles it is better to preserve to the community one old established business than to add two new business enterprises," Chamber Vice President Clarence Bement wrote to Auto Body management.

The efforts to put Auto Body back on solid financial footing, however, were largely unsuccessful and a few years later the North Lansing plant stood empty.

Most other businessmen, however, looked ahead to the future with definite optimism. "Lansing, I am sure, is to be one of the fortunate cities during the reconstruction era," banker B.F. Davis stated. "If our factor-

ies can get the materials they need, a wonderful prosperity is to be our lot."

A housing shortage faced Lansing's business community, one that had plagued the area since R.E. Olds began employing large numbers of auto workers in the early 1900s. When Oldsmobile announced its intent to build additional facilities in the spring of 1919, General Motors president W.C. Durant issued a warning to city leaders.

"Lansing offers the best opportunities of any of the 40 localities in which the General Motors corporation has established itself," he told the Chamber of Commerce. "But there is a shortage of houses everywhere. There aren't the homes in Lansing for workmen necessary to the Olds Motor Works expansion."

The Chamber, the Lansing Real Estate Board and the *Lansing State Journal* responded with the vigorous promotion of an "own your own home campaign" and local real estate firms began to develop subdivisions throughout the area. The Standard Real Estate Company, for example, announced a new subdivision between St. Joseph and Michigan avenues in the summer of 1919 and company president L.B. Ayres admitted that the Olds expansion was a major reason for the development.

In addition to the new subdivisions, the 20th-century's third decade brought significant new non-residential construction to the Lansing area. The architecturally significant Strand Theater (later named the Michigan Theater), the Prudden Building, the Masonic Temple, the Lansing YWCA, West and Walter French junior high schools, the Porter Hotel, and a football stadium on the college campus were just a few of the structures built soon after the war.

Others include the State Office Building (which was named the Lewis Cass building after a 1950s fire which considerably altered the structure), the Durant Motors Plant, and Fisher Body (now BOC - Lansing Product Team).

One of the most far reaching industrial decisions in the early 1920s, however, was the consolidation of the Prudden Wheel Company, Gier Pressed Steel, the Auto Wheel Company and the Weis and Leah Manufacturing Company to form Motor Wheel Corporation. Success was almost instant as Motor Wheel turned out a million wheels in 1920 – its first year of operation. By 1924, Motor Wheel laid claim to being the world leader in the manufacture of both wooden and steel wheels.

Chapter 4

Boom & Bust

Mural in the MSU Auditorium painted by Charles Pollock during the 1940s under WPA. Photo by David Olds

1930 Oldsmobile Roadster

Courtesy of Oldsmobile

Except for a brief post-war slump, the 1920s were a period of prosperity and growth, and the Lansing Chamber of Commerce took every opportunity to brag about Michigan's capital city. In it's 1926 "Lansing: A Progressive City" booklet, the Chamber told about the city's 450 acres of parks, its 160 miles of sewers and its many paved streets. And, as an added incentive for prospective companies, the publication stressed that "Lansing is totally free from union influence, there being no organization in the automobile, metal and woodworking

Davis Ice Cream Co. Lansing

Courtesy MSU Archives

trades. Less than one-half of one percent of Lansing's workers are union members." Not surprisingly, the Chamber stated that labor costs were significantly lower than most other municipalities.

Two years earlier, H. Bond Bliss, in an article for the "Michigan Manufacturer & Financial Record," had reported that "Lansing, Michigan is not merely a capital city. It is also an industrial and financial center, a leader in automotive manufacturing; substantial, prosperous, growing; a place for business or pleasure."

The employment statistics Bliss included in his article confirmed what most people already knew – Lansing's economy was dependent on the automobile. With the exception of the 2,000 Lansing workers employed by the state, Reo with 4,600 employees, the Olds Motor Works with 4,200, Motor Wheel with

2,000 and the Durant Motor Works with approximately 1,000 workers were by far the area's largest employers. Bliss also took the opportunity to introduce a new Lansing manufacturer, Fisher Body, to Michigan's business community. Fisher Body, he wrote, "was established this year (1924) on the grounds of the Olds" and is currently "turning out bodies for the new Olds cars and is employing about 200."

Not all Lansing businessmen, however, were convinced that motorized vehicles had completely replaced the horse in commercial ventures. N. H. Winans & Sons, long-time Lansing milk dealers, still used 17 horse-drawn wagons (along with 26 motor trucks) to deliver its dairy products.

"Why, an automobile has to be stopped and started," a company spokesman told "Lansing – This Week" in 1925. "We couldn't use them on the routes. We even have one horse that stops for traffic signals. We can't say he knows when to go ahead and when not to, but at the sound of the traffic gong, he stops stark still until the driver says it's all right to go ahead. And there's another horse that can turn the wagon around without the aid of his driver when he comes to the end of the street."

The Winans' firm was in the minority, however, as most Lansing companies had not utilized "real" horsepower in quite some time – and most were doing quite well in the world of metal, machines and the latest in 20th-century technology. Reo executives took out large ads in the *State Journal* in the mid-1920s, pointing out the firm's growth during the past 20 years. From 1905 to 1926, the ads claimed, Reo employment increased from 304 to 5,209, factory space went from 182,000 feet to more than 2,455,000 and vehicles produced jumped from 864 to 32,650.

In December of 1923, Reo had announced that R. E. Olds was stepping down as company president to take the somewhat honorary position of chairman of the board. For the next several years, Olds would concentrate on developing his Florida land holdings as well as investing in hotels and other real estate projects throughout the country.

Courtesy of Lansing Public Library

The company's new president was Richard Scott, Olds' long-time ally and friend. Scott soon began adding new models to the company's line – at prices both above and below the existing Reos. The Flying Cloud, the Wolverine and additional models of the Speed Wagon were all introduced in 1927 as total production jumped to more than 40,000 vehicles. While Scott's decision to diversify paid off handsomely in 1927, it later contributed to major power struggles between Scott and Olds, and was blamed by some as the major cause of Reo's eventual decline a decade later.

The Olds Motor Works completed a plant expansion program in 1927, investing $3,500,000 in new buildings and equipment. Experiencing a 20 percent sales increase, president and general manager Irving J. Reuter predicted even better things for 1928. "Oldsmobile's New Year's gift to Lansing is the prospect of the greatest year's business in the history of the company," he proclaimed.

Reuter was right. Oldsmobile's new F-28 was advertised as being "Built to Go 50,000 miles with Only Minor Attention." A record 84,635 F-28s were built, selling for a very reasonable $875. The next year, over 100,000 F-29s were produced, coming in such color schemes as Sumatra beige, Algerian blue, Dustproof gray and Locust cream.

Business was also good over on the corner of Hosmer and Hazel streets where the Duplex Truck Company had set up operations. Originally located in Charlotte, Michigan, the firm moved to Lansing in 1917 and had built a reputation for its heavy-duty trucks, frequently picturing road scrapers marked "Ingham County Highway Department" in its advertisements.

Many of Lansing's smaller firms were also finding commercial success in the decade of the 1920s. The Atlas Drop Forge reported "heavy sales, heavy production, heavy employment"; the Lansing Ice & Fuel Company doubled the capacity of its ice plant; and R. E. Olds' Ideal Power Lawn Mower Company (Olds had been issued a patent for a power mower in 1915) was finding a market for its mowers on many of the Midwest's golf courses.

The mid-1920s were also kind to North Lansing as both new buildings were constructed and new businesses were opened. The Bank of Lansing built a new branch office on the corner of Grand River Avenue and Center Street, while Motor Wheel, Reliance Engineering and the Melling Forging Company all expanded existing facilities. The Sherwood Paint Company, the Michigan Fertilizer Company and Capital Aircraft Corporation all moved into Lansing's north end during

1927. The *State Journal* expressed delight that so many good things were happening in the area, writing that "The North Lansing shopping district holds a prominent position in the history of Lansing as it was the city's first business street. . . ."

Lansing was achieving some success in exporting its products to foreign markets and, in a 1927 issue devoted almost entirely to foreign trade, the "Michigan Manufacturer & Financial Record" mentioned several Lansing companies. In addition to the foreign business generated by Reo and the Olds Motor Works, the Hill-Diesel Engine Company sold $108,000 during the past year to foreign countries; the Novo Engine Company had business in Europe, Latin America, Australia and Asia; the United Engine Company sent cream separators world wide; and the Ideal Power Lawn Mower Com-

Hermann Tailor Shop Lansing, 1951

Courtesy MSU Archives

pany had extensive business in Canada. Two Charlotte companies – the Hancock Manufacturing Company and the Jordon and Steele Manufacturing Company were also mentioned for their foreign trade.

A year later, the same business journal ranked Lansing as the state's sixth leading industrial center

Lansing's Roy Chapin after his famous cross-country trip.

ROY CHAPIN

It was on October 27, 1901, that Lansing's Roy Chapin began one of the most remarkable journeys in automobile history. Driving a 1902 curved-dash Oldsmobile, Chapin spent seven-and-one-half days traveling between Detroit and New York in an attempt to prove that a car that sold for only $650 was sturdy and reliable.

While Chapin's cross-country venture received considerable attention from newspapers throughout the country, it was his later accomplishments that enhanced his reputation as a financial genius and a conscientious public servant. A founder and president of the Hudson Motor Car Company, Chapin also served as President Herbert Hoover's Secretary of Commerce in the 1930s, acting as "President for a Day" in 1932.

Roy Chapin was born in Lansing on Feb. 23, 1880, at the family home on Ionia Street. His father was noted Lansing attorney, Edward Chapin, and his mother was Ella King Chapin.

Somewhat sickly as a child, Chapin had to fight off several serious attacks of pneumonia. As a result, he could not participate in sports with the other boys his age, but had to settle for less strenuous activities.

His favorite hobby was photography, and his first camera was one he made himself – a square box with a pinhole in front and a viewfinder on the top. Using glass plate negatives which he developed in his self-constructed darkroom, Chapin took pictures of anyone who would pay for a print. It was later estimated that he made between $3 and $4 a month from his photographic pursuits.

Whatever project Chapin undertook, he seemed to turn it into a financially profitable venture. While a student at Lansing High School, he took over as business manager of the yearbook, The Oracle, and made the publication a money maker. He also took a job selling ads for the Lansing State Republican, delivered orders for a local grocery store and collected rents for the owners of the Hollister Building. Probably his most unusual job, however, was working as the local reporter for the U.S. Weather Bureau in Lansing. Each day, he would fly a kite carrying a thermometer at the end of about 1,000 feet of piano wire, reel the kite in, and take the temperature readings.

Chapin entered the University of Michigan in February of 1899, but left school in 1901 after receiving an offer to work for the Olds Motor Works in Detroit (Olds Motor Works and Roy both moved to Lansing a year later). He worked at odd jobs, then tested cars and, using his photographic skills, took the pictures for the Olds catalogue. By 1904, he was the company's sales manager.

Chapin's 1901 trip from Detroit to New York covered 860 miles, used up 30 gallons of gas and 80 gallons of water and averaged 14 miles-per-hour. When he arrived in front of the Waldorf Astoria hotel, he was so covered with mud that the doorman refused to admit him, insisting he enter by the service entrance. Chapin's boss, Ransom E. Olds, later publicized the trip in many of his advertisements and claimed the trip played a major role in the sale of approximately 750 curved-dash Oldsmobiles to New York City residents in 1902.

"He was young, but already experienced in the whys and wherefores of the business," automotive historian Chris Sinsabaugh wrote about the Roy Chapin of the early 1900s. "He was energetic to the point of restlessness; always looking ahead, always on the watch for new ideas."

Chapin left the Olds Motor Works in 1906 to help form the E.R. Thomas-Detroit Company (later to become the Chalmers-Detroit Motor Company). In 1909, along with Detroit businessman J.L. Hudson, he founded the Hudson Motor Car Company. Hudson served as the firm's first president, but retired in 1910. Chapin, then only 30 years old, took over the top spot.

During his years at Hudson, Chapin produced cars that had a reputation for acceleration, speed and power, and Hudsons were frequent winners at stock car races during the 1930s. The company was absorbed by American Motors in 1954.

While Chapin seemed to have a knack for making profits in the private sector, he was also a dedicated public servant. For most of his professional life he was a strong supporter of public efforts to promote good roads and auto safety. During World War I, he headed the nation's motor transportation committee that was responsible for organizing shipments of munitions and men to embarkment points. In 1931, he became President Hoover's Secretary of Commerce. The State Journal reported that on Nov. 7, 1932, Chapin unofficially became "president for a day" when the president and all the other cabinet members were out of Washington.

Chapin, even though he lived in Grosse Pointe Farms during his days as Hudson president, retained an interest in Lansing. His contributions, for example, built the east wing of Sparrow Hospital – called the Edward C. Chapin wing after his father.

Roy Chapin died on Feb. 16, 1936 of his childhood nemesis, pneumonia. At the time of his death he was the country's oldest automobile executive in terms of service, having presided for 26 years as president of the Hudson Motor Car Company.

The State Journal ran the story front page, under the headline, "Roy D. Chapin, 'Boy Wonder' of Auto Industry, Former Lansing Man, Dies."

"Lansing mourns Roy Chapin because he honored the place of his birth and the long continued home of his parents," the paper's main editorial on Feb. 18 concluded.

D. Thomas

behind Detroit, Grand Rapids, Flint, Highland Park and Hamtramck, and ahead of Saginaw, Muskegon, Pontiac, Kalamazoo, Jackson and Battle Creek.

The city's downtown stores also reported an ideal business climate. One firm, John Herrmann's Sons, at 218 N. Washington, had been founded by John Theodore Herrmann in the late 1870s and was still prospering 50 years later. Richard Herrmann, the great grandson of the founder, had joined the company in 1927 and was being groomed to eventually manage the family business. "The firm maintains a workday force of 35, including Conrad Herrmann, brother of Richard, and to the credit of the house, the labor turnover is remarkably small," the *State Journal* reported. "The average period of service with the company is 23 years, and in one instance 43 years, an enviable record and one which reflects a harmony of goodwill between employer and employee which is admirable."

At 401 N. Cedar, the Lawrence Baking Company announced it was planning to install new baking units in 1927 and would spare no expense in bringing the people of Lansing the finest in baking goods. "As one of the oldest business houses in Lansing and one of the largest of its kind in the state, the Lawrence Baking Company is proud of the fact that it has grown with Lansing and looks forward to continued growth with the city," company president Charles Lawrence said.

Construction, which had been steady if not spectacular during the first part of the 20th century, flourished in the 1920s. One of the most impressive structures was the Strand Theatre and Arcade (later called the Michigan Theatre) at 215 S. Washington. Originally designed by well-known theatre architect John Eberson, it opened in 1921 and featured a 1,774 seat auditorium, crystal chandeliers and Turkish carpets as well as a grand ballroom and a basement bowling alley and billiard room. The adjoining arcade contained 14 fashionable shops.

A leader in Lansing's construction industry was the

Eastern High School
Courtesy Reniger Construction Company

Reniger Construction Company which began business in Lansing in 1916. The Masonic Temple, St. Lawrence Hospital, Eastern High School, the Olds Motor Works administration building, the Maplewood School and residences for Ray Potter (vice president of the Michigan Screw Company) and I. G. Reuter (president and general manager of the Olds Motor Works) were just a few of the company's projects. The best known, however, was probably the Hotel Olds.

Opened in 1926, and financed by a group of investors headed by R. E. Olds, the hotel had experienced a steady increase in business, and by 1931 was housing 80,000 guests and serving 250,000 meals yearly. Known as one of the state's top convention centers, the Hotel Olds had hosted 21 large conventions during 1930 – including 400 Oldsmobile dealers and 300 members of the Michigan Retail Dry Goods Association. Hotel manager George Crocker also entertained the Michigan Livestock Exchange, the Michigan Education Association, the Michigan Photographers' Society, the Michigan Prosecuting Attorney's Association and special meetings for Reo.

"The hotel was a popular stopping place for tourists during the summer months on their way to the Michigan playgrounds of the north and during the football season it was patronized by scores of persons en route to Ann Arbor to the University of Michigan football games," the *State Journal* reported.

In 1929, Olds began work on a 26-story office building on the corner of Capitol and Allegan. Opened in 1930, the Olds Tower (now the Michigan National Tower) housed the Capital National Bank as well as the R. E. Olds Company, created to manage the Olds family investments. For many years the Olds Tower was the tallest building between Detroit and Chicago.

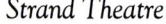
Strand Theatre
Courtesy of Lansing Public Library

The possibility of making Lansing an aviation center was a major theme of the Chamber of Commerce in the early 1920s. It wasn't until 1927, however, when Lansing's Driggs Aircraft Corporation located on West Saginaw Street, that Lansing could legitimately claim any kind of aviation industry. Started by Ivan H. Driggs, a graduate of Lansing's Central High School and already an accomplished airplane designer, the company designed both the Dart and the Skylark aircraft before the firm's demise in 1931 because of financial difficulties.

1928 was even more significant in Lansing's aviation history as the Capital City Airport was officially dedicated, a Lansing-made airplane motor (the Rover) was designed and tested by the aeronautical division of the Michigan Screw Company, and the Capital Aircraft Corporation was established.

The aviation event that probably received the most attention, however, was the arrival on July 5, 1928, of Lansing's first air mail delivery at Capital City Airport. When the Stinson-Detroiter plane set down on the runway, Mayor Laird J. Troyer, Chamber of Commerce President Alton J. Hager, Chamber secretary C. W. Otto and Chamber airport committee chairman Clyde B. Smith were all on hand to greet the city's first mail plane.

Even though Lansing never emerged as a force in the aviation industry, two mid-Michigan flyers are still remembered for their accomplishments in the 1920s and 1930s. East Lansing's Arthur Davis had 9,000 hours of flying time and 143 first-place honors in state and national flying competitions by 1931. In Lansing, Talbert (Ted) Abrams was a pioneer in the field of aerial photography and the aerial survey company that he established in 1923 was known worldwide for its innovative efforts in the field.

Lansing, of course, wasn't the only mid-Michigan community that housed impressive industrial plants. One of the most interesting manufacturing towns was Grand Ledge. Three factories – the Grand Ledge Chair Company and two industrial potteries – are especially noteworthy. Founded in 1883, the Grand Ledge Chair Company was purchased by Edward Turnbull in the late 1880s and stayed in the Turnbull family until 1972. As early as 1901, Turnbull and his company received significant attention in the statewide press. "In eight years he

Grand Ledge Lion

Old Lansing City Hall

(Turnbull) more than doubled the size of the plant, and 100 men are now regularly employed in an effort to keep pace with a demand extending from the Atlantic seaboard to the Golden Gate, and from King Ed's domains on the north to the land of Diaz," the *Detroit Free Press* reported.

Grand Ledge Chair Company chairs have filled the men's and women's dorms at Michigan State University, the University of Michigan and the University of Indiana, provided seats at the coffee shop in Lansing's Hotel Olds and been placed at the Executive Office Building in Washington. For many years the company had a salesroom on the fifth floor of the Blodgett Building in Grand Rapids.

Grand Ledge's industrial potteries produced high-quality sewer pipe and drain tiles from nearby sources of sandstone and clay. It was, however, the lions, turtles, alligators, frogs, coiled snakes, lamp bases and ashtrays that were made by workers at both the Grand Ledge Sewer Tile Company and the Grand Ledge Clay Products Company between 1901 and 1940 that have made

Grand Ledge Clay Products Workers   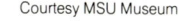 Courtesy MSU Museum

Grand River in the 20s, 40s, 50s
Courtesy of MSU Archives

the two firms famous today.

"Undoubtedly," Michigan State University Museum Director Kurt Dewhurst says, "the Grand Ledge lions and the other creations became an outlet for artistic expression by the workers who were accustomed to rigorous nine-hour work days." Dewhurst, and MSU folk art curator Marsha MacDowell, were so impressed by the clay pieces that they featured the works in an MSU Museum exhibit in the early 1980s.

North of Lansing, St. Johns had been known for the tables made at the St. Johns Table Company around the turn of the century and for wheels made by the Hayes Motor Wheel Company during World War I. In the 1920s, the F. C. Mason Company, which started as a blacksmith shop in 1898, briefly made automobile frames as well as its main product – agricultural implements.

While East Lansing didn't have much in the way of manufacturing plants, it was becoming one of the favorite residential areas for Lansing's middle class. Over the next few years, numerous subdivisions were opened in the area, including Brookfield on the east side of East Lansing in Meridian Township. In the fall of 1926, Brookfield's first model home, completely decorated inside by the F. N. Arbaugh Company, was opened, and ads announcing the event were placed in local newspapers. Interest was high, as more than 2,000 people visited the house on a single Sunday afternoon, the papers reported.

It had been a long time since East Lansing had been a community that was populated exclusively by people connected with the adjacent college. There were strong

Lansing ties. In 1925, the city council included Michigan Millers' executive Luther B. Baker as mayor and Christman Company engineer Fred Dodge as an alderman (there were no college employees on the council). Even police chief John P. Hackett was a former Lansing patrolman and a captain in the Olds Motor Works police force.

The city was also providing lucrative opportunities for Lansing builders. The Reniger Company was building East Lansing's new high school, the Christman Company was constructing the new business block on the corner of Abbott Road and Albert Street as well as Peoples Church and the Horticulture Building on the college campus, and Bowd and Munson were in charge of designing the plans for the new bank building and theater at Grand River and Abbott. An East Lansing firm, Lockwood & Son, had secured the contract for East Lansing's new fire station.

Even though East Lansing did not officially become a city until 1907, its business roots went back much further.

"Mr. John Joy, in 1851, was probably the first man to

do business within the present limits of the city," East Lansing historian J. D. Towar wrote in 1936. "In his log house, located near the corner of Haslett Street and Grand River Avenue, he made, mended and tapped boots and shoes for the pioneers."

Seventy years later, East Lansing's business district was concentrated on Grand River Avenue and catered to both the new Lansing residents and to the established college community. One of the best-known businesses was Hunt's Food Shop, located at the present location of Green's. Opened in 1922 by the four Hunt sisters (Ada, Clara, Agnes and Florence), the shop had a bakery and delicatessen on the first floor and a restaurant upstairs.

"We were known primarily for our Sunday dinners and we catered to families," an 80-year-old Ada Hunt Whithouse told the East Lansing *Towne Courier* in 1973. "If we went below the 1,000 mark on Sundays, something was wrong.

Other popular East Lansing businesses during the 1920s included the M.S.C. Restaurant, the College Drug Store, Our Gift Shop, Fox Brothers grocery, J. H. Tompkins jewelry store and Washburn's Smoke Shoppe.

The good times, however, were not destined to continue forever and many Lansing businessmen were introduced to the 1930s in much the same manner as J. Gottlieb Reutter.

In his 56-page memoir which he penned in 1947, the former Lansing mayor, Chamber of Commerce president and businessman remembered his initiation to the economic downturn of the early 1930s.

"In 1929 I was getting along finely, selling real estate and building houses," Reutter wrote, "when a certain very popular local citizen, connected with a local brokerage firm, came into my office one day and brought me two thousand shares of a local stock, at $34.00 a share, which totaled $68,000. He told me to hold on to it, and he would sell it for me and make me some money. I should have remembered the statement in the Book of Matthew: 'Beware, let no man deceive you.' I knew nothing about stocks, as all I had ever done was to work. In ten days he came back, and brought me two thousand more shares of the same stock at $32.50 a share, which totaled $65,000.00. That made a grand total of $133,000.00. A few years after buying the four thousand shares of stock, Blanche, my wife, and I sold it for $3.00 a share, which meant a loss of $121,000.00."

As in the rest of the country, the 1929 stock market crash officially signaled an end to Lansing's prosperity of the 1920s and plunged Reutter and most of the city's other businessmen into the worst economic crisis of

J. Gottlieb Reutter
Lansing Mayor
1912–1917

Courtesy Lansing Public Library

their lifetimes.

As if the tumbling stock market had not already made mid-Michigan residents uneasy, the December 21, 1931 news of financial difficulties in one of Lansing's largest banks shook the populace even more. "The American State Savings bank did not open for business Tuesday morning, the board of directors having decided to protect its depositors through future administration of its affairs through the state banking department," the *State Journal* reported the next day.

Bank president J. Edward Roe, explained that "The deposits have been withdrawn in such unusually large volume that in our judgment the best interests of our depositors are served by conserving the assets and closing at this time." Bank officers attributed the withdrawals to the similarity in names between a closed Detroit bank, the American State Bank of Detroit, and the local bank. There was no connection.

The closing was short-lived, however, as the American State Savings Bank, as did all other mid-Michigan banks, bolstered by shipments of cash during the night, opened for business the next day. "A small group had collected at one bank and were promptly given their funds at the stroke of 9 o'clock," the *State Journal* reported. "Another bank opened before the customary, paid on withdrawals and at 9 o'clock, when business would ordinarily be taken up, the bank was virtually deserted."

The Junior Chamber of Commerce immediately issued a statement assuring depositors that Lansing banks were sound: "The Junior Chamber of Commerce carries deposits of its funds in five Lansing financial institutions. It proposed to use those funds in the normal transaction of its affairs. We urge all citizens to do the same." The assurances and the banks' willingness to let customers make withdrawals was apparently successful, because the *State Journal* reported in its New Year's edition that banking in the city had returned to normal.

Michigan Central Station, now Clara's

It wasn't only Lansing's businessmen who faced though times after the stock market crash of 1929. During the next few years thousands of mid-Michigan workers found themselves facing either permanent or temporary layoffs and Lansing, which had traditionally faced labor shortages, was now trying to figure out how to take care of large numbers of unemployed.

The "Michigan Manufactured & Financial Record" released information in 1932 that showed employment in Lansing's 18 leading industries in April 1931, was 9,571. A year later, employment had dropped to 7,570 – a decrease of 2,001. There were similar drops in both the ranks of government employees and workers employed in small firms.

The auto companies and their suppliers were especially hard hit as the buying public could not do without food, but could postpone buying a new car. The Olds Motor Works, which employed more than 4,000 workers in the 1920s, announced in late 1931 that its work force had hit a yearly high of a little more than 2,000 workers. Curtailed working hours, sometimes only three days a week, further reduced the auto workers' income. New job applicants were not even being considered for work in the plant as preference was being given to laid-off Olds workers.

Rumors of worse times to come frequently spread through the city. Reports that the Olds Motor Works and Fisher Body were in the process of moving many of their departments to other cities, for example, prompted the *State Journal* to run a front-page story on April 21, 1932, under the headline, "Olds, Fisher Are Not Leaving City." Three weeks later, the company confirmed its intentions of staying in Lansing by announcing that the engineering staff of the Muncie Products Company (it made transmissions for General Motors) was being transferred to the Lansing Olds plant.

An example of the serious situation of Lansing's poor was reported by the *State Journal* on December 12, 1930.

"Evidence of the poverty which exists in Lansing was brought to light early Friday morning when officials of the unemployment registration bureau came to their new quarters at 104 North Washington Avenue. They had occasion to visit the basement of the building and there found a man sleeping on two packing boxes with an old overcoat and a few newspapers drawn over him to keep him warm. Police were called and the man awakened. He said that he formerly had been employed at a store in the building, has lost his job, but his former employers had told him he could sleep in the basement. He was not arrested."

Unemployed men selling pencils and thread, or simply begging, on Lansing streets were a common sight in 1931. Even children were pressed into a beggar's role by desperate parents. To help the situation, the Volunteers of America printed up tickets to be used by downtown shoppers and merchants when approached by someone asking for money for food. The tickets could be exchanged for meals provided by the Volunteers.

With few resources available from state and federal programs, the city of Lansing bore much of the responsibility for taking care of the poor.

". . . the city welfare department found itself catapulted almost overnight from a minor branch of the city government caring normally for less than 300 families, to one of the biggest branches of municipal activity with nearly 2,000 families on its lists," the *State Journal* reported in early 1932.

For many years the fire department had been the city's biggest expense. By early 1932, however, the Depression had turned the city budget upside down. Welfare was costing Lansing more than $388,000, 24.5 percent of total city expenditures. The fire department was in a distant second place with a budget of approximately $202,000, while sewers received $172,000 and police were allocated $156,000.

City welfare director Dan Riordan implemented a

welfare strategy that favored not just handing out money, food and clothes, but putting welfare clients to work. Recipients were given jobs shoveling snow, repairing streets, cutting wood at the city timber tract near Lake Lansing, maintaining city parks and working in the city potato patch near Francis Park. The welfare department also distributed large quantities of seeds in the summer so recipients could grow vegetables in their backyards.

"When any of the welfare charges become ill he is removed to a local hospital where he is treated at city expense," the *State Journal* reported. "In case of death in a family receiving help from the city, the welfare department sees to it that the death victim receives a Christian burial. There is no such thing as a Potter's field in Lansing."

Street Steam Roller, Lansing

Courtesy MSU Archives

Private agencies and individual citizens also lent a hand. The Volunteers of America, for example, quickly remodeled their hall at 122½ Ottawa to provide free lodging for the unemployed. Remodeling efforts were assisted by a $100 gift from American State Savings Bank President J. Edward Roe and the free installation of a large water and gas tank for the shower by Consumers Power Company. The Volunteers also provided temporary jobs for four unemployed men to help with the remodeling.

One Lansing man, J. W. Sanderson, offered 3,700 acres he owned north of Lansing for gardens for the unemployed. "He says that the use of this tract for garden purposes should enable many unemployed of Lansing to raise most of the food they need," the *State Journal* explained.

On September 23, 1932, one of the first shipments of federal government relief arrived in the city – 23,000 yards of flannel shirting, gingham and other materials to be made into clothing. A Reo truck picked up the material at the train station and took it to the Red Cross offices for distribution to area welfare agencies.

A month later, a committee composed of J. W. Brophy of the Olds Motor Works, Lee Benner of Motor Wheel and Father John Gabriels of the Church of the Resurrection organized a city-wide clothing drive for needy families. When the drive ended, 3,000 pairs of shoes, 2,000 men's shirts, 350 overcoats as well as large numbers of men's suits and women's dresses were collected. Trucks and drivers to haul the clothing were provided by such local companies as Olds Motor Works, Motor Wheel, Novo Engine Company, the Hugh Lyons Company, Consumers Power and the Fireproof Storage Company.

While the large number of unemployed had a definite impact on Lansing businesses, reduced working hours for many of the workers who were able to keep their jobs also hurt the local economy. Many state employees were only working on a part-time basis, and in July of 1932, Michigan State College officials announced an average eight-percent salary reduction for staff and faculty. In St. Johns, the *Clinton County Republican* announced in 1933 that school would end May 5 instead of June 9 because "it would be financially impossible to carry on beyond May 5, due to the unusual tax delinquency." Teachers and staff had already seen their pay cut by 50 percent on March 1.

A similar situation existed in Okemos as the school board cut teachers' salaries, but increased the workload by 20 percent. In addition, according to the *East Lansing Press*, "Approximately 40 percent of the annual transportation expense was eliminated when buses were

Consumers Power

Smith Floral's display window at
117 S. Washington, its home from 1921 to 1935.

turned over to teachers and janitors."

Because residents had significantly less money in their pockets to buy goods, shopowners had to work harder to attract customers. In April of 1932, for example, 80 Lansing stores participated in "Dollar Days," an event that had not been held since 1927. "It was good to be on the streets of the business section of Lansing Thursday of this week," the State Journal editorialized. "It was like old times. There were so many people out to take advantage of the bargains of 'Dollar Day' that one could not feel otherwise than that goods were moving."

Two months later city merchants tried again, this time sponsoring "Lansing Day." Factory whistles throughout the city all simultaneously shrieked at 8 a.m. to remind residents of the bargains that could be found in downtown stores. Even though the fire and police departments were swamped by hundreds of calls from people thinking the whistles were announcing some kind of catastrophe, the day was apparently a success. "Lansing Day" also provided some of the unemployed with a day's wages as many stores hired temporary salespeople in anticipation of the increased number of shoppers.

While most of Lansing's downtown merchants were struggling to make a living during the early 1930s, businessmen selling second-hand goods could barely keep up with customer demand. At 511 East Michigan, Harvey E. Wilcox was finding that his used ice boxes, typewriters, desks and a variety of household furniture appealed to Lansing families facing uncertain economic futures. Usually Wilcox employed four men to take care of his stock, but sometimes things got so busy that he would increase his staff to 15.

Elmer Keys was also finding that his furniture repair shop on Marion Street had almost more business than

could be handled, forcing himself to work many evenings in 1932 just to keep up with a backlog of orders. Keys didn't just repair and re-upholster furniture in Lansing, but also had customers in Owosso, Battle Creek, Jackson, Saginaw and Grand Ledge.

Even during the worst days of the Depression, Lansing exhibited an amazing amount of optimism. The State Journal was continually reporting stories that predicted better times were "just around the corner," and for many months ran a front-page column called "Bright Spots in Business." Businessmen (publicly at least) tended to talk about excellent prospects for the future and downplay their losses of the past.

At Michigan State College (since 1925, MSC was no longer the Michigan Agricultural College), President Robert Shaw told the 1932 freshman class that the bad economic times also had their positive side. "Adversity," he said, "causes us to think and ponder upon our objectives as to their adaptability, possibility of attainment or their need for revision. During the world orgy of unprecedented prosperity the world has not done much thinking of the right sort."

There was no shortage of plans by Lansing residents to end the Depression.

One idea to aid the disadvantaged was proposed by R. E. Olds at a 1932 Junior Chamber of Commerce dinner in his honor. Olds suggested passing a "back-to-the-farm" law that would give every unemployed family 10 acres of land and a ready-cut house which the family could put together itself. The land would be tax exempt for five years and, in lieu of the present welfare payments, the cities and villages would provide seeds for planting.

"The state of Michigan has thousands of acres of reclaimed land which can be divided into ten-acre tracts and listed so that first come could have their pick of locations," Olds told the Chamber. "The lumber for the ready-cut houses could be made up by local mills, thus starting this industry as well as the lumber business. The ten acres would produce all the food that any one family could use and they could sell vegetables enough to get spending money.

"I let one man use two city lots on which he raised enough to take care of his family and sold about $1,200 worth a year, so I know 10 acres will give one man a start and livelihood until better times." Olds' proposal was not enacted into law, but it probably made sense.

Farmers, as the industrialists and the factory workers of the city, were also facing troubled times. "The drop in farm income in the last two years has been due primarily to choking of demand by a worldwide Depression rather

Pollock Mural in MSU Auditorium

than to fresh mistakes of overproduction," the "Michigan Farmer" reported in 1932. "Shrinking of public buying power everywhere has necessitated lower prices to move as large a volume of goods into consumption as formerly."

Price declines for the farmers' crops were staggering. According to U.S. Department of Agriculture statistics, corn had dropped form $1.06 a bushel in 1924 to 28 cents a bushel in 1932, while wheat fell from $1.38 to 38 cents, oats went from 48 cents to 17 cents and potatoes from 35 cents to 24 cents. "Michigan farmers are undoubtedly facing at the present time the most serious economic situation ever encountered in the State," the USDA commented.

Still, drastically reducing their operating expenses and becoming even more self sufficient than ever, many mid-Michigan farmers survived. One example was Clinton County mint farmer E. A. Livingston, who was honored for his efforts by the "Michigan Farmer" in 1931. Harvesting 85 acres of mint in 1930, he also raised a dairy herd, drew 120 gallons of syrup from his maple trees and grew onions, carrots and parsnips. Livingston remained convinced that a living could be made from Michigan's farm land despite the bad economic times. "I think success is a matter of looking after the details of the business, of not letting an opportunity pass that holds a chance for profit," he said.

Interestingly, it was frequently the farmers, needing help during the harvest season, who supplied Lansing's unemployed factory workers with the chance to find temporary employment. Farmers could frequently only pay by sharing part of the harvest, but to the unemployed worker, it helped feed the family.

"My husband didn't have work in the shops," Lansing resident Sadie Smith remembers about the depression years. "Reo wasn't doing much. But he went out and worked for a farmer south of Williamston. The farmer had a lot of trees he wanted cut down. He (her husband) took our oldest son and they went out and cut trees. We had an old Studebaker car and they took the back seat out and they filled it up with wood and made enough to buy gas and have a little left over. He worked for different farmers at threshing time. One farmer gave him a bushel of wheat. He took it to the milling company in Lansing and had it ground up for flour, so we had bread. Another farmer gave him a bag of beans, so we had beans."

Area farmers received good news in 1932 when the Lansing Beet Growers Association and the Crystal White Sugar Company decided to reopen the Lansing sugar plant on North Street. Originally begun in 1900

Elwin C. Holmes and daughter Luvenia polishing tomatoes from their garden in the early 1930s.

by the Kilby Manufacturing Company of Cleveland, the plant had been idle since 1928. "Probably no plant in this city has distributed more money to more persons than the Lansing sugar factory," the *State Journal* commented. "Its operations affect many persons and many industries. It leaves thousands of dollars right in the area where it operates. This year hundreds of men found employment in the beet fields and thus were able to support themselves and their families without asking public aid."

Mid-Michigan residents were so excited about the opening of the sugar plant that they hosted a "Sugar Festival" on September 28. Complete with a parade, the main events took place near the bridge at the corner of Grand River Avenue and Turner Street and featured band, orchestra and vaudeville performances as well as an address by Lansing Mayor Peter Gray. "Everybody who uses sugar can help," Gray said. "It's really the only business proposition I ever heard of where every householder has a chance to help financially and still benefit from the help themselves."

The Lansing Sugar Company wasn't the only new business to open its doors during the early 1930s. On December 13, 1930, the W. T. Grant Store held its grand opening on Washington Avenue in downtown Lansing. The next year, the Liebermann Trunk Com-

Cannell & Edmonds (1897)

pany began its Lansing business in a vacant store formerly occupied by the J. W. Edmonds Company at 107 South Washington Avenue.

In East Lansing, the Kroger Grocery & Baking Company held its grand opening in October of 1931, complete with a free grocery bag for the women and balloons and suckers for the kids. One of the chief attractions of the new store was the new vegetable counter. "The vegetable and produce stand includes a fine-mist spray to keep the merchandise always fresh. This mist spray is electrically operated and is the latest development in vegetable display known," the *East Lansing Press* reported.

But the news that probably created the most excitement was the 1932 announcement by the J. C. Penney Company that it had leased the first three floors and the basement of the Prudden Building for the next 15 years. In making the announcement, Penney president E. C. Sams said that his company's decision to open another store "reflects faith not only in Lansing's present retail trade outlook but also in the city's future business potentialities."

Actually, despite significant unemployment in manufacturing plants, the construction industry seemed to be one of the few bright spots in Lansing's economy. Buildings completed in the early 1930s included the 15-story City National Bank Building (currently the home of the Bank of Lansing), new post offices in both Lansing and East Lansing, the remodeling of the old Capitol National Bank quarters in the Hollister Building into retail shops and manufacturing plants for Melling Forge Factory, Reo and Atlas Drop Forge. On the MSC campus, Mary Mayo Hall and a new wooden basketball floor were completed. In East Lansing, new construction included a $30,000 house for the Kappa Kappa Gamma sorority, an addition to the city hall and fire station and several business establishments on Grand River Avenue.

Chapter 5

Recovery & World War II

One-time Governor Kim Sigler 1947-48

Courtesy Michigan State Archives

*from 1932
Calendar
Lyman Body
Company*

Longtime Lansing businessman John Affeldt always knew that Lansing would come back from the Depression. "I have been in business for half a century and have seen Lansing flat broke a number of times," he told a *State Journal* reporter in 1933. "But the old town never yet took the count and always came out of her troubles stronger and better than ever."

Affeldt was right. Lansing did come back. It's not always only the governmental statistics and the pronouncements of business leaders that signal the coming of better times. In October of 1934, for example, the Ingham County Kennel Club held its annual all-breed dog show at Demonstration Hall on the MSC campus.

"Fanciers throughout the state report a substantial recovery in the sale of pedigreed dogs of all breeds," the *State Journal* reported. "Prices obtained this year were much higher than for several years past. From all indications the breeding and sale of pedigreed dogs is getting back to something near normal and breeders and fanciers are beginning to realize the usual profits."

Official statistics, of course, also indicated that by 1934 mid-Michigan was beginning to experience a substantially improved business climate. Lansing's employment, according to the Chamber of Commerce, stood at 15,163 in May compared to just 7,175 at the same time in 1933. Building permits issued by Lansing's city building department totaled 490 in 1934 as compared to 282 in 1933 and 326 in 1932.

By 1934, area industrial plants were experiencing significant sales gains. Motor Wheel reported net earnings of $500,000 for 1934 – an increase of approximately $380,000 over the previous year. The firm also announced it had 33 percent of all the wheel business in the country, more than "any other single builder of wheels," and had reached a peak employment total of 2,550 employees – 42 percent above 1933. Oldsmobile also saw its sales dramatically improve, producing 75,574 cars in 1934, the highest number since 1929. Production got better in the next few years as 91,357 units were produced in 1935, 120,317 in 1936, and 179,830 in 1937. Employment in the Oldsmobile and Fisher Body plants increased from approximately 9,000 workers in 1935 to more than 12,000 in 1936.

The good times also brought expanded public relations programs at Oldsmobile. In early 1936, the *State Journal* reported that "For the first time in many years the people were asked by Mr. McCuen (president and general manager C.L. McCuen) and his factory executives to visit the plant and see for themselves how Oldsmobiles were built. In a three-day open house thousands took advantage of the opportunity to see the factory in full production."

In August of 1936, when the plant was shut down for model changeover, thousands of Oldsmobile employees were guests of management at an outing at Lake Lansing. Billed as "Lansing's largest picnic," workers spent an entire day and evening "playing as hard as they worked."

Despite a severe drought in 1934, the income of Michigan farmers was improving. In Lansing, the reopening of the sugar beet plant in 1932 did not turn out to be a one-year experiment. By 1934, 1,200 beet growers were producing 85,000 tons of sugar beets and 250 carloads of beets had arrived at the plant by railroad. Plans for 1935 included a complete overhaul of plant facilities, providing jobs for a "considerable force of skilled and unskilled labor."

Mid-Michigan was getting substantial help in its recovery from President Franklin D. Roosevelt's New Deal programs. In 1935, for example, the removal of street car tracks from Lansing's city streets was started under the Civil Works Administration, continued under the Federal Emergency Relief Administration and completed under the Works Progress Administration.

"Although the three alphabetical agencies were involved with the city engineering department in the car track removal, the project provided jobs for hundreds of men over a long period of time," the *State Journal* reported. "In some instances the pavements were torn up and relaid for the second time after tracks were removed. This provided additional work."

Factory in Production

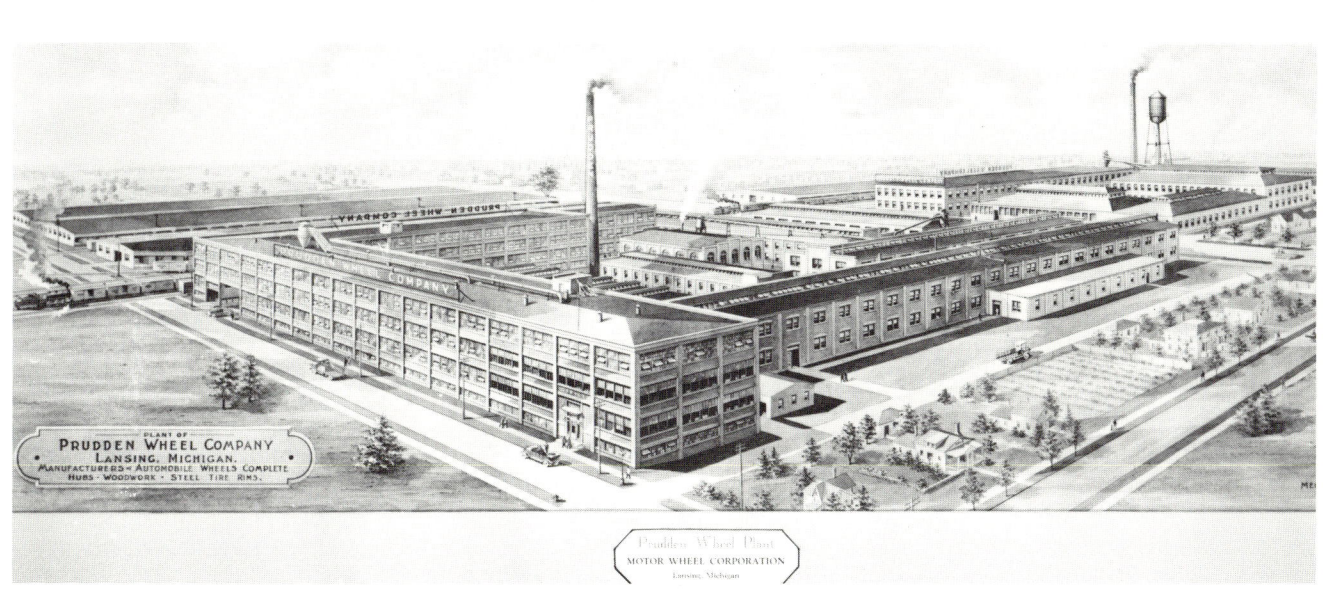

The Prudden Wheel Company was one of the forerunners of Motor Wheel Corporation.

MOTOR WHEEL

The future of Motor Wheel – one of Lansing's largest and most respected firms – was decided to a great extent by three broken match sticks.

Back in 1920, prospects of a growing and expanding wheel market brought together Lansing industrialists Harry Harper, D.L. Porter and B.S. Gier to discuss a possible merger. Harper chaired the Prudden Company, Porter headed Lansing's Auto Wheel Company and Gier operated the Gier Pressed Steel Company.

A fourth company – Weis and Lesh – produced cured hickory spokes.

On Jan. 17, 1920, the four companies became one – Motor Wheel Corporation.

Who would be president? Harper won after it was decided to draw match sticks to decide on division of $1,000 in stock.

There were 100 shares – par value of $10 each, so Gier, Harper and Porter agreed that the man drawing the shortest of the three broken matches would get 32 shares, and the other two would each get 34.

Harper drew the long stick from the hand of Porter. Gier also drew a long one, leaving only the short match for Porter. Porter sided with Harper, who was elected president. Gier became a vice president and secretary, and Porter, with "only" 32 shares, was designated vice president.

Doug Pearson

Other post-Depression projects completed with the help of federal funds included the expansion of Lansing's sewer system (PWA), remodeling of the Michigan Avenue bridge (WPA), expansion of city parks (WPA), and constructing an addition to the Walnut Street School and a third floor to Eastern High School (PWA). In smaller communities such as St. Johns, federal monies helped finance construction of railroad crossings on Clinton Avenue (WPA), build a baseball field, bleachers and dugouts at St. Johns City Park (WPA), and erect the city's new city hall-library (PWA).

In early 1941,, state WPA administrator Abner E. Larned reported that during the previous 12 months in Ingham County WPA-funded projects had installed or improved 6,000 feet of sanitary sewers, 700 feet of storm sewers, 32 manholes, 21 catchbasins and 115 sewer connections. In addition, the new Lansing water conditioning plants, a new Lansing city garage and service building, and additions to three hospitals, 25 schools and 6 town halls were all constructed with WPA funds.

Not everyone, however, survived the Depression in good shape. Reo had been experiencing problems even prior to the stock market crash. While the auto industry was enjoying record sales in 1929, Reo's sales of cars and trucks were declining. "Ransom E. Olds had apparently had doubts for some time about the wisdom of (Richard) Scott's diversification program, and the events of 1929 only served to convince him that he had been right in feeling that Scott had over-extended the limited resources of the company on the program that had failed to achieve the anticipated amount of increased sales," wrote auto historian George May.

The economic depression of the early 1930s, of course, further slumped sales and Reo reportedly lost more than $6 million when the Reo Royale failed to sell as expected. In 1932, Reo did not pay its stockholders a dividend – the first time that had happened since 1911. The company's unstable management direction undoubtedly also contributed to the company's problems (Scott, William Robert Wilson, Donald Bates, and R. E. Olds all took turns running Reo between 1930 and 1936).

In 1936, Reo announced it was dropping its production of passenger cars to concentrate on the truck market. Reo, taking a positive approach, said its decision was based on the growth potential of truck production rather than declining car sales.

"The decision to devote all efforts to the manufacture and sale of trucks and busses was made after an exhaustive study of the automotive field," according to the *State Journal*. "The results of this study indicated that, even though the bus and truck business had expanded to a remarkable degree over a period of years, the expansion had only started and the opportunities in this field

WPA Crew, Comstock Park, Lansing

were limitless."

May, however, saw it somewhat differently: "Reo, like nearly all other small producers of automobiles that had survived into the thirties, had found the competition from the Big Three, combined with the enormous drop in sales resulting from the Depression, made it impossible for them to stay in business."

Although the company was having financial difficulties, Reo trucks enjoyed an excellent reputation and the firm was considered an industry leader. The February, 1936, issue of *Michigan Trucking News* gave Reo a two-page spread in the center of the magazine and called the new truck model, "a line of smartly stream-lined trucks, meeting approximately 98 percent of all commercial transportation requirements."

The Depression was even harder to Durant Motors which had operated its Lansing plant since 1921. Employing as many as 2,500 workers before the Depression to produce the Star automobile, the Durant plant shut down in 1931. While the Durant closing had a harsh impact on the Lansing economy in the early

R.E. Olds & Governor Frank Fitzgerald 1930s

1930s, the old plant ended up playing a positive role in the city's economic recovery a few years later. In the spring of 1935, General Motors purchased the Verlinden Avenue factory as the new home for Fisher Body. GM immediately transformed the plant into what the *State Journal* called the "most modern body building factory in the world." The revamped facility soon began turning out bodies for both Oldsmobile and Chevrolet and employed more than 3,500 in its first year of operation.

On December 11, 1934, as Lansing was struggling to emerge from more than four years of economic troubles, a non-economic disaster hit the city's downtown area – fire destroyed the Hotel Kerns.

"Unfortunately, the hotel was a blazing inferno when fire trucks arrived," a *State Journal* reporter wrote. "Caught like rats in a trap, guests of the hotel stumbled over each other in the halls and many more were unable to get out of their rooms because of the flames."

The fire that destroyed the 17-year-old structure left more than 30 people dead and leveled at least a temporary blow to Lansing's attempt to attract an increasing number of conventioneers and tourists. Still, the city was seeing thousands of tourists' cars heading up to the state's northern resorts, frequently stopping at such local attractions as the Capitol, the college campus, and Potter Park. The city tourist camp between Michigan Avenue and Kalamazoo Street was attracting dozens of travelers pulling "modern type trailers equipped with every modern convenience."

While the Hotel Kerns was an unfortunate casualty of the early 1930s, Lansing's downtown section soon gained a most imposing structure – the new home for the J.W. Knapp Company. Designed by Bowd & Munson and built by the Christman Company on the site of the old Hotel Downey on Washington Avenue in 1937, the five-story Art Deco building created considerable attention in both the statewide and national press for its architectural innovation.

Lansing employers had traditionally taken a protective approach toward their workers, rewarding them in good times and caring for them in bad. Reo was especially active in providing its employees with incentives to identify with company management, believing that cooperation increased efficiency and that "good will was sure to follow." To maximize cooperation between management and labor, the company created a promotional magazine, "Reo Spirit," and sponsored sports teams, fairs, speakers, movies and encouraged its foreign employees to learn English and become American citizens.

The Reo fairs began in 1917 and became one of the city's biggest fall events, attracting 22,678 visitors in 1921 and 28,511 in 1922. Both Reo and other area businesses supplied premiums to entries ranging from photographs to pickles. In one early fair, according to the elaborate premium book published by Reo, the best knitted mittens won a white enamel dresser tray from the Jury-Rowe Company, the best white onion won a box of candy from the Perry Barker Candy Co., and the handsomest baby boy took home "$1.00 in trade" from the J. W. Knapp Co. Only Reo employees and their families could enter.

Labor organizations had traditionally played very minor roles in Lansing's industrial heritage, but things changed dramatically in 1937. On March 11, Reo employees, upset over the firing of 15 fellow workers and a reduction in pay, staged what was probably Lansing's first official sit-down strike. The strike lasted a month and didn't end until 75,000 striking Chrysler workers settled 12 hours earlier.

"A parade of 6,000 Lansing auto workers led by the Dodge union band of Detroit marked the end of the Reo strike on April 8 in what was up to that time the largest labor demonstration in the city's history," the *State Journal* reported.

A little more than a month later, on May 21, UAW-supported employees at the Capital City Wrecking

1940 Oldsmobile "Woody" Station Wagon.

Courtesy of Oldsmobile

Company went on strike, shutting down the nine-year-old firm at 719 E. St. Joseph St. Then, on June 1, Judge Leland W. Carr issued an injunction to prevent picketing. Six days later, action taken by Ingham County Sheriff Allan MacDonald and the vigorous response of organized labor put Lansing on the front pages of papers all across the country.

"The demonstration was ordered in protest against the arrest of two women and six men, seized at 2 a.m. in their homes on warrants charging they interfered with operations of the Capital City Wrecking Company, where a strike has been in progress for several weeks. One of the women was the wife of Lester Washburn, UAW official," the Chicago *Daily Tribune* wrote on June 8. "Declaring a labor holiday, union leaders closed all automobile plants here and brought sympathetic delegates from Detroit and Flint. The unionists flocked to the downtown district and blocked off with rows of cars an area which included the city-county building and state capitol."

In an editorial the next day, the Chicago paper compared the Lansing strike and similar activities in Ohio to incidents during the Russian Revolution, and concluded that "The outlook for the law abiding people of Ohio and Michigan is dark." Eighteen months later, however, the *State Journal* reported that things had not become as "dark" for Lansing's citizens as the Chicago *Daily Tribune* had predicted. "In contrast with 1937, there were no strikes or major labor disputes in Lansing during 1938," the paper reported.

As the decade of the 1940s approached, Lansing's economy was showing marked improvement over the Depression years of the early 1930s. By 1939, many of the city's veteran companies were again doing record business. The 54-year-old Simon Iron and Steel Corporation, founded in the 1880s, was shipping millions of pounds of scrap metal from Lansing factories to far-away steel mills. The Novo Engine company, possibly the oldest gasoline engine maker in Michigan, was experiencing high demand for its engines in such places as the

West Indies and South America. And the city's oldest firm, the Lansing Company (started in the early 1880s as the Lansing Wheelbarrow Works), had long ago ceased specializing in wheelbarrows and had branched out to include dozens of other products as well.

Lansing was also experiencing a 12-year high in construction during 1940 with 1,450 building permits issued and building costs estimated at more than $6,000,000. Among the major construction projects were expansions for Oldsmobile, Motor Wheel, Piatt Products Company, and the Duplex Truck Company. On the college campus, Mason Hall, Abbott Hall, the Auditorium, Campbell Hall and Jenison Field House were built between 1938 and 1940.

Machine Gun Manufacturing at Oldsmobile in 1943.

Courtesy of R.E. Olds Museum

Suddenly, everything changed. On December 7, 1941, the Japanese attacked Pearl Harbor and Lansing's biggest companies almost immediately converted their peacetime facilities to defense plants. By year's end, most Lansing firms were either involved or planning to be involved in the production of war goods. One of the earliest recipients of federal defense contracts was Motor Wheel. "The dawn of a new year (1942) finds the corporation working day and night on three contracts and speeding preparations for the production of 75 millimeter and semi-armor-piercing shot," the *State Journal* reported.

The Nash-Kelvinator Corporation took over the old Duplex Truck Company plant (also used at one time by Reo for truck manufacturing) at the corner of Mount

Hope and Washington avenues in 1941 for the construction of parts for the Pratt-Whitney aircraft engines. In another old Reo plant on South Cedar, Nash-Kelvinator began building Hamilton Standard propellers for bombers. It was predicted that as many as 8,000 people would be hired for the work.

Oldsmobile, of course, became a major supplier of defense goods and its battle cry on the assembly line was "Keep 'Em Firing." While precise production figures were classified, it was estimated that Oldsmobile was producing $2,000,000 worth of war materials each day and many new workers had been hired to replace the 2,255 Olds employees in the armed forces. By the war's end, statistics later released by Oldsmobile indicated the company produced 48 million rounds of ammunition, 140,000 aircraft machine guns and tank cannon, 175 million pounds of forgings for military guns and vehicles and nearly 350,000 aircraft engine parts.

"A trip through Lansing war plants today reveals many startling changes, especially in personnel," the *State Journal* wrote in early 1943. "Men who formerly operated retail business establishments, salesmen, gas station attendants, housewives, clerks, and people from many of the professions are working together along assembly lines."

A year later, in its special New Year's edition in 1944, the *State Journal* reported that 40 Lansing companies, employing approximately 33,000 workers, were producing goods for the war effort. Lansing's top manufacturers of war goods were Oldsmobile, Nash-Kelvinator, Reo, Motor Wheel, and Atlas Drop Forge.

World War II ended in late summer of 1945 and, on October 15, the first automobiles were already rolling off the Oldsmobile assembly line. "Not surprisingly, they were warmed-over versions of the 1942 models," Oldsmobile historians wrote on the company's 75th anniversary in 1972. "This was typical practice throughout the industry; time, of the essence, had dictated stop-gap measures."

Lansing industrialists seemed to have few problems in converting their physical plants to peacetime use. Motor Wheel, for example, immediately announced a $2 million expansion plan that would raze its old plant between the New York Central and Pere Marquette railroads and replace it with a new facility designed exclusively for the storing and shipping of passenger car wheels. Additions were also planned for the company's Duo Therm division which already had enough orders on file to operate for a year and a half at its pre-war capacity.

Finding peacetime jobs, however, for the approximately 33,000 employees (including 2,600 women) who worked in Lansing's war-time factories, and for the 13,000 people returning from the armed services could have been a serious problem. Luckily, Lansing products were in sharp demand after the war, many women who had held war jobs chose to return to household duties, and many "migrants" (workers who had migrated to Lansing for work in the defense plants) returned home. By 1947, the Lansing employment picture looked good as the Chamber of Commerce reported 24,000 workers were employed in 25 leading industries – an all-time peacetime high.

"Barring a new wave of strikes or other difficulties that might retard production, the city's industrial leaders look forward to new records and steady employment

Don Norris with political cartoon for Oldsmobile's newspaper in 1940s.

1950 Oldsmobile "88" Hardtop Coupe (Holiday).

Courtesy Oldsmobile

for thousands during the coming year," a *State Journal* reporter wrote in early 1947. "As rapidly as materials are available in greater quantity there will be a marked increase in output at the plants of Oldsmobile, Fisher Body, Motor Wheel, Reo Motors, Inc., John Bean, and many smaller industries."

The transition from war-time to peacetime manufacturing was slow for some. Oldsmobile, for example, sold 180,908 units in 1947 – 78,000 more than the previous year, but short of its peak year of 1941. Behind the "Futuramic" new designs of Harley Earl's styling crew and the new Rocket V-8 engine, however, Oldsmobile turned out 282,885 cars in 1949 and approximately 396,757 in 1950.

While Oldsmobile was proud of its increasing sales totals, it also took pride in its "Valiant" program for the benefit of disabled and handicapped veterans. Oldsmobiles, equipped with hydramatic drive and special driv-

---

Lansing Industries Employing In Excess of 100 Workers That Produced War Goods During World War II

Abrams Aerial Survey Corporation – aircraft instruments and air mapping equipment

Atlas Drop Forge – forgings for tanks and bombers

Centrifugal Fusing Co. – castings

Duplex Truck Co. – trucks and searchlight equipment

Federal Drop forge – forgings

Fisher Body – aircraft parts

Hill-Diesel Engine Co. – engines for the Navy

Hugh Lyons & Co. – miscellaneous

Industrial Metal Products Co. – tools, dies and gauges

John Bean Manufacturing Co. – fire fighting equipment

Kold-Hold Manufacturing Co. – low temperature testing equipment

Lansing Company – miscellaneous

Lansing Drop Forge – forgings

Lansing Machining Co. – tank and truck parts

Lansing Paint & Color Company – paints and materials for explosives

Lansing Stamping Co. – steel products

Lundberg Screw Products – screw machine parts

Lindell Drop Forge – forgings

Melling Drop Forge – forgings

Motor Wheel – wheels and oil-burning appliances

Nash-Kelvinator – propellers

Novo Engine Company – gas engines, machinery and small electric plants

Olofsson Tool & Die – tools and dies

Oldsmobile – ammunition, aircraft cannon and forgings

Reo Motors – trucks, transmissions, axles and tank parts

Wohlert Corporation – machine parts

Source: the *State Journal*, January 1, 1944

ing controls, had been made available to handicapped veterans since 1945. By the end of 1947, 26,000 special cars had been produced and many were used in rehabilitation programs at government hospitals.

In the countryside, area farmers found that despite low yields due to spring floods, summer droughts and early fall frosts, 1947 still turned out to be a pretty good year.

"The harvest was much better than anyone had hoped for," MSC Agriculture Dean Ernest L. Anthony told the *State Journal.* "We had a bumper wheat crop, and although the total corn crop was the smallest since 1936, the money loss wasn't great because the price was so high." Anthony said that two new developments – an oil-burning anti-frost machine and improvements in chemical weed control – had great potential for the farming community. The anti-frost machine, developed by the college's agricultural engineering department, was expected to be ready for widespread use by early 1948, while chemical weed control was used extensively in Michigan in 1947 and was "generally accepted."

As mid-Michigan moved toward peacetime prosperity, its greatest industrialist, R.E. Olds, died of "complications of old age" on August 26, 1950. Although he had not been active in the city's business affairs for a number of years, the 86-year-old auto pioneer was still regarded as the "elder statesman" of the business community and the primary reason for Lansing's development as a manufacturing center.

"Death came to the production genius in his rambling Victorian mansion in downtown Lansing," the Detroit *Free Press* reported on August 27. "He passed away amid the noisy rumbling traffic he helped develop." In an editorial two days later, the *Free Press* wrote that "Mr. Olds, last of the mechanical Mohicans, was a kindly Christian man not given to the wars of the giants that followed in his wake."

Olds' death was not just a Michigan event, but carried in newspapers throughout the world. The Chicago *Tribune,* for example, wrote that "His curiosity and love of 'tinkering' led him to experiment with a horseless carriage powered by an internal combustion engine, a device which in the 1890s was like rocket powered space ships today, merely an engineering dream."

By the beginning of 1952, the Lansing industrial sector that R.E. Olds had so greatly influenced was called one of the "bright spots" in Michigan's economic picture by the *Michigan Manufacturer & Financial Record.* In addition to the strong manufacturing base anchored by Oldsmobile, Motor Wheel and Reo, one of the reasons cited for the optimistic outlook was the opening of a

Ransom Eli Olds
". . .last of the mechanical Mohicans."

new fertilizer facility in town. "Further impetus to Lansing industrial activity was provided last December when the Davison Chemical Corp. of Baltimore, Md. purchased the fertilizer assets of the Michigan Fertilizer Company," the journal commented. " The present output of the Lansing plant is between 60,000 and 65,000 tons of commercial fertilizer for farm use annually. Starting in July, Davison is planning an expansion program for the plant which will include installation of machinery to manufacture fertilizer in granulated form as well as in powdered form."

Construction was also booming as a record 1,338 building permits were issued for single-family residences in 1950 in the Lansing area, and another 945 in 1951. "Enough new homes and apartments were started in the Greater Lansing area last year to house the population of an entire city the size of Eaton Rapids, Mason or St. Louis," the *State Journal* reported in early 1952.

The newspaper itself contributed to the city's construction activity as it moved into its $2,000,000 facility on Lenawee Street in August of 1951. The new two-story high presses could print up to 55,000 copies per hour.

Other major 1951 building projects in what was one of the city's biggest ever expansion years included the $5,000,000 General Motors engine plant on West Saginaw Street (completed in 1952); a new home for the Auto-Owners Insurance Company at the corner of Kala-

Lansing Product Team facilities in Lansing and Lansing Township. Looking northwest, the facilities include the former Fisher Body plant on Verlinden (lower right) and Plants 2 and 3.

mazoo and Washtenaw streets; a J.C. Penney Store on Washington Avenue; the new YMCA building on Townsend Street; the $385,000 St. Vincent's home for orphans; additions to plants at Melling Forging, Atlas Drop Forge, and Industrial Metal Products; drive-in branches for Michigan National and American State Bank; and new Market Basket grocery stores on North Larch and West Saginaw streets.

Sports got much of the attention on the Michigan State College campus in the early 1950s as the football team went undefeated and the boxing team won the national championship. The event that probably had the most long-range impact, however, was the completion of the $2,000,000 Kellogg Center for Continuing Education. Built with the help of more than a million dollars of money from the W. K. Kellogg Foundation of Battle Creek, the facility featured a 193-room hotel and facilities for adult education, conferences and special training programs.

Former MSU president John Hannah wrote in his 1980 memoirs:

"I remember very well the day I first went to Battle Creek to talk to the Kellogg Foundation and to ask Dr. Unary Morris, who was then its president, to provide a substantial grant to build the continuing education center (now known as the Kellogg Center) and to finance the operations of the program

for the first few years. A great deal rested on the outcome of that visit, and about all I had going for me was the fact that I had come to know W.K. Kellogg pretty well. After he became blind he put his great interest in Arabian horses and in agriculture and had developed his farm near Augusta, which eventually became part of the MSU Bird Sanctuary and Farm.

"Fortunately, the foundation gave us the grant and we started on a program that was almost immediately copied by other land grant universities. The MSU Kellogg Center and the Kellogg program at Michigan State were both widely imitated, not only by public universities, but by private institutions all over America. The Kellogg Foundation subsequently financed several of them."

While new structures were dotting the Lansing landscape, other buildings saw their last days in 1951. On Feb. 8, Lansing experienced its greatest fire – the $8 million dollar burning of the state office building (later called the Lewis Cass Building after being rebuilt). Started by a 19-year-old state highway department employee who set fire to maps in his office "because I thought it would keep me from being drafted," the fire, water and later ice (temperatures were below zero) destroyed vast amounts of government records and forced state employees to find temporary working quarters throughout the city.

66

While 1951 was significant for the great changes in the physical make-up of the city, it also saw Lansing once again convert much of its manufacturing facilities to make goods for the Korean conflict. This time, however, it wasn't just "guns," it was "butter" too. Oldsmobile estimated that 21 percent of its work force was employed in defense activity in early 1952, while the rest were involved in automobile production. A plant originally designed for steel storage was converted to the production of 90-mm, high-velocity cannon for tanks, and Oldsmobile's 6-cylinder engine plant was converted to the production of bazooka shells.

When more than $236 million in defense contracts were awarded to Michigan in early 1952, the *Michigan Manufacturer & Financial Record* reported that Oldsmobile, Reo, Motor Wheel, Kold-Hold Manufacturing Company and the Abrams Instrument Corporation were all recipients. Kold-Hold received one of the largest contracts – $3,298,261 – to build components for the M114 bomb.

While Lansing industrialists had traditionally measured their success on production, profits and levels of employment, both private residents and city officials were insisting that manufacturing plants also had an obligation to protect the surrounding environment. Apparently, Lansing manufacturers were taking their environmental responsibilities seriously as city pollution control engineer E. K. Piatt reported in 1954 that

State Office Building smoulders (later the Lewis Cass Building)

Courtesy of Reniger Construction

compared to other cities of the same size in the United States, Lansing had the cleanest air.

By 1955, city officials estimated that Lansing had more than 100,000 people. The Chamber of Commerce's Industrial Directory of Metropolitan Lansing for the same year reported 73,826 city telephones, births (2,672) outgaining deaths (865) by a wide margin and industrial employment standing at 32,200 (total employment was reported at over 79,000). The city's top industrial employers were listed as Oldsmobile, Fisher Body, Motor Wheel, Reo, Atlas Drop Forge and John Bean.

In its January 1, 1957 review of business, the *State Journal* pointed out that while Lansing was traditionally recognized as an automobile town, a recent survey had indicated a much more diversified economy. "Lansing's chief industrial recognition is as the home of Oldsmobile division of General Motors, and historically it is among those recognized as the birthplace of the modern assembly of motor cars," the paper reported. "However, many smaller industries in the city are growing and some have gained worldwide importance."

Lansing companies identified as having national or worldwide recognition included the Paul Henry Company (toys); Farm Bureau Services, Inc. (fertilizer); Ranaud Plastics, Inc. (industrial tools and plastics); Jarvis Engineering Works (structural steel fabrication); Kish Industries (plastic tools and dies); Centrifugal Fusing Company (brake drums); Phillips Manufacturing Company (screw machine products); Tranter Manufacturing Company (plate type evaporators); and Ray Sablain, Inc. (ready-mixed concrete).

The Duplex Division of Warner & Swasey (the Duplex Truck Company had merged with Warner & Swasey in November of 1955) was also producing goods for a national market. The merger was apparently successful as the Duplex Division increased production by 50 percent between 1955 and the end of 1956. Trucks, cranes and special engine generator sets for defense installations were the primary products, and general manager Howard L. Walker predicted another record year in 1957.

Soon after Duplex joined Warner & Swasey, Reo was purchased by the White Motor company. Reo General Manager John C. Tooker saw the 1957 purchase as a good move for Reo's financial future. "White has provided a real opportunity for Reo and its employees," Tooker said, "particularly since White is maintaining Reo's general offices here and strengthening manufacturing facilities at the present South Washington Avenue location." Two years later, Tooker's optimism had

forge, Atlas, Lansing, Federal, Lindell and Melling forging have made Lansing one of the world's foremost forging areas.

In 1972, Oldsmobile took time out to celebrate its 75th birthday. Buoyed over the previous two decades by such popular automobiles as the F-85, Cutlass, Delta, and the 4-4-2 (four hundred cubic feet, four barrel carburation and twin exhausts), the company had been placing consistantly in the top five in sales in the automobile industry.

Company publicists wrote in a booklet published especially for the anniversary celebration:

"Today Oldsmobile employment rolls number some 16,000 – and factory floor space has grown from the million square feet of the early 1900s to almost seven million, over a million square feet of which has been added just in the last five years. The Oldsmobiles being built within these awesome facilities . . . are as different from the little one-cylinder runabouts that launched the company as might be devined by the broadest of imaginations. The Oldsmobile still 'Goes' (referring to the old slogan of the 'The Oldsmobile Goes'), but rather more gracefully than in the era of past decades."

Five years later, in 1977, Oldsmobile became the third automaker in history to sell one million cars during a single model year. In 1978, with the opening of the Lansing Cutlass Assembly Plant, the division became the largest passenger car assembly complex in North America.

While Lansing was reveling in its role as an established automobile manufacturing center, one of its pioneer firms, the Lansing Company, announced in 1967 that it was discontinuing operations. Founded under the leadership of Lansing banker Benjamin F. Davis in the early 1880s as the Lansing Wheelbarrow Company, the

not diminished. Reo sales manager George R. Collins reported that sales had increased by 71 percent for the first 10 months of 1958 over the same period in 1957. Exports for trucks had increased 62 percent, not including an unannounced number of military vehicles for the government of Pakistan.

While Lansing's business leaders liked to talk about the tremendous diversification of the city's manufactured goods, Lansing was still an automobile town. In early 1960, *State Journal* Automobile Editor Carlisle Carver pointed out that one in every four mid-Michigan workers was employed in plants "directly or indirectly on paychecks earned by their contributions to the production of a 1960 car."

Carver also reported that:

. . . Oldsmobile and Fisher Body employed more than 15,800 men and women in their plants and Motor Wheel employed another 2,642; automobile workers received an average wage of $5,616 a year; Oldsmobile built 366,305 cars in 1959, while Fisher Body assembled 233,803 bodies and Motor Wheel made 4,750,000 automobile wheels; on March 23, 1959, Oldsmobile built its 6,500,000 automobile; the work of Oldsmobile

1966 Olds Toronado

Courtesy R.E. Olds Museum

Capital City Airport

firm claimed at one time to be the nation's largest manufacturer of wheelbarrows – some which were said to have been used in the Yukon gold rush. In later years the company manufactured chiefly industrial carts and racks at its plant on North Cedar Street.

Seven years later, Reo (then called Diamond Reo) met the same fate and was declared bankrupt on May 30, 1975. The reasons, summarized several months later by the *State Journal,* included the economic downturn, the loss of military contracts and "their own overambitious selling program."

A 1976 promotional book published by the Greater Lansing Board of Realtors stressed the diversity of Lansing's economy. "But there is another important side to Greater Lansing Industry. The production of automobiles and auto-related items are by no means the sole mainstay of that industry, even though the combined payrolls of the General Motors Oldsmobile division are estimated to be over a quarter of a billion last year, and Motor Wheel, world's largest manufacturer of styled wheels, has a cumulative payroll of $24 million. The typical manufacturer, however, employs 25 or fewer workers – and the items run the gamut from candied apples to prefabricated homes. These diverse products provide about 40 percent of the industrial employment."

While Lansing had originally been an aggressive recruiter of new businesses in the early 1900s, much of its industrial growth after 1930 came from existing firms. The 1983 "Metropolitan Profile," a comprehensive statistical study by the Lansing Regional Chamber of Commerce, indicates that many of Lansing's biggest employers were the same firms that had been dominating the employment picture for the past several decades. Such veteran companies as Lindell Drop Forge, the Oloffson Corporation, Motor Wheel Corporation, Bank of Lansing, the J.C. Penney Company, Federal Drop Forge and, of course, the General Motors plants were all still key Lansing-area employers. Oldsmobile (17,000), Fisher Body (5,000) and Motor Wheel (2,607) were at the top of the employment lists.

In the early 1980s, General Motors announced plans to convert its Lansing assembly plants to produce a totally new line of GM cars – the Buick Somerset Regal, the Pontiac Grand Am and the Oldsmobile Calais. The new cars made their debut in the 1985 model year.

In 1984, a reorganization completely changed the structure of General Motors' North American car operations. A General Motors reorganization phased out the Fisher Body Division (its plant at 401 N. Verlinden is now called BOC Lansing Body Assembly Operations) and made both Oldsmobile and the new BOC plant part of the Buick – Oldsmobile – Cadillac Group.

Public sector employment also looks much the same as it did in past years, only the numbers are greater. According to 1985 statistics, approximately 15,000 state employees are scattered across Ingham, Clinton and Eaton counties, while approximately 8,000 people work at MSU, and 5,600 more are employed by the Lansing School District.

In communities surrounding Lansing, companies such as Federal Mogul and Sealed Power (St. Johns), Dart Container Corporation (Mason), Owens – Illinois Glass Container Company (Charlotte), and Meijer Distribution Center (Delta Township) contributed significantly to local employment.

St. Johns Main Street and Courthouse

While it's the big manufacturing companies and government that account for most of the jobs in the mid-Michigan area, several Lansing-area craftsmen are making products in the old-time manner of bygone days. On the outskirts of Okemos, for example, Richard Hanley is using the skills he learned as an apprentice to Detroit stained-glass maker Andrew Maglia to craft windows for such local establishments as Clara's, Win Schulers, The Sheraton Inn and the Crossroads Cafeteria on the MSU campus. Hanley's stained-glass windows at Clara's (Lansing's old Michigan Central Railroad Station) are especially interesting as they are replicas of the windows that once adorned the home of R.E. Olds.

Outside Haslett, Hungarian-born clockmaker Karl Barathy crafts reverse glass paintings with century-old methods for use in antique clocks, supplying hundreds of clock collectors throughout the United States and Canada with old-looking glass.

In East Lansing, Australian native George Blaze, a former student of the late Lansing violin maker Nolan Bartow, carves musical instruments in a style reminiscent of 19th-century European masters. Two other local firms, White Brothers String Shop and Elderly Instruments, have developed national reputations for their careful restoration of old musical pieces.

The economic picture in Lansing is, of course, dependent on the success of selling cars. Tough times in the auto industry during the early 1970s and 1980s had harsh impact on Michigan's capital city. But as businessman John Affeldt said in 1933, "the old town never yet took the count and always came out of her troubles stronger and better than ever." He could have been talking about 1986.

For the past 80 years, the accomplishments of firms such as Oldsmobile, Reo and Motor Wheel have been carried in the black, bold headlines and the front-page stories of Lansing papers. Nineteen eight-six is no exception. In the June 5 edition of the *State Journal*, the headline once again told of the remarkable success of a Lansing industry – "Olds scores best month in history."

"Lansing-based Oldsmobile sold more cars in May than any other month in its 88- year history," Oldsmobile General Manager William W. Lane was quoted as saying. "These are outstanding accomplishments. We are confident that we're well on our way toward our fourth consecutive 1 million-plus (sales) year."

A long time ago, Ransom E. Olds said that "It's funny how an idea sticks when you once get it in your head." Luckily, Olds' idea to build a horseless carriage 'stuck', and Lansing was the place he chose to do his building.

Olds scores best month in its history

Incentives play big role in sales

Thursday June 5, 1986

By CAROLYN K. WASHBURN
Lansing State Journal

Lansing-based Oldsmobile sold more cars in May than any other month in its 88-year history, Oldsmobile General Manager William W. Lane said Wednesday.

The General Motors Corp. division sold 115,598 cars last month up 2.5 percent from the 11... units it sold in May 198...

The old recor...

Part II

Chapter 6

Commerce & Finance

Downtown Lansing, Michigan Avenue *Courtesy Michigan State Archives*

by Sallie Mossman Manassah

Fire Station #2

Although Lansing is blessed with the mixture of state government, higher education and heavy industry such as car building, the history of the city can be traced through the small, medium, and large businesses created to serve the people who work for the state, university and Oldsmobile. Many of these businesses had their roots at the time Lansing became the capital.

Lansing developed early as a financial center. As undeveloped as Lansing was when the Capitol was built, there was a need for a local bank. Joseph C. Bailey, a deputy state treasurer, opened the doors of "J.C. Bailey & Co." in a little frame building on the northeast corner of Washington and Michigan avenues in 1850. It was really more of an exchange than a bank, a place where merchants and residents came to sell or swap their credit in one form or another with a minimum of cash involved. Sometimes the banker made a loan; and he kept some cash for depositors. Within five years, the banking business was successful enough for Bailey to leave his job with the state and to build a two-story brick building on the same northeast corner of Washington and Michigan avenues.

By 1864 Lansing was growing as a business and industrial area and ready for a full-fledged bank. Shortly after the federal government provided for federally chartered banks, Bailey and several other wealthy men organized the First National Bank while James I. Mead, a prominent merchant, and several of his contemporaries, were planning a Second National Bank. Ironically, Lansing never got a First National Bank despite efforts by Bailey. After receiving his charter, Bailey purchased the northwest corner of Washington and Michigan and built a new three-story brick building. But Bailey died unexpectedly and his bank never opened.

Meanwhile, the Second National Bank, which bought Bailey's first brick building from him, opened its doors on April 1, 1864, and was the only chartered financial institution in Lansing for eight years, although private banking continued.

In Clinton County, the First National Bank of St. Johns was chartered on August 28, 1865, to take advantage of the new banking laws. Twenty years later it was reorganized as the St. Johns National Bank and served

the St. Johns area until February 21, 1961, when it was consolidated with the State Bank of St. Johns to form Clinton National Bank and Trust Company. Other mergers of local banks with the Clinton National Bank followed and in 1983 the bank affiliated with CB Financial corporation, a holding company with corporate offices in Jackson, Michigan.

Although business continued to grow in Lansing, there was talk in the late 1860s about moving the state capital, particularly since the Capitol needed to be replaced. Passage of a bill on March 16, 1871, to build a new Capitol ended speculation and spurred interest in financial institutions. The Lansing National Bank was the next to be formed in 1872, with John Bush as presi-

dent and Orlando M. Barnes as vice president. It was situated on the southeast corner of Washington and Michigan avenues. Three years later Barnes organized Lansing's first state bank in the rear of the Lansing National Bank and became its first president. In 1879 it was moved to the northwest corner of the main crossroads into the building of the never opened First National.

But the city's most powerful combine to be formed during the century, according to Lansing historian Birt Darling, was the $100,000-capitalized City National Bank, started in 1886 with Edward W. Sparrow as president. The directors leased the same building that held Lansing's first bank and which later served the same purpose for the Second National Bank. The City National Bank was strong enough to survive the Panic of 1893 when four local banks failed, but it succumbed during the Depression.

The 1880s were prosperous years. Two other financial

institutions started the same year as the City National still exist. The Farmers' Bank of Mason was organized June 8, 1886, with 30 shareholders. One hundred years later the bank is known as the Mason State Bank located at 322 S. Jefferson St. The other institution was the Union Building and Loan Association, started by a group of prominent Lansing citizens for home financing. The association provided a systematic, extended plan with low interest rates and installments gauged to meet the borrower's income. In 1983 the Union Savings and Loan Association received a federal charter and changed its name to Union Federal Savings.

In 1890 the Capitol Investment Building and Loan Association, the forerunner of Capitol Federal Savings and Loan, was started with a similar interest in making Lansing a home-owning community. Shares sold for 75 cents and the association's original capital was $352.50. By 1895 mortgage assets of the company reached nearly one million dollars, the same amount paid in dividends to its customers 35 years later. By 1940 the firm expanded to the Detroit area and the company celebrated its 50th anniversary without ever missing or delaying a semi-annual dividend. The name was changed to Capitol Federal Savings in 1982 when it received a federal charter.

One of the other banks to survive the Panic of 1893 was the Lansing State Savings Bank. Incorporated in 1892 with 82 shareholders, the directors purchased the southeast corner of Washington and Michigan avenues from the Lansing National Bank. In 1917 one of the most modern and complete banking houses of the time was built on that site. Forty years later an extensive expansion and remodeling program resulted in the present structure. In 1921 the Lansing State Savings Bank merged with the American Savings Bank, whose building was destroyed by fire, to form the American State Savings Bank. A merger in 1958 with the Central Trust Company resulted in the bank's name being changed to American Bank and Trust Company. In 1978 the bank joined the First American Bank corporation in Kalamazoo and in 1983 the bank became known as First of America Bank – Central.

By the early 1900s, the town around Michigan Agricultural College was becoming organized and incorporated as East Lansing in 1907. A few years later a group of investors decided the 2,000 residents of East Lansing needed their own bank and organized the East Lansing State Bank on May 31, 1916, with capital stock of $20,000. By late 1916, the bank's assets totaled approximately $200,000. As of 1986, ELSB is the largest locally owned bank in Ingham County with assets of more than $160 million.

American Savings Bank (left) City National Bank (right) circa 1904

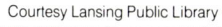

In nearby Mason, the Dart National Bank was founded in 1925 by Doc Campbell Dart and his father, Rollin C. Dart, who formerly operated his own private bank. Dart National was the third national bank in Ingham County and the first in Mason to hold a charter since 1890. The bank opened its doors at 100 Ash St., and, in 1936, bought the assets of the First State Savings Bank and moved into a larger building on the northwest corner of Ash and South Jefferson streets. Today Dart is the oldest national bank in Ingham County.

The north end of Lansing was developing a strong commercial and business community, feeling a need for its own bank. In the fall of 1928, J. W. Wilford, president of Melling Forging Company, and other businessmen met to discuss the organization of a neighborhood bank for an area that was composed of Poles, Germans, Italians, and Greeks. On October 1, 1928, in the twilight of the "Roaring Twenties," the doors of the Bank of Lansing opened at Grand River and Center with capital of $100,000. The new bank prospered while others teetered. City National was building a new headquarters on the corner of Washington and Michigan when it almost folded. It was bailed out temporarily by Capital National and the building was completed, but neither bank survived. In 1932 the Bank of Lansing moved its main office into the new City National Bank Building, where it still is today, and kept its original location as a branch bank. In January 1981, the Bank of Lansing was sold to the Detroit-based Manufacturers National Corporation, part of Northern States Bancorporation.

The demise of the Capital National brought a successor in the Lansing National which purchased certain acceptable assets of Capital National to form a reserve for an initial liquidation dividend for its depositors. But the real salvation for some banks occurred in 1941 when the Michigan National Bank was organized. It was formed through a consolidation of Lansing National Bank, whose charter it retained, with five national banks in out-state Michigan. Howard J. Stoddard came to Lansing in 1940 to take over the presidency of the Lansing National Bank and stayed on to head up the new Michigan National Bank.

Stoddard was a part of the Reconstruction Finance Corporation, a commission set up by President Franklin D. Roosevelt in 1933-34 to help banks through the crisis. Stoddard was sent to Michigan to help resolve the financial condition of the banks and came up with a plan that would revolutionize Michigan banking – organize the money and expertise of several banks throughout Michigan into a branch banking operation. The idea worked and at the time of Stoddard's death in 1971,

Hollister Building
Courtesy of Lansing Public Library

Michigan National was one of the 50 largest banks in the United States.

One of the most recent banks to be formed locally is the Capitol National Bank, 200 N. Washington Square. The bank was organized November 22, 1982, by local investors to meet the needs of small to medium size businesses. The bank is no relation to the old Capital National Bank, which never reopened after the bank holiday of 1933.

As banking was one of the earliest enterprises, the practice of law was one of the earliest professions. Many lawyers came to Lansing from New York to set up a practice in the county seat of Mason and later, after 1847, in Lansing near the Capitol. Col. John Weasel Burchard was one of the first practitioners of law in Ingham County. He studied at Rochester, N.Y., and settled in Mason in 1839. He gave up law in 1843 to engage in other business in Lansing. He erected a dam across the Grand River in 1843. A year later he drowned while inspecting the dam following high water. Daniel L. Case was another early settler and attorney who settled at Mason in 1843. He, too, studied law near Rochester, N.Y., and later gave up the legal profession in favor of a mercantile business which he started in 1845. He was elected auditor general of the state in 1858.

Other early lawyers have familiar historical names, because these people went on to make major contributions to the city and state. John W. Longyear, who prac-

DANIEL BUCK

*O*n Aug. 1, 1872, the Lansing Republican *reported that "A handsome counter from the furniture store of D. W. Buck was placed in the land offices of the J.L. and S. Railroad. It shows that there is no necessity for leaving Lansing to obtain first-class furniture."*

And first-class furniture was what the Buck family supplied to Lansing residents for almost 100 years. The tradition began with Daniel W. Buck. Of Irish descent, he was born in Lansing, N.Y. on April 28, 1828 and was destined to live all his life in towns with the same name. He arrived in Lansing, Mich., on Oct. 8, 1847.

Trained as a cabinetmaker (he served five years as a cabinetmaker's apprentice in New York), Buck built a furniture shop on the corner of Washington and Michigan Avenues in 1849. With the help of a hired man he began making and selling a wide variety of handcrafted furniture.

Around 1855, Buck moved his business two blocks north to the northeast corner of Washington Avenue and Ionia Street where it remained until its closing 75 years later. The business rapidly expanded and Buck was soon employing 10 workers and had a separate factory on North Grand Avenue. Buck's furniture was a frequent winner at the Agricultural Society fairs held throughout the state in the 19th century.

By the 1880s, the competition of the Grand Rapids furniture industry had become formidable and Buck ceased producing his own furniture and became largely a retail merchant.

Furniture making and selling, however, were not Buck's only interests in life. Funerals and theater also filled much of his time. Adept at making coffins as well as sofas, Buck combined his furniture business with one of the city's first undertaking establishments and for years his ads identified him as "D.W. Buck, Furniture and Undertaking."

An interesting item appeared in the March 7, 1872 edition of the Lansing Republican which demonstrated the potential hazards of operating both an undertaking and a furniture business. It read, "D.W. Buck, the enterprising furniture dealer, has given prominence to coffins in his advertisements in the Republican for several years past. He promises to soon rewrite his advertisement and make a speciality of cradles, baby jumpers and children's carriages which are more in demand in Lansing than burial-cases and hearses."

Buck was known as much for his kindness as he was for his ability as a businessman. "Daniel Buck was doing works of charity long before society was organized along such lines," said Daniel Mavis, one of Buck's contemporaries. "Many an early Lansing man, woman and child was buried by Buck free of charge, if young Dan saw the survivors were pressed for money. His books could tell the story of many an unpaid account which was never pressed."

In addition to funerals and furniture, Buck ventured into the arena of commercial theater. In the early 1870s, he built Lansing's largest and most elaborate opera house just south of his furniture store (on the site of what became the Gladmer Theater). Called Buck's Opera House, it seated 1,060 people and took up the upper three floors of a four-story building. The ground floor contained a grocery, music store and clothing shop.

The opera house opened in March of 1873 with Edwin Booth, a noted Shakespearean actor and brother of Lincoln assassin John Wilkes Booth. The performance was Hamlet and it was a sellout.

Daniel Buck played a prominent role in Lansing politics, serving as mayor in 1874, 1875 and 1886. He retired in 1890 and the business was continued by his sons until about 1925.

D. Thomas

ticed with his brother Ephraim Longyear, was a U. S. Representative from the Third District. George Peck, who moved to Michigan in 1839, was a state representative and served as the first postmaster of Lansing, a Michigan Secretary of State, and a U.S. Representative. George I. Parsons, also from New York, came to Lansing in the 1850s and was elected prosecuting attorney for Ingham County in 1856, serving until 1860.

The earliest court held in Ingham County was the Circuit Court, held in the school house at Mason November 12, 1839. The Hon. Wm. A. Fletcher was the presiding judge. Simon Ford furnished a large share of the business before the court for the docket shows three entries against him. The first attorney admitted to practice was Augustus D. Hawley. Among the cases presented was "The People against Elijah Woodworth," indicted by the grand jury for disturbing a religious meeting. In 1839 the county fixed the salary of the prosecuting attorney at $150 per year, which increased to $1,000 by 1874. By then a probate judge was making $1,025 per year.

The *History of Ingham County and Eaton Counties of Michigan* by Samuel Durant lists 54 attorneys in 1880 who practiced in Ingham County since 1859. Among them was a Jason E. Nichols of Lansing, whose name might be remembered by some living in Lansing today. According to a eulogy following his death in 1946, Nichols was born in a log house in Clinton County in 1851. During a career of 70 years, he served as a president of the Lansing School Board, the local board of health, chairman of the local committee that built the Carnegie Library, and was one of the organizers of the first bar association, also serving as a president of that

*Jason E. Nichols
Prosecuting Attorney*

organization. He was elected prosecuting attorney in 1883 and later served several judgeships.

One of the oldest law firms in the mid Michigan area is Fraser Trebilcock Davis & Foster, P.C. which traces its roots to the private practice established by Rollin H. Person in 1883. In 1913, Person was joined by Edmund C. Shields and Harry A. Silsbee to form the firm of Person, Shields and Silsbee located in the Hollister Building. Person left the firm in 1915 when he was appointed to the Michigan Supreme Court. After a series of name changes to reflect the various partners, the firm reorganized in 1958 under its present name of Fraser Trebilcock Davis & Foster, P.C. It is located on the ninth and tenth floors of the Michigan National Bank Building.

Another of the oldest firms is Foster Swift Collins & Coey, P.C. which traces its history to 1903 when Walter S. Foster began practicing law. Shortly after World War II, his son, Richard B. Foster, joined the firm. The law firm reorganized as a professional corporation in 1970. In 1978 the company's shareholders formed a separate partnership to acquire and renovate two old downtown buildings as offices as part of the Plaza I – II – III project. The firm is now located at 313 S. Washington Ave. in the old Home Dairy building.

As banking and the legal profession have grown in more than a century in Lansing, the city has also become home for a number of insurance companies. Although the business climate was good in the 1880s, the average businessman had other worries, ranging from the stability of the local banks to floods and the threat of fire. Insurance was expensive, especially for millers whose mills and elevators were vulnerable to fire. Lansing flour millers met at the old Lansing House to discuss prohibitive rates and agreed to try to insure each other from fire. In 1881 the legislature passed an act enabling them to set up their own insurance firm and the Michigan Millers Mutual Fire Insurance Co. was born, an event that also launched Lansing as an insurance center.

The first president of the Millers company was D.L. Crossman, who was also its first policyholder. But the real impetus behind the company was Arthur T. Davis, a retired merchant, who accepted the job of administrator. According to "After Fifty Years," a brochure published by the company in 1931, "Mr. Davis was able, resourceful, and energetic, and during the 16 years of his management the company made a creditable growth. For seven years he constituted the entire office and field force. In order to impress potential customers with the size and dignity of the company, he virtually became two men by assuming, while in the field, the name of

Early Fire Engine now in front of Michigan Miller Headquarters

Courtesy of Michigan Millers

A.D. Thomas." Davis recorded his expenses carefully, and noted the average hotel bill was 50 cents and a trip covering eight cities in the state cost the company $8.05. At the outset the losses were optimistically lettered A,B,C. etc., in the hope, if not the expectation, that the alphabet contained enough letters to designate all the losses.

Davis was the uncle of A.D. Baker, who joined him in 1903 and eventually served as president during his 64 years with the company. The two men worked in Michigan Miller's first home office at 120 W. Ottawa St. in a building designed by Darius Moon, now listed on the National Register of Historic Places.

By 1886 the business extended into Ohio, Indiana, and Illinois and was writing general business insurance at the beginning of the century. In 1929 the company built the Mutual Building at 208 N. Capitol Ave., which was in 1986 the site of the Michigan State Museum and various state offices. Still visible are the old millstones embedded in the sidewalk in front. Two are 118 years old and came from Monroe. Two others from Alma date to 1881.

The growing use of the automobile after the turn of the century created special insurance needs. In response Vern Valentine Moulton started an insurance company in Mount Pleasant called Auto-Owners in 1916. Moulton was an experienced businessman who operated his own farm in LeRoy, attended Michigan Agricultural College and Lansing Business University, and was a township clerk at the age of 21. A year after he started, he literally carried the business to Lansing under his arm and in his pocket, for at that time it consisted of one block of policyholder's names and $174.25 in assets.

His early offices were in the Hollister Building. But rapid expansion, paralleling with the automobile industry, forced the company to move six times before building its current headquarters in Delta Township. The company wrote in Michigan exclusively until 1935-36 when it was permitted to write policies in Ohio and Indiana; it now writes in 18 states. In 1940 the company began writing general casualty insurance. The Auto-

Owners Insurance Group of companies surpassed the $1 billion in assets milestone in 1984 and ranks among the largest in the nation.

Jackson National Life is also based in Lansing. It was started in 1960 by A.J. "Tony" Pasant, who worked for insurance companies since his college days at Michigan State University. He became frustrated with conservative insurance company practices and was certain that better products and values could be offered to policy holders. On his birthday on August 29, 1960, he founded Jackson National Life, in Jackson. He named the company after Andrew Jackson, the seventh U.S. President, whose dictum "One man with courage makes a majority" is the company's motto.

Pasant spent that first year traveling the state to raise capital, which was one of the toughest sales jobs for Pasant – convincing people to invest in an unproven company that had not yet opened its doors or sold a single policy. Finally the doors opened on August 30, 1961, and the first policy was sold on September 5, 1961, to restaurateur Win Schuler, marking the start of the first life insurance company formed in Michigan in nearly three decades. Through the sale of individual life insurance and avoiding mergers or acquisitions, the company grew substantially over the years, passing the $100 million insurance-in-force milestone in 1969, and its first $1 billion in 1976. On its 25th anniversary, it had $31 billion in force, and it is licensed to do business in 45 states and Washington, D.C. In 1976 the company outgrew its building in Jackson and moved to Lansing where its office was outgrown in five years, leading to the construction of a three-story building at 5901 Executive Drive in the 252-acre Midway Park that Jackson National helped develop.

Other insurance companies have had an impact on Lansing. Blue Cross was incorporated in December 1938 as the Michigan Society for Group Hospitalization. It was established by the Michigan Hospital Association and modeled after other plans to provide prepaid hospital benefits. Among the benefactors in the original plan were two prominent Lansing citizens: R.E.

Early Floral Christmas Display

CHRISTMAS, 1882

*L*ansing businessmen had especially fond memories of the 1882 Christmas season.

"The holiday sales are reported by our merchants to be larger than ever before experienced by them at this season," the Lansing Republican reported. "A great many people must have been happy if happiness depends on the giving of good gifts."

The Lansing of the 1880s was no longer a "city in the forest" that offered only practical gifts. The variety and quality of holiday merchandise that could be found in local stores was probably somewhat reminiscent of goods that were sold in the bigger cities such as New York and Chicago

"For weeks prior [to Christmas], the windows and shelves of the tradesmen are converted into perfect museums, in which every possible variety of shape and color meet the eye in the most ingenious and beautiful combinations," the Republican said on December 13, 1882.

U.H. Forrester's shop on North Washington Avenue featured a tea party near its entrance in which the "guests" were elaborately crafted Japanese dolls. Forrester also carried photograph frames, Christmas cards, albums, lacquer boxes and Japanese tableware.

A block south was the giant drug store and bazaar of the Davis brothers. Claiming to have "the largest display of five and ten cent goods ever offered in the city," the store also had a large selection of books, Swiss music boxes and dressing cases.

Charles Broas, "the wide-awake clothier," at 100 S. Washington Avenue, "had just returned from a trip to the East, bringing back the latest in neckwear, handkerchiefs, hats, caps and men's underwear."

Nearby, jeweler Watson Raplee claimed to have the best selection of French clocks and Swiss and American watches in the area. Like most other Lansing jewelers, he also carried diamonds, rubies, pearls, garnets and fine cameos.

The firm of Shull & Alsdorf had opened its doors at 102 N. Washington Avenue on December 1, 1882, and Lansing shoppers were excited about the magnificent toys the new store had stocked. The "kicking and squalling" mechanical doll in a baby carriage was a popular item, and customers also liked the wooden hobby horse which sold for $6 and the huge dolls that were bigger than the little girls who would someday own them.

Possibly the most elaborate display of the 1882 Christmas season, however, was found in the Grand Ledge store of W.L. Carter where an ingeniously constructed pyramid of revolving shelves loaded with goods was propelled by a small steam engine that "exhausts its steam into the street."

Christmas over one hundred years later might start the same way in North Lansing at Washington Avenue, furnishing the home from Estes Furniture, Schaberg's Lumber, and Bunday's. Then on to Kositchek's and Holden Reid you'll find men's clothes, buying for the ladies from Suites and Maurices; gifts from Liebermann's, Mr. Toad, and the Mole Hole; flowers from Barnes, Belen's, Van Peenen's, and Smith Floral. Then out Saginaw to Toy Village where the annual meeting of doll collectors on the last Sunday in June is a highlight of this local toy store.

D. Thomas

Olds, the automaker and a trustee of Edward W. Sparrow Hospital, and Joseph G. Gleason, who was affiliated with St. Lawrence Hospital and was president of the Silver Lead Paint Company. In 1939 the Michigan State Medical Society loaned $10,000 to start Michigan Medical Services, which later became known as Blue Shield. In 1974 the "Blues" consolidated into one corporation, known as Blue Cross and Blue Shield of Michigan.

Delta Dental Plan of Michigan was organized as Michigan Dental Service Corporation in 1957. The first office, employing only a handful of people, was located in the Stoddard Building downtown. Today the company is located in Okemos and covers 1.8 million people with dental benefit programs.

The Michigan Farm Bureau Insurance Group is one of five affiliates of the Michigan Farm Bureau, which was formed in 1919 as an advocate for farmers in the legislature. The Farm Bureau Mutual Insurance was born January 3, 1949, and the Farm Bureau Life Insurance arrived on September 20, 1951. Together the affiliates offer a multiple line of coverage to its members. The Michigan Farm Bureau is a non-governmental, voluntary organization comprised of more than 90,000 member families working together through 69 county or county-combination "local" Farm Bureaus.

The Michigan State Accident Fund was started in 1912 when the workmen's compensation law was created. The company, now known as Accident Fund of Michigan, broke ground in 1986 for a six-story addition to its building at the corner of West Washtenaw Street and South Capitol Avenue. Two other important companies were the Wolverine Insurance Company which moved to Battle Creek in December 1950 and the

This building now houses Accident Fund of Michigan Courtesy of Reniger Construction Co.

Grange Life which was absorbed by the Michigan Life Insurance Company of Detroit in 1930.

While insurance relieved some of the early residents' concerns, the developing community had other needs. By 1880 Lansing was a city requiring improved communication and ways to heat and light the growing number of government buildings and homes. In 1880 William A. Jackson, general manager of the Telephone and Telegraph Construction Company of Detroit, agreed to establish a Lansing exchange if 50 subscribers signed up. Sixty responded and by the end of the year Lansing boasted 100 telephones. The first commercially used telephone was installed in the old Lansing House, later known as the Downey Hotel. By 1883 Lansing was connected to Detroit, Ionia, and Battle Creek. At the turn of the century, the Citizens Telephone Company was formed, followed by the Michigan State Telephone Company in 1923. A year later the company became Michigan Bell and purchased the Citizens Telephone Company. By 1956, more than 90 percent of Lansing's households had telephone service.

But the real concern in the 1880s was how to meet the needs of a growing community for clean water and better fire fighting techniques. Fire was a constant threat to the predominantly wood constructed buildings and this hazard, as well as cramped quarters, prompted the building of the present Capitol in 1879. It was an auspicious decision, because three years later residents watched helplessly as their primitive fire equipment failed and the old Capitol burned to the ground.

In 1883 the City Council ordered a water survey and found that Lansing was situated over a basin of pure water which could be tapped by deep wells. Following a debate whether the system should be private or public, the public voted on January 26, 1885, overwhelmingly in favor of the city bonding itself for $100,000. The Lansing Board of Water and Light had its beginning Feb-

Early Michigan Farm Bureau Courtesy Lansing Public Library

ruary 16, 1885, when Lansing's Common Council passed an ordinance establishing a Water Board. The first plant was located on Cedar Street south of Michigan Avenue, and within a year, two pumping engines were operating.

Electric light and power were introduced into Lansing by a private organization in 1883. At first arc type lights were used for streets, stores, industrial shops, and public buildings, but soon the company installed equipment that made incandescent lamp electric light possible in private homes. Again the city debated whether or not

Photos Courtesy of Michigan Bell

Above: *An operator switchboard in use in 1885.*
Left: *A Michigan Bell telephone equipment truck photographed in front of the state capitol in Lansing in 1946.*
Below: *Lansing Fuel and Gas Light Co. was able to generate 300,000 cubic feet of gas daily during the early 1900s.*

Courtesy of Lansing Public Library

electrical energy was best supplied by a public or private company. Putting it to a vote, the taxpayers decided to issue $60,000 in bonds to purchase a power plant in 1892, and the money was used to purchase and improve the Lansing Electric Light and Power Company.

The municipally owned power plant was not the only electricity supplier. By 1907 the Michigan Power Company began challenging the city's right to bar private companies from supplying electricity for lighting. They took the city to court and the city lost, and both competed in the light and power fields. However, during a recession around the time of World War I, the Michigan Power Company went into receivership in 1918. To assure adequate electrical coverage for Lansing, the city purchased the company.

To meet the needs of the increase in housing and

Board of Water & Light

the next 25 years, service was expanded to some outlying areas including Delta and Delhi townships.

Today the Board of Water and Light is a $122 million-a-year operation. In 100 years the number of electric customers grew from 136 to more than 82,000. There are now 127 wells that pump an average of 22 million gallons of water per day to almost 44,000 customers through 500 miles of mains. It is the largest municipal electric utility in Michigan and among the 20 largest in the United States.

Another major supplier of energy to metropolitan residents is Consumers Power. It was founded in 1886 by W. A. Foote, who had a vision of a network of power lines linking communities and rural areas. Consumers Power was a pioneer in extending lines to farm families. In 1927 an extension of the existing line was run adjacent to 33 farms in the Mason-Dansville area, later extending the lines to 100,000 farms in Michigan. Consumers Power also provides natural gas to area residents, a service that was started around 1925. The company was located then at 110 E. Michigan Ave., next to Jim's Tiffany Restaurant. Until the 1930s, gas was manufactured from coal. However, in 1936 the Lansing division became the first to be converted to natural gas. Today more than 41,000 homes and businesses in Lansing receive natural gas from Consumers Power and the company serves nearly 65,000 electrical customers in the tri-county area.

The Lansing Ice & Fuel Company developed out of people's need for something taken for granted today – clean ice. The only way to keep milk cool and butter hard in the summer was to harvest ice from the rivers during the winter. Men wrapped in their heaviest coats would cut the ice with a plow saw pulled by a horse.

building following World War I, the Eckert power plant was built in 1922 east of the Moores Park Dam. Two years later combined offices, shops, warehouse, and garage were constructed on South Pennsylvania Avenue. Outgrowing its location in City Hall, the board erected its own six-story office building at 116 W. Ottawa St. in 1928. The building is now privately owned and still in use today. The Board of Water and Light offices moved into their present location across the street at 123 W. Ottawa St. in 1962. In 1939 the Cedar Water Conditioning Plant was put in operation. A milestone occurred in 1940 when the new $4 million Ottawa Street Station was constructed. It was built without a bond issue and without federal aid. During

Then the large cakes would be pushed to the bank where teams of mules would haul the ice out and take them to ice storage buildings. There they were packed in sawdust which would prevent them from melting until they were sold by peddlers door to door during the summer. Around the 1880s there were a number of companies that were in the ice business, but as the city grew, it appeared that not enough river ice could be stored. Also people were beginning to question how clean the ice from the river might be. In 1906 J. Gottlieb Reutter, a local butcher and later mayor of the city, organized the Lansing Pure Ice Company with several other prominent citizens. He took advantage of an ice making machine that had recently been invented. By 1912 he was manufacturing his own ice in great freezing compartments from "the purest water available," using river

Lansing Pure Ice (forerunner of Lansing Ice & Fuel)

ice only for commercial cooling. In 1916 the business was expanded to include retail coal sales, changing the name of the company to Lansing Ice and Fuel. The advent of natural gas for heating purposes started a decline in the coal business, and by 1958 the company added fuel oil and gasoline delivery. Today the company is headed by James L. Reutter, grandson of Gottlieb.

One of the earliest firms to develop in the electrical contracting business was the Bohnet Electric Company, founded in 1906 by William F. Bohnet at 114 E. Ottawa St. Five years earlier, George Bohnet, his brother, had developed a steam powered car. In spite of encouragement from some local businessmen, Bohnet made only two more vehicles. The Bohnet Electric Company was incorporated in 1913, moved to 326 N. Washington Ave. in 1916 and began selling washing machines and ironers. In 1941 the business moved across the street

W.F. Bohnet Electric Co. - 1908

and began carrying major appliances. The company is still owned by the Bohnet family.

Another electrical company formed in the early 1900s was the beginning of the Barker Fowler Electric company. W. Fred Barker was working at the Capitol Electric Supply company in the motor division when he decided to venture into business. He heard of a man in Ionia named B.C. Fowler, who was doing a one-man electrical job, and the two teamed up. Their first major job was at Oldsmobile. The flood of 1913 put the *State Journal* out of commission and Barker Fowler got the newspaper back in operation by repairing the presses. After several locations, the firm moved in 1921 to 116 E. Ottawa, with the motor shop and warehouse at 500-508 N. Larch St. A retail outlet flourished on East Michigan Avenue between Grand and Washington avenues. Presently, all offices are located on Larch Street.

Hayes Electric Co. was founded by F. D. Hayes of Ontario in 1923. Besides founding a conventional full-service electrical firm, Hayes patented, and later manufactured, an electric garage door opener that featured a buried electric sensor which, when triggered from the car, would open the door. It was years ahead of its time. Currently, Hayes Electric is owned by Mike and Pat Hayes, and Ken Lutz, who purchased the firm from F. J. Hayes, Mike's and Pat's father and son of the founder.

One supplier in the building business for nearly 60 years is Capitol City Lumber. Starting out as Capitol City Wrecking Company in 1928, the wrecking business was discontinued in 1953 in favor of millwork and retail lumber. Today Capitol City Home Center, Inc., includes the lumber firm at 700 E. Kalamazoo St. and Capitol City Hardware and Home Center in Holt. Located on six acres near downtown, the company operates a large retail store, an architectural mill for custom made cabinets, shelves, and other items, and nine warehouses for lumber storage.

The development of Lansing can also be attributed to a number of prolific builders. Among them are the

Christman Company, Reniger Construction Company and Foster-Schermerhorn-Barnes. Granger Construction Company has given rise to several other companies and the Eyde Company has become involved in adaptive uses of outdated buildings as well as residential and commercial construction. F.J. Corr, Inc., built, among other things, Frandor Shopping Center, one of the first shopping centers in Michigan in 1954. Frandorson Properties received its name from Francis Corr, his wife Dorothy, and their four sons.

The introduction of electricity and other power sources were not the only factors in developing new commercial enterprises. The advent of the car not only brought jobs in manufacturing, but sales as well. The first independent automobile dealership was started as early as 1898 by William E. Metzger in Detroit. At first customers were expected to plunk down cash for a car, but by 1905 cars were being sold on credit. The manner in which cars were sold in those days varied depending upon the manufacturer – and there were many different manufacturers then. Cars were often sold as a sideline to another business. One of the pioneer firms in Lansing to deal exclusively with car sales was Capital Auto Company, organized in 1906 with J. Edward Roe as president, George Bohnet (the bicycle repair man who experimented with a steam powered car) was vice president, and O.R. Starkweather as treasurer. The firm first handled the line of Reo products, but later sold out to the Reo Motor Car Company upon the latter's decision to open a branch office here. The men then switched to carrying cars built by the Dodge Brothers. The directories of 1910 list several other automobile dealers including Lansing Auto Sales, the R. M. Owen Company, and the Standard Motor Sales Company which sold Oakland cars.

Surprisingly, the car that was manufactured in

Lorenz Brothers Buick between 1926 and 1933 Courtesy of Lorenz Buick

Lansing did not have a dealership here for nearly a quarter of a century. Instead there was a factory branch, owned, operated, and managed by the Oldsmobile Division of General Motors. In 1923 the company decided to discontinue this factory branch operation in favor of a dealership. The first dealers were J.I. Van Keuren, F. N. Arbaugh (the department store owner), Smith G. Young and Bruce E. Anderson, and, interestingly, R. E. Olds, who formed the Lansing Oldsmobile Company. This group of men sold Oldsmobiles at 315 S. Capitol Ave. for the next 21 years. In 1944 the dealership owners sold the business to Herbert E. Trevellyan, then general sales manager at Oldsmobile. Ten years later Trevellyan retired and sold the business to Karl Story, then vice president and general manager for Fincher Motors in Miami. According to an article in the *State Journal*, the business was one of the largest Oldsmobile dealerships in the world. Story moved the dealership to a four-acre site on East Michigan Avenue adjacent to Frandor in 1960. A few years later he built University Oldsmobile now located at 6520 S. Cedar St.

Diversifying his business with an eye toward improving Lansing, Story purchased the 400 block of South Washington Avenue and in 1975 remodeled the former Arbaugh Department Store into offices, including the headquarters for Story, Inc.

Another of the older dealers is Lorenz Buick. R. K. and Harold Lorenz gave up dairy farming in the 1920s to open a garage to house other people's cars. This idea expanded into a gas station and then into a wrecker service. In 1922 they were franchised as dealers for White trucks and Franklin cars and in 1923 for Buicks. During those early days the owners sold cars, taught mechanics and driver education, and financed automobile sales. "We'd sell

Car Built by George J. Bohnet, June 6, 1900 Courtesy of Bohnet Family

people cars, and after they'd bought the car they'd say, 'I never drove a car,'" R. K. Lorenz said, "so the salesmen had to teach them," R. K. purchased his brother's interest in 1955 and was joined by his sons.

McClintock Cadillac, the original Cadillac dealer in town, was founded in 1936 by F. H. McClintock, who sold it to his son William 30 years later. It was originally located at 2400 E. Michigan Ave. and moved to 5901 S. Pennsylvania Ave. in 1969. The dealership was sold in 1981 and the name was changed to Capitol Cadillac.

One of the other General Motors dealerships is Lee GMC Trucks, Inc. Bill Lee purchased the 40-year-old firm in 1983 from Vic Rhynard. Lee recently moved the dealership from Larch Street to west Lansing at 6333 Lansing Road. The service department is said to rival the Reo plant.

Communicating the business, social and political interests in the early years of the capital was the local newspaper. In the same year that Michigan State University was chartered and Abigail Rogers opened the doors on her Michigan Female College, Henry Barns

WSYM – newest on the media scene

Courtesy of Lansing Public Library

State Republican, 1880, located on north side of W. Michigan Ave. between Washington and Capitol Avenues, where police station is today.

came to Lansing. He was a man with a mission – to start a Republican newspaper to appeal to the followers of a new Republican administration in Lansing and to counteract the views of the six-year-old Democratic newspaper, the *Lansing Journal*. Thus the first edition of the *Lansing Republican* rolled off a flat bed press in a cramped log cabin on April 28, 1855. Barns, who has been considered by historians as a "Johnny Appleseed" of journalism, had already started seven other newspapers before arriving in the state capital. A strong abolitionist, he had been a founding member of the Republican party in Michigan a year earlier in Jackson. He was apparently a smart businessman, too, because after publishing only two editions, he sold the paper to Rufus Hosmer and George Fitch.

A succession of owners and editors followed over the years. *The Republican* became a daily in 1886 and changed its name to *State Republican*. In February 1911 the paper absorbed its Democratic competitor and became *The State Journal*, a name that stuck until 1980 when it was changed to *Lansing State Journal* to "more positively identify the newspaper with the Greater Lansing area that it serves," stated an announcement at the time. In 1914, partners Ard E. Richardson and Charles N. Halsted bought the paper and moved it to new headquarters at Grand Avenue and Ottawa Street, where it remained for more than 30 years. The only other serious competitor in this century was the *Capital News* which began daily publication in 1921. It faltered during the Depression and was also absorbed by *The State Journal* in 1932. In 1928 *The State Journal* became a part of the newly formed Federated Publications, headquartered in Battle Creek. The *Journal*'s first newspaper plant, housing all aspects of the newspaper operation, was built in 1951 at 120 E. Lenawee Street, where it continues today. In 1972, the Federated Newspapers were acquired by Gannett Co., Inc., which is the nation's largest communications group as of 1986.

It seemed that the 1920s was a time for new media. Besides the *Capital News*, radio came to town. WREO, which was based at the Reo Motor Car Company, signed on the air November 1, 1924, and could be received with relatively simple, crystal headset equipment. It was only on the air a few hours a day and ceased operation August 31, 1927. Meanwhile, the forerunner of radio WKAR at MSU had experimented with the airwaves. In 1922 Michigan Agricultural College received a broadcast license from the Department of Commerce. The call letters were picked at random and assigned by the government. It was originally 8YG, a station built and operated by student engineers who made the transmitter from borrowed and homemade equipment. The station, which added FM operations in 1948, has been housed in a variety of locations, from the Engineering

March of Dimes Broadcast

Courtesy of MSU Archives

Building to the Home Economics Building, but presently enjoys a modern new home in the Communication Arts & Sciences Building. The fourth oldest of all radio stations in the state, WKAR Radio is a member of the National Public Radio Network and operates one of 17 public radio communication satellite transmission stations.

The first full scale commercial radio effort was undertaken by Harold Gross in the 1930s. He named his station WJIM after his then toddler son, who later ran the stations. In 1950, Gross Telecasting introduced television to Lansing when WJIM-TV Channel 6 became one of the first 100 stations in the country to go on the air. During the 1950s, local stations could select programming from any of the national networks, and Lansing residents were treated to a variety of offerings. When WJIM-TV moved to its new and current headquarters at E. Saginaw and Howard Street in 1953, the station produced a number of local programs. In 1984, Backe Communications purchased WJIM-TV and changed the call letters to WLNS-TV. The radio station was purchased in 1985 by local investors and moved to a studio in the Frandor shopping center keeping the WJIM call letters.

Soon after WJIM began broadcasting those flickering black and white images, WKAR-TV at MSU went on the air. Going on the air in 1954, WKAR is the second-oldest public-TV station in the country. Originally the signal came on UHF Channel 60 – at a time when less than 15 percent of the homes could get UHF. Consequently, WKAR reached a cooperative arrangement with a new commercial station, WILX-TV, in 1959. WILX would lease the university's transmitter and the two stations would share the day on Channel 10. WKAR, called WMSB during those days, had 39½ hours of program time, but WILX had evenings and prime time. Eventually both stations wanted more air time and Clifton Wharton, then MSU President and a member of the Public Broadcasting System Board, recommended a full-time operation. The station sold its old transmitter to WILX and built a new one. In 1972 WKAR returned to its own call letters and went on the air as Channel 23. In September 1981 the station moved to the new Communication Arts building on campus where it takes up part of three floors and has three studios.

In recent years Lansing has become the home of a number of new media, including television and radio stations, cable television systems and weekly newspapers. The community is fortunate to have a diverse business climate as well as a variety of investment opportunities. In many ways, these financial and commercial interests have set the stage for the Lansing of the future.

The Onlooker
By Jim Hough

If you played a word association game with me and said "Lansing," my one-word response would be "heart."

It is probably ironic that Lansing became known as a pioneer in open heart surgery because this city's heart has never needed an operation. Lansing's heart beats loud and strong. Best of all, it beats with a warmth and compassion uncommon to cities this size.

When my family moved here about 40 years ago from a very rural area of Michigan's Upper Peninsula, I was a 16-year-old boy who was sure he'd hate the big city. Where among such masses of people would one find the warmth and caring so common to rural folks who had learned to depend on each other?

But I will always remember the early days in our very modest first home in Lansing and how the neighbors came over to welcome us, offer help and assurance. It has been like that ever since. Lansing is a city newcomers grow to love — not because of its industry, its great colleges, its prestige as the state capital but because of its heart, the warmth of its people.

We'd never put a knock on other great cities of our state — Grand Rapids, Flint, Saginaw and others — but I fear they'd be hard pressed to match Lansing, a big city with a farm community approach to daily life. You can't see it, you just feel it after you live here awhile.

As a daily newspaper columnist here for nearly 25 years, I've been privileged to get a much closer look at the city's heart.

I recently produced a book called *The Onlooker Looks Back.* It is a collection of 60 of the 8,000 columns I've written over the past 25 years. Believe me, the effort was not an ego trip. It was an emotional experience to review those columns. Re-reading all that evidence about the warmth of a big city and its people had me in tears many times.

I recall when there was talk about closing Potter Park Zoo because that city-owned facility was underfunded and becoming a distasteful place to display animals. Before the movement to close the zoo got strong, I went to the pen of Herman, a white Mexican burrow who had lived in the zoo

for 20 years. I interviewed Herman, patriarch of the city's animal kingdom. I went back to the office and reported what Herman had said — that Lansing needed a Friends of the Zoo Society. Herman called for a meeting. It was attended by nearly 200 persons. The zoo society was born. Since then, hundreds of thousands of dollars have been raised to improve the zoo. Children went door-to-door selling Herman buttons until they raised $6,000 to buy a baby elephant. Adults got the message. Today, the zoo is the city's leading attraction with more than a half million visitors per year.

The city had opened its heart.

And there was the time I made a one-sentence mention during the Vietnam War that our soldiers liked to have unpopped popcorn but couldn't get it over there. Labor unions, Jaycees, school kids and airlines jumped to the for. Suddenly, Lansing had sent a ton of popcorn to Michigan soldiers in Vietnam. Each got a two-pound package. it was so much fun that we did it again the next year.

The city had opened its heart.

I remember the time I mentioned in a column that the State Home and Training School at Mount Pleasant — a state facility for mentally retarded adults — needed some women's formals for a dance to be held there for the retarded residents. Lansing women sent more than 1,000 formals there.

The city had opened its heart.

I remember the time I mentioned in a column that Indian children on a reservation near Sault Ste. Mare were heading into winter in need of warm coats. Two days later, this community had filled the Lansing State Journal's lobby with heaps of kids coats. Two truckloads of coats went north to those kids.

Lansing had opened its big heart again.

And there was the day I opened the Onlooker column mail and saw ten, crisp $100 bills dumped out of an envelope. With the money was an anonymous note from a reader asking that the money be used to take some needy kids on a shopping trip. The writer recalled being embarrassed in school as a child because of inadequate clothing.

Lansing's heart was open again.

And so it goes, on and on. All that and more — a city that always makes its United Way goal, always responds to the slightest cry of need.

As that old song says, "you've gotta have heart." This city has it.

Readers of the Onlooker column have read thousands of words under my byline extolling the virtues of my native Upper Peninsula. While there is honesty in all of that U.P. ballyhoo, I always will be incredibly proud to call Lansing my home.

Courtesy GayMarie Granger

Chapter 7

A Cultural Renaissance

Lansing City Club—Once Brauer's 1861 House

Gladmer Theatre

Courtesy Michigan State Archives

Culture has always been an important aspect of life in Lansing. As the community prospered at the turn of the century, many of the prominent businessmen decided to do something about the quality of life.

Theaters were built and well-known performers from around the country were brought to Lansing. Even Mark Twain made it here in his lecture tour of the 1890s. As films became popular, grand movie houses were built. The depression years did not interrupt this interest as 1929 saw the birth of the Lansing Civic Players and the Lansing Symphony gave its first performance in 1932. Interest in a library occurred as early as the 1860s and the forerunner of the state museum was in place by 1879. Timber barons, local politicians and those associated with the young automotive industry in the early 1900s made certain that their city had plenty of trees, parks, and recreational facilities.

This momentum has continued today. The city can boast five community theater groups, a resident equity company, many art galleries, dance troupes, an opera company, four museums with others in the developing stages, and numerous smaller groups associated with the arts. Lansing maintains 113 parks for the public's enjoyment, athletic facilities, specialty nature centers with miles of hiking, and a zoo with more than 400 animals. There are more than 260 restaurants to please every taste, including Greek, Italian, Mexican, oriental and Mediterranean. This is a long way for a community whose cultural life began with local theater in people's homes and when the only restaurants in town were in boarding houses or hotels.

There was not much opportunity for cultural life in the wilderness. Early settlers were so busy clearing the land and fighting off the timber wolves that the theater and other cultural endeavors were not foremost in their minds. However, when the legislators arrived in January of 1848, they became lonely for the lights and laughter of Detroit. About the only theater the town knew in this time were the wandering "Olympic Players" who presented "dramatic entertainment" at the Benton House hotel that same year. Lansing had no real hall fitted for dramatic performances until 1862 when Capital Hall was opened over the two stores at 109 and 111 S. Washington Ave.

The inventive settlers also formed many of their own groups for cultural purposes. Local theater groups would perform in people's homes and literary groups would meet to discuss classical literature or to invite noted speakers to town. Groups such as the Calliopean Society of Michigan Agricultural College, the Young Men's Society, and the Lansing Library Association flourished in the 1870s.

Lansing acquired its first legitimate theater in 1865. Mead's Block, a three-story arch-roofed building, at the southeast corner of Washington Avenue and Ottawa Street housed the Star Theater. James I. Mead, who had been in the milling business on East Shiawassee Street, built Mead's Hall shortly after the Civil War. The first floor was devoted to retail establishments while the theater, with a sizable stage, scenery and balcony, was upstairs.

The building which became Lansing's elite entertainment mecca was Buck's Opera House, located on the southwest corner of Washington Avenue and Ionia Street. The building, under different names, was the scene of Lansing entertainment, both live and on film, for more than a century. The building was erected in 1872 by Daniel Buck, who was in business with his brother at Buck's Furniture Store/Funeral Establishment just across the street. The Opera House was a grand building, four stories high in the popular Second Empire or Mansard-style. Three commercial shops were located on the first floor: a grocery store, a clothing shop and a music store. The upper stories were occupied by the theater itself, which seated approximately 1,060 people. Shakespearean actor Edwin Booth, brother of the infamous John Wilkes Booth, performed in Macbeth on opening night.

Lansing Women's Club   Courtesy Lansing Public Library

In 1890, James J. Baird bought the building, remodeled it and changed the name to Baird's Opera House. The building was purchased in 1905 by Fred Williams and Frank Stahl, who in turn renamed the building the Gladmer. The name was selected from the names of the children of the two families – Gladys Williams and Merritt Stahl. The Gladmer became a motion picture theater in the 1920s, and the front facade was remodeled in the contemporary Beaux Arts style with marble and bronze trim. The Gladmer closed in March 1979 and was partially torn down in 1984.

When small movie houses began springing up around the business district in the early 1900s, the Mead Block and the Gladmer became focal points. In addition to the Mead's Star Theater, which later became the Garden, the Plaza opened in 1914 and later housed the Baudette, The Garden, and the Orpheum theaters on the ground floor. It was later renamed the Palms and then the Downtown Arts Theater. The Mead Block was a victim of the wrecking ball in 1968 to make way for downtown redevelopment.

Another movie house during this period was known as the Theatorium and later the Empress, located in the 200 block of North Washington Avenue. It was operated by Joseph M. Neal, a famous showman of the time. In 1921 the Empress was acquired by Claude E. Cady, who changed its name to the Capitol. Cady also leased the Gladmer for a movie house. The Capitol closed in 1955 and was later the site of the Eagle Restaurant in the early 1960s.

One of the grandest theaters of its time in the state was the Strand, opened in 1921 by the Butterfield organization, which was developing a chain of theaters in the region. It was designed by prominent architect John Everson, complete with a long arcade that featured two levels of shops. The Strand was renamed the Michigan Theater after major remodeling in art deco style in 1939. The theater closed in 1980 and was sold by Butterfield to two Detroit entrepeneurs. An effort was made by a group called DeCapo to save the building and keep it as a cultural center. Unfortunately, the group was not able to raise the $450,000 needed to buy the building. The theater was renovated into office space by its new owners, but much effort was made to preserve some of the special architectural touches of the original European design. The balcony of the theater was used for the rear facade of the building.

Theater, whether on stage or screen, has long been a major interest in Lansing. In the year of the stock market crash, 1929, an important marriage took place. The Players Guild and the Civic Theater joined to become

Civic Players Firehouse Headquarters

the Lansing Civic Players, the only live show in town. The fledgling group made its debut by staging "Captain Applejack" in the Eastern High School Auditorium. During the depression, the Players struggled for survival. Dr. Karl and Ione Brucker kept the group alive by paying many of its bills from their own pockets. Mrs. Brucker, who had acted and directed professionally, had a stage in her home and often coached aspiring actors. During World War II theaters around the country were closing and the Civic Players considered doing the same. However, the group was encouraged to keep going to provide some "escape" for residents from the war for at least a few hours.

The Civic Players has had its headquarters and its performances in a variety of locations around town. For more than 20 years the group was headquartered at the Prudden Auditorium before it was razed for state buildings. In 1960 it was relocated at 300 N. Washington Ave., where the Community Services Building is today. Then the group moved to 408 N. Washington Ave. where a Lansing Community College building is now located and plays were produced at West Junior High Auditorium. For a while the Civic Players rented quarters at the Lansing Industrial Center on South Washington Avenue. In 1977 the Civic Players bought their own headquarters – a one-time firehouse at Michigan Avenue and Hayford Street – and began performing at the Harry Hill Auditorium.

A group that has been performing for 50 years is bound to have its stories and the Civic Players has its share. On its golden anniversary, the *Lansing State Journal* recounted some of the more humorous incidents on stage. In the 1950s in "Strange Bedfellows," an actor had to make a quick change between acts. He forgot to button up his pants and the audience tittered while he and his wife argued. To top it off the actor's punch line was: "And that will show you who wears the pants in the

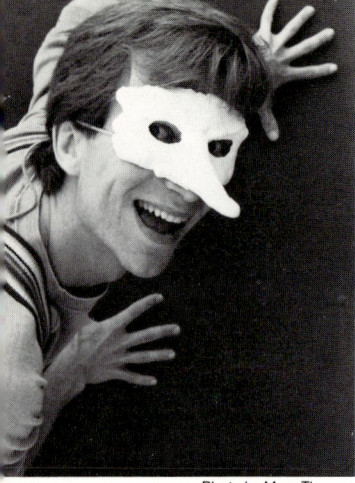

*David Kropp,
Director of Lansing
Community College's
"Comedy of Errors,"
Summer 1985*

Photo by Marc Thomas

family." Another time an actor opened a door on stage and announced loudly, "There's no one there!" only to find an actress on all fours, peering through the keyhole to see the play. In another play an actor's putty chin fell off. And once a "corpse" in full view of the audience, reached down to pull the sheet over his head.

The Community Circle Players organized in 1958 and presented its first shows in a 124-seat auditorium in a warehouse on Sheridan Road. Leaders dreamed of having a theater of their own, but expected that would be years away. Then along came Karl and Bee Vary, who had spotted two barns along Okemos Road that they felt had potential. One was just the right size for a theater while the other could be used for storage and as a rehearsal hall. People laughed, including the farmer who leased the buildings to them, but in the fall of 1964, about two months after the acquisition, the Community Circle Players opened at the Okemos Barn Theater. In that very hot and short summer, haymows were emptied, a well was dug, plumbing put in, and manure shoveled out. Since the group moved it has been nicknamed "The Barn." In 1986 the group lost the lease on the barns and moved the theater to an empty warehouse next to Impression 5 Museum on Museum Drive in downtown Lansing.

From its humble beginnings in Fitzgerald Park at Grand Ledge in 1966, the BoarsHead Theater developed into the principal regional theater in the state with a solid national reputation. Known as the Ledges Playhouse then, it was founded by John Peakes and Richard Thomsen as a summer theater. They had bought the Ledges from a faculty member at the University of Iowa where they were Ph.D. candidates in drama. For five summers they left their college teaching jobs to do shows ranging from Shakespeare to Miller, from Ibsen to Neil Simon. Their wives, Connie Peakes and Barbara Thomsen, provided costumes and props and ran the office while their husbands and a troupe of students, young professionals and theater buffs acted, directed, designed and built sets.

With some moderate successes, both men gave up

their teaching jobs – Peakes at Iowa and Thomsen at the University of Vermont – and rented a church in Grand Ledge for a year-round operation in 1971. At about the same time, the theater became a non-profit corporation. The mixture of scripts continued to be eclectic and a number of fine actors now working in New York and regional theaters as well as films received their start at BoarsHead. Oscar winner William Hurt, his former wife Mary Beth Hurt, Anthony Heald, Rich Reilly, and John Hammond are just a few who spent three to five years in the company.

In 1975, Thomsen and Peakes worked with a committee to design a theater in the new Center for the Arts in Lansing and BoarsHead moved from Grand Ledge to a permanent facility. By 1979 BoarsHead had its first Equity Letter of Agreement and its first managing director. Now the resident equity company comprises about

Okemos Barn Theatre

Photo by Ginger Sharp

75 percent of each production. In addition to producing American classics and recent New York productions, the theater has focused some of its resources on producing new work and has become especially interested in Michigan and other Midwestern writers. In addition to a full schedule of seven plays in the winter, the company of BoarsHead: Michigan Public Theater, produces a statewide tour and has expanded its education programs to include workshops, school performances, and a theater program at Blue Lake Fine Arts Camp as well as a summer series in Muskegon.

Theater has not been the only show in town. Music also attracted much of the populace during the development of cultural life. Although there had been earlier community orchestra and choral groups, it was really the dream of John Stevens to have a symphony orchestra. The director of the school orchestras at Central and Eastern high schools, Stevens invited all the instrumentalists in the Lansing area to a meeting to organize the

a professor of conducting at the University of Michigan. In 1983 the Symphony moved its performances to the new Wharton Center on the Michigan State University campus.

Another form of music, the opera, has gained popularity. After traveling together to other communities to see performances, a number of opera devotees decided to form their own group here. In 1973 the Opera Guild of Greater Lansing was organized and produced La Traviata. Within a year, membership grew to 175 families and the guild produced Carmen. In 1977 the name was changed to Opera Company of Greater Lansing and the following year the company sponsored a two-opera season. One of the company's highlights came during the 1983-84 season when it joined forces with the Greater Lansing Symphony Orchestra for a production of "The

Left: *Carmen Decker and Allen McCoy in "Sister Mary Ignatius Explains It All For You" at BoarsHead Theater.*

Left:
Carmen Decker plays an intense card game with John Peakes in "The Gin Game."
Photo by Connie Peakes

symphony. Fifty responded, and in 1929 the organization began to take shape. However, it was March 1932 before the first program was presented – a free Sunday afternoon concert in the old Prudden Auditorium which some 1,800 people attended, and $500 was raised by passing collection plates. Stevens had wanted to conduct that first performance, but because of an illness, Izler Solomon, a Michigan State College violin instructor, took his place. In 1934 Solomon became the first permanent conductor, until he moved on to the Illinois Symphony in 1936. A well-remembered conductor is Romeo Tata, music professor at Michigan State University, who took over in 1941 and served for 20 years. When the symphony celebrated its 50th anniversary in 1979, it also welcomed a new conductor, Gustav Meier,

Right:
Buck Schirner and Jeffrey Dougan in "Time Steps."

LCC Production of Grease

Photo by Harley Seeley

Photo by Robert Killips

Right: *(Left to Right) Maria Mills, Christina, Rosa Lopez Killips are three of the four choreographers for the "Reflections of Spain" concert.*

Photo by David Olds

Above: *Lansing dance teacher Marcia Smith, owner of Studio De Danse, relaxes after a hard day.*

Merry Widow." The official title was changed again in 1984 to the Opera Company of Mid-Michigan to reflect the scope of the organization and the more than 500 supporting families and individuals.

Dance has developed in recent years to become a major part of the Lansing cultural scene. In 1965 local people formed the Greater Lansing Area Dance Council (GLADC) to promote dance activity and a wider appreciation of dance in the Lansing area. At that time, there were no dance companies in town. The members launched the Modern Dance Workshop and the

Young Ballerinas at Turner Dodge House

Photo by Bonnie Zell

Lansing Ballet Company. The council membership includes private dance teachers, members of the faculty of Michigan State University and Lansing Community College, area dance students, representatives of various dance groups and people interested in dance.

Among the independent dance groups are Happendance, a contemporary troupe started in 1976; the Pashami Dancers, a local troupe founded in 1969 by Dorothy Jones to study and perform African dance; and the Children's Theatre, a ballet troupe that gives Christmas and spring performances. The 10-year-old Michigan Dance Association is committed to stimulating the growth of dance as a cultural, educational and recreational resource in communities throughout Michigan. All this is not unusual in a community that welcomed one of the greatest dancers of all time to the spotlight at the opening of the Gladmer Theater in 1910 – Anna Pavlova, the Russian dancer who made ballet known around the world.

Lansing has been fortunate to have many talented artists associated with the university and in the community. Among the most remembered is Leonard D. Jungwirth, the MSU art professor who created the "Sparty" statue, the symbol of the school's athletics. He taught sculpture at MSU for 23 years before his death in 1963. He also did stone reliefs for the MSU Alumni Chapel, a figure for the Capitol Avenue outer wall of the Lansing City Hall, ceramic reliefs for Landon Hall dor-

La Bohème Courtesy of Mid-Michigan Opera Company – Photo by Alan Suits

mitory and the Stations of the Cross for St. Thomas Aquinas Church.

The Lansing Art Gallery was started around 1965 by a group of local teachers, businessmen and artists with the support of city officials. Known as the Lansing Community Gallery, its first home was at 124 W. Ionia St. in a building erected in 1911 and which formerly housed the Lansing Business University. One of its unique features was a "Salon des Refuses" room available to artists whose works are rejected by the judges. This was patterned after the room established by Napoleon III at the Salon des Beaux Arts in Paris in response to artists' complaints of rejection due to political prejudice. Several years later the gallery moved to the second floor of Jim's Tiffany Restaurant, where it remained until it moved into its new quarters in the Center for the Arts at the corner of Grand and Lenawee. As the first permanent art gallery in the Lansing area, it is dedicated to the promotion of visual arts in an effort to increase community awareness and appreciation of various art forms. Art competitions, special events, art workshops, and seminars are a few of the services. The exhibits feature individual and collective shows by Michigan artists. Competitions are held throughout the year.

The Kresge Art Center was constructed during a massive building program on the Michigan State University campus. It opened in 1958, the gift of the Kresge Foundation. It houses the university's permanent art collection, which includes African, Mexican, Middle Eastern and Western art from the prehistoric period through the present. Works of Andy Warhol, Morris Lewis, William Bailey, Alexander Caulder, Theodore Roszak, and George Rickey have been seen there.

Nowhere is there a greater focal point for the evolution of the cultural scene than the Arts Council of Greater Lansing. In May 1962 the Lansing Fine Arts Coordinating Committee was formed by nine capital area arts groups to foster better communication, avoid scheduling conflicts, and better inform the general public of events. The group also initiated a community arts festival, which was an annual event for 15 years. In 1965 the group incorporated as the Metropolitan Lansing Fine Arts Council and became the first arts group in Michigan to hire an executive director in 1974.

At the same time, a study committee of the Junior League of Lansing identified a need for a central location for arts activities. An independent Founders Committee was established and a campaign to secure a fine arts facility for metropolitan Lansing was launched. The committee envisioned a center for the community – a theater, an art gallery, meeting rooms and offices. The vacant O'Shaugnessey auto dealership at Lenawee Street and Grand Avenue was proposed as the site, and the Junior League sold its building on Walnut Street in 1974 and donated $30,000 to obtain the center. Major gifts from Ransom Fidelity, the Lansing Foundation, Gannett Foundation, Michigan Council for the Arts, the City of Lansing and many businesses and individuals helped.

In April 1975, a board of directors representative of the diverse interests of the metropolitan Lansing area was appointed to administer the project. On June 23, 1975, the Center for the Arts was incorporated and a managing director was hired. Individuals and corporations were members of the center and a representative from the center joined the Metropolitan Fine Arts Council. The facility developed into a 266-seat theater for small theatrical and musical performances, meetings and other activities; an art gallery and administrative offices; and a meeting area and kitchen. The resident organizations include BoarsHead Theater, The Lansing Art Gallery and the Junior League. Space is

Center for the Arts Photo by K.R. Cranson

also rented to interested groups. The center evolved into a producer of events in which it develops, promotes and administers programs featuring performing and participatory arts.

In the fall of 1978, the staffs and boards of the arts council and the Center for the Arts began to realize the need for one arts group in the community. After much review the two groups merged in 1978 and became the Metropolitan Fine Arts Council at the Center for the Arts. Later the name was changed to the Arts Council Center of Greater Lansing. The merger of the two groups brought greater strength to the cultural community.

Yehudi Menuhin, Violinist Featured at Wharton Center

While community groups, volunteers and business people were forming the Center for the Arts, the idea for one of the largest science museums in the state was germinating in the mind of a local resident. Marilynne Rosenberg Eichinger, the founder of Impression 5 Museum, was talking with a friend over coffee in 1972 about the need for more cultural attractions in the community. "Why not start a museum," she said. "All we have to do is put up a poster asking for interested people to come to a meeting, find ourselves a lawyer for incorporation purposes and sell the idea."

That idea launched her into a project that would occupy much of her next 13 years. It also would involve a wide part of the community in planning and development. Eventually she was given a room at Marble School to hold classes after school for students on

such diverse science topics as ventriloquism, kitchen chemistry, magic, kite making, and simple electronics. By 1975 the museum had gained credibility and some money, and it was ready for its own building at 1400 Keystone Blvd. With the help of the Junior League of Lansing and the Jaycees, Impression 5 became a reality.

From that converted warehouse, dreams and ideas continued to emanate. Local foundations became enthusiastic and offered their help. In three years, the museum had outgrown its new home and began looking for larger quarters. In 1979, a 135-year-old warehouse known as the Reniger Building was purchased. After much renovation, including volunteer labor from various organizations, the museum opened in its new home on June 5, 1982.

Today the museum is a major attraction in the area. More than 200 "hands-on" exhibits demonstrate basic principles in geometry, physics, chemistry, electronics and many other science areas.

Another museum in Lansing was an outgrowth of community planning and involvement. Named after automotive pioneer Ransom Eli Olds, Lansing's R.E. Olds Museum opened August 21, 1981, on the 84th anniversary of an enterprise that became Oldsmobile. A task force was created in the late 1970s to determine the need for local history representation – what is the city known for and what would make the city unique today. After investigating several possibilities, the idea emerged for a museum that would illustrate the part Lansing played in the development of transportation, with special emphasis on the automobile and its effect on the community and its people. Millions of cars and trucks that have been used in countries around the world have their origins in Lansing. Other vehicles, such as carriages, bicycles, and airplanes have been manufactured here over the years. R.E. Olds was experimental and unique and left behind decades of

R.E. Olds Museum

Photo by Leavenworth Studios

New State of Michigan Library

ideas and products worthy of preservation.

The Chamber of Commerce task force developed into the core of the R. E. Olds Museum. Several of the key forces behind the museum were Richard Neller, George Clemison and Eugene Wanger. A search was started to find a building, and one was located downtown in the old CATA bus facility at 240 Mill St. It was spacious and garage-like, just the way a transportation museum should be. Besides, the building itself had historical importance. A small two-story brick structure on one side was part of the Bates and Edmonds Engine Company, which produced some automobiles around the turn of the century. In the 1930s and 1940s the building was owned by the Hill-Diesel Engine Company that later built the south building. Wood-laminated beams were used rather than steel because of the shortage of steel during World War II.

When the museum opened in 1981, it featured 20 cars ranging from a sporty little 1907 curved-dash sportster to a powerhouse '69 Toronado. Today, in addition to Oldsmobiles and Reos (the car built by R.E. Olds after he left Oldsmobile), other Lansing-built vehicles are recognized; the Duplex Truck, the Durant, the Star, and the obscure, turn-of-the-century Bates. Other features are the "Wall of Wheels" from the Motor Wheel Division of Goodyear, displays of the fabulous Victorian home of R.E. Olds, displays of vintage auto advertising, a special license plate collecton, vintage clothing, posters, pictures and more.

Lansing residents have long enjoyed the advantage of the Michigan Historical Museum in their midst. The museum provides a close look from the time of the Indians and early explorers to the industrial age. The museum has had several locations in its 100-plus years. The original museum can be traced to the Michigan Pioneer Society that displayed its collections in two rooms in the Capitol in 1879. Mrs. Marie B. Ferrey was the society's clerk and was responsible for the early development of the museum. In 1913 the Michigan Historical Commission was created by the Legislature and appointed by Gov. W.N. Ferris. The Pioneer Society's collections were transferred to state ownership and the Michigan History Museum was born. In 1922 the museum was relocated in the State Office Building (now known as the Lewis Cass Building), and in 1944 to the former Turner family home at 505 N. Washington Ave. Dubbed temporary quarters, the Turner home was sold to Lansing Community College, and in 1980 the museum moved to its present quarters in the lower level of 208 N. Capitol Ave.

The Michigan Historical Museum will have a new home in 1987 when the five-story State of Michigan library-museum-archives is completed at Allegan and Sycamore streets. In addition to the museum, the 258,000 square-foot building will house the State Archives and Publications, Historic Preservation and Archaeology sections of the Bureau of History, Department of State. The Office of the Great Seal, Department of State, will reside in this $39 million structure, as will the Library of Michigan, supervised by the Legislative Council of the Michigan Legislature.

The idea for the heritage center originated with the Bureau of History and the Library of Michigan. Both were faced with dwindling space and growing collections. They also needed more control over environmental factors such as temperature and dust to preserve their collections. And they wanted to be in a location that was more accessible to the public.

The project was launched in 1983 with a planning document, and the architectural design was completed

MSU Museum's Gift Emporium

in June 1985. Groundbreaking on the 14-acre site was held October 3, 1985, and was called "a celebration of Michigan's past and a commitment to Michigan's future." It is reported to be the first state library patterned after the Library of Congress.

The oldest museum in the Lansing area, and, in fact, one of the earliest museums on a university campus in the Midwest is the Michigan State University Museum, organized in the 1860s. Currently housed in the former University Library, the museum's curatorial divisions include anthropology, folk arts, history, mammalogy, vertebrate/paleontology, life science, education and interpretation of exhibits. Its attractions include life-like diorama of Michigan wildlife and three-dimensional re-creations of such 19th century institutions as the old country store. Other areas of interest within the museum are the Michigan Bird Hall, the culture of Great Lake Native Americans and dinosaur skeletons.

Museums were not the only means for satisfying intellectual curiosity in the early days. As the capital attracted more people, an interest developed in establishing a library. A society known as the Lansing Library and Literary Association was started in the early 1860s with capital of $1,000 and a store building on West Michigan Avenue. The library continued until 1882 when the books were donated to the Lansing Board of Education. They were to be housed in the Lansing High School and made available to the students and the public.

Increasing use of the book collection forced a move to more spacious quarters in the new city hall at the

corner of Capitol Avenue and Ottawa Street in 1897. But even this proved inadequate in a few years. Through the efforts of Mary C. Spencer, the state librarian, the Carnegie Public Library was built. It opened February 22, 1905, with a collection of 13,000 volumes. By 1929 the library's collection grew to 74,000 volumes.

According to long-time library director Virginia Summers, who wrote a history of the library, it has been noted for expanding services beyond its doors. In 1944, the library established a branch library at Sparrow Hospital along with two temporary industrial libraries in Reo and Oldsmobile plants to accommodate industrial workers during World War II. Also, during the 1940s, the library personnel broadcast 15-minute book reviews. In 1947 the library promoted book services to the seriously ill through the addition of ceiling projectors and filmed books. A telephone reference service was added in 1949 and has continued.

The boom in business and industry after World War II placed new demands on the library. In the early 1950s, business services were offered that included business and investment services, directories, specialty periodicals and a business librarian. The old Carnegie building was unable to accommodate these and many new trends in library science and services, not the least of which was use of audio-visual aids. The building was also inaccessible to many handicapped people who often had special need of its services.

The Library Citizens Committee was established in the late 1950s to study the prospects of a new building which opened at the corner of Kalamazoo Street and Capitol Avenue in 1964. Designed by architect Kenneth Black, the structure made many new services possible as well. Among the new services were a new LP

Postcard view of Lansing's Carnegie Library

record collection, art print collection, film service and a public gallery. A local history room opened in April of 1969 and was decorated and furnished in Early Victorian style, symbolizing the period of Lansing's settlement. It houses a collection of books and other materials related to Lansing, Ingham County and Michigan. The Lansing Public Library currently houses more than 223,000 volumes and continues to be associated with the Lansing Board of Education.

The early businessmen had a general interest in leisure time activities that extended beyond theaters, the arts and a library. They wanted to ensure that the community offered outdoor recreational opportunities – for themselves and for generations to come. They saw the community growing, ,and with that, a decline in the availability of recreational land near the city.

Although there were plenty of greenspaces at the turn of the century, there were only two designated parks in Lansing. One was the old Third Ward Park between South Capitol Avenue and Townsend Street, which had been obtained from the state. It later was renamed Central Park, and finally, in 1943, Reutter Park, in honor of J. Gottlieb Reutter, a former mayor. In 1929 he donated the $30,000 fountain of water and lighting effects as a memorial to his wife Mary Catherine Reutter. The other park was Oak Park on East Shiawassee Street. Oak Park was originally established in 1852 as a cemetery and was used for that purpose for 25 years until Mt. Hope Cemetery was purchased. Graves in the old cemetery were moved to Mt. Hope Cemetery between 1877 and 1900 and Oak Park was designated as the second recreation area.

J. Henry Moores, one of Lansing's great timber kings, believed Lansing needed more park space and in 1909 he donated Moores Park (known then as Belvedere Park), a sprawling area of 18 acres. Soon after, Reasoner Park was started in North Lansing.

But what Lansing needed now was not more parks, but a parks department to care for the increased recreational area and to make certain the "city in the forest" did not become treeless. A citizens' committee was formed and recruited a director who left after only two months. The city took over the parks and recreation program from the citizens' committee in 1913 when H. Lee Bancroft was hired as city supervisor of parks and as forester. Bancroft was working in the Michigan Agricultural College landscape division and was one of the two men who had been instrumental in developing Moores Park in its formative stages.

Soon after Bancroft took over, he inadvertently acquired a zoo. The James M. Turner estate, located on

Courtesy of State Journal

Zoo attendant Kristen Swanson of Haslett bottle feeds a 9 week old deer named "Bill" at Potter Park Zoo.

the Grand River in North Lansing, was home for a herd of elk that had been transplanted there by Turner. His estate turned over the herd around 1915 and Bancroft moved them to Moores Park. He had not thought much about a zoo, but he assumed the elk would attract more people to the park, and he was right.

James W. Potter did not want to be outdone by his fellow timberman. Potter, whose hardwood timber kingdom was in the area that is now Potterville, had established a plant that came to be known as the Hugh Lyons Company. He decided that a tract of land near his plant would make a good park for the city. In 1912, he carved out a sizable chunk of the tract and deeded it to the city. He was so excited about the possibilities that he later turned over another major portion to the city and contributed $25,000 toward the construction of a pavilion. The park was dedicated in 1915 and the pavilion was completed in 1921. Of course, today it is known as Potter Park.

The park system continued to grow. When Moores died in 1918, he willed another wooded strip of land to the city's park system. Named Frances Park after his wife Sarah Frances Goodman, it was located west along the banks of the Grand River from his Moores Park tract. Today, the park is noted for its beautiful rose gardens and excellent facilities.

Meanwhile, the zoo at Moores Park was growing, with a steady stream of donations. Bancroft decided to move the zoo to Potter Park where there was more space. In addition to the elk, he had acquired a bear, a pair of raccoons and some other native animals.

Today, the zoo is Lansing's No. 1 tourist attraction with more than half a million visitors a year, and home to more than 400 animals and about 120 different species. These include elephants, lions, tigers, kangaroos, elk, bears, llamas, wolves, alligators, giant tortoises, monkeys, mountain goats, and many varieties of birds and snakes. In 1969, the Friends of the Zoo Society was formed and it has stimulated a major redesign of the zoo with emphasis on enabling the visitor to better see and even touch animals.

In 1972 a contact area was developed to give children and others an opportunity to examine animals at

Francis Park

Photo R. Nolin

close hand. A farm area was constructed with the help of Karl Story of Story Oldsmobile along with a deer and elk exhibit donated by a Lansing General Motors Corporation plant. Another development in recent years is the aviary for native birds. In 1974, a train was added to travel the perimeter. Most of the $500,000 in improvements since the society launched its fund drive in 1972 have been made with public contributions.

Bancroft continued as head of the Parks Department until he retired in 1957. During his tenure, other personnel helped shape today's park system. William Atchison, as the city's landscape architect, supervised the building of Frances Park, Potter Park's monkey island, bird house and bear dens, and Evergreen Cemetery as well as the remodeling of Moores Park. Atchison first worked with Bancroft in 1914 while a student at Michigan Agricultural College. After graduation, he ran his own landscape business until the Depression and later rejoined the city.

Carl Fenner, who took over the department from

Bancroft, spent the first three decades of his career as assistant city forester. In his 39 years with the department, Fenner played a major role in shaping the park system and in developing a tree care program. He started the program in 1932 after driving his Model-T to Washington, D.C., to view its tree-lined avenues, each featuring a different species. During the Depression Fenner had more than 500 men planting 3,000 trees a year with pick axes and shovels under federal work programs. By the time Fenner retired in 1962, 93 percent of Lansing's streets were lined with trees.

Fenner's legacy will include not only the treees, but the arboretum that bears his name on East Mt. Hope Avenue. He planned the park as a nature-lover's paradise. The 120-acre farm land was purchased in 1952 by the city for $60,000 from Scott Turner, a former resident who operated an engineering firm in New York City. Turner was the son of James M. Turner, one of Lansing's first settlers, who owned the 1,200 acre Springdale Farm along East Mt. Hope Avenue. In the 1920s the area had been planted with white, red, Austrian and Scotch Pines, spruce, tamarack and other evergreens. Development of the park began in 1958 and it was open to the public in August of 1959. Part of the land is used to grow hay for the Potter Park Zoo. The park offers several nature trails, a nature center and educational programs.

Another park area acquired about the same time was Scott's Woods. This 70-acre park, located on South Clifton near the Sycamore Golf Course and Mt. Hope Cemetery, was purchased from the Scott family in the early 1950s. The property was acquired many years ago by the late Richard H. Scott to save it from commercial interests. He was a prominent businessman who was associated with Reo, Atlas Drop Forge, Novo Engine, Michigan Screw, and National Coil. A strong advocate of beautification, he did not want to see the timber cut or the sand and gravel removed from the property.

One of the major developments in the Lansing park

Riverfront Park

Photo K.R. Crans

system in recent times is the Riverfront Park. The park was officially opened during the Fourth of July weekend in 1976 amid an ethnic festival, parade and bicentennial activities. Stretching along both sides of the river in downtown Lansing, the park was the culmination of years of planning and work, beginning in the mid 1960s. The centerpiece is the area along Grand Avenue across the street from Lansing Community College where the park takes up a full block west of the river, between Saginaw Avenue and Shiawassee Street. Some of the key attractions are a broad open area for outdoor games; The Rollie Stebbins Riverwalk, a series of wooden docks, river walkways and lookout areas; picnic and rest areas; and amphitheaters.

Another park that appeared on the drawing board about the same time as the Riverfront was Woldumar Nature Center. In 1963 the Nature Way Association was formed "to acquire natural lands, to establish an educational nature center, and to foster the preservation of native animals and plants." During that time the association sponsored a Camp Discovery program for school boys and girls at the Rose Lake Wildlife Experimental Station. In May of 1966, Mrs. Gladys Olds Anderson, daughter of Lansing auto pioneer R. E. Olds, offered the idle farm located near her former home along the Grand River to the association. A year later the American Oil Company donated an eight-acre tract bordering Woldumar on the southeast at Lansing Road and Highway 27. In 1968 the huge barn at Rose Lake yielded its siding and timbers for a gift shop and office at Woldumar. Woldumar's habitats include White Spruce and Pine plantations, hardwood forests, streams, ponds, the river and field areas. One can hike for five miles over primitive, rustic trails.

An addition in recent years is the Moon log house. The house was built in 1854 by Sands and Mary Moon, soon after they moved to Delta from New York State with their nine children. The two-story log house was hewn by Sands and his sons from elm and basswood trees on their property. Sands Moon died in 1864 and his son Andrew took over the family farm. Another son, Darius, became Lansing's most noted Victorian home designer and several of his works still stand. Delta Township acquired the house from its owners, Canal Associates, so it could be placed in a natural setting. Oldsmobile provided for the moving of the cabin to Woldumar.

The Friends of Cooley Gardens and Other Greenspaces was formed in 1984 to restore Cooley Gardens. The garden was located at Main and Townsend streets in 1938 and was "dedicated to the horticultural education and pleasure of garden lovers." Its rose garden, peony collection, assortment of trees, shrubs and perennials graced Lansing as a horticultural showplace. However, in the late 1960s the freeway cut between the gardens and downtown and the city funneled parks dollars to other sites. The grandeur of Cooley Gardens faded until the Friends group planted more than 2,000 spring bulbs and put in an annual display. A master plan for the restoration and replanting of many of the plant materials which have been lost or damaged over the years was begun to restore Cooley Gardens.

Another important project to preserve local heritage is the revitalization of the Turner-Dodge House located at 100 E. North Street, high on the bank of the Grand River. After serving as the campus for the Great Lakes Bible College, it was acquired by the City of Lansing for use as a park in 1974. Refurbishing began with the

Woldumar Log House

Photo Sallie Manassah

Merry-Go-Round (Now owned by MSU) Courtesy David Thomas

help of the Jaycees and the Green Thumb program.

The classical revival style house was the home of prominent Lansing merchant James Turner. The original house built for him in 1859 had two central stories balanced by one-story wings on either side. A businessman from New York, Turner opened a general store in the first hotel in North Lansing at the corner of present day Turner Street and Grand River Avenue. Turner's daughter, Abby, married Ohioan Frank L. Dodge in 1888 and they purchased the house from Turner's widow in 1889. Dodge served in the Michigan House of Representatives and as a commissioner of the United States Court.

Between 1900 and 1906 Dodge hired local architect Darius Moon to enlarge and re-design the house to accommodate 11 family members. Moon's eclectic design resulted in a three-story building featuring stately wooden Ionic columns, a decorative cornice, porches, and an additional two-story west wing. The Friends of the Turner-Dodge House and Park, Inc., is helping to preserve this facility for the public.

An interesting history can also be found at a public park outside the city, Lake Lansing. Lake Lansing Park South, known for its fine beach and picnic areas, was once the premier amusement park in mid-Michigan. The southwest side of the lake, which was known as Pine Lake a century ago, first became a popular gathering place in 1883 when Spencer Shaw purchased the land and set aside a portion of it for spiritualist camp meetings. He added an auditorium, dancing and horseback riding. Around the turn of the century, interest in

the park waned, partly because there was no convenient transportation, and Lansingites turned to Waverly Park, an amusement park on the west side. Lansing's trolley line was then extended to Lake Lansing with a loop at the campgrounds.

To boost passenger business, the Michigan United Railways constructed a roller skating pavilion. Soon afterward, the Michigan Catering Company started an amusement park. The real impetus for the attractions came from William "Al" Sprague, who was hired as superintendent in 1916. Al Sprague was a balloonist who gave exhibitions around the United States from 1900 to 1930. In 1923, he bought a 1921 Curtiss Seagull pontoon plane that attracted crowds on Sundays when he would fly it from Pine Lake to a spot on Grand River in Lansing. Under the Sprague ownership, new rides were added or exchanged; live entertainment from lion tamers to trained poodles performed there; and the casino became a nightclub called the Mayfair.

Al Sprague eventually sold the park and by the early 1970s much of the interest had died. There was also competition from some of the bigger amusement parks within driving distance. In 1972, Lake Lansing Park's carousel was sold to Cedar Point and a year later, the park closed. In 1974, Ingham County purchased the land to prevent condominiums from being built. Remaining rides were sold or demolished, but the building that housed the carousel remained intact. Three years later the lake was dredged and a public beach was created.

Meanwhile, Thomas and Kimberly Wolf of Lancaster, Pa. were looking for a place to put the carousel Kimberly had inherited from her grandfather's defunct amusement park in Pennsylvania and they heard about the building at Lake Lansing. When the Wolfs found out that their carousel was a twin to the one previously located at the park, they knew their unit would fit perfectly. In May of 1983, six tractor trailer loads brought the carousel to Michigan. With the help of many volunteers, it was reassembled in time for Memorial Day and it has become a focal point at the lake. A small ferris wheel and a riding track coupled with the generous beach and recreation area returned Lake Lansing to a popular leisure spot.

Although the early parks offered an opportunity for family recreation, there was a desire by some for more sophisticated leisure activities. By the turn of the century, boating for pleasure and golf were becoming popular. The Lansing Boat Club, founded in the 1870s, was the center of social life, including rowing regattas, amateur theatricals and billiard parties. Golf, which first gained national prominence in the mid 1880s, didn't surface formally in Lansing until 1906 when the Riverside Country Club, a six-hole golf layout, was built from Moores Park to Waverly Park to boost a real estate development. James H. Moores donated the land and built the original clubhouse, a small, frame, one-room building in 1910 and rented it to the club for $100 a year. By 1921, the course had increased to 18 holes and a new clubhouse was opened. In 1922, the name was changed to the Country Club of Lansing. During the past 60 years, the clubhouse has been expanded, renovated and redecorated on numerous occasions and the golf course has been modernized and improved.

About the time that the Riverside Country Club became the Country Club of Lansing, a second club was being formed. A group of Michigan State College professors known as the Campus Golf Club had been playing golf on a small plot of ground near where Demonstration Hall and Spartan Stadium are today. The college was growing and needed the additional land. Consequently, the group formed the Inter-City Club and moved to new land near the intersection of M-78 and Grand River Avenue. A nine-hole course was constructed there but it soon proved to be inadequate for all those who wanted to play. Again the group moved. The members purchased the old Carl farm located on Lake Lansing Road. It included part of Chandler's Marsh where rattlesnakes nested, and they had to be burned out with kerosene.

The club was given the name Walnut Hills from the walnut trees that dotted the landscape, and the course was formally opened July 4, 1929. The original clubhouse was a picturesque English Tudor style that burned to the ground in 1961. The present structure was built the following year. In 1984 the club celebrated its 55th anniversary.

The City Club followed close on the heels of the other two clubs, but its focus was not golf or other sports but primarily a gathering place for businessmen. The club now serves both men and women and is a favorite spot for government and business leaders. Although the idea had been brewing since 1919, the club became organized in 1924 when the Hotel Olds was being built across from the Capitol. A lease with the hotel was negotiated and the club facilities opened in 1926, consisting of a suite of four rooms on the club floor of the hotel. In 1979 the club moved to 213 S. Grand Ave., the 1861 House, which it purchased in 1981 from Stanley Brauer who had operated a restaurant there.

The University Club, formed as a male faculty club, was organized in 1929 and located in the Alumni Memorial Union Building. Known as the State College Club, the organization was noted for its luncheon meetings with prominent speakers that included Michigan governors, sports figures and international scholars. The name of the organization was changed to MSU Men's Club in 1955 when the college received university status. As the university grew, the club outgrew its quarters and formed a committee in 1960 to consider a faculty club facility. Plans began to take shape with the donations of two friends of MSU: Dr. Floyd Owens (B.S. 1902 and Ph.D. 1930), who left the bulk of his estate for a clubhouse, and Forest Akers of Detroit, who donated land adjoining the MSU golf course which is named after him. The organization became the MSU Faculty Club in 1967 when women were admitted as members. Groundbreaking for the

MSU Canoeists at the Red Cedar River

new clubhouse took place on the nine-acre site in 1969 and the clubhouse opened in 1970. The new location also enabled the club to have a swimming pool and tennis courts. In 1971 the name changed again to the University Club of MSU. Ironically, the location of this facility was placed within the city limits of Lansing to avoid the dry laws still in place in East Lansing when the facility was built.

The community today is known for a variety of athletic outlets. The first YMCA was organized around 1877. Over the years it has served thousands of youths and adults in several buildings. The main building at Lenawee and Townsend streets was built in 1950. The Oak Park branch serves southwest Lansing and the Parkwood branch serves East Lansing.

Public golf courses and tennis courts abound. There are more than 25 golf courses open to the general public. In addition, Lansing maintains 65 tennis courts in its 113 city parks, and private indoor facilities are offered at the Lansing Tennis Club in Okemos and the Racquet Club in Lansing. The Lansing Ice and Gymnastics Center offers programs in ice skating, hockey, dance and gymnastics for all ages. Bicyclists will find 35 miles of marked routes that are both functional and scenic.

The Red Cedar River and the Grand River offer opportunities for canoeing, setting the stage for two famous canoeists. In December 1983, Verlen Kruger and his son-in-law, Steve Landick, completed a 28,000-mile, three and one-half-year journey by canoe, ending at Lansing's Riverfront Park. Starting from the headwaters of the Missouri River at Red Rock, Minn., in April 1980, the pair crisscrossed the United States and Canada; paddled on the Atlantic, Pacific, and Arctic Oceans; and traveled the Gulf of Mexico and up the Grand Canyon. Other sports such as hiking, cross country skiing and nature walks are available in many of the area parks.

Restaurants appeared late in Lansing, although taverns surfaced early to handle the great influx of pioneers along the Grand River. Tavern keepers offered bed and meals to the weary traveler. With the establishment of the capital in Lansing in 1847, several hotels were built, and boarding houses came into existence. The latter were often convenient to the boarder's job. As a result of boarding houses and hotel dining rooms, "pure" restaurants generally were not needed. Establishments which performed no other function than the serving of food were not even given a separate listing in Charles F. Clark's "Michigan Gazeteer" of 1863-1864.

The coming of the railroads to Lansing in the 1860s and 1870s and the beginnings of industrialization increased demands for more eating establishments. According to *"Brown's Directory of Lansing"* (1873), there were at least five "eateries" operating here, ranging from a "depot restaurant" to a "saloon and bakery" to a "confectioner."

By 1880, at least one daring soul had started a full fledged restaurant in the downtown area. He was Grover E. Chapman, native of Putneyville, N.Y. who was a Civil War hero and a former Great Lakes sailor. But the hotel dining rooms continued to flourish and among the more popular was the Hotel Downey. In the early 1900s, a new type of eatery arrived on the scene known as the "armchair" restaurant. Patrons would get their food from a table in the center of the room and eat it in armchair seats with an oversized right arm rest for trays.

Also making their debut at the turn of the century were a number of ethnic restaurants. The first Greek restaurant was "Antanoko's." The owner came from Sparta, Greece, as did many others in this field in the following years. Alex Andros and Tom Gikas started the Sugar Bowl, a restaurant-confectionary at 106 S. Washington Ave. Candy Land, a similar place, went into business at 221 N. Washington Ave. The Famous Grill, 539 E. Michigan Ave., was not established until 1931, but it thrived on the same corner previously occupied by a small eatery, Al's Coffee Shop. Stephen Scofes, father of George Scofes of Scofes Restaurant, was in business with his brothers Nick and Peter at the Famous Grill at Michigan Avenue and Cedar Street for more than 40 years.

By 1921, there were seven restaurants in the 100 block of East Michigan Avenue, including cafeterias and soda fountains. Estill's Cafeteria became a leading downtown cafeteria along with the Home Dairy. Estill's was located in the basement of the old Elks building where Russell Estill served free lunches on the anniversary of the cafeteria's opening. Home Dairy, now the Foster Building, was closed in 1970 after 50 years of business.

Since the early days, saloons, billiard places and even places for bowling had flourished, and these often sold food as a convenience to their customers. Prohibition put a damper on these places, but many found a way to survive. On December 5, 1933, the twenty-first amendment repealed prohibition of alcoholic beverages. However, that did not completely solve the problem in Lansing. The post-prohibition temperance people still attempted to curb liquor sales, established early closing hours and prevented sales on Sunday. For four years after the repeal, Lansing remained dry as far as the sale of spirits in taverns was concerned. Then the city council began granting licenses to private

recording stars known as Rare Earth. Malcolm X once worked there as a dishwasher. Alex Vanis, the current owner, bought the place around 1967.

Another place that became popular due to East Lansing's liquor laws was Grandmother's, which today is the Silver Dollar Saloon. Actually, the big building just outside East Lansing's city limits began life in 1941 as a bowling alley, Spartan Lanes. Redesigned by the designers of Disneyland in 1978, some familiar names who have performed there are Peter Frampton, REO Speedwagon, Ted Nugent, Bob Seger, and even Kiss.

Several Lansing restaurants that started downtown in the 1920s have survived, although their locations may have changed as well as their owners. One of these is Weston's Kewpee's, originally known as Kewpee Hotels Hamburgers, and the city's first drive-in restaurant.

Coral Gables Fire

Courtesy of Alex Vanis

clubs. Established institutions like the Elks and the Lansing Country Club easily obtained private licenses, but many of the more popular establishments were those that drew their membership from society at large. For about $10 a year, a person could join a club like the Tally Ho Club or the Club Lebanon. The Tally Ho Club became the Hunt Club when the city overturned the dry law around 1947. Later it became Dine's and finally Alex's at 321 E. Michigan Ave.

One of the popular hot spots in the area in the late 1940s was the Coral Gables. At the time, East Lansing was still a dry town, so the Gables was located just beyond the city limits and offered the nearest liquor and dance floor. In the 1940s and 1950s it featured big dance bands. After a major fire, it was rebuilt in 1958 and became a popular rock spot. The restaurant can boast the employment of some young people who later made names for themselves. One of its one-time regular groups was the Sunliners, who later became the

The famous Kewpee jingle is still on a 50-year-old plaque with the Kewpee doll; "Hamburg-pickle-on-top. Makes your heart go flippity-flop."

Another local restaurant that has stood the test of time is Jim's Tiffany Place. The original restaurant was known as the Lansing Cafe and was established by Jim Vlahakis at 203 S. Washington Ave. in the summer of 1914. In 1937 the restaurant moved to its present location at 116 E. Michigan Ave., two blocks east of the Capitol. Angelo Vlahakis later inherited it from his father and changed its name as well as its appearance, adding a distinctive collection of turn-of-the-century memorabilia. In 1980, Craig DeHaven bought the restaurant.

Greek restaurants have been popular in Lansing. The Eagle was started by S. Spanos, who served the first meals at 427 E. Michigan Ave. In 1916 it was purchased by the the Lianos brothers. Pete Pappas bought it in 1922 and sold it to Gus and Steve Vanis in

1926. In 1947 Steve Vanis's brother-in-law, James Stajos, came to Lansing and entered a partnership with them. The Eagle moved to the old Capitol Theater building in the 200 block of North Washington Avenue. Also caught in Lansing's urban renewal, the Eagle moved to 300 S. Capitol Ave. in 1971. David Zarkas, Stajos's son-in-law, now owns the restaurant. Although Scofes Restaurant, another Greek restaurant, is only 18 years old, its owner George Scofes has been in the business since the 1940s. His father Stephen introduced Scofes to the restaurant business at the Famous Grill. The Parthenon Restaurant arrived later on the scene, but with all the enthusiasm of the earlier establishments. George and Maria Kafantaris, co-owners, immigrated from Greece and had a long-time dream of owning their own restaurant. The Parthenon opened August 1, 1977, at 227 S. Washington Square. Starting at about the same time was another Greek restaurant,

Beggar's Banquet

or rather, restaurants – Theios. Savvas Nicolaou came to the United States in 1969 as an exchange student to Charlotte High School and lived with his uncle Andy, who owned a restaurant in Charlotte. He sold his business in 1976 and helped his nephew start "Theios," which is the Greek name for "uncle."

The America's Cup, in the University Mall at the corner of M.A.C. Avenue and Albert Street in East Lansing, features gyros and other Greek specialities served in a nautical setting. Lebanese co-owners George and Louis Eyde entered the restaurant business in 1972, diversifying from their real estate activities,

and added "B'Zar" directly downstairs. Also Lebanese with Italian specialities as well is the family owned Corey's Restaurant on Cedar.

A popular restaurant in the East Lansing area is Beggar's Banquet. Started in 1973 by Bob Adler, Chuck Rose, Christopher Blunt, and Martin Richard, the restaurant attracts a variety of people from shoppers, students and faculty to professionals and townspeople.

Other ethnic restaurants have flourished. Italian food is popular and some Italian restaurants were among the early establishments. Emil DeMarco's first venture in the food business was a fruit stand at 2012 E. Michigan Ave. in 1922, and later a neighborhood saloon. Although he died at the age of 70 in 1973, two Italian restaurants still bear his name – Emil's East and Emil's West. Some of the other Italian restaurants in the area are Coscarelli's, Casa Nova and Pasquale's.

Mexican restaurants have made great strides in recent years. The Torres Taco House at 734 E. Grand River Ave. is the oldest "original" Mexican restaurant in town, being in business for 30 years, according to Rogelio and Hortencia Torres, the owners. Another Mexican-America restaurant is Ramon's. Margarita and Ramon Fuentes started the Mexico Cafe in 1971 across from Fisher Body. Seeking a better location and larger building, they sold the Mexico Cafe and opened Ramon's on Grand River Avenue in 1976 as well as other locations.

Oriental cooking has captured the taste buds of many Lansingites and there are more than 10 restaurants serving Chinese, Japanese, Polynesian, Vietnamese and other types of Oriental foods. One of the earliest was the Foo Ying Cafe on downtown Washington Avenue, started by the Lum family in 1914. The restaurant burned in 1969 and Wing Dot, the son of one of the original owners, moved the operation to East Michigan Avenue. He now operates a restaurant in downtown DeWitt.

Many of the Oriental restaurants were started by persons who immigrated to the United States. Anna and York Wang came to Lansing by way of California. Born in the Chinese province of Shantung, both moved as youngsters to Korea where their fathers were working. They came to Lansing and started the Peking Restaurant offering Mandarin style cooking in 1977. Another couple who moved to Lansing to start a new life are Dat Luu and Hanh Phung of South Vietnam. They arrived in Lansing in 1975 after the Vietnam War and in 1981 they opened Aux Delices Restaurant in downtown Lansing.

Many of the area restaurants today are in buildings

The "Pop" Musicians

The field of music in the Lansing area has had strong leadership from the musicians union and several charismatic musicians, among them Dar Hart, Red Van Sickle, and Bryan Grinnell. Bryan has been a favorite at the Harley Hotel for more than 18 years – probably the longest "gig" in musical history. Grinnell is often joined by fellow band leader Max Swick of the Dixieland Express. Both Max and Bryan are known for the mellow style of 40s music and Dixieland jazz that made them the favorites on the famed Delta Queen and Mississippi Queen riverboats. Currently joined by Dick Fizzell and Dale Kinsler, the group has included the talented Mike Sweeney and Paul Cullins. A group of businessmen who get together often to

Josh White Jr.

VANGUARD
RECORDINGS FOR THE CONNOISSEUR

Kitty Donahoe

entertain are the Basement Five with Judge Robert Drake, Ted Hacker, Sy Lurie, Sandy Izenson, and Bud Steele.

Campus celebrities are the Geriatric Six + One consisting of Bill Faunce, Maurice Crane, "Sandy" Sandefur, Owen Reed, Jim Smith, Owen Brainard, Don Thornburg, Milt Ponell, and Wally Keller. The mainstay of the Lansing Country Club is longtime performer Lee Talboys, while the Shriner Band is led by Dick Long. The Roger Clark Band combines both men and women: Old and New. And two popular singers are Country music performer Kathy Ford and Patsi Richards performing regularly first at the Village Market, then by invitation to the Montreaux Jazz Festival in Detroit.

J. Moffett

that began life as something else. Clara's was once the passenger station for the Michigan Central Railroad. Built around 1903 on East Michigan Avenue, the depot sported cut stone arches and towers that were designed by Detroit architects Spiers and Rohns who gave several Michigan railroad stations a similar dash of Romanesque design. The building was last used as a depot in 1971 and its new owners, Peter Jubeck and R. W. Swartz, refurbished it using a number of antiques from the period. A similar restaurant, The Depot, was located in the old Grand Trunk Western Railroad station on South Washington Avenue. The 80-year-old building featured 40-foot high cathedral ceilings and is listed as a state historic site and in the National Register of Historic Places. Started by Vince Malcangi and later sold to Don Schuitema, the restaurant's theme was railroading with luggage wagons, signal lanterns, rails and a cast iron "Lansing" sign which was salvaged from the station on East Michigan Avenue before it was refurbished. The Depot was a stop on President Gerald Ford's whistle stop tour during the 1976 Presidential elections.

Restaurants located in rather unlikely structures include The Pan Tree which opened in 1976 in the old red brick building that had been the East Lansing Post Office. The Frontier at 820 Filley St. is noted for a 50-year-old cabin structure. The rustic flair outside lends itself to a roaring fire in a fireplace inside. And Harrison Roadhouse, a popular college spot at 720 Michigan Ave., was once a gas station.

The Pretzel Bell at 1020 Trowbridge Road boasts unique design combining an ultra modern exterior with an antique interior. Lawrence R. Brink, a former student of Frank Lloyd Wright, designed the building, installed a copper bar and made extensive use of tempered glass. More than 350 photographs of MSU campus life decorate the walls.

Some Lansing residents will remember several other area restaurants that made a name for themselves in their day. Archie Tarpoff's Restaurant at 124 E. Kalamazoo St. opened in 1959 at one of the gala events of the year. Over the years this restaurant attracted a number of celebrities – from Danny Thomas and Jerry Lewis to Betty Hutton and Gordon McRae. McRae came with the "Oldsmobile Shows" to promote new model Oldsmobiles.

Celentino's Lounge and Restaurant was another Lansing tradition. The family had been in the city since before the turn of the century and three generations were in the restaurant business. Joe Celentino operated the restaurant at 1016 W. Saginaw St. until

1980. Since then it has been known as El Azteco Restaurant.

Among the newer restaurants in the area creating their own traditions are The Pour House between Lansing and Charlotte and Pistachio's Restaurant on Grand River Avenue in East Lansing. Both are operated by Ronald Gibson and are noted for their fresh sea foods. Hobies, Inc., is a five-restaurant chain with operations in Lansing, East Lansing and Kalamazoo. Established in 1968 by a 26-year-old Michigan State University student, the Lansing company is marketing its line of soups made with Michigan products in grocery stores. Hobies President, Ernest G. St. Pierre, said the name comes from a combination of the name "Dobie" from the 1960s television show "Dobie Gillis" and "hoagie," the popular name for submarine sandwiches in Ohio and Pennsylvania.

Another of the newer downtown restaurants is the Knight Cap. Opened in 1969 by George Sinadinos, the establishment is his answer to the "big city, little bar and restaurant" that can be found in Chicago and New York. Sinadinos was on the only national championship wrestling team to date at MSU in 1967 and his restaurants (he also owns the Knight Cap Two in Haslett) attract many visiting sports celebrities.

The Lansing of today is a far cry from the lonely wilderness that greeted the early legislators. Residents and visitors can find plenty of sights, sounds and tastes to satisfy their appetites for fun, leisure and culture, and the aforementioned are only a sample.

Chapter 8

A Caring Community

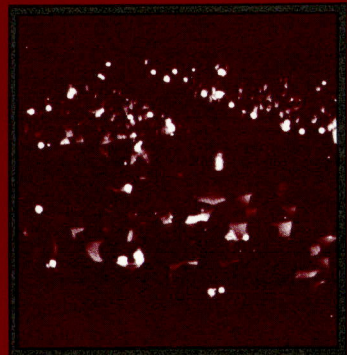

. . . A Place where Faith Grows

St. John's Student Center

Photos Matt Burton

Central Methodist Church

Lansing has always been known as a community that cares. Nearly 400 churches, major health care facilities, and social service organizations evolved to respond to the needs of its people. The social needs of the early settlers were often met through the church. Within 10 years of becoming the capital, Lansing was blessed with at least seven denominations. It seemed that everyone who came here had some religious affiliation and if not, developed one, at least as a means of social contact.

The following appeared in the *Jackson Patriot* on August 3, 1847:

"We are informed that Rev. Mr. Brown organized a Congregational Church in Lansing last Sabbath. The day is described by travelers as one of great interest. The minister's text was, 'See that thou make all things after the pattern,' from which he preached a most eloquent discourse – setting forth the adaptation of Congregational principles to our form of civil government."

"This was the first religious organization upon the Capitol grounds. The inhabitants of Lansing are generally anxious that the moral atmosphere of that rapidly increasing community should be of the most healthful character.

"A division of the Sons of Temperance is soon to be organized. The number of families is constantly increasing – so that by the next meeting of the Legislature there will be upon the ground a population of five or six hundred."

In spite of the diversity of religions, there was a great interest in ecumenism – a spirit that prevails today. In early times many congregations shared the same buildings, held celebrations together, and formed joint Bible societies. The early Senate, rather than selecting a chaplain, invited the clergy of Lansing to arrange among themselves to officiate in turn in the opening of the deliberations.

Later, many established congregations, needing larger quarters, sold their buildings to other denominations. Thus, the German Methodist Church sold its church to the Seventh-Day Adventists and the Main Street Methodist Church sold its building to the Catholics to use for a Spanish-language parish.

One of the earliest group efforts was in the development of a meeting place. Joab Page, who had come here in the mid-1840's from south of Mason to complete work on a North Lansing dam, organized a small group into the "First Methodist Class" and meetings were held in his home around 1846. Sermons were delivered by Rev. Frank A. Blades, a Methodist circuit rider known as the "boy preacher".

A year later the Presbyterians organized what was to become the First Presbyterian Church at a meeting held at the old First Ward schoolhouse on North Cedar Street. Both Page's small group and the Presbyterians were beginning to feel the need for a public meeting place. James Seymour, who owned the dam, had a barn on the north side of Wall Street between Center and Cedar streets which he sold to the two societies. They set out to remodel it into a church. "Remodeling" may be too sophisticated a term for the barn's transformation; records describe it as a long building with a double row of pillars holding up the roof and obstructing the view. The walls were plastered inside and painted white, although they soon took on a dingy grey hue from the smoke. The high back seats were made by the men of the congregations. The hard seats were softened by cushions made by the women. These were crude at best, being made from sharp edged marsh grass which cut the women's fingers as they stuffed it into fabric sacks.

Because the barn could not be called one religion's or the other's, it took on the name "God's Barn."

Recognizing the importance of religion and education to the community, the Legislature of 1848 granted lots near the Capitol to religious denominations and organized school districts, provided that a church or schoolhouse be built. Within five years, eight lots had been granted to churches, including the First New Church Society, the First Baptist Church, St. Paul's (Episcopal), the Methodist Episcopal, Central Presbyterian Universalites, and Plymouth Church (Congregationalist).

"God's Barn" continued in use until the Presbyterians built a 68-by-38-foot structure in 1852 and the Methodists put up a wooden church on the southeast corner of East Grand River Avenue and Cedar Street in 1870. The illustrious "meeting place" was sold and resumed being a stable before it was torn down.

The church built by the Presbyterians was the first church building on the southwest corner of Washington Avenue and Genessee Street. Dedicated in 1852, it was expanded in 1868. What is believed to be the first church bell in Lansing was placed in the belfrey in 1856. The Presbyterians used the church until 1889, when they moved to their new brick church on the

First Presbyterian Church with 1st church bell.

Photos Courtesy Michigan State Archives

southwest corner of Capitol Avenue and Allegan Street.

The first meeting of the new First Baptist Society was held February 1, 1851, at the First Ward Schoolhouse on North Cedar Street. The Grand River was a frequent baptismal scene. The old Presbyterian Church was rented for $10 a month to the First Baptists, who used it until 1894 when they moved into their new church on the corner of Capitol Avenue and Ionia Street. The original group became the parent of South Baptist Church (1905), Pennsylvania Avenue Baptist Church (1912), Judson Memorial Baptist Church (1930), and Olivet Baptist Church.

Because the Presbyterians were one of the first to have a structure, it was said to have been shared with the Congregationalists. The Congregationalists made a clean break in 1864 when Plymouth Congregational Church was founded. They erected a chapel on their Capitol Square lot at Capitol Avenue and Washtenaw Street in 1865. At the time the location was undesirable due to the swamp, stables and foundry that surrounded the chapel. They bought a site on the southeast corner of West Allegan and Townsend streets in 1866 and built a brick structure with a Gothic spire in

Sleighing in front of Capitol

Plymouth Congregational on right

First Presbyterian in center

THE OLD CONVENT

*T*he Second Empire residence which Walter D. Sabin built at 311 Seymour in 1879 has been private housing for over 100 years. Most of that time its occupants have been teachers.

When Sabin built his 3900 sq. ft. house, he was a prosperous hardware merchant who may have held the contract on the hardware for the new Capitol: the doorknobs and hinges and backplates in the house are a rare cast bronze like that in the Capitol. The techniques and designs of the plastered floral wainscotting and the carved glass in the front doors are also similar and were probably done by Capitol workmen. The three-story house also contains patterned flashed glass in red and blue and some of the earliest large sheets of window glass.

James B. Judson, an attorney and land speculator, bought the house in 1882 for $10,500. He and Mrs. Judson, who had been a teacher of French and German at the High School (now Old Central) when it opened in 1875, raised three sons there. After Judson's death the house was leased to Supreme Court Justice William Carpenter and his family for a few years. Both families were active in Lansing civic affairs.

After the death of Mrs. Judson, St. Mary Parish bought the house and double lot in 1910 to use as a convent. For sixty years the teaching nuns continued the studious tradition. For a time in the 70's, the building housed the Education Offices for the Diocese of Lansing.

In 1982, City Visions, Inc., in a major adaptive re-use design project, began to turn the building into a luxury condominium, known as The Old Convent.

Robert J. Morris, a former English professor and now a restoration designer and president of City Visions, first restored the Sabin-Judson House. He rebuilt wall surfaces, installed baths in hallways, and turned the nuns' ironing room back into the master bedroom. In the wings added to the house by the Church for a chapel and kitchen and dining room and more nuns' rooms, he began building three more period houses.

These three townhouses blend new spaces and new and old materials within the restored structures. For example, the chapel area is now the high-Victorian Chapel House. It contains borrowings from many other reworked Lansing houses: woodwork and doors from 314 N. Walnut, now a dentist office; radiators from 1003 N. Washington, the Michigan Podiatric Association; a staircase from a Hillsdale Street house, razed for Capital Commons; a pedestal sink from 403 Seymour, the American Lung Association Building. The new entry porch, a replica of the 1879 porch, contains a door from the Capitol.

The design of each house is unique to its original function. The Kitchen House, with its spare lines, restored maple cabinets, and a solarium, is now a Scandinavian country house. The Refectory, with its 33' living room, original oak staircase, and fanlight windows, is an elegant urban 20's Mediterranean.

Spared from demolition by its private use, The Old Convent is typical of a nationwide return to gracious downtown housing. Such houses carry their history in their architecture, the past lives in their walls. Such houses were built for their quieting perspectives and spaces; the owners are the keepers, temporarily, of a life that will outlast them.

Linda Peckham

Above: *Pilgrim Congregational*

1876. Two other Congregational churches were founded by Plymouth: Pilgrim in 1892 and Mayflower in 1903. Pilgrim's Church burned down the day of dedication, Jan. 9, 1899, but was quickly rebuilt.

In addition to sharing meeting houses, many of the early churches met at the Capitol in the House or Senate chambers. One of these was St. Paul's Episcopal Church. Between 1850 and 1853, Rev. Brown guided the families of the church in Lansing in the formation of an Episcopal society. In 1853 Rev. Brown celebrated the first communion in the parish. At the diocesan convention held in 1856, St. Paul's was admitted as a parish with 15 communicants.

Schoolhouses were also popular meeting places and the First Ward Schoolhouse often set the stage for Baptists, Presbyterians and Lutherans. The Lutherans migrated to Lansing in the early 1850s and, in 1855, some 52 men

Right:
Plymouth Congregational 1876 –

113

signed a constitution to organize "The First Evangelical Lutheran Congregation of Lansing." Now known as Emanuel First Lutheran Church located at Capitol Avenue and Kilborn Street, the congregation celebrated its 125-year history in 1980.

The Roman Catholics may have predated all other religions in the area. According to Lansing historian Birt Darling, Indian mounds unearthed in the 1870s revealed silver crosses among the decaying bones of the Indians who had lived and died before the Revolutionary War.

Early records show that in the 1840s Catholic missionaries came to Lansing from Detroit, Corunna, Westphalia and Ionia. According to *Pulpit and Prayer in Early Lansing*, published by the Historical Society of Greater Lansing, the first mass was said in 1854 in the cabin of Thomas Saier at Lenawee and Townsend streets by Father Kellert, a German missionary from Westphalia.

After a year or so, the local Catholics decided to erect a church of their own. Saier presented two lots at Madison and Chestnut streets and work began on a frame structure. But funds soon were exhausted and the contractor dismantled the building before it could be used. A brick edifice was begun in 1859, but it was not completed for two years. A committee called upon the bishop of Detroit, seeking additional funds and a permanent pastor. The bishop donated personal funds and the work continued. In 1866 he appointed the first resident pastor, Rev. Louis Van Driss, and the history of St. Mary began.

Walking from Detroit with all his personal belongings in a red bandana handkerchief tied to a stick, Lansing's first resident priest arrived to find a half-finished church, a debt of $400 and no rectory, cemetery, sisters' house or school. He made a decision to complete construction and did so with the loyal support of his small congregation. The church was expanded in 1870 and in 1873 two rooms were added for the first parochial school.

In 1897 the Rev. Father Lafayette I. Brancheau took over the parish and he realized the need for a larger and more centrally located parish center. He started work on the new church in the 200 block of North Walnut Street; it was used for the first time on New Year's Day 1904. This structure soon proved inadequate and plans were laid for a new massive Norman-Gothic building with towers of gray sandstone. The cathedral-like building was started in 1911 and consecrated in December 1913. In 1937 the Diocese of Lansing was established by

St. Mary Church under construction circa 1913

attracted persons from a wide area who would live at the campgrounds for the duration of the meetings. The *Lansing Republican* in 1876 reported that 1,500 people attended the annual meeting.

Under the leadership of Elder Levi G. Moore, those who became interested through the evangelistic meetings organized and purchased in 1895 the German Methodist church building at the corner of Saginaw and Seymour streets. It was moved to the 600 block of West Washtenaw Street where a new church was constructed in 1931. In 1969 the Adventists built a new

were too small to organize a synagogue. The *Lansing Republican* of September 22, 1876, reported that the Jewish New Year was celebrated by local Hebrew residents at the home of D. Behrendt, 16 Hillsdale St., their first religious service in Lansing.

Individual families that included both German and Russian Jews continued to settle in Lansing in the late 1880s. Because of their differences in philosophy and world views, there was a great deal of antagonism between them, according to Jewish historian Daniel Jacobson. In 1902 David Friedland arrived in Lansing

Congregation Shaarey Zedek

K. R. Cranson

church at 2400 W. St. Joseph St. and the University Seventh-Day Adventist Church bought the East Lansing Church of the Nazarene at 149 Hyland Avenue in 1971. The meetings at camp grounds in Grand Ledge continue to be an important part of the church's activity.

The Christian Scientists were latecomers on the religious scene. The First Church of Christ Scientist, one of the Capitol Square churches on the northwest corner of Walnut and Allegan streets, was built in 1910 after several years of meeting in people's homes and at the Women's Club rooms. The First Church of Christ Scientist was established in East Lansing in 1941, with services held at a variety of non-sectarian locations until the construction of the church at 709 East Grand River Avenue.

Followers of the Jewish faith have lived in Lansing since the capital was established, but their numbers

and he was able to soothe the differences between the two groups to form the Congregation Shaarey Zedek (Gates of Prayer). The articles of association were signed Nov. 10, 1918, one day prior to the signing of the armistice which ended World War I.

Some of the congregation's first services were held in a frame house at 523 S. Capitol Ave. In 1932 a new synagogue was dedicated in the presence of other religious leaders at the southwest corner of North Pennsylvania and Linden Grove avenues – the current Salvation Army building. A further effort to unite the Jewish community occurred in 1939. The members of Temple Beth El, which had been formed in 1932, merged with Shaarey Zedek on a conservative basis. The congregation now worships in a contemporary designed synagogue that was constructed in 1968 at 1924 Coolidge Road.

In recent times, a significant number of Spanish-speaking persons have chosen Lansing as their home. In October 1961 Cristo Rey began as a Catholic mission church to serve this population in the old Main Street Methodist Church. Six years later when the church relocated due to the construction of I-496, it was decided that a community center was needed and the church could work in conjunction with it.

The cement block structure at 1314 Ballard St. has become more than a social center: it offers Spanish-speaking people a place to mingle with others of their own heritage, to share in their native cultures, worship in their mother tongue and benefit from the services offered. In 1978 the Parish Council of Cristo Rey purchased the Capital City Baptist Church on South Washington Avenue for its church services and the Ballard Street building remains a thriving social center.

The Greater Lansing Council of Churches represented another step in the direction of interfaith cooperation, being formed in the early 1930s as an outgrowth of the Lansing Sunday School Association. The council has expanded into suburban areas.

In 1982 the Lansing Council of Churches changed its name to ACTS (Area Congregations Together in Service), following the lead of many other church councils to signify, through the use of an acronym, a more action-oriented organization. Since the organization is not associated with the National Council of Churches, the name change also expresses greater individuality.

ACTS represents about 50 member churches in encouraging cooperative ministries, such as the nursing home ministry. It has worked toward assuring that every nursing home in Lansing has a religious service on Sundays and has been involved with the Pastors Council in joint seminars and ministry at the Ingham County Jail. In 1985 ACTS accepted responsibility for the annual CROP (World Hunger Appeal) Walk, to raise money for food for the needy in Lansing and the rest of the world.

The emphasis in churches today is on ecumenism and social action – including peace movements, alleviating poverty, sponsoring food banks, developing crisis centers and advocating political action. With the change in the makeup of the traditional family, many churches have initiated programs concerned with the problems of the feminization of poverty, single parenting, and marriage counseling. One of the more tangible signs of this new ecumenism occurred in October 1985 when many area churches participated in a State Ecumenical Forum in Lansing.

The churches in Lansing have shown concern about

Courtesy of Arts Council

Lady of the Lake:
(l to r) Carrie Potter, Pooh Stevenson, & Wanda Degen.
Ten Pound Fiddle Coffee House – part of United Ministries.

the needs of the underprivileged. When a severe economic crisis hit Michigan in the late 1970s, many churches began food programs. In 1978 the Ingham County Food Bank was started to serve as the main clearinghouse and coordinating office for a network of emergency food closets. As of July 1985 there were 26 food closets in the Lansing area and eight in smaller out-county communities. The Michigan Agenda, an interreligious program sponsored by Protestant, Catholic and Jewish groups, advocates justice for all citizens, especially the poor and unemployed. The group communicates with elected officials on public policy issues and provides a networking center for advocacy groups concerned with justice issues.

Another example of ecumenism is the United Ministries in Higher Education at the University United Methodist Church at 1118 S. Harrison Road. Other congregations and denominations include the Christian Church (Disciples of Christ), the Church of the Brethren, the United Church of Christ, the Episcopal Church and the Red Cedar Friends Meeting (Quakers). The United Ministries staff offers programs to Michigan State University students on such topics as cults and religious freedom, stress, conflict resolution, communications skills, and suicide prevention. The Wesley Foundation Student Center houses the East Lansing Peace Education Center, the Women of Faith Action Center, the Ten Pound Fiddle Coffee House and the English Language Program of the Haslett / East Lansing Adult Education Center.

Many Lansing area churches participate in other ecumenical ventures including summer Bible school programs and interdenominational worship services. The Catholic Diocese extends beyond its doors through the Catholic Community Services / St. Vincent's home, two organizations that were merged in 1985. Catholic Community Services provides a variety

St. Katherine's Chapel

ST. KATHERINE'S CHAPEL
This building was erected about 1887 for John Forster, an early surveyor in the Lake Superior Copper Country. In 1888 the chapel, named in memory of Forster's daughter Kitty, was presented to the Protestant Episcopal Diocese of Michigan. Simple in design and workmanship, the chapel seems to be the work of an unsophisticated country builder. The interior is completely panelled with naturally finished pine with black accents.

Photos David Thomas

of programs including leadership in the social teaching of the church and the development of family life. St. Vincent's Home provides custodial care to approximately 30 children who are emotionally impaired. The home describes itself as a "change agency" and is concerned with changing negative behavior and returning these children to their families and to the community.

To describe in detail the various denominations and churches would require volumes. A survey, however, shows the flourishing religious community that exists in Lansing today.

There are about 400 churches in the area with more than 60 denominations represented. About 22 percent are minority churches, including black and Hispanic. There are nine interdenominational churches and 17 nondenominational ones. Korean, Latvian and Indochinese congregations also worship here. One church offers services in German.

Eighty Baptist congregations, which are independent or affiliated with one of nine different conferences, worship here; and there are 21 Roman Catholic churches. Also represented are United Methodist, Episcopalian, Nazarene, Congregational, Lutheran, Presbyterian, Wesleyan, and Anglican.

In addition, there are African Methodist Episcopal,

Christian Methodist Episcopal, Assembly of God, Apostolic, United Church of Christ and Seventh-Day Adventist. There are also Church of the Brethren, Christian Reformed, Churches of God, Churches of God in Christ, Pentecostal, Quakers (Friends), Full Gospel, Mennonite, Churches of Christ, Christian Church (Disciples of Christ), Christian and Missionary Alliance, Independent Fundamentalists of America, Free Methodist and Unitarian-Universalist.

Others are the churches of Jesus Christ of Latter-day Saints, Reorganized Churches of Jesus Christ of Latter-day Saints, Churches of Christ Scientist (Christian Science), Baha'i Spiritual Assemblies, Jehovah's Witnesses, Bible Churches and Spiritual Episcopal Churches.

The area has two Greek Orthodox churches, two Jewish synagogues, a Salvation Army Church and chapel, the Islamic Center in East Lansing for Moslems, and yearly Sikh religious ceremonies for the eight to 10 Indian Sikh families here.

Other organizations that contribute to the community's religious life include Lansing Area Christian Educators, Church Women United of Greater Lansing, Women's Aglow Fellowship and the Full Gospel Businessmen's Fellowship Association.

Related groups with statewide influence include the Michigan Council of Churches, Michigan Interfaith Disaster Response, Michigan Farm Worker Ministry Coalition, and the Michigan Peace Network.

As the churches care for spiritual condition, the area's hospitals care for bodily health. Hospitals did not arrive on the Lansing scene until the late 1800s, and then their appearance was usually due to religious influence or to the work of concerned women's groups.

The Daniel Case residence, also known as the home of the late supreme court Justice Howard Wiest, at 827 N. Washington Ave., served briefly as a hospital under Catholic auspices in the 1880s. It was the first building in Lansing designated a hospital.

In April, 1896, 100 local women met in the Hotel Downey and formed The Women's Hospital Association. There were prominent Lansing names like Mrs. James Turner, Mrs. Orlando Mack Barnes, Mrs. H.M. Longyear and Miss Mary Buck.

The hospital was started first in a red brick fortress-like home called the "Deviney Place" at 310 W. Ottawa St. It was a 12-bed facility that was named Cottage Hospital. Dr. Rush Shank brought in the first patient, a man needing a leg amputation. It was to the credit of these early doctors that no surgical infection was reported during the first 2-1/2 years.

In May 1899 the hospital was relocated at the John S. Moffett home, 205 S. Grand Avenue. Six months later, the facility was moved to the James Mead home at 429 N. Cedar St. and renamed Lansing City Hospital. The Mead home was bought on contract at $65 a month, but it was in poor condition. The superintendent's pay was increased to $25 a month in an effort to get better administration. In the long run, the Mead home proved inadequate and the women were constantly raising money from bazaars and recitals to keep it going.

At the turn of the century, the demand for hospital services mounted as the city grew. The women decided to approach prominent citizens who could support the hospital with larger donations. In 1900 they received an appropriation from the city and in 1901 they began organizing a hospital staff of local physicians and planning a nurses' training program.

Samuel L. Kilbourne, son of Joseph H. Kilbourne, the man who had played a major role in attracting the capital, began raising substantial sums from merchants and industrialists. Among those who became interested was Edward W. Sparrow, a Lansing real estate and lumber tycoon. He offered to provide a new steam heating plant and operating room. However, he soon realized that the old Mead building could not be refurbished and decided to provide $100,000 for a new

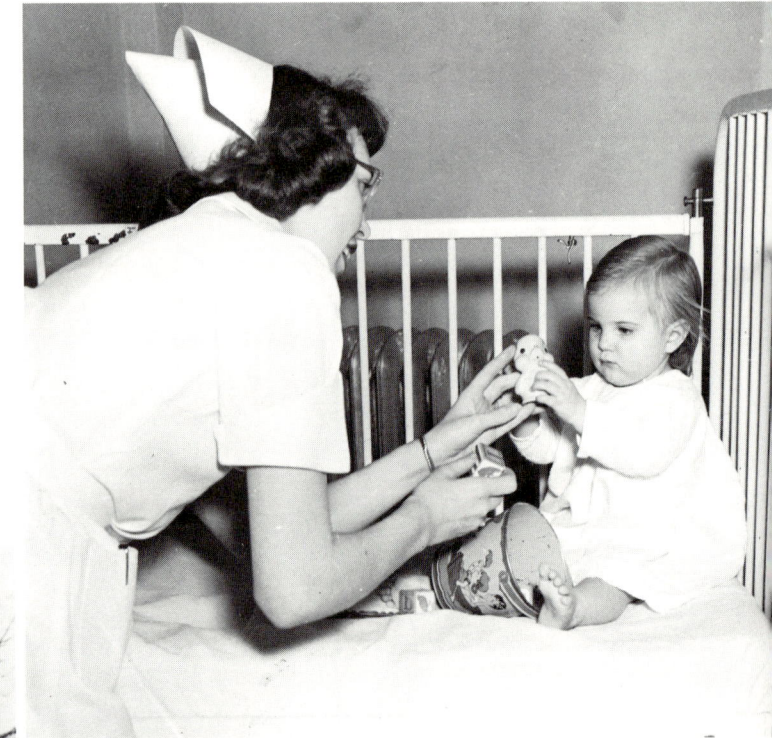

Above:
*St. Lawrence
circa 1955*
Left:
*Original Sparrow
Hospital*

building. He also donated a large tract of land in the 1200 block of East Michigan Avenue.

To equip and furnish the hew hospital, Mr. and Mrs. W. K. Prudden offered $5,000 if the hospital board women would raise a like amount; and they did. The doctors themselves equipped the laboratory and the hospital was dedicated on June 1, 1912, completely furnished.

Originally, Sparrow had requested that the facility be run by an all-male board. However, he was so impressed with the work of the women, that he declared, "The women whose efforts have meant so much for hospital activities in the past will have charge of the conduct of this new hospital and there will be dual control. Trustees will be responsible for the business and the Women's Board of Managers will control the School of Nursing, guide volunteer groups and care for the personal side." A school of nursing, started by the hospital in 1899, operated until 1959.

Within a few years after the hospital opened, expansion efforts were underway. A new wing for a children's department was donated by Roy Chapin, the automotive leader who started in Lansing. His gift of $115,000 was followed by one for $52,000 by Dr. Julius Post in 1916 to erect another wing.

In 1927 the hospital's main structure was rebuilt and enlarged. In 1942 additions were made to both the Chapin and Post wings. Ground was broken on a $2 million West Wing addition in 1957 and a year later the $1.6 million Foster Wing opened. Construction on the South Wing began in 1965 and opened a year later.

In the early 1980s Sparrow officials began construction of the new West Wing and renovation of existing areas of the hospital. This included construction on a five-level, 170,000 square-foot addition attached to the South and Foster wings. The project, the largest for a hospital in Lansing's history, brought total bed capacity to 502 and provided new units for intensive and cardiac care, burn treatment, surgery, recovery, emergency, radiology and central supply.

Although the Sparrow Hospital of the early 1900s provided Lansing residents with some measure of sophisticated health care, it was not able to meet all the needs of the sick. Within a year after Sparrow's dedication, a 10-bed tuberculosis sanitarium was started; it was the forerunner of today's Ingham Medical Center.

The public's fear of what was known as the "white plague" made isolation of those with tuberculosis a requirement. The only things that people understood about the disease were that it was often fatal and it was contagious. Consequently, when a hospital specifically for the afflicted was built, it was located as far away as possible – in this case, outside the south city limits. When the hospital opened in 1913, the staff consisted of a nurse, who also did the cooking, a maid and a janitor.

In 1917 a second building known as the Dakin cottage was constructed to provide eight beds for ambulatory patients. The capacity was doubled in 1921 and 13 years later the building was moved a block east of its original site to be used as an employees' residence until it was torn down in 1958.

By 1924 TB case-finding techniques had improved and there was a new public awareness of tuberculosis treatment. Overcrowding at the Ingham Sanatorium resulted in the construction of a 30-bed infirmary. It became the children's building in 1930 and was converted to a nurses' residence in 1938. It was removed in 1956 to make room for the new staff residence.

In 1930 expansion occurred again. A four-story, fireproof building was constructed to accommodate 100 patients. In 1938 a thoracic surgery department was approved and the following year saw the addition of a surgical department and the conversion of lounges to increase bed capacity to 135. Improvements were made in 1948 and in 1954 the surgical south wing was added. That same year the name was changed to Ingham County Chest Hospital.

In the late 1950s an official report of the administrative and medical staff of the hospital predicted the future of the facility:

"Further growth of the hospital as a chest surgical center is anticipated as newer methods for the detection and treatment of such diseases as lung cancer and heart disease are developed . . . The facilities necessary for adequate medical and surgical treatment of chest disease often are adaptable and sometimes necessary to the treatment of other diseases . . . It is conceivable that the hospital will become a general hospital with a well organized 'chest department' so as to retain its present identity as a chest center."

In 1960 the facility became known as the Ingham Medical Hospital and formally opened its doors for treatment of all types of ailments. The next 14 years were important ones as Ingham changed its image from a chest hospital to a general hospital. In 1966 it became the first hospital in the area to perform open heart surgery. The first procedure was done to close a hole in the heart of a 15-year-old. Other sophisticated techniques in the areas of thoracic and orthopedic surgery followed as well as a complete rehabilitation program for patients treated in these areas. A new medical facility was completed and dedicated in 1972, providing the hospital with 254 beds. In 1974 the name was changed to the Ingham Medical Center. In 1980 a prototype facility for arthroscopic surgery was opened and has been visited by thousands of orthopedic surgeons from around the world.

The third major hospital to be established was St.

Lawrence who suffered martyrdom at the hands of the Romans about 258 A.D. for offering the sick, poor and crippled as the church's greatest treasure.

Since the former Lange sanitarium was only a temporary structure, a campaign for a new hospital was launched in 1922. Local attorney Edmund C. Shields led the campaign to raise funds for the new institution

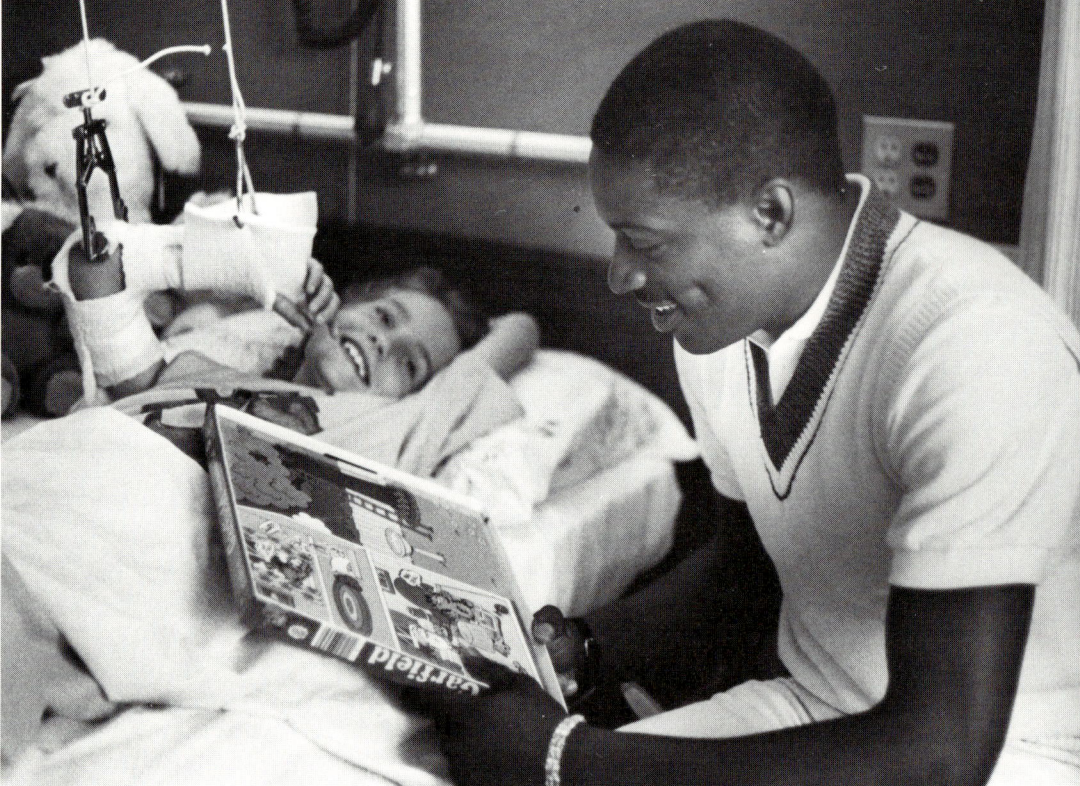

Former MSU basketball star Sam Vincent visits 9-year-old Renee Rathbun of Lansing at St. Lawrence Hospital.

Courtesy of St. Lawrence Hospital

Lawrence Catholic Hospital. In 1917 the Sisters of Mercy were invited by the Rev. Fr. John O'Rafferty, pastor of St. Mary Catholic Church, to start a hospital. Sister Mary Assisium Hynes led a group of nuns to Lansing and set up a hospital in the former Lange Sanitarium on Willow Street and Washington Avenue. With a capacity of 26 beds, the hospital opened on Jan. 20, 1920, in the midst of the post- World War I flu epidemic. By the next day, the hospital was filled to capacity and additional cots were brought in.

Fr. O'Rafferty and Edward VerLinden, then general manager of the Olds Motor Works, were among the key figures associated with the hospital; and the early financial support came from a man who died three years before the hospital doors opened. Lawrence Price provided a $100,000 legacy for the hospital under the direction of the Sisters of Mercy. He also selected the name "St. Lawrence," after the patron Saint

and the subscription totaled more than $200,000. Particularly helpful was the donation of nearly four acres of land on West Saginaw Street by Mr. and Mrs. Joseph Gleason, the founders of Silver Lead Paint Co.

The cornerstone was laid in 1923 and the new 125-bed hospital opened prematurely when an expectant mother could go no further and delivered a baby boy the night before the official opening of March 10, 1924.

As the community grew, the hospital expanded numerous times. By 1970 it added a community mental health center geared to local treatment of the mentally ill.

However, in 1971, the staff, trustees and advisory board decided that they needed to rebuild the present facility. A community campaign followed that raised a million dollars toward the new hospital. Ground was broken in May 1976 and the building was dedicated on

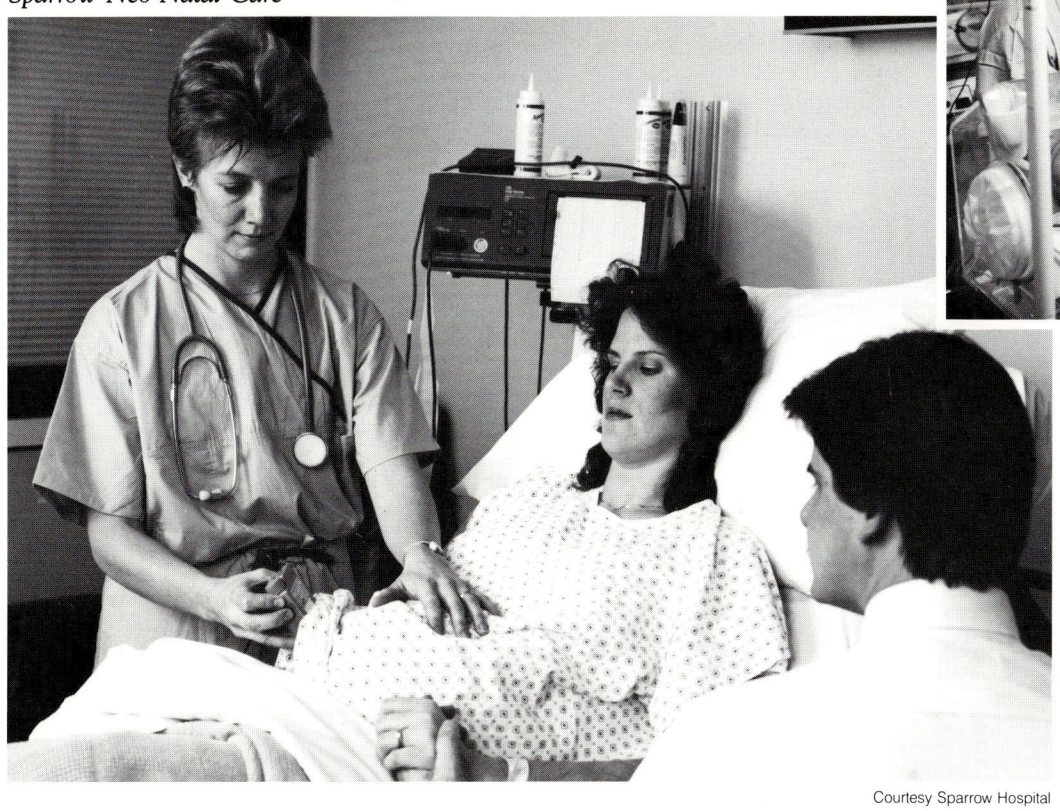

Courtesy Sparrow Hospital

June 3, 1978. Today, St. Lawrence is a 259- bed facility and is noted for its work in mental health.

Newest of Lansing's hospitals is Lansing General, which was started in 1941 to provide osteopathic physicians with a place specializing in osteopathic care. It was originally called McLaughlin Osteopathic and was started by Dr. Lawrence M. Jarrett and his wife, Dr. Harriett Jarrett. It was incorporated in 1942 by the Jarretts and Mr. and Mrs. C.J. McLaughlin of Hollywood, Fla., Mrs. Jarrett's parents.

When it opened at Townsend and St. Joseph streets, the hospital had only eight beds. The hospital was actually a converted 23-room mansion that had been constructed by R.E. Olds for one of his daughters. In spite of the small number of beds, the hospital reported 297 admissions, 50 babies delivered and 126 surgeries in its first year.

The hospital's capacity was expanded to 25 beds in 1943, and two years later a three-bed pediatric department was added. By 1956, the hospital had increased six-fold. In 1958 the hospital moved to its new building, a 243-bed hospital at 2800 Devonshire St. and the name was changed to Lansing General Hospital.

In the late 1950s the city's hospitals launched a $6,300,000 expansion program. The United Hospital Expansion campaign received more than $4,300,000 in pledges from residents and businesses. Other monies came from the federal government. This program was responsible for the new osteopathic hospital and for bed increases at St. Lawrence and Edward W. Sparrow

Hospitals.

Construction projects in the 1970s brought Lansing General Hospital to its present 243-bed capacity. In 1972 Lansing General Hospital and Michigan State University arranged for an affiliation with the College of Osteopathic Medicine. In recent years the hospital opened a residential drug and alcohol treatment facility, sleep disorders center, and medical rehabilitation center.

Health care today in the tri-county area of Ingham, Eaton and Clinton is provided by seven hospitals. Lansing's four hospitals work with the smaller ones – Hayes-Green-Beach in Charlotte, Eaton Rapids Community Hospital, and Clinton Memorial in St. Johns. The medical colleges at Michigan State University serve the community with additional health care resources and advanced research and technology. University physicians practice in all the hospitals and in the Clinical Center on campus, an outpatient facility open to the public and staff. Olin Health Center provides student health care. All seven hospitals have emergency rooms and the four Lansing hospitals have the largest and most sophisticated intensive care and cardiac care units.

MSU, through its Speech and Hearing Clinic, offers diagnostic, therapeutic, and consultative services for speech, hearing, and language disorders in infants, children, and adults. The College of Veterinary Medicine, the only veterinary school in Michigan, serves the public through its Small Animal Clinic, Large

(Grand Ledge, Neff Elementary School) — Ben Scypher, age 5, has his height recorded by his teacher while fitness for youth program originator, Dr. Guy Reiff of the University of Michigan, looks on and other five year olds wait for their turn. Height and weight measurements and physical performance tests are recorded yearly, comparing students to themselves as well as nationally-known norms.

Fitness for Youth

Blue Cross and Blue Shield of Michigan's commitment to the citizens of Michigan extends beyond offering quality health care coverage. The corporation also aids the public through a variety of less well-known programs. Approximately one million dollars a year is spent to support community educational and social programs in Michigan. "Fitness for Youth" is one such program.

Introduced in Stockbridge, in southeastern Ingham County, Fitness for Youth encourages children to adopt healthy lifestyles. The program was developed by the University of Michigan. While stressing exercise and good nutrition, it introduces concepts designed to make students aware that fitness is ultimately their personal responsibility.

Each week, a physical education teacher provides students with two 30-minute periods of vigorous, aerobic exercise and nutrition information. Tests measuring biomedical and physical performance levels are administered yearly. Results are compared to national norms as well as those obtained in a particular school. The measurements show that, as a general conclusion, children between 5 and 12 years of age will nearly always improve their level of fitness as a result of participation in Fitness for Youth. A dozen school districts now offer the Fitness for Youth program, benefitting approximately 30,000 children. In addition to Stockbridge, Fitness for Youth is offered in the Grand Ledge and Mason school districts.

Dennis Larson

Animal Clinic, Ambulatory Clinic and Emergency Clinic.

Most area hospitals have obstetrical services. Sparrow has the regional center for neonatal intensive care which provides special care for newborns with problems. Infants are transferred to Sparrow from a wide area. Lansing General Hospital has an alternative birthing suite. Ingham Medical Center has a pediatric intensive care unit for children.

The four Lansing hospitals offer complete x-ray services as well as computerized axial tomographic (CAT) scanners, the latest advance in x-ray technology. Meridian Instruments of Okemos also provides a highly sophisticated diagnostic service through the use of a unique cell-sorter, developed through basic research at Michigan State University.

All seven tri-county hospitals and the MSU Clinical Center provide specialized care and treatment for cancer patients. The oncology unity of Sparrow Hospital has earned recognition as one of the most advanced research and treatment facilities in the nation, while intensive cancer research is the ongoing concern of the MSU Carcinogenesis Laboratory.

The four Lansing hospitals have developed many programs to treat particular diseases. Since it evolved from a chest hospital, it is only natural that Ingham Medical Center now specializes in emphysema and other lung diseases and in open heart surgery. Lansing General also developed specialized services in respiratory disease and treatment.

St. Lawrence has a 50-bed residential facility in Dimondale for treatment of persons suffering from alcoholism and/or drug abuse (this is in addition to Lansing General's treatment program). St. Lawrence houses the 60-Plus Medical Center for senior citizens and the area's Poison Control Center, a 24-hour hotline which provides the community with poison information and instruction in emergency situations.

Kidney patients can receive dialysis at a special center at Sparrow, but kidney disease patients may be hospitalized in any area hospital. Arthroscopy, a new type of knee surgery that involves puncture incisions instead of the conventional cuts, is performed at all Lansing hospitals. Ingham Medical Center has a special suite for this procedure. All hospitals treat burn cases, but the most severe are transferred to Sparrow which treats more than 80 persons a year.

Lansing General, the only osteopathic hospital in the area and one of the largest osteopathic hospitals in the country, offers osteopathic manipulative therapy, which is a specialty of osteopathic physicians. Lansing

General also has a Sports Medicine Clinic for professional or amateur athletes. Sports injuries are evaluated and clinic experts can suggest when an athlete may return to sports activities.

Sparrow is one of only six complete regional tissue banks in the United States. Established in 1978, it is able to provide approximately 25 different kinds of tissue organs for transplants from donors to patients in need.

The Lansing area also has two health maintenance organizations (HMO). HMO plans differ from traditional fee-for-service plans in that the medical provider contracts to deliver health care at a fixed prepaid fee per member without regard to the frequency or type of services utilized.

Health Central, Inc., started in 1977, became a subsidiary of Blue Cross/Blue Shield of Michigan in 1979. It has more than 50,000 members. As a group practice model, its physicians work for the HMO. Patients are also referred to community physicians specializing in medical services not available at Health Central. Because of its emphasis on "wellness," Health Central offers a variety of preventative services and health education programs.

The Physician's Health Plan originally was sponsored by Sparrow Hospital in 1981 to open access to health care at a lower cost. It has expanded to include all the hospitals and 98% of the physicians. Participating doctors continue to operate their private practices as well. In addition, there are more than 30 clinics that provide emergency and general practice care to patients throughout Lansing and its suburbs.

Social awareness was one of the signs of the times as the Community Chest movement started in 1919. What was to grow into the Greater Lansing Community Chest was started at a meeting October 22, 1919.

"Smile Day" Sponsored by Delta Dental   Delta Dental

Members of the first board of trustees were: Ray Potter, chairman; Charles W. Nichols, vice chairman; W. K. Prudden; F. N. Arbaugh; C.E. Bement; and Donald E. Bates. Growth of the fund is seen in a comparison between the 1919 list of 3,000 contributors and the 1948 roster containing 35,214. The organization was set up primarily to coordinate 11 agencies and consolidate their appeals.

Today the organization is known as the Capital Area United Way. More than 1,000 volunteers are involved in the annual campaign to raise more than five million dollars to support 51 area agencies. There are dozens of other organizations not associated with the United Way that provide social services to make Lansing a better place to live.

From a few small groups of people meeting in homes in a wooded and swampy area over 125 years ago, Lansing has grown into a community that reponds to its people's needs – whether religious, economic or social.

Participants start on the CROP walk

Photo Vaughn Gurganian

Chapter 9

An Educational Mecca

Lansing Community College Library

Marble School Early School in East Lansing, built in 1861

Courtesy East Lansing Public Library

The residents of the newly cleared area in the forest quickly got down to the business of educating their offspring shortly after the state Legislature began using its hallowed halls in 1847.

This concern not only led to strong local public and private primary and secondary education, but served as the springboard for one of the nation's finest universities that now exists along side one of the state's largest community colleges as well as one of the nation's fastest growing schools of law. In the days in between, Lansing saw noble attempts to establish specialized private and public institutions as the residents struggled to shed the pioneer image and move into a sophisticated era. Most efforts succeeded, but even the futile efforts laid the groundwork for successful institutions.

First came the local primary schools. Although the Capitol was to be the center of a well-organized community, the people settling the proposed town of Michigan were so far-flung and separated into three centers of commerce that three school districts were organized.

The first school building was built in the spring of 1847 in what was then known as Lower Town near the present site of the Cedar Street School. Serving the north end of the city, this first schoolhouse was a crude, one-room building with holes cut in the sides for windows and a door hung by leather thongs at the top for hinges. It was replaced by a larger structure that fall, and by 1851, a four-room, two-story brick building costing $5,000 was constructed, which lasted for nearly 25 years.

The next school district was organized in 1848 in what was known as Middle Town with a school at the northwest corner of Townsend and Washtenaw streets not far from the Capitol. By 1851, the third school district was organized to cover the area known as Upper Town, south of Michigan Avenue and east of the Grand River.

It wasn't until the spring of 1861 that the public schools were consolidated under the provision of the city charter, forming an early beginning of the Lansing School System. The City of Lansing had been incorporated only two years earlier with a population of about 3,000.

In 1986, the Lansing Public Schools celebrated its 125th anniversary. It has grown into a system of more than 40 schools and includes many specialized educational programs – from vocational education at Harry Hill High to bilingual education. The special needs of mentally impaired youth have been met in recent years by the Beekman Center. Opened in 1968, it was the result of a 10-year effort by parents and special education professionals to establish such a facility. With $500,000 in federal funds from the Mental Retardation Construction Act and $1 million from the Lansing School District, the center was built on the southeast side of Lansing. It was named in honor of Marvin E. Beekman, a nationally known pioneer in the field of special education who was instrumental in the development of the center. He served for more than 36 years as a teacher and director of special education programs

State Superintendent of Public Instruction Henry R. Pattengill (far right) around 1893

Courtesy Lansing Public Library

A class in Cherry Street School, 1907 Courtesy of Mrs. George Stucky

for the Lansing Board of Education and was later state director of special education.

Private schools proliferated in early Lansing for three or four decades. Some historians believe this was a result of the importance placed on education by the highly educated early settlers from the east who snubbed public schools as lacking in refinement. One of the first private schools was started by Mrs. Laura Burr in 1847. She was assisted by her husband, who was one of the earliest physicians in the community. Unfortunately, an epidemic of "brain fever" (what is believed now to have been meningitis), killed many of the pupils as well as Mrs. Burr's husband.

The most ambitious and memorable of the private schools was the Michigan Female College, established in 1855, by Abigail and Delia Rogers. They had come to Michigan from New York in 1847 and taught at Albion College and the State Normal School at Ypsilanti. Arriving in Lansing, they tried to convince the state legislature to establish a college for women in the capital city. When they met with no success, they decided to start one on their own. Investing their entire fortune of several thousand dollars, together with contributions from some of Lansing's leading citizens, they erected buildings on the present site of the Michigan School for the Blind.

For nearly 15 years, they taught girls from the best families in Lansing, Jackson, Detroit and other Michigan cities. Their aim was to prepare them for entrance into the University of Michigan and other academic institutions. In 1869, Abigail died, and Delia felt incapable of running the school by herself. She disbanded the college and later donated much of its equipment to the Lansing Public Schools.

The same year that the Rogers sisters established their college, the state legislature passed an act which founded the first agricultural college in the nation. However, it was not without struggle. In 1837, Michigan's first year of statehood, the legislature established

what it believed to be the premier institution for higher learning, the University of Michigan at Ann Arbor. Although it served people in almost every field, there was one important omission – the scientific teaching of agriculture. In the early years of the state, 90 percent of the population was engaged in some aspect of farming. To address the needs of those involved in this work, the Michigan State Agricultural Society, comprising 60 members of the house and senate, was organized at Lansing on March 23, 1849.

The society petitioned the State Legislature in 1850 for a college dedicated to instruction in agriculture. Low on finances, the Legislature petitioned Congress for a grant of 350,000 acres to foster agricultural education in Michigan. This was the first time such a petition had been made by a legislative body and it led to the college land-grant concept.

But the supporters of the college were not willing to

Marvin E. Beekman

Courtesy Beekman Family

wait for Congress to decide its fate. A revised constitution for the State of Michigan in 1850 specifically provided for the college. The next five years witnessed a great debate on where and how the college should be established. John C. Holmes, a Detroit horticulturist and secretary of the State Agricultural Society, secured passage in 1855 of an act authorizing the purchase of not less than 500 acres of land within 10 miles of Lansing as a site. Lansing was chosen as a compromise among a number of legislators who wanted the college in their districts.

On February 12, 1855, Gov. Kinsley S. Bingham signed the law which founded the Agricultural College of Michigan. Unfortunately, the bill limited the cost of the land to $15 per acre, which reduced the possibilities to unimproved woodland. Various sites were offered, including DeWitt on the north, Pine Lake (Lake Lansing) on the east, and Delta on the west. But

Faculty at M.A.C. (Kedzie 5th)

Robert Clark Kedzie
"Consumer Advocate of the '80s"

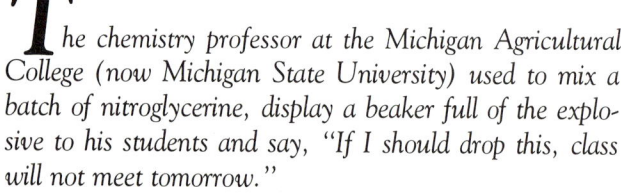

The chemistry professor at the Michigan Agricultural College (now Michigan State University) used to mix a batch of nitroglycerine, display a beaker full of the explosive to his students and say, "If I should drop this, class will not meet tomorrow."

Luckily, Robert Clark Kedzie never dropped the container and was able to teach at the college until his 80th birthday, dying in 1902. His accomplishments as an educator and scientist during his 39 years at MAC fill many pages in the history of the college.

A graduate of the University of Michigan's Medical School in 1851, Kedzie practiced medicine for 11 years at Kalamazoo and Vermontville. When the Civil War broke out, Kedzie joined the 12th Michigan Infantry as an assistant surgeon. During the Battle of Shiloh it was said that Kedzie refused to leave the wounded Union soldiers even though Confederate troops were rapidly approaching. Captured, he was shortly released and, because of poor health, resigned on Oct. 8, 1862.

Returning home, Kedzie decided to leave his practice of medicine and, in 1863, accepted a position as professor of chemistry at the Agricultural College. Although a popular teacher, it is Kedzie's pioneering efforts in science and consumerism that are best remembered today.

One of his most famous consumer crusades was the battle against a mysterious toxic poisoning, occasionally causing death, that was occurring in some of Michigan's older homes. Studying the strange happenings, Kedzie discovered that a certain type of wallpaper called "Paris green" was tinted with arsenic. Over the years, as the color gradually came off the wall, the arsenic would infect people living in the house. As part of his effort to stop the distribution of the wallpaper, Kedzie cut up 80 rolls of the arsenic-tinted paper, bound them into books and sent copies to libraries throughout Michigan. The book, titled "Shadows from the Walls of Death," helped stop the sale of "Paris green" wallpaper.

Other Kedzie campaigns included persuading the legislature to require safety standards for kerosene; fighting for the passage of a law that provided for the inspection of commercial fertilizers; and convincing the legislature to reduce the taxes for people who plant roadside trees in an effort to replenish Michigan's dwindling forest lands.

Kedzie has been credited with the first use of electric lights on the MAC campus, installing an Olds engine in 1884 to generate the power to light the chemistry laboratory. He is also remembered as the father of Michigan's sugar beet industry.

While Robert Kedzie's accomplishments are obviously significant, he was not the only Kedzie who made major contributions to the Lansing area. His son, Frank Stewart Kedzie, served as president of MAC from 1915 until 1921. Frank's wife, Kate Marvin Kedzie, was Lansing's most prominent turn-of-the-century music teacher. A daughter-in-law, Ella Kedzie, was a painter who had studios in Lansing's old city hall; while two other sons, William and Robert F., were on the faculties of Kansas State and Mississippi State respectively.

D. Thomas

the 676 acres of woodland that stretched from what is now Harrison Road to Bogue Street and from the Grand River Plank Road to Mount Hope Road was purchased.

According to the history of the college as written in the catalog of 1900, the site had its limitations:

"It was a herculean task to transform the wild forest into an orderly home for a great agricultural school, and the conditions seemed by no means promising. Lansing itself was at the time but a little clearing in the woods, accessible only by stage and surrounded by dangerous swamps. The College Farm was three and one-half miles from town. Of the 676 acres, only three were cleared, and for much of the year, the road from Lansing to the building site was bottomless. It is small wonder that nearly two years elapsed before the first buildings were completed and the beginnings of school work were made."

The first building, College Hall, was also the first structure in the U.S. for instruction in the science of agriculture. The four stories were built from bricks that were made by hand and baked upon the campus grounds. The only other original structures were a dormitory (later to become known as "Saint's Rest" for its sober juniors and seniors), and a barn. The faculty of a half dozen scholars included Holmes as superintendent of horticulture and college secretary. John R. Williams of Harvard was recruited as the college's first president.

On May 13, 1857, the college was formally opened and welcomed 63 students, a sizable opening enrollment. The college year ran from late February until November, when field experiments were halted by cold weather. This schedule continued for 40 years. Many students taught school in their home communities during these winter months to earn money for their education.

Every effort had been made to make the cost affordable. Tuition was free to all students in the state and $20 for those from out-of-state. Board was $2 per week and room rent was $4 per year. Everyone was charged a matriculation fee of $5 and had to pay $10 in advance to the treasury to help settle accounts at the end of the term. These figures changed very little in the first 40 years of the college. An early catalog estimated that a student should expect to spend $150 per year to attend college.

To assist with their expenses and to aid in the work of the young college, all students were required to work three hours per day. Depending on "ability and fidelity," students could expect to earn anywhere from 4 cents to 8 cents per hour, which was applied to their board. No one was exempt from this work, regardless of

their financial status. The catalogue of 1861 eloquently stated the purpose of this work: "It is believed that the three hours labor which every student is required to perform on the farm or in the garden besides serving to render students familiar with the use of implements and principles of agriculture are sufficient also to preserve habits of manual labor and to foster a taste for agricultural pursuits."

In reality, the work in the early years was difficult. A letter written home by Charlie Jewell in July 1861, reveals,

"I have been logging considerable – clearing for the 'breaking'. Yesterday I logged four hours . . . the old calico shirts are entirely 'used up' and I shall have to wear my fine shirts, I suppose. If I had expected to do such dirty work, I would have brought a pair of 'hickory' (striped) shirts."

Holmes and his colleagues had given careful consideration to the curriculum. Although they left the classical studies to the University of Michigan, they filled the schedule with courses such as chemistry, animal and vegetable physiology, geology, and veterinary science, a rigid curriculum for students who had come to campus from a variety of educational experiences.

In another letter home, Charlie Jewell related,

"Some of the class think this is not so difficult a year, as some in the course, but I have never found so little time for writing letters and reading. We have got through to practical economy and are reviewing at the rate of 20 pages per day

Agriculture Building

Courtesy MSU Information Services

. . . Then we spend 2-1/2 hours each day in the laboratory; while the third study, anatomy and physiology, is the most difficult of the three."

In April 1861, the first shots of the Civil War were fired at Fort Sumter. The first class from the college graduated in September 1861, two months early so they could all enlist in the Union Army. In the midst of the Civil War, educational advancement was not forgotten. MAC President Williams, continued to press for a federal land-grant to support agricultural colleges like MAC.

In 1862, President Abraham Lincoln signed into law the Morrill land-grant act to support a college in each "loyal" state that should include agriculture, engineering and military tactics in order "to educate the industrial classes in the several pursuits and professions in life." Michigan received a quarter of a million acres of land, which was sold, and the proceeds deposited in a perpetual endowment fund.

With MAC's financial future more secure, the State Board of Agriculture recruited more faculty and expanded the curriculum and enrollment. Attracted to the college in the next 40 years were people who shaped its future, like Theophilus C. Abbot, an English professor from Maine who served as president of the college from 1862 until 1884. Another was Dr. Robert Kedzie, professor of theoretical and commercial chemistry, who was a member of the original state health department. He and his son Frank, who later became president of the college, worked on chemical compounds to destroy insects that ravaged Michigan farmland.

William James Beal, botanist, who discovered the secret of modern hybrid corn, planted a grass garden in 1873 that evolved into one of the few botanical gardens of the 1880s. Liberty Hyde Bailey, who first worked as Beal's assistant, founded and edited the first campus newspaper, the *Speculum*. Later, returning from a stint at Harvard, he established the first horticultural school in the United States at MAC in 1885 and became famous for his pursuit of new plants.

With little fanfare, women gained admittance to the college in 1870 when 10 women (daughters or relatives of faculty or local residents) enrolled; they usually lived at home since dormitories were for men only. In 1896 a Women's Course was added to provide women, according to the catalog, "the capability to take prompt hold of life on the side of its material tasks. What science has done for the workshop, it can also do for the household." The Women's Course included algebra, English, botany, cooking, calisthenics, geometry, elements of chemistry, entomology, meteorology, and bacteriology.

Two other programs were initiated to comply with the stipulations of a land grant college: the Department of Military Science and Tactics in 1884 and the Department of Mechanic Arts in 1885 to teach,

M.A.C. Coed Room at the turn of the century

MAC Professor William Beal in Beal Gardens.

Courtesy MSU Archives

BEAL BOTTLE EXPERIMENT

*S*omewhere on the Michigan State University campus, in a spot known only to a few university scientists, six one-pint bottles have been buried for more than 106 years. The bottles, a part of the nation's oldest continuing agricultural experiment, will remain undisturbed until 1990 when one will be removed from its secret hiding place.

It started back in 1879 when Michigan Agricultural College (now MSU) botany professor, William J. Beal, buried 20 bottles, each containing the seeds of America's most common weeds, in an undisclosed campus location. Then, like a pirate marking the spot of his buried treasure, Beal prepared a map indicating the hiding place of the bottles.

Professor Beal's original plan was to dig up one bottle every five years and attempt to germinate the seeds. In 1920, however, the interval was changed to every 10 years in order to extend the length of the experiment. The last of the six bottles now in the ground is scheduled for removal in the year 2040.

The purpose of the experiment, in Beal's own words, was to "learn something more in regard to the length of time seeds of some of our most common plants would remain dormant in the soil and yet germinate when exposed to favorable conditions."

Beal's decision to bury the seeds of common weeds instead of well-known flowers or vegetables was apparently intended to test the practice of 19th-century farmers of leaving their fields fallow for a time in hopes that the weed seeds would die off and make future plantings weed free.

The results of the Beal experiment indicate that the farmers would have had to wait many decades for this to happen. In 1950, for example, 47 of the then 70-year-old seeds germinated within two weeks after planting. In 1960, three species of the seed germinated. In 1970, only one seed germinated – Verbascum Blattaria, a weed commonly called moth mullein.

In 1980, 101 years after Beal began his experiment, three MSU professors dug up one of the buried bottles, returned to their laboratory and planted the seeds. Two of the seeds germinated within the first two weeks and three more seeds germinated in the following three weeks.

"Obviously we've already proved that farmers can't leave their fields fallow enough to rid them of weeds," MSU botany professor Robert Bandurski said after the 1980 part of Beal's experiment. "But the fact that the seeds have been buried for so many years has given us a unique opportunity. The seeds collected from the 100-year-old weeds will be planted to determine what mutations have occurred from the seeds being exposed to 100 years of natural radiation. We're learning more about how the life processes continue for a very long time. After all, they're living on their own reserves."

Dr. Alexander Kivilaan, retired MSU botanist, holds bottle from 1980 dig.

MSU scientists plant seeds from 1980 dig.

Dave Thomas

according to the catalog, "the principles upon which the leading industries of the country are based with a full line of instruction in the use of tools and the construction of mechanical products."

Because of the college's vacation schedule and the students' work activities, inter-collegiate athletic encounters were rare. In 1888, MAC joined the Michigan Inter-Collegiate Association (MIAA), now the oldest athletic conference west of the Allegheny Mountains. Besides MAC, the other members were Albion, Hillsdale, and Olivet, all similar in size then. In 1896, the long winter vacation was changed to summer and football became popular. Interest in intercollegiate sports grew and an athletic-physical education staff was developed.

The shift in vacation schedule led to the disappearance of manual labor and the increase in required laboratory work. At the turn of the century, college enrollments increased everywhere. At MAC the number of students went from 400 in 1895 to 2,000 in 1915. Through the promotional efforts of college President Jonathan LeMoyne Snyder, people were beginning to understand the diversity of the curriculum at MAC. A further boost came in 1907 when President Theodore Roosevelt gave the annual commencement address. He discussed the federal responsibilities for rural people and asked the land-grant colleges to fulfill them. He urged these colleges to reach out and be part of the community in which they were located. With much planning and legislation, the Extension Service was developed as a way to take the laboratory to rural Michigan, teaching farmers better methods of production and sharing homemaking skills among their wives.

There were other important changes in the academic program in the early 1900s: in 1902, the forestry curriculum was added and in 1910 veterinary medicine became a four-year program. This was a natural addition to an agricultural school, but it provided the impetus for the eventual and unprecedented founding of two additional medical schools. In 1924 the State Board of Agriculture created new Divisions of the College: the Division of Applied Science and the Division of Liberal Arts. Through this means, major degrees in most of the fields traditional to American universities were offered and more students were attracted to study at the college.

Because of this expansion of the college's mission, the name Michigan Agricultural College was no longer suitable. In 1925 the state Legislature changed the name to Michigan State College of Agriculture

and Applied Sciences, a name that was quickly abbreviated to Michigan State or MSC. The athletic teams traded "Aggies" and "Farmers" for the "Spartans" nickname and the student newspaper became the *State News.* That same year the first Doctor of Philosophy degree was conferred and business administration, hotel management and police administration were introduced.

Enrollment continued to rise, from 2500 in 1925 to 3300 in 1930, in spite of the beginning of the Great Depression in autumn of 1929. That same year John Beaumont (class of 1882), a Detroit lawyer and a student in the first class that President Kedzie had taught, wanted to commemorate the location of College Hall – the first building in America for the teaching of agriculture. He and Mrs. Beaumont donated the campanile tower that houses a 47-bell carillon.

The Great Depression did not stop what seemed to be a constant building program. The college made allowances to survive – cut salaries across the board

Beaumont Tower at M.S.U. Courtesy East Lansing Public Library

Jack Nutter
Pitcher, MSU Baseball
Now baseball coach at
Ovid-Elsie High School

Judi Brown-King
Silver Medal
Olympics 1984

Above: "Magic" Johnson
& Kyle Macey
Below: Carrying the Olympic
Torch thru East Lansing

Art Brandstatter
East Lansing and
MSU Star Athlete

1985-86 MSU Hockey
Mike Donnelly

135

without dismissing a single faculty member, reduced tuition and developed a network of area wide freshman colleges for those who could not afford to go away to college. In 1931 the first bond-financed dormitory, Mary Mayo Hall, was built. Nine other major buildings, including the Auditorium and Fairchild Theatre, the Health Center and Jenison Gymnasium and Field House, were erected during the next 10 years through bonds and federal grants.

In 1941, John Hannah became the 12th president of the college, following his father-in-law, Robert Shaw. He had served as secretary of the college since 1935 and was instrumental in the building program. That momentum continued through his 28-year presidency, particularly to accommodate the influx of World War II veterans. MSU historian Madison Kuhn wrote:

He watched over every detail of an institution that was growing from seven thousand to thirty thousand students, from a half square mile of teaching and research buildings to almost two square miles, from a college with a few strong departments to a university with many distinguished ones, a university with a reputation for leadership in science and applied science in general education and continuing education, and in innovations that culminated in a community-oriented College of Human Medicine.

In 1948, the college was admitted to the Big Ten and Michigan State qualified for the Rose Bowl where Clarence "Biggie" Munn's Spartans defeated UCLA, 28-20, on January 1, 1954. When Munn became athletic director, his assistant and successor, Hugh "Duffy" Daugherty, returned to the Rose Bowl in 1956, again defeating UCLA, 17-14.In 1951, the Kellogg Center for Continuing Education, one of the foremost adult educational centers in the nation and the largest laboratory for hotel, restaurant and institutional management schools in the nation, was opened.

The College of Education was raised from the status of a department and ground was broken for a $4,000,000 library. Today that library houses more than three million volumes. Robert Vincent founded the National Voice Library in 1962 and collected more than 8,000 recordings spanning 75 years. Today it is known as the G. Robert Vincent Voice Library, the largest academic voice library in the nation and has more than 40,000 recordings of the voices of such people as Adolph Hitler, Ty Cobb, and Woodrow Wilson. In 1954, WKAR-TV, the third educational TV station in the nation and the first east of the Mississippi,

Duffy Daugherty with Northwestern's Alex Agase

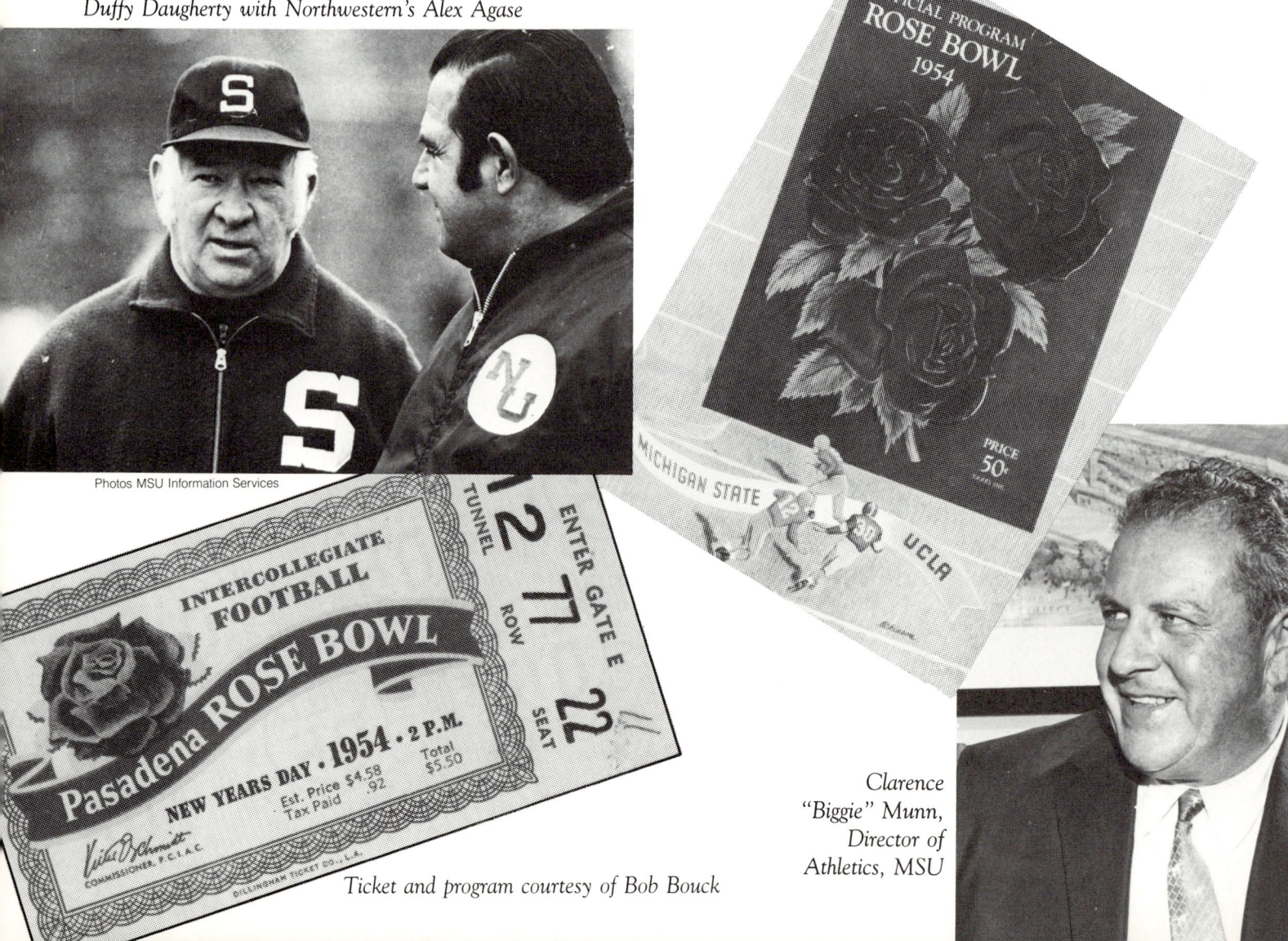

Photos MSU Information Services

Ticket and program courtesy of Bob Bouck

Clarence "Biggie" Munn, Director of Athletics, MSU

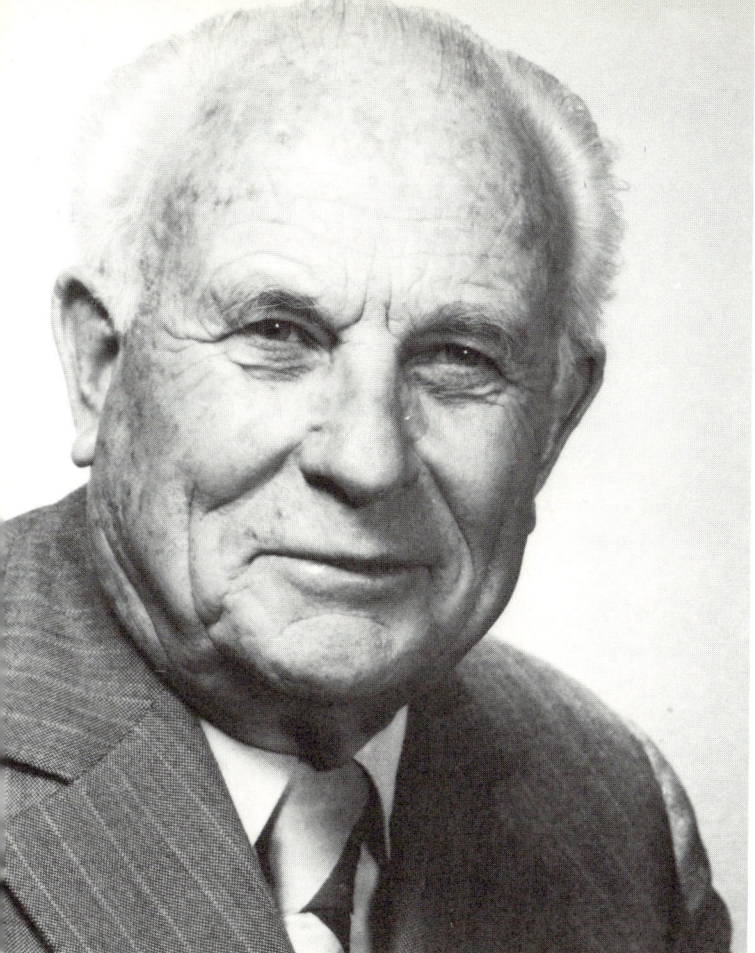

John A. Hannah

Photo by Douglas Elbinger Studios
Courtesy MSU Information Services

began operation.

But the most memorable event of Hannah's tenure came in the institution's centennial year. In 1955 the name was changed from Michigan State College of Agriculture and Applied Science to Michigan State University of Agriculture and Applied Science by an overwhelming vote in the Michigan Legislature. This name was officially shortened to Michigan State University in 1964.

There was seemingly no end to the advances of the Hannah years. In 1955 the College of Communication Arts and Sciences was established, the first of its kind in the nation. A year later, a dean of International Programs was named to direct MSU's expanding foreign assistance programs that would coordinate research and teaching projects in such countries as Costa Rica, Okinawa, Colombia, Vietnam, Brazil, Nigeria, Turkey, and Pakistan.

While the institution was taking a prominent place among universities, interest in the athletic program continued to increase. Spartan Stadium, constructed in 1923 to seat 14,000, was expanded for the third time in 1957 to accommodate 76,000 spectators, making it the 10th largest university-owned football stadium in the country.

In the final decade of Hannah's presidency, enrollment rose from 20,000 to 44,000, and MSU achieved status as one of the top 10 largest universities in the United States. The university attracted more National Merit Scholars than any other institution and was the first to establish an Honors College on a university-wide basis. Fifty-six new buildings or major additions appeared, including a science complex featuring a cyclotron, food science building, and the Eppley Center for the College of Business. The Kresge Art Center was constructed in 1958 with a gift from the Kresge Foundation to house the university's art department and maintain a collection of work from antiquity to

Abrams Planetarium

Courtesy MSU Information Services

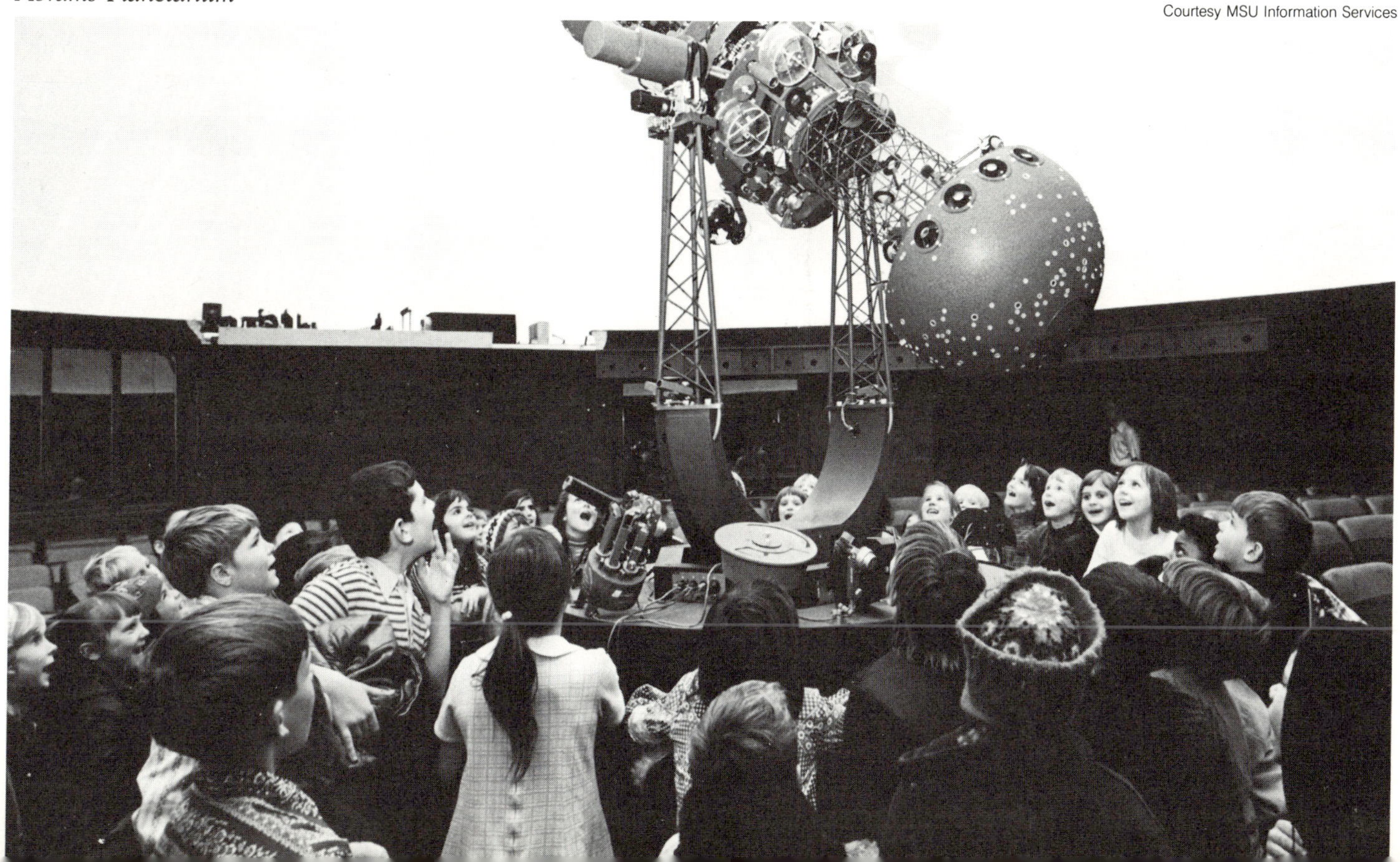

Dedication of Sparty with MSU Band

the present. The Abrams Planetarium, financed by alumni and friends with a major gift from Talbert and Leota Abrams of Lansing, was constructed in the mid 1960s to provide programs in space science in the 360-degree sky theater.

The constant construction led some wags to joke that "the concrete never sets in the Hannah empire."

The College of Human Medicine was founded in 1964 to emphasize community and family practice as more than specialization. Also emphasizing community medicine, the College of Osteopathic Medicine, the first state-supported and university-based school of its kind, became part of MSU in 1969. It was started as the privately chartered Michigan College of Osteopathic Medicine in Pontiac. Medical school classes began in East Lansing in 1971. Joining with the College of Veterinary Medicine, these two colleges make MSU the nation's only university with three medical colleges.

The decade of the 1970s brought important academic discoveries and national acclaim to campus. Three presidents – Walter Adams, Clifton Wharton, and Edgar Harden – led the university from 1969 to 1979 (they were succeeded by MSU's sixteenth president, Dr. Cecil Mackey). Work was begun on the heavy-ion cyclotron in 1977, and in 1979 on the National Superconducting Cyclotron Laboratory. Today it is a major national facility for nuclear physics research, and is funded by the National Science Foundation and the Department of Energy. The laboratory is also building the world's first superconducting cyclotron for hospital use.

In recent years, cisplatin, the most widely used anti-cancer drug developed in the United States, was discovered at MSU, and researchers in the Carcinogenesis Laboratory are working to develop more methods to uncover the cancer-curing potential of chemicals. Much research is occurring in the field of genetics engineering though the use of such experimental techniques as recombinant DNA, monoclonal antibodies, and plant cell fusion. These efforts resulted in the development of new ornamental plant varieties, in the genetic mapping of cancer- causing viruses, and in the development of bacteria that produce bovine growth hormone. The work in the Pesticide Research Center, the Mass Spectrometry Laboratory, and the National Institute for Research on Teaching brought national recognition to campus.

Construction continued in the 1970s including Munn Ice Arena, the MSU Clinical Center, and the Communications Arts and Sciences Buildings, the latter completed in 1981. The Wharton Center for the Performing Arts, with the 2,500-seat Great Hall and the 600-seat Festival Stage, was started in 1979 and completed in 1982 mainly through faculty and private donations.

MSU boasted a banner sports year in 1979 by winning an unprecedented triple crown: Big Ten football, baseball, and basketball championships. Much of the success of that year's basketball team can be attributed to the incomparable Earvin "Magic" Johnson. "Magic," a Lansing native, went on to be a star in professional basketball; teammate Jay Vincent, another Lansing native, became a professional player as well.

The 1980s have observed a campus building boom reminiscent of the 1960s. One of the largest structures erected at MSU is the new $29 million Plant and Soil Science Building. This building consolidates the major units of the departments of horticulture and crop and soil sciences scattered throughout campus for more than 50 years. Four new athletic facilities are on the drawing board or completed, including the Jack Breslin Student Events Center with its 15,500 seat multipurpose arena, the East Campus Intramural Facility, the Indoor Football Practice Facility, and the Indoor Tennis Facility.

The Michigan State University of today combines a distinguished academic program and sophisticated high tech research with many of the traditions of the past. With all the changes in its more than 130 years, some things still survive. Beal Gardens, now more than 110 years old, are today considered some of the finest in the world. The six acres of 5,000 plant species are organized in economic, systematic, landscape, and ecological groupings and are used as an outdoor teaching lab. The MSU Museum, one of the oldest on a college campus, provides insights into Michigan heritage, culture, and natural history. Cowles House, built in 1857 as one of 10 homes used by the faculty and once the home of botany professor Beal, serves as the official residence of the president. A major restoration and interior design program has been undertaken to establish a permanent and cohesive design representative of its original period.

The university has long established itself as a leader in almost every academic field, and yet agriculture remains an important educational focus. The 3,000 acres of MSU farms provide support for the university's many agricultural projects. MSU researchers, along with those from nine other American universities, are involved in a massive project to help prevent famine in 12 developing countries through improvements in the production and use of dry beans and cowpeas.

When John A. DiBiaggio became 17th president in 1985, he came to a campus that boasts a consistent enrollment in excess of 40,000 students, a campus of 2,100 acres considered to be one of America's most beautiful college facilities, and a campus with 538 buildings and $186 million in planned and current construction. The MSU of today claims more Rhodes Scholars than any other public institution, attracts more National Merit Scholars, and leads in the number of students who win National Science Foundation fellowships. MSU spreads its influence throughout this country and the world through its research, its gradu-

ates, and its direct applications of scholarly research to solving life's problems.

While Michigan Agricultural College was offering an education in farming and scholarly pursuits, there were many men coming home from the Civil War who needed training for wage-earning jobs. The Lansing of 1867 was a bustling capital city of nearly 10,000 people. State government was expanding and industry such as carriage manufacturing and mill work was developing. However, many of these men wanted more than these laboring jobs, but work in state government required skills.

That year Henry P. Bartlett and E.P. Holbrook opened the Lansing Commercial College in the Lansing Academy, located in the old Benton House at the northwest corner of Washington Avenue and Main Street. The Benton House was Lansing's first "fine hotel", but it was being converted to apartments and commercial use. The school was started to "train young men for positions in the counting houses," by means of courses in bookkeeping, penmanship, commercial arithmetic, commercial law and business correspondence. By 1880 Bartlett, who taught most of the classes himself, was also offering courses in grammar, algebra, and geometry. He also changed the name to Bartlett's Business College. Bartlett sold it to W.A. and C.E. Johnson in 1887, and the brothers changed the name to Interlake Business College.

In 1898 Herbert J. Beck purchased the school, naming it Lansing Business University and adding A.C. Wessel in 1904 as a teaching partner. Competition appeared in 1905 when the Central Michigan Business College was incorporated. Competition between the two schools was intense, but they settled their differences in 1907 with a merger. In 1914 Charles E. Ebersol took over and combined the operation with the Lansing Commercial Institute.

William Dowden acquired the school in 1920, broadening the curriculum and in 1923 moved the

MSU Museum

school to 130 W. Ionia Street where it remained for more than 30 years. He continued as president and manager until his death in 1932, and he was succeeded as president by his wife. Mrs. Dowden continued until 1951 when she sold the school to Robert Sneden of Grand Rapids.

In 1961 Clark Construction Company built an eight-story building at Capitol Avenue and Ottawa Street to house the school and other offices. In August 1977 the school moved to its own building at East Kalamazoo Avenue and Cherry Street. In 1979 the school was acquired by Davenport College of Business, a Grand Rapids institution that grants two-year associate business degrees, and the name was changed to the Davenport College of Business.

Today Davenport is a two-year college with 600 students specializing in business careers. It offers associate degrees and diplomas in the secretarial, management, computer, accounting, fashion merchandising, retail and travel fields. There are majors in more than 20 different areas ranging from receptionist/typist to computer programing. Students are able to receive extensive "hands on" training on state of the art office machines from electric typewriters, to personal and mini computers.

The Lansing Business University was a leader in business education in the community in the mid 1950s, but job training needs were changing. After World War II and continuing in the 1950s, the industrial facilities around Lansing were growing rapidly, creating a demand for draftsmen and other skilled tradesmen. This need and the initiative of industry representatives were instrumental in the inception of

*Groundbreaking for Arts and Sciences Building
(l to r) John Dart, Lee Trumble, Mayor Max Murninghan, Phil Gannon and Frank Benedict*

Lansing Community College. They met in August of 1956 and plans were made to establish a "Community Technical College."

Meanwhile, a young man named Philip Gannon was working on his doctorate degree in higher education and administration at Michigan State University. A former teacher in Battle Creek, he had become involved in researching the educational needs of communities. Thus, he was employed as a special advisor to the superintendent of the Lansing School District to study whether or not Lansing needed and could support a community college. The big question to be answered was whether a community college could exist next door to a major state university. MSU President Hannah gave an unqualified endorsement and advised that the curriculum be broadened as soon as possible to include the arts and sciences.

By April 1957, Gannon completed the study and recommended that a college be established as a technical institute offering training in mechanical, electrical and civil technologies, apprenticeship programs, and licensed practical nursing. The Lansing Board of Education accepted Gannon's report and wanted to call the institution Capital City Community College and Technical Institute. However, the superintendent of public instruction recommended the college be called Lansing Community College. By fall LCC welcomed 425 students to its facilities located in the Technical High School (formerly old Central High School). By the end of the first year, 54 practical nurses had graduated and Gannon was named dean of the college.

In those first years Gannon did everything from hiring the faculty to registering students. "We worked out of a cigar box," he said. "At the end of the first week of registration, we balanced our books to a penny." But Gannon had a plan that led LCC to become one of the top urban community colleges in the country.

By the second year, the curriculum was broadened to include liberal arts transfer courses and secretarial training. The third year a cooperative program was established with the St. Lawrence School of Nursing, and the student newspaper, the *Lookout,* was first published.

Enrollment increased to 2,124 by 1962, and the board of education recommended expansion in downtown Lansing. Accelerated enrollments in business, liberal arts, civil technology, mechanical technology, practical nursing, and the sciences created more space problems the following year. Two mobile office and classroom units were installed next to Old Central. Administration, faculty, and counseling moved into

Aviation Course at LCC

the old Lansing Library building. But space problems and increasing enrollments are a symptom of success in the academic world, and in 1964, the college was accredited for 10 years by the North Central Association of Colleges and Secondary Schools.

Enrollment jumped again in the fall of 1964 to more than 3,000 students, and a citizens committee was appointed to study the feasibility of establishing a county-wide community college district. Voters approved the district in a December 1965 election, along with an "all-purpose" one mil assessment for capital outlay and operation. A board of trustees of six members was elected and Gannon was appointed college president.

The separation from Lansing Public Schools was completed in 1966 and the first annual college operational budget was $2,225,730. With enrollment up to 4,000, several buildings were being renovated and expanded; and contracts were awarded for construction of the health sciences and liberal arts and sciences building which opened in 1968.

New programs had been added every year, usually to meet the demands of the business community. In addition to the original technical courses and liberal arts transfer courses, the college by 1968 was offering classes in law enforcement, fire science technology, truck driver training, court and conference reporting, hotel-motel management, data processing, library technology, heating and air conditioning, commercial art, appliance service and repair, radio and television servicing, auto parts counterman, aviation maintenance technology, small engine repair, as well as other programs with direct applications to business.

"The college started as an education and training institute," said Jacqueline Taylor, vice president of community and public relations. "We have always had a partnership approach with business, industry and government and have responded to their needs." Many of the area businesses look to LCC for training at all lev-

els – from the trades to management training programs for existing personnel.

The arts were not to be overlooked. In 1971 the Department of Performing and Creative Arts was established in the Technology Division with extensive programs in art, music, theatre and dance and in 1979 the large group instructional facility opened with the auditorium dedicated in the name of Charter Trustee John H. Dart. Cable TV Channel 33/21 was established in 1975 and media radio and television was added to the curriculum. A year later, with its own TV studio, LCC was "on the air." In 1978 the first telecourse, "Child Development" was offered on this channel. Today some 60,000 homes throughout Lansing and East Lansing have access to programming on this station.

Health careers such as respiratory therapy, nuclear medicine technology and radiation therapy technology were added during the 1970s. In 1980 the vocational-technical, health careers and physical education building was dedicated as the Gannon Vocational-Technical Center, a tribute to the man who has been the only chief administrator of the college.

LCC has made registration easier through its innovative program which registers about two-thirds of its students by telephone through a computer. First used in 1975, the system provides control over all elements of student information and contains on-line facilities which handle everything from seat reservations to "drops and adds." The computer has also revolution-

Dart Auditorium

Lansing Community College

Photo by Dianne Schwartz

ized LCC's library system and office operations. Patrons of LCC's three libraries use a computer terminal instead of card catalogs to locate materials on and off campus.

Although called "community college," LCC's influence is far from provincial. In 1977, the Nigerian government sent 46 students to LCC for technical education. LCC students have studied at Kongju College in Korea and Shiga Prefectural Junior College in Japan. An international studies committee was appointed in 1979 and the following year Gannon was appointed a consultant to the Technical Education Research Institute and the Ministry of Education in the Republic of Korea. In the 1980s the college has cooperated with Motor Wheel Corporation of Lansing in developing a tour of seven Japanese manufacturing plants by five top Motor Wheel Executives and Gannon. Gannon served as consultant in 1985 for polytechnical education in mainland China for three months under the auspices of the World Bank.

Gannon said he became interested in international programs when he noticed that his contacts in business and industry were constantly referring to their world markets. "If we were to continue to serve them, we needed to expand our educational opportunities beyond this country," he said. ". . . we had to learn how to train people to produce quality products at competitive prices."

LCC programs have been utilized by foreign governments. The LCC Airframe and Powerplant Program was selected by the Saudi Airlines Corporation for the training of its personnel. Students and staff members from colleges in other countries have visited the campus to observe the curriculum. As of 1985, the college maintained sister college arrangements with Belize, Japan, the Republic of China (Taiwan), and the Repub-

lic of Korea. In addition, LCC has conducted the Japan Adventure, an overseas academic work-study program in conjunction with Japan's Biwako-Kisan Steamship Company for the last four years. It has offered 100 students the opportunity to learn the Japanese language and work overseas.

In 1985 LCC's enrollment was more than 23,000 students, but more than 40,000 persons are engaged in various programs offered through the college. LCC occupies 14 buildings on the downtown campus plus an Aviation Center at Lansing's Capital City Airport and a Truck Driver Training Center at Fort Custer in Battle Creek.

In addition, LCC has extended the campus to 25 off-campus instructional centers in communities within the service area of the college. The college also has taken its campus to the people in factories, government offices, banks and other businesses. LCC has served business, labor, industry and government by developing training programs, offered through the Management Development Center and the recently established Business and Industry Institute. LCC instructors and consultants combine work place visits and instruction with campus-based training classes to make programs accessible.

LCC is one of three licensed CADAM (Computer Augmented Design and Manufacturing) training centers nationwide. Lockheed Corporation donated the CADAM equipment to LCC in 1984 and the recent designation as an official training site means CADAM users throughout the Great Lakes region and the nation have access to an approved training facility. The computerized system allows draftsmen to design, diagram, calculate, and perform other drafting functions.

Among the other programs receiving statewide attention are the Criminal Justice Center, the only state-certified Police Academy in Mid-Michigan that provides in-service training for area law enforcement agencies as well as corrections and security programs; the data processing curriculum that is one of the most comprehensive in the state; and the apprenticeship and skilled trades programs offered in cooperation with 158 area organizations.

Recognized as a leader in the development of diversified programs and renowned for its excellent standards of education, it is the eighth largest college in Michigan and ranks in the top 10 percent in size and complexity among all colleges in the United States. In addition to business, four other academic divisions offer more than 300 career programs and liberal arts education. They are Arts and Sciences, Student Personnel Services, Technology and Applied Sciences and TeleCommunication and the Arts.

Although there were many educational institutions in Lansing by the mid twentieth century, there was no instruction for those who desired a career in the church.

On September 21, 1949, the first classes were held for eight students of the Great Lakes Bible College in a one-room log cabin at Rock Lake near Vestaburg north of Lansing. In 1959, the college trustees purchased the eight-acre Turner-Dodge estate on East North Street in Lansing from the heirs of Frank Dodge, a 19th century civic leader.

Although this location was highly beneficial to the college, its growth ultimately made another move to larger quarters necessary, one that could expand with the college. In 1968 the trustees chose the 40-acre Frank Huxtable farm at Creyts Road and West Willow Highway. Buildings were constructed and the campus was occupied in the fall of 1972. It is fully accredited by the American Association of Bible Colleges (AABC).

One of the best known contributions of the college to the community's cultural life comes through the annual Madrigal Dinner-Concert Series. The program features dinner, a court jester, a drama in rhyme and is climaxed by a concert of authentic madrigal songs.

Lansing's newest educational institution is the Thomas M. Cooley Law School. What began as a simple letter written 15 years ago by a justice of the Michigan State Supreme Court to the State Board of Law Examiners has developed into a thriving and nationally recognized law school.

In 1971 Justice Thomas E. Brennan wrote the members of the board and pointed out that there was a definite need for more legal education. There had not been a new law school chartered in Michigan in more than 40 years and none was located outside the southeastern part of the state. Also, the state's law schools were turning away many potential students for lack of space.

Brennan and his colleagues wanted to create a law school which, like the English Inns of Court, would function as an educational arm of the legal profession, rather than a legal curriculum within an education institution. The name Thomas M. Cooley Law School was selected to honor a Michigan Supreme Court Justice of a century ago who is remembered as one of the state's outstanding jurists. He served on the Supreme Court bench from 1865-85, was a dean of the University of Michigan Law School and was the first chair-

man of the Interstate Commerce Commission and president of the American Bar Association.

According to Brennan, Stanley E. Beattie, the chairman of the Board of Law Examiners was enthusiastic, but wrote a terse and eloquent prescription for success: "All you need is a dedicated faculty and two million dollars."

"We didn't have two million dollars, of course," said Brennan, "but we did have a list of over 300 prospective students who wanted to go to law school."

After one and a half years of planning by a dozen other judges and lawyers and a long battle on the State Board of Education, Cooley began operations with 76 students on the night of January 17, 1973, in rented quarters above a vacated engraving shop on South Grand Avenue. However, before the first year was over, the student body had grown to over 200, the school had purchased the building at 507 S. Grand Ave. and the State Board of Law Examiners had given the school its accreditation. By 1976, Cooley was approved by the American Bar Association.

Today Cooley Law School owns three buildings – the 80,000 square foot former Masonic Temple at 217 S. Capitol Avenue, the three-story administration building on South Grand Avenue where the school began, and the 65,000 square foot former J.C. Penney building

Cooley Law School   Courtesy Judge Brennan

on South Washington Avenue that is being renovated into a law library.

As of 1986 Cooley Law School is the 22nd largest among the 173 accredited law schools in America – one of only 28 law schools with an enrollment of more than 1,000 students. From a regional law school primarily serving mid-Michigan, Cooley has developed a national reputation and stature. More than 40 percent of its students come from outside of Michigan. Cooley has continued its commitment to provide legal education for working people in America by year round operation, reduced class load curriculum with a choice of morning, afternoon or evening sessions, and opportunities for practical experience.

Another school that started in downtown Lansing with an idea and a lot of determination is the Institute

Courtesy of Linda Knapp

of Merchandising and Design. Organized in 1977, the school opened with only seven students and has grown to more than 100 students today engaged in the study of merchandising, management, interior design and fashion design. Judy Merrill Clinton and Linda Petroff Knapp, who were associated with the Lansing Business University, started the institute. It is one of the few schools in the Midwest offering post-secondary training in this field.

While at LBU, the pair received inquiries from people about courses in fashion and merchandising but were not able to direct them to an appropriate school. They decided to start their own fashion and merchandising school and originally called it Merrill Fashion Institute. In 1982 they changed the name to the Institute of Merchandising and Design and moved to 116 W. Allegan St. The institute is accredited by the National Association of Trade and Technical Schools and is licensed by the State of Michigan, Department of Education.

Some education has evolved in Lansing to meet special needs. The oldest of these is the Michigan School for the Blind, developed from the single building which was the old Michigan Female College. After the college closed in 1869, it was purchased by the Oddfellows Association. This organization leased it to the state in 1880 when the blind program was separated from the deaf program in Flint. For 100 years it was the boarding school for Michigan's brightest blind children, and held an international reputation for excellence in its special role. The school's programs included music, home economics, industrial arts, and sports. Although there were vocational programs in such things as broom making and piano tuning, the school offered blind children a basic education that enabled many of them to pursue college studies. It has graduated judges, factory workers, journalists, teachers, and even talented recording artist and musician Stevie Wonder.

The school had football, basketball, swimming, and wrestling teams playing other small high schools like Williamston and Webberville. One year MSB won a state championship wrestling championship and the football team was well respected. The school had marching bands, proms and plays.

A major change took place at the school in the 1970s. State and Federal special education laws moved the majority of Michigan's blind children back to their homes and community schools. Multiply handicapped children were taken out of mental institutions and sent to school for the first time in history. Today the school serves blind, partially sighted, deaf-blind and multiply handicapped children and young adults. Students get the same kind of basic education offered in the regular public schools, but the teaching methods and materials are different. Cooperative programs with elementary and secondary schools in the Lansing area offer courses not included in the MSB curricula.

Lansing, East Lansing and beyond

It has been the privilege of the Lansing Regional Chamber of Commerce to serve this area for 85 years and during that time to share, with many, many others, responsibility for fostering the growth of this three county region.

We welcome the reader to this beautiful documentation of our area's business history and quality of life.

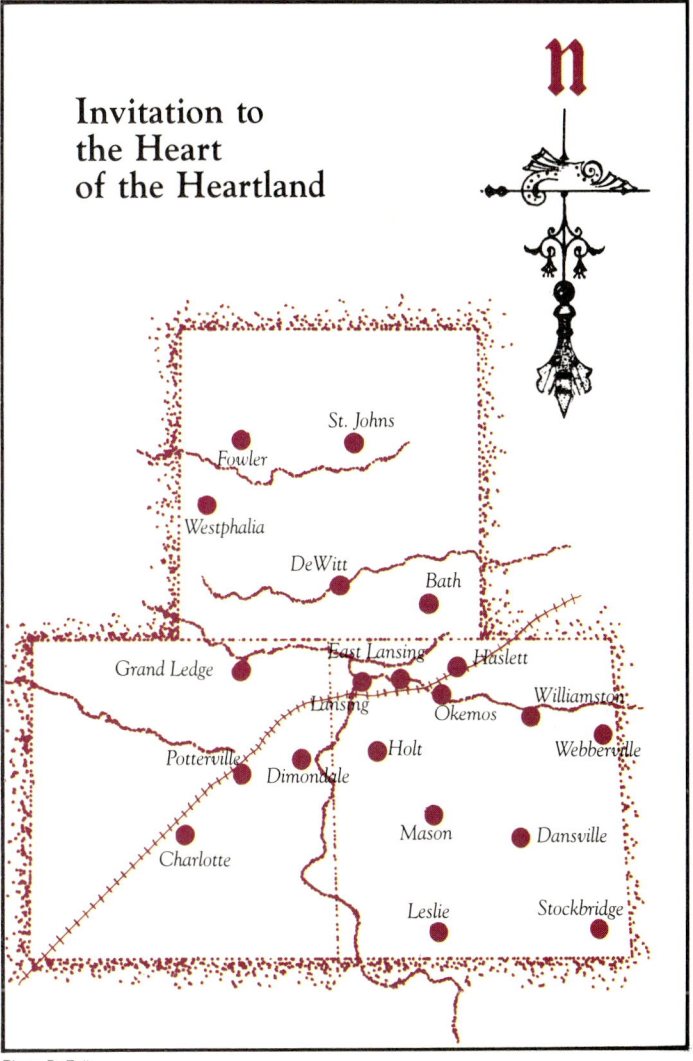

Invitation to the Heart of the Heartland

Photo B. Zell

Commerce and Trade Building

Oldsmobile Headquarters

Sealed Power, St. Johns

Business & Industry

The Atrium

Motor Wheel Corporation

Federal Mogul, St. Johns

Roberts Corporation

Plaza One, Story Inc.

One Michigan Avenue

Michigan Millers Original Office (above) (LWC is Lansing Women's Club) in contrast to their current headquarters (left).

Services & Hospitality

Auto-Owners Atrium

The 70,000-square-foot Home Office of
Jackson National Life Insurance Company

Auto-Owners Headquarters

Photo Balthazar Korab

Sheraton Inn by night

Photo John DeLong

St. Lawrence Hospital

Photo B. Zell

People Who Care

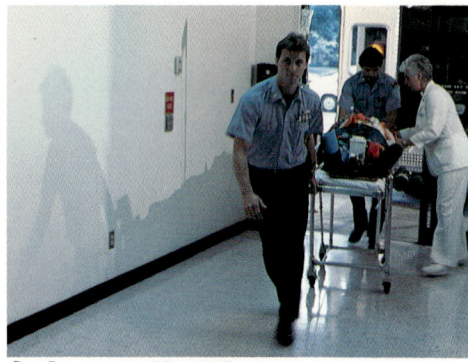
St. Lawrence Hospital

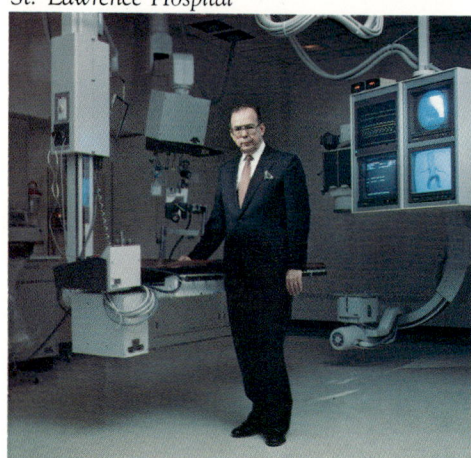
Edward McRee, president of Ingham Medical Center, stands in one of the hospital's three cardiac catheterization suites.

Ingham Medical Center

Health Central

Health Central

Sparrow Hospital

Photo G. Boynton

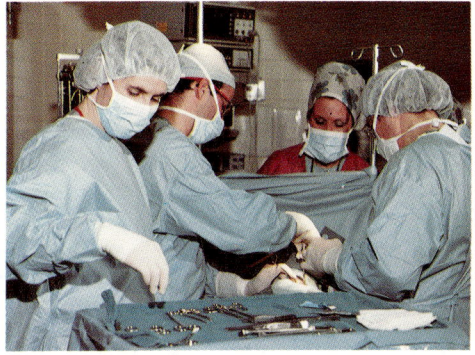

Sparrow Hospital

Photo G. Boynton

Lansing General Hospital

MSU Clinical Center

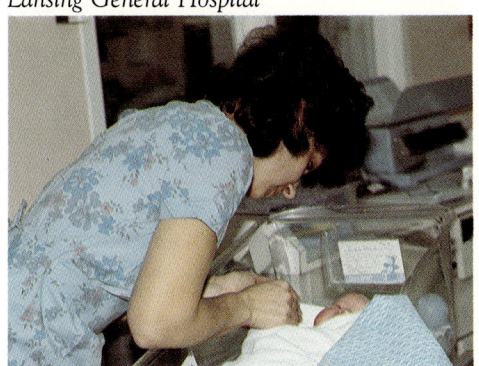

Lansing General Hospital

In addition to traditional labor and delivery rooms, Lansing General Hospital offers unique Alternative Birthing Suites.

Delta Dental

Photo B. Zell

Photo B. Zell

Places to Go
People to See

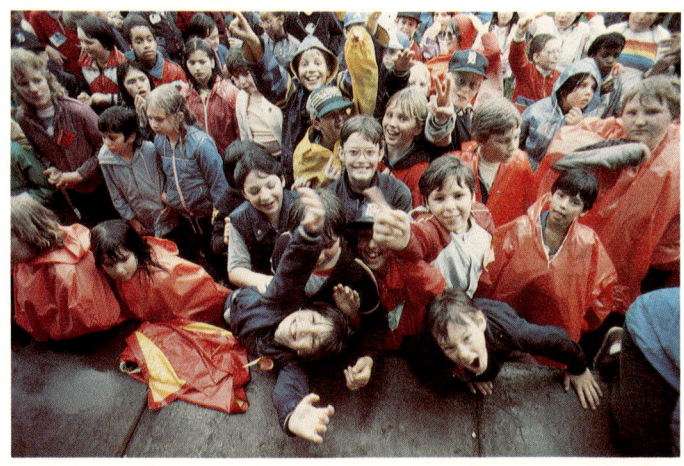

Photo B. Zell

Photo Charles Smith

Photo William Mitcham

154

Photo William Mitcham

Photo William Mitcham

Sports

Mid-Michigan Opera Co., The Mikado

Photo B. Zell

The Arts

BoarsHead Theatre, Jacque Brel

Turner-Dodge Ballet Class

Photo B. Zell

Wharton

Riverfront Park sculpture Windlord III

Kresge Art Museum

Yehudi Menuhin at Wharton Center.

Local ballerinas perform at Wharton.

Lansing Art Gallery, Visions '86

Photo: B. Zell

Future Images of Lansing

General Motors Warehousing and Distribution

Courtesy B-O-C

Beal Gardens at MSU
Photo B. Zell

Approximately 425,000 people live in the Ingham, Eaton and Clinton tri-county area with 130,000 residing in Lansing. The "Heart of the Heartland" is today within 90 minutes of 90 percent of Michigan's population. MSU, the agricultural college built on the "cheap" woodlands of the 1850s, is today considered one of the most beautiful – and important – universities in the country. Where Pliney Olds produced his one horsepower, stationary boiler engine in 1880, is the community that is known for building quality automobiles that are sent all over the world.

The effect of "Capital, campus and cars" has made Lansing what it is today. Businesses developed to support all three – from clerical services and supplies for state government, to retail and service industries for the campus, and parts manufacturers and suppliers for the automobile industry.

But the Lansing of tomorrow will go beyond these arenas. Already the city has given birth to a number of high technology companies. It has become a home base for several prominent financial and health care institutions, and it has laid the groundwork to become a cultural and tourist center.

The road map for this new Lansing is being plotted by several organizations. Among them are the Lansing Regional Chamber of Commerce and a special off-shoot committee of community leaders called "Lansing 2000" as well as Governor James Blanchard. Each has something special to offer the future of this community.

"Our goal is economic development," said Jim Jordan, Executive Vice President of the Chamber, "as well as improving the economic, educational and cultural environment of the Greater Lansing area. We are concerned with bringing in new companies as well as retaining what is here. We are also interested in working with individuals and organizations such as Michigan State University in creating new companies." (The Chamber surveys companies periodically to ask about future plans and to see if there are problems that the organization can help solve.)

The Chamber represents area business and industry in every facet. More than 40 committees involve 500 individuals in projects designed to improve the business climate in the region. Approximately nine of these committees are concerned with the complex issues of governmental affairs.

A major factor has become the Regional Economic Development Team, commonly known as the "Red Team," which joins Ingham, Eaton and Clinton counties, Delta and Meridian townships, East Lansing and Lansing, into one organization to recruit new business or to help solve the problems of existing ones. The Red Team is pooling its resources, from data to people, to compete with other markets throughout the country. The target industries of the Lansing of tomorrow, according to Jordan, will continue to be light industry, such as automobile and industrial parts, and agriculture related, such as food processing and packaging. But the real potential lies in advanced technology and service industries (which include professional services), warehousing and distribution (due to Lansing's central location), tourism and convention services and facilities (such as restaurants, hotels and entertainment businesses).

"The most important thing the Red Team has done is open the lines of communication," Jordan said. "If a business does not locate in one area, it still might be interested in another in the tri-counties. Our purpose is to serve as a catalyst."

Jordan feels the area offers much to a new business, including a high quality of life for employees, power sources, transportation systems, trained labor forces, and the ability to use people from Michigan State University, Lansing Community College, and Cooley Law School as resource people. "A Chamber is people working together doing what no one can do alone," Jordan said.

The Lansing/East Lansing area has already experienced considerable success in the spin-off of high technology and biomedical companies. A partial list of companies located in the area which produce advanced

Board of Water & Light Eckert Power Station

162

Hannah Research and Technology Center

Photo Courtesy of Zell

technology products or research are: Abrams Instruments, producers of electro-mechanical equipment and military electronics; Barros Research Institute, which is conducting molecular biology research on the aging process; Bio-Gas Detector Corporation, which is working on agricultural instruments to improve crop yields; Data Communications Technical Services (Burroughs), which offers consulting and programming services; and Dialog Systems, Incorporated, which produces support system software.

Other high tech companies are: Eaton Medical Group which is involved with biomedical instruments; Eaton Stamping Company, makers of circuit boards; Forest Computer, makers of software; Furda Biochemical Labs, Inc.; Gateway Systems Corporation, which produces systems software; Institute for Advancement of Prosthetics, which researches and manufactures prosthetic devices; ISO-E Chemistry Lab, Inc., a medical reference laboratory; and Keck Geophysical Instruments, maker of geophysical logging instruments, groundwater sensing and sampling equipment.

Also on the list are: the Laboratory of Clinical Medicine, which is developing bio-analytical lab materials from living organisms; Martin Electric, an electronic control systems company; Meridian Instruments, which is developing biomedical instruments; Neogen Corporation, a developer of genetically engineered vaccines and pharmaceuticals; Plas-Labs Inc., makers of isolation chambers and equipment; Recomtex Corporation, developer of various genetic engineering products; Republic Plastics, involved in the research and development of thermoplastics; Residuals Management Technology Inc., an environmental and pollution control consulting operation; Snell Environmental Group, which offers bioengineering and consulting; Spartan Research Animals, which is involved with laboratory research animals; Sys-

tems Research Inc. (Burroughs), supplier of front-end processors; Technisoft Systems Corporation, producer of computer software; Technitron Inc., electronic components and custom prototype equipment assemblies; Technology Venture Management, which is involved with computer related projects and business start-ups; and Toxicology Laboratory Center, which offers analysis of toxic substances for industry, agriculture and medicine.

In addition to these companies, there are more than 85 computer-related firms in the tri-county area that are involved in some aspect of software or hardware development, programming, retail service, systems design or training.

Foremost among these high tech companies is the Michigan Biotechnology Institute. It is a non-profit corporation, established in 1982, for the commercialization of biotechnology in Michigan. This research institute emphasizes industrial applications of biological sciences and focuses on the development of new processes and products. It fosters research and technology transfer to industry and promotes commercialization and collaboration between industrial, university and national laboratories. Included in these potential areas are agrifood,

LCC's designation as the Midwest Training Center for CADAM (computer augmented design and manufacturing) means this specialized training is available.

LCC Archives

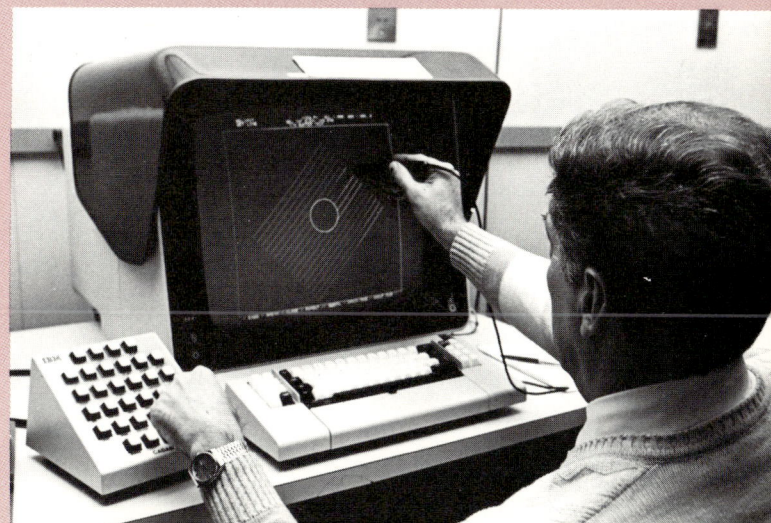

Governor Blanchard and Mayor McKane discuss Revitalization

Photo J. Fish

energy, chemical products, waste treatment, forestry products and pharmaceutical industries. Examples of projects planned or underway include new processes for producing gasoline octane additives from wood, improved waste treatment processes, production of new sweetening agents, and production of improved tree plantlets.

For the future, MBI is building a 120,000-square-foot center adjacent to Michigan State University. Through its combined research, development and technology transfer activities, MBI will provide development of new biological factories in the twenty-first century for chemicals, foods, ingredients, fuels and structural materials production, improved utilization of resources, enhanced conservation techniques, and increased jobs and industrial diversification.

The Lansing area can also lay claim to 10 percent of the state's fastest growing private firms – 10 out of the top 100 – according to a survey done by Michigan Business Magazine, Arthur Young & Co., a public accounting firm, and Durocher and Co., a Detroit-based public relations firm. The list highlights the diversity of the area's economy and includes companies in data processing, advertising, marketing, printing, systems management and building materials.

The companies are All-Star Printing (13th fastest growing); Datamatic Processing, Inc. (17th); Marketing Resource Group Inc. (24th); Massoglia and Assoc. Inc. (29th); Getaway Travel 'n' Tours (42nd); Spartan Paper &

Office Supply Co. (54th); Caspers Systems Corporation (67th); Beurmann-Marshall Corporation (75th); Telecheck Michigan (81st); and RBK corp. (93rd).

To provide the leadership that is needed for major developments to take place in any community, a special group has been organized known as "Lansing 2000." This 40-person board is composed of business as well as governmental representatives who meet to resolve problems that impede the city's progress. While the chamber focuses on the tri-county area, "Lansing 2000" is concerned with making downtown a vibrant business, tourist, entertainment, and cultural center.

"We are currently concentrating on bricks and mortar because there is a void," said Joe Reid, a local attorney who is chairman of the group. He was referring to the efforts to see that current building projects such as the Radisson Hotel, the Exhibition Center and several office buildings, progress as planned and that facilities be developed near them.

"Our only interest is downtown," he said. "We believe if we can increase pedestrian traffic through such things as office buildings and hotels, the rest, such as restaurants, specialty stores and entertainment, will fall into place."

Other plans for the future include the establishment of a Women's Hall of Fame in the Cooley-Haze House and the Railroad Museum in North Lansing. The historic district potential can be witnessed in Blue-Cross/Blue-Shield's restoration at Pine and Ottawa. Neighborhoods and personal values are still the core of this "Hometown."

"Lansing 2000" and the Chamber actively support Governor James Blanchard's Task Force to Study the Revitalization of Downtown Lansing, which presented major recommendations to the Lansing City Council in February of 1986. This task force encourages a partnership between the two governments "to create a thriving capital city which offers a variety of entertainments and which attracts visitors, new businesses, and residents to the area." Among the highlights of this plan is a $880,000 commitment through the Department of Transportation to redesign and improve Michigan Avenue from the Grand River to the Capitol; to dedicate the Capitol complex as a public park; to improve and beautify the major gateways to the Capitol; to preserve and restore the Capitol as the dignified and functional structure it once was; and to establish a "Yes! Michigan" center to encourage visitors to take advantage of all that "The Capital City" has to offer.

"We have only begun," Governor James Blanchard said of the improvement plan he believes will not only attract tourists, but will provide "for solid neighborhoods, for investment in jobs and for improved quality of life."

Partners In Lansing's Progress

Turn of the Century Advertising Art

LANSING REGIONAL CHAMBER OF COMMERCE

Lansing Regional Chamber Of Commerce

In 1901 a Lansing group called the Businessmen's Association organized itself for the express purpose of bringing a company into Lansing from Detroit.

The new Association was so enthused about the project that when the State Fair moved from Lansing to Detroit, they purchased the vacated Fairgrounds and gave it to a young inventor named Ransom E. Olds who then located his automobile company here.

It was a good trade — the defunct state fairgrounds for a piece of the infant auto industry. That small company, the "Olds Motor Works" has grown into today's Buick-Oldsmobile-Cadillac Group of General Motors.

After this success, the Association began working to increase cooperation among area businesses. Early presidents of the group included R.E. Olds himself and W.K. Prudden, founder of Motor Wheel Corporation donor of the chamber's first offices.

After a series of name changes beginning in 1914, the original Businessmen's Association is now the Lansing Regional Chamber of Commerce, active in the three county metropolitan area of Clinton, Eaton and Ingham Counties.

In addition to its intensive community involvement the Lansing Regional Chamber of Commerce has accomplished something no other local chamber of commerce has ever done.

It created a program, "The Chamber ATHENA," refined it, and with sponsorship of the Oldsmobile Division of General Motors, has made it successful nationally.

The ATHENA is a beautiful bronze sculpture, commissioned by The Chamber to an East Lansing artist, awarded annually to outstanding women in business, recognized for their business acumen, involvement in community matters, furtherance of women's success in the business world and the contribution which they make to the mission of their chamber of commerce.

In 1985-86, its first year of offering, The Chamber ATHENA was used by 300 chambers of commerce in the United States to recognize their women in business.

Today's Lansing Regional Chamber of Commerce represents area business and industry in every facet of the region's business climate. It has more than forth committees involving 500 individuals in projects designed to improve the economic, educational, political and cultural environment of the region.

The Chamber also serves as headquarters for the three-county, sixteen-organization Regional Economic Development Team designed to work with local and incoming business and industry.

The Chamber stresses regional cooperation as the vehicle for growth and development, which like its original success, will benefit all who live and work throughout the region.

Athena Winner MSU's Dr. Marilee Davis, Athena designer Linda Ackley, General Sales Manager of Oldsmobile James Mattox, and 1986 Chamber President Martha Mertz.

PARTNERS IN LANSING'S PROGRESS

The sponsors and contributors of *Out of a Wilderness* represented the corporate names and faces that were there as history was being made. This new group of sponsors for *Lansing: Capital, Campus, and Cars* includes many of those corporate giants like Oldsmobile and Motor Wheel who traditionally have been the backbone of the community. We've been privileged to see the growth of a few young progressive companies who had the vision then, and now five years later we see that vision realized. Joining these stalwarts are additional progressive, new and enthusiastic leaders who have Lansing "on the go again." Our thanks to you – the sponsors – for making this book possible. Your stories parallel the spirit of the past and deserve being told in the following pages:

Auto-Owners Insurance

Leadership + Quality Products + Service = Success

The evolution from birth to maturity of successful corporations is dependent on a number of factors. One of the most important is leadership.

It's not surprising then, that Auto-Owners Insurance, a business resident of Lansing for all but the initial year of its existence, has evolved into the largest property and casualty insurance company domiciled in Michigan.

Auto-Owners' success can be traced back from its present management to the early leadership of Vern V. Moulton who, in 1916, organized Auto-Owners Insurance Company in Mt. Pleasant, MI. The infant Company had no capital and was housed in one room of a bank building.

Auto-Owners operated in Mt. Pleasant for a little less than a year. In 1917, V.V. Moulton literally picked the Company up, placed it under his arm and in his pocket (The Company consisted of one book of policyholders' names and $174.25 in assets.), and moved Auto-Owners to the Hollister Building in Lansing — an environment that would prove to be ideal for future growth.

As the Company grew, both in volume and confidence, it also expanded physically. By 1922, Auto-Owners occupied part of the fourth floor of the Bauch Building in downtown Lansing but soon filled the entire floor.

By 1927, Auto-Owners was writing in excess of $1 million a year in insurance premiums and purchased one of Lansing's stately mansions on North Capitol Avenue for a home office. The young Company continued to grow by leaps and bounds and, in 1929, a two-story addition was completed.

It wasn't long before the Depression began, and Auto-Owners weathered even the lowest point of that era — the bank holidays of February, 1933. The Company demonstrated its corporate toughness and financial stability by paying all claims promptly, daily, and IN CASH! The firm was then writing more than $2.5 million in insurance premiums.

Despite the Depression, the Company continued to grow. In 1934, an additional building on East Shiawassee Street was leased and, in 1940, a two-story building on West Shiawassee was acquired.

Auto-Owners entered the general casualty insurance field in 1940 (only automobile insurance was written previously) and, during the next five years, found it necessary to acquire three more buildings in the vicinity of its main office on Capitol Avenue, because of continued growth.

The first completely self-contained underwriting and claim office established outside of Lansing was in Detroit in 1947, when the Company purchased a nine-story office building at the corner of Shelby and Congress Streets. This branch began servicing the Detroit area, Southwestern Michigan, and Ohio. Today, full facility offices operate in St. Paul, MN, Peoria, IL, Montgomery, AL, Marion, IN, Lima, OH, Lakeland, FL, Brentwood, TN, and W. Des Moines, IA, with claim offices in 24 additional cities.

The original plans for building a home office to replace the five Lansing locations were begun in 1941 but World War II delayed construction until 1949. When the home office at 303 West Kalamazoo Street was built, it was constructed of reinforced concrete, faced with Indiana limestone, and was contemporary in design. This building served as the home office from 1951 through 1976.

Auto-Owners' growth didn't result from Michigan sales alone. The Company wrote business in Michigan, exclusively, from 1916 until 1935 when it began writing insurance in Indiana and Ohio. In the forties, Auto-Owners extended operations to include Illinois and Minnesota and, during the fifties, Iowa, North and South Dakota, Florida, Missouri, Alabama, Tennessee, and North and South Carolina. The Company began operations in Wisconsin in 1969,

Auto-Owners Insurance Group corporate headquarters building in Delta Township, just west of Lansing, anchors a 120-acre complex called Verndale. The A-O development is comprised of a Sheraton hotel, office buildings, a branch bank, condominiums, apartments and single family dwellings.

Georgia in 1973, Nebraska in 1978, and Arizona in 1982.

Because of Auto-Owners' rapid growth in the 60's and 70's, the Company outgrew the Kalamazoo Street quarters and preparations were made to construct a new home office as part of a business and residential complex called Verndale, in Delta Township, west of Lansing. Construction began in 1975 and employees moved into the 207,000 square foot facility in December, 1976. By 1985, continuous growth produced a need for a major building addition to its corporate headquarters so a three-story 50,000 square-foot addition was built onto the east side of the existing structure, with completion in early 1986.

The Lansing corporate office serves not only Auto-Owners Insurance, but its subsidiary companies: Auto-Owners Life Insurance, Home-Owners Insurance, Owners Insurance, and Property-Owners Insurance. The Michigan Branch Underwriting and Lansing Branch Claims offices are also housed in the structure.

Auto-Owners' growth evolves from its loyal employees, agents and policyholders. The Companies are represented by approximately 3,000 independent agencies, marketing personal and commercial property / casualty and life and health insurance in 18 states. Total employees number more than 1,600 with over 700 in the Lansing area.

Since its beginning, excellent employee relations has been an important business philosophy at Auto-Owners. As a result, there exists an atmosphere of team spirit that has enabled the Company to achieve above-average productivity from its employees.

Contributing to its reputation as being an employer that understands employee needs has been the Company's employee benefits program. Auto-Owners was among the first companies in the area to adopt pension and group life and health insurance plans for employees. An employee credit union has existed since 1948.

The Auto-Owners Insurance Group of companies surpassed the $1 billion in assets milestone in 1984. The Group ranks among the largest in the nation.

With nearly two million policies in force, the Group's annual premium writings exceeded $800 million in 1986, its 70th anniversary year. The Companies also enjoy the highest possible ratings assigned by nationally-recognized independent rating authorities.

Auto-Owners Premium Income Growth	
1916 -	$ 2,060
1926 -	1,120,000
1936 -	2,091,000
1946 -	7,904,000
1956 -	24,605,000
1966 -	59,717,000
1976 -	270,172,000
1986 -	820,000,000
	(Projected)

SHERATON INN-LANSING

A highlight of Auto-Owners' Verndale complex, just west of Lansing, is the Sheraton Inn-Lansing. The five-story hotel, meeting and entertainment center was opened June 30, 1982, and features 221 guest rooms and 18 meeting rooms with facilities to accommodate up to 1,800 persons.

The Sheraton Inn (owned entirely by Auto-Owners as a part of its investment program) also features The Royale Ballroom, with banquet seating for up to 600; The Reo Theatre, seating 114; Scandal's nightclub; Christie's dining; and Cafe Caraval for light dining and cocktails.

Other hotel facilities include a swimming pool, racquetball court, exercise equipment, whirlpool and sauna.

The Sheraton Inn-Lansing has earned the reputation of being Lansing's foremost hotel for quality entertainment, dining and hospitality.

The three-story atrium is the most striking feature of Auto-Owners corporate headquarters building. It provides not only beauty, but also a means of increasing efficiency and energy conservation within the building.

The Lansing Sheraton Inn is located within Auto-Owners Verndale complex, adjacent to the Creyts Road I-496 exit, just west of Lansing.

Blue Cross and Blue Shield of Michigan

Building on a 48-Year Tradition ...

Since 1939, Blue Cross and Blue Shield of Michigan has helped business, organized labor and individuals pay for their health care needs. The corporation is as proud of its historic ties to Lansing as it is of the many innovations in health care coverage it pioneered.

The corporation's roots are in both Detroit and Lansing. Incorporated in December, 1938, as the Michigan Society for Group Hospitalization, it was established by the Michigan Hospital Association and modeled after other Blue Cross plans to provide prepaid hospital benefits. The arrangement assured hospitals prompt payment in return for guaranteed care of its members.

The plan started with a $10,000 loan from Ford, Harper and Grace hospitals in Detroit and $5,000 from two prominent Lansing citizens: R.E. Olds, the automaker and a trustee of Edward W. Sparrow Hospital, and Joseph G. Gleason, who was affiliated with St. Lawrence Hospital.

On March 8, 1939, the first office of the Michigan Society for Group Hospitalization opened for business in a small room on the 10th floor of the Washington Boulevard Building, Detroit. There were only three employees. The Society's entire staff consisted of John Mannix, the director, John Begley, his assistant, and Elizabeth Kay, their secretary.

The first contract was sold March 17th, 1939, to John F. Houlihan, Detroit manager of John Hancock Mutual Life Insurance Company. For $1.90 a month, Houlihan, his wife and six children prepaid for 21 days of hospital care in a semi-private room.

In 1939, the Michigan State Medical Society unveiled a prepayment plan covering medical and surgical services. The medical society loaned $10,000 to start Michigan Medical Service, which later became known as Blue Shield. Michigan Medical Service opened for business in February, 1940, sharing office quarters and field staff with the Michigan Society for Group Hospitalization.

The medical plan became operational considerably sooner than originally anticipated in order to help the Michigan Society for Group Hospitalization obtain the Ford Motor Company contract. Ford required that the health coverage also include surgical benefits.

The contract between Ford, the Michigan Society for Group Hospitalization and the Michigan Medical Service, was the forerunner of a complete hospital-surgical health package which was sold to any employer with 25 or more employees.

The plans grew rapidly and several branch offices opened in outstate areas. A Lansing branch office was opened at 511 Mutual Building on Capitol Avenue with Edgar C. Ryan serving as branch manager.

In February of 1940, a group of Lansing and central Michigan business and professional men announced that they would support the Michigan Society for Group Hospitalization by serving on the local sponsoring committee. This committee included:

Herbert R. Bush, Howell

Arthur J. Clark, head of the Chemistry Department of Michigan State College and president of the East Lansing State Bank

Murl DeFoe, editor of the Charlotte Republican Tribune *and a state liquor control commissioner*

Dr. Fred Drolette, chief of staff, Hayes-Green Memorial Hospital, Charlotte

Walter S. Foster, attorney

Joseph Gleason, president of the Silver Lead Paint company

Harry F. Harper, president of Motor Wheel corporation

Dr. Harry Huntington, Howell

Dr. O.M. Randall, chief of staff at Sparrow Hospital

Ard E. Richardson and E.C. Shields, local attorneys

The Michigan Society for Group Hospitalization enrolled 90,000 persons within ten months, including employees of 675 organizations state wide. Among these organizations were many local concerns: Michigan State College (now Michigan State University), the S.S. Kresge Co., Hotel Olds, Neisner Bros., Piatt Products Corp., Michigan Sugar Co., Warren S. Holmes Co., Loose Wiles Biscuit Co., Edward W. Sparrow Hospital, Superior Brass and Aluminum Casting Co., St. Lawrence Hospital, Advance Realty Co., and the Nehi Beverages, Inc. The plan offered services at 93 nonprofit hospitals in Michigan, including the two Lansing hospitals which played such a prominent role in its founding.

In 1946, the corporation sold its first individual or nongroup contract, confirming a commitment to making health care accessible to all Michigan citizens. The first 65 year old nongroup member was enrolled in 1959, affirming those same principles. When Medicare came into existence in 1966, the corporation began selling coverage to supplement those services not covered by the federal program.

Physicians once dominated the board of Michigan Medical Service (later known as Blue Shield of Michigan) and hospital representatives were in the majority at the Michigan Society for Group Hospitalization (later Michigan Hospital Service and then Blue Cross of Michigan). Each organization acted voluntarily — Blue Cross in 1964 and Blue Shield in 1971 — to create a customer majority on its governing board. In 1974, the "Blues" consolidated into one corporation, known as Blue Cross and Blue Shield of Michigan.

The benefits received by today's Blue Cross and Blue Shield subscribers are substantially more extensive than those enjoyed by early customers. In addition to 365 days of hospital care, compared to the original 21 days, typical contracts now include dental services, vision and hearing benefits, out-patient psychiatric treatment, care in skilled nursing facilities and home-care programs.

Blue Cross and Blue Shield of Michigan's market share rose to nearly 58 percent of the state's population by 1977. Alternatives to the traditional benefit packages began to appear in the late 1970s. Health maintenance organizations sprang up throughout the state and, in response, Blue Cross and Blue Shield of Michigan organized a network of seven HMOs as subsidiaries. Lansing's Health Central is one. The newest health care alternative now being offered to cost conscious employers is the Preferred Provider Organization. BCBSM established the first statewide PPO in 1985. Offered first to the auto companies, it became available to other organizations in 1986.

In addition to the alternative delivery systems and self insurance arrange-

An 1889 photo of the Morgan B. Hungerford home shows original owners.

Restoration — originally purchased by local realtor Marguerite Moore — with 2 story and garage additions by BCBSM.

the corporation has increased its employment to more than 8,000. It contributes more than $240 million a year to the state's economy in paychecks and purchases.

Since the first office in the Mutual Building, Lansing employees have worked at six different locations: Washtenaw and Capitol in a building now housing the State Accident Fund; 1111 Michigan Avenue and 27 Woodland Pass in East Lansing; 313 South Washington, downtown; and the present facilities at 4802 Willoughby Road, Holt, and 602 West Ionia, Lansing.

The Ionia street office houses 21 employees working in legislative liaison, government marketing, legal services and public relations. It is located in a beautifully restored Victorian home designed by Darius Moon, a self-taught Lansing architect. Built in 1880 by Morgan Hungerford, it is designated a Michigan Historic Site.

Some 240 employees work in marketing, provider and hospital record review and regional customer service departments at the Holt office, including 127 in the State of Michigan Dedicated Service Unit which services more than 57,000 State of Michigan employees and retirees.

Blue Cross and Blue Shield of Michigan also operates Health Central, a health maintenance organization with medical facilities at 2316 South Cedar in Lansing, 1401 South Creyts Road, Delta Township, 1525 West Lake Lansing Road, East Lansing and 210 North Oliver, Charlotte, in the office wing of Hayes-Green Beach Hospital.

The concern Blue Cross and Blue Shield of Michigan shows for its subscribers as well as other citizens of Michigan will assure the corporation a place in the state's health care market for years to come, even in the face of increasingly intense competition.

While change now seems to be a constant, Blue Cross and Blue Shield of Michigan is confident it can survive the challenges of the changing business environment by concentrating on the health care needs of its customers and meeting those needs in the most responsive and cost effective manner possible.

ments, there are more than 300 insurance companies presently competing directly with Blue Cross and Blue Shield of Michigan for health care customers. As competition increased and the auto industry contracted, membership dropped to 4.6 million.

Blue Cross and Blue Shield of Michigan has expanded its facilities and capabilities several times in the past 48 years. From its original three employees,

Board of Water and Light

A Century of Service

It began in 1885 out of a need for adequate fire protection and safe drinking water. It evolved in 1892 through a desire for cheaper and more reliable street lighting. It grew with Lansing to become the largest municipal electric utility in Michigan and among the 20 largest in the United States.

What eventually became the Lansing Board of Water and Light began simply as the Water Works Board. Initially, the question facing members of Lansing's Common Council was whether to issue a franchise and allow a private concern to build and operate a water system, or

have come a long way in the last century. The utility that was begun for $100,000 a century ago is now a $122 million per year operation. The water utility has grown from 16 miles of mains to 500 miles. From a single well to 127. From a capacity of 2½ million gallons a day, to an average pumpage of 22 million gallons per day delivered to almost 44,000 customers.

From 136 electric customers to more than 82,000. From an initial capacity of 90 kilowatts to 580,000 kilowatts, total annual sales of more than two million megawatt hours, and steam sales to some

to. The foundation was laid in 1885 when two critical decisions were made by the Common Council and the voters. First, they decided that the essentials of water and electric service were important enough to everyone that the utility should be owned by the people it served. Second, they decided that this publicly-owned utility should be separated from normal political channels and operated independently, like a business.

The Board of Water and Light derives its authority from the Lansing City Charter. Its affairs and policies are governed by an eight-person board of com-

Board of Water and Light line crew, circa 1900.

Inside the Brush Electric System Operating Center, where computers monitor and control output to the BWL's 82,000 electric customers.

whether it should be publicly owned and maintained. The concern was that Lansing citizens would be unwilling to pay for the $100,000 it would cost the city to build its own system. The fear was unfounded. Placed on a ballot, the vote was 445 to 49 in favor of public ownership.

Seven years later, taxpayers voted on another bond issue, this time for $60,000 to purchase a power plant. The city expanded the duties of the Water Works Board to include the new electric utility, and on December 1, 1892, Lansing entered the electric utility business with 110 arc street lights and 136 customers. One of its first actions was to reduce rates ten percent and offer all-night electric service.

Lansing and its municipal utility

430 downtown industrial, commercial and residential customers.

The electric utility today stands in excellent financial condition, has substantial reserve capacity to accommodate economic growth, and features energy rates that are the envy of the midwest. An annual poll of the nation's 30 largest cities consistently shows only three with electric rates below Lansing's. Closer to home, BWL rates for residential, commercial and industrial customers range from 30 percent to 65 percent below those of large neighboring investor-owned utilities.

Lansing's municipal utility has benefited from the efforts of solid leadership and dedicated employees, with some good fortune tossed in. But in essence, it has thrived because it has been allowed

missioners whose members are appointed by the mayor and confirmed by the city council. The commissioners establish rates under procedures outlined in the charter. Board policy is implemented by a staff of 900 employees under the direction of a general manager appointed by the board of commissioners.

The people who organized the Board of Water and Light couldn't have envisioned the incredible growth that would occur over the utility's first 100 years. The next century undoubtedly will bring changes and developments at an even more accelerated pace. The BWL and its planners will look to the future and to the world around us, as well as to the past, to ensure that Lansing's municipal utility will continue a leading role in helping our community to grow and thrive.

Clinical Center
Michigan State University

A Provider of Quality Outpatient Health Care

Carlos J. Caguiat
Clinical Center Administrative Director

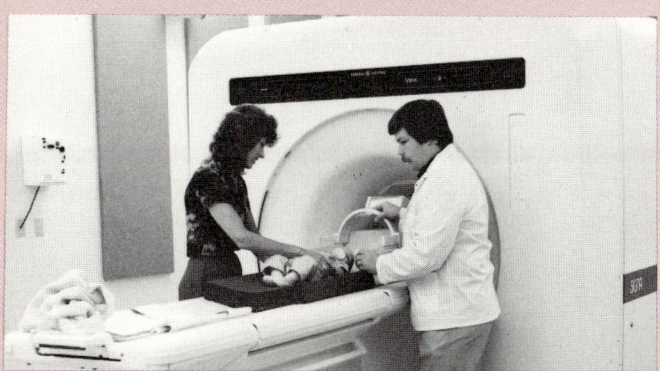

Mother preparing baby daughter for diagnosis by Magnetic Resonance Imager.

The Clinical Center was dedicated in October, 1976. The $18.1 million, three-building complex has 153,000 square feet, and the distinction of being the nation's first university health care facility jointly utilized by both allopathic and osteopathic medical colleges as well as a College of Nursing. The patient care building houses a complete array of services available for the patient. A full range of both primary care and consultive services are offered by allopathic and osteopathic faculty, resident physicians, and nurse clinicians. Additional services include a Laboratory, Pharmacy, Radiology, and a Minor Emergency Clinic.

In the College of Human Medicine, emphasis continues to be upon defining more precisely the knowledge, skills, and attitudes that a physician should possess, and helping students to acquire these skills as efficiently as possible. In the College of Osteopathic Medicine, early clinical involvement in patient care enables the students to study the biological and behavioral sciences that are relevant to what they are seeing and doing in the clinical area. The College of Nursing includes clinical nurse specialists who use specialty skills and knowledge in providing care to clients of all ages and stages of develop-

ment in primary care settings. The entire teaching program emphasizes the important cooperative relationship between basic sciences and clinical practice.

The Clinical Center identifies state-of-the-art technology with the newly dedicated Magnetic Resonance Imaging service. It is one of the most sophisticated medical scanning systems in Michigan. The Magnetic Resonance Imaging service is particularly adept in diagnosing conditions of the spine, head, heart and circulatory system. The diagnostic "tool" draws patients to the Clinical Center from communities beyond the Lansing area including Detroit, Saginaw, Traverse City, Muskegon and Kalamazoo. Officially called a General Electric 1.5 Tesla Whole-Body Imaging and Spectroscopy System, the unit produces internal body images via magnetic interaction with radio frequency waves. Superior in many ways as compared to CT scanning, magnetic resonance imaging can show early changes in soft tissues. College of Human Medicine

and College of Osteopathic Medicine physicians staff the department.

Technology aside, the Clinical Center has maintained the tradition of the Children's Corner since its beginning. The Children's Corner has been providing "drop-in" care for healthy children of patients at the Clinical Center for over ten years. Parents of children two-years and up find quality short-term care in an environment which is warm and caring as well as educational. Activities include arts and crafts, dramatic role playing, and assorted other recreative activities. This service has always been provided at no cost to the patient.

From the Clinical Center's present developmental state, it will grow into a much larger teaching facility with an anticipated volume to exceed 125,000 patient visits per year, and an expanded research model for testing ambulatory care delivery systems. The growing emphasis on ambulatory care provides an extremely bright future for the Clinical Center.

Consumers Power

Serving Lansing since 1925

W.A. Foote was an entrepreneur who dreamed big during Michigan's frontier days. He foresaw the role electricity could play in turning the Michigan frontier of the 1880s into one of America's most powerful manufacturing centers. His determination to build a network of power lines linking communities and rural areas provided the power for that industrial transformation to take place. The growth, in turn, created a greater demand for Foote's electricity.

But even Foote, with his grand vision, probably never dreamed that the modest electric company he founded in 1886 would, 100 years later, serve millions of people from the Straits of Mackinac south to the Indiana and Ohio borders. It would make life easier for people from the shores of lakes Huron, St. Clair and Erie, west to Lake Michigan.

Consumers Power Company is celebrating its centennial in 1986. It has grown to become one of the nation's leading energy utilities, a major force in developing Michigan into an industrial power. It serves giants like General Motors and Dow Chemical, Upjohn and the Kellogg Company, manufacturers of vital automobile parts and just plain Michigan folks. The company led the nation in developing rural electric service, was one of the first utilities to take steps to protect the environment, and was one of the first nuclear utilities in America.

Consumers Power was a pioneer in extending its lines to farm families. In 1927 an extension of the existing line was run adjacent to 33 farms in the Mason-Dansville area, just outside Lansing. Even though the action was taken at no cost to farmers, there were few takers for the "new-fangled" service.

Once the idea took hold, the Company would become the first and only utility anywhere to extend its lines to 100,000 farms.

But Consumers Power is not just an electrical utility; it also provides natural gas service to Michigan residents.

Until the 1930s, the gas sold by Michigan utilities was "coal gas," or gas manufactured from coal. In 1931, the company began buying newly discovered Michigan natural gas. The Lansing divi-

sion became the first division to be converted to natural gas in 1936, bringing to an end the era of gas production in the local coal gasification plants.

Lansing and Consumers Power have been tied together throughout the development of the company. Records show efforts were underway to establish a gas industry in the City of Lansing as early as 1859. Various companies assisted in the development of the industry until it eventually became the property of Consumers Power in 1925. In those early years, 75 customers were served with gas through the Lansing division.

Consumers Power Company opened its doors in Lansing in 1925 at 110 East Michigan Avenue. The building housed city and county governments in the late 1800's; the site is now a parking lot next to Jim's Tiffany Place. Consumers Power's service operations were located in a separate facility on Hazel Street.

As the Lansing division was organized, it took over parts of the electrical distribution system for the surrounding areas, though the company both then and now has only provided gas for the city itself. In the late 1920s Consumers Power also supplied electricity for the Lansing street railway system.

The original Lansing office of Consumers Power was located downtown at 110 East Michigan, now a parking lot. The appliance showroom occupied the first floor with office and clerical space taking up the second and third floors. The present service center at 530 West Willow, the site of a former coal gasification plant, was constructed in 1958.

Today, more than 41,000 homes and businesses in Lansing receive natural gas from Consumers Power. In the tri-county area, the company serves 64,700 electrical customers and 102,200 gas customers. Consumers Power employs more than 430 people at their Lansing office.

Systemwide, Consumers Power today supplies electricity and natural gas to almost 6 million people in 67 of Michigan's 68 counties in the Lower Peninsula. W.A. Foote would have been proud.

The present Lansing Service Center at 530 West Willow Street was built in 1958 on the site of a former manufactured gas plant.

Davenport College

Big Traditions in a Small Building

Davenport College has been in existence since 1866, but for the first 113 years operated only in Grand Rapids. Over the last 20 years, Davenport has become the largest independent college in Michigan and was the first regionally accredited two year business college in the state. But, in the fall of 1979, when they took over the old Lansing Business Institute building on the corner of Kalamazoo and Cherry, they inherited less than 130 students and very little public awareness. In 1985 they are serving over 600 students.

Davenport is a two year college specializing in business programs. It offers Associate Degrees and diplomas in over 20 different areas ranging from Receptionist/Typist to Computer Programming. And through the college's double major program students can virtually tailor a curriculum to their own career goals.

Davenport's small, individualized classes are attractive to students. Easy access to instructors who can work individually with students ensures mastering the skills necessary to succeed on the job. Davenport's equipment classes provide students with an opportunity to work on state-of-the-art office machines including electronic typewriters, IBM Personal Computers, Dictaphone Transcription equipment and the IBM System/36 mini computer.

All machine classes are limited to the number of pieces of equipment available in the classroom, thus allowing students to receive extensive "hands-on" training.

Most of Davenport's students are from the mid-Michigan area, although there are a few from as far away as the Upper Peninsula and two from Brazil. In age they range from 17 to 68 and while most are right out of high school, many are older persons returning to upgrade their skills before re-entering the job market.

Because Davenport draws students from all over the state, the Lansing branch maintains a dormitory located at 525 Seymour in Lansing. This apartment building provides housing for 68 students. Even dorm life is a learning experience at Davenport College. It provides a stepping stone in the difficult transition between living at home with parents and striking out on their own.

At a school as specialized as Davenport, the placement rate is crucial. Because the college offers a specialized business curriculum, it attracts students who, for the most part, have already made up their minds as to the type of career they want. They choose Davenport because it offers the kind of training that is necessary to enter their chosen field. But once they receive the training, they still need to land that first job in order to begin to put those newly acquired skills to use. That's where the Placement Office comes in. Davenport is very pleased with the acceptance their graduates have received in the business community.

Davenport graduates are eligible for lifetime job placement assistance through any of Davenport's nine locations. Being a Davenport graduate also allows them to return and brush up on any class, or their entire program, at no cost.

Davenport is involved with providing business training to a variety of groups. Since it first opened in 1979 the college has worked closely with local JTPA agencies, helping to train and place disadvantaged or displaced workers. In the fall of 1983, Davenport-Lansing branched out and began operating an attendance center in Alma, Michigan, which now serves over 80 students in the surrounding area. Students at the attendance center are able to complete Certificate programs in six areas and credits may be applied toward Degree Programs.

Beginning January in 1983, students at Great Lakes Bible College are able to earn a minor in business through Davenport College. Classes are offered primarily at the Great Lakes facility and Davenport instructors go onsite to teach. Several of the GLBC students have continued their education and earned Associate Degrees from Davenport.

Davenport-Lansing also provides business education to area high school students. In conjunction with the Eaton Intermediate School District and the Clinton County Intermediate School District, area high school students who successfully complete their EISD or CISD program earn both high school and college credit. By continuing their education at Davenport, they can earn an Associate Degree in as little as three terms after they graduate from high school.

Davenport holds classes just four days per week which leaves Fridays free for meeting with instructors, working in labs or just putting more hours in on the job.

Developing and maintaining programs that fill the changing needs of business, training individuals in those skills, and then assisting those individuals in putting those skills to work are the primary functions of Davenport College. But the college motto best sums up what Davenport is all about: Make A Living; Make A Life; Make A Contribution.

Delta Dental Plan of Michigan

A Tradition of Quality & Service

Smiles around the state have been brighter since Delta Dental Plan of Michigan, a nonprofit dental service corporation, was created in 1957. Its goal: to make dental care available to more people in Michigan through the help of dental benefit programs.

Originally called Michigan Dental Service Corporation, the organization was allowed to sell only nonrisk programs. In 1963, enabling legislation was passed to permit sales of programs on a risk basis. Dental Care, Inc., was formed to handle those programs, which emphasized preventive care. The first office, employing only a handful of people, was located in the Stoddard Building in downtown Lansing.

During the '70s, Delta experienced tremendous growth — from 111 groups covering 48,000 subscribers in 1972, enrollment increased to more than 1,000 groups covering over one million people. School business sold through the Michigan Education Special Services Association contributed significantly to Delta's early growth and its present mix of business. By the end of the decade, Delta had become the largest dental benefits carrier in Michigan and had moved its corporate headquarters to a newly constructed building in nearby Okemos.

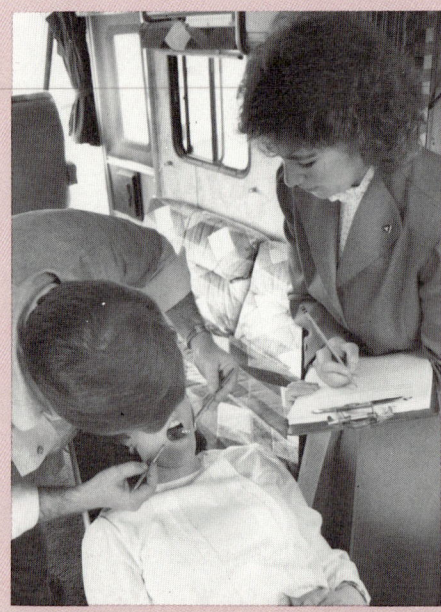

A computerized system helps Delta Dental Plan employees process claims quickly and efficiently. Nearly $200 million in benefit payments for dental treatment was made in 1985.

A tested cost and quality assurance program, which includes reviews by dentists of treatment received by subscribers, is an important Delta feature.

Delta Dental Plan of Michigan

Responsible in large part for Delta's growth boom were the benefit programs negotiated by the UAW-represented employees of General Motors, Ford, and Chrysler. These programs, which began in 1974, were jointly administered by Delta and Blue Cross/Blue Shield of Michigan. At that time, Delta's present Southfield office was opened. Two years later, in 1976, Delta was selected as sole administrator of the programs covering General Motors' and Chrysler's Michigan UAW-represented employees, retirees, and surviving spouses.

While General Motors and Chrysler remain Delta's largest groups, coverage is available to employee groups with as few as 10 people. Delta's programs feature sound benefit design, coupled with effective cost and quality controls. A key feature is the service agreements Delta has with 90 percent of the state's dentists; these agreements provide unique protection to Delta's customers and subscribers.

Today, dental benefit plans are well-accepted, and Delta remains the leader, covering 1.8 million people. The realization that good health includes a healthy smile has had a positive impact on Delta as well as the people of Michigan.

Delta Dental Plan's corporate headquarters is located east of Lansing in Okemos.

Diocese of Lansing

Remembering, Renewing and Reaching Out

Bishop Kenneth J. Povish

Bishop Kenneth J. Povish declared the months from May 22, 1986 to August 4, 1987 as a Festival of Faith: Remembering, Renewing and Reaching Out for the over 227,000 Roman Catholics of the ten county Diocese of Lansing. Over a century after the faith had been brought to this area, Pope Pius XI created the Diocese of Lansing on May 22, 1937. From 1833 to 1937 this area had been under the jurisdiction of the Bishop of Detroit.

Joseph H. Albers, the auxiliary bishop of Cincinnati was chosen to lead the diocese and chose as his cathedral the church of St. Mary at the corner of Seymour and Ionia in the city of Lansing. Bishop Albers lead the diocese for over 25 years till his resignation in 1964. He was the brick and mortar bishop so needed at that point in time. During his tenure as bishop there was unprecedented growth. Schools increased, new parishes were founded, numerous new schools, convents, rectories and churches were built. The spiritual welfare of his flock lead Bishop Albers to foster the building of the Portiuncula in the Pines retreat at DeWitt. Franciscans run the facility for the use of the laity and for the annual priest retreats.

Upon Bishop Albers' resignation

Alexander M. Zaleski, former auxiliary of Detroit, lead the diocese from 1964 to 1975. This decade was characterized by change. The Second Vatican Council called for changes in the way the sacraments are celebrated, in the role of the laity, and in the lifestyle of clergy and religious. Fr. William Rademacher organized the "Renewal Through Vatican II" program to help the parishioners through study groups to understand the documents and implications of the council. For youth, Fr. Matthew Fedewa developed the now national Teens Encounter Christ or TEC program.

Bishop Zaleski as a respected theologian was chosen head of the national bishops committee on doctrine. He was often consulted by national figures. His academic orientation lead to the development of professionally staffed diocesan offices to support parish efforts. The offices of education and catholic charities as well as others moved to full time direction with support staffs.

On a very stormy night in December, 1975, Kenneth J. Povish was installed as the third Bishop of Lansing. He shepherds a diocese very different than the one Bishop Zaleski came to in 1964. In 1971, Kalamazoo was created a diocese and the southwestern portion of the old diocese became part of the new one. At the same time, the counties of Washtenaw and Lenawee were incorporated into the Lansing diocese.

The major cities of the diocese are Adrian, Ann Arbor, Flint, Hillsdale, Jackson, Lansing, Owosso, St. Johns and Ypsilanti. The Lansing parishes and their establishment dates are as follows: St. Mary Cathedral, August 4, 1866; St. Casimir, September 17, 1921; Resurrection, June 15, 1922; Holy Cross, September 21, 1924; St. Thomas Aquinas, October 4, 1940; St. Therese, July 1, 1949; Immaculate Heart of Mary, July 1, 1949; St. John Student Center, December 24, 1957; St. Gerard, June 25, 1958 and Cristo Rey, October 6, 1961.

St. Mary Cathedral

East Lansing, Michigan

Allé, 1982.

A Cosmopolitan City with a Hometown Flavor

Grand River Avenue looking west, October 1985.

Grand River Avenue business district, 1919.

East Lansing is a 9⅓ square mile residential community offering a small-town atmosphere for workers in the Greater Lansing and Tri-County area as well as for employees and students at world-renowned Michigan State University.

East Lansing began as a college town which devploed around "faculty row," a group of homes built in the late 1850's specifically for the MSU faculty. "Collegeville" grew to serve the needs of students and faculty.

By 1901, the population had grown enough to warrant the formation of a school district and the erection of Central School which at that time served only eight grades. Growth in the college, especially in faculty, resulted in a community with high educational expectations, and East Lansing soon became known for its quality of education offered. This is still the case today, as East Lansing is served by one high school, two middle schools and seven elementary schools and boasts of 17 semi-finalists for National Merit Scholarships and one semi-finalist for the National Achievement Scholarship Program for Outstanding Negro Students.

By 1907 the area had grown to the point where the lack of sewer and water facilities, street lighting and paved streets had become a problem. Residents voted to incorporate and the state legislature approved the proposed charter in May, 1907. The Michigan House and Senate were divided over the name, but "East Lansing" won over "College Park." East Lansing today is a thriving community of about 50,000, 45% of which live in the university housing on campus.

M.S.U. (Michigan Agricultural College at the time) celebrated its 50th anniversary the same year that East Lansing became a city. The celebration drew distinguished guests such as presidents of many colleges and universities, congressmen, members of the Cabinet and others. A crowd of over 20,000 attended the Commencement on the last day of the celebration to listen to President Theodore Roosevelt. This was a huge crowd considering that most of the people had arrived by streetcar or by foot.

Growth of the city was highly influenced by the phenomenal growth of the university in the 1950's and 1960's. Several neighboring areas were annexed into the city during these two decades. Total annexed expansion from 1944-1982 has resulted in East Lansing being over eight times larger now than at its founding.

East Lansing's council-manager form of government was established in 1944 when residents voted to amend the city charter to change from a fourth-class city to a home rule city. This allowed for five councilmembers to be elected at large with the mayor elected among the council, and for the appointment of a city manager to administer the daily operations of the city. Since 1944, East Lansing has had only four city managers.

East Lansing residents have always tried to promote a high standard of living in the community, and throughout its history, city officials have striven to maintain this standard by charter and ordinance provisions covering such things as yard and street parking, noise and nuisance parties, and strict code requirements to insure that health and safety standards are met in all buildings and rental units in the city.

When the city Charter was drawn up in 1907, city "fathers" included a Prohibition provision which was enacted to help maintain this standard of living. The Charter stated that no liquor or beer be manufactured or sold within the city. Through the years, the question of the sale of alcoholic beverages came before the voters many times and failed. In November, 1968, however, following a vigorous campaign led by the Committee for a Better East Lansing (pro-liquor) and the Committee for a Best East Lansing (anti-liquor), 83.6% of East Lansing's registered voters turned out to vote approval of the sale of alcoholic beverages within the city, thus ending East Lansing's era of prohibition.

In a more recent attempt to protect the health of its residents and visitors, elected officials adopted the state's first local ordinance to regulate smoking in public and retail establishments, restaurants and the office work place. A "Right to Know" ordinance which regulates the storage of hazardous materials was also adopted recently and is the first such ordinance to be passed by a municipality in the state.

Citizen involvement in East Lansing's history has been paramount in its development, and citizen involvement continues today as the city looks at economic development to expand the tax base while preserving the charm of residential neighborhoods and the excellence of city services and at programs to meet the needs of residents for leisure and educational activities and to further the integration of the arts into the community.

East Lansing State Bank

A Commitment to Quality Service

East Lansing State Bank (ELSB) is the largest locally-owned bank in Ingham County with assets over $160,000,000. On May 31, 1916, the bank was formally chartered with capital stock of $20,000. By late 1916 the bank's assets totaled approximately $200,000.

From the eighteen incorporators, the first board of directors was elected: Addison Makepeace Brown, President; Jacob Schepers, Vice President; A.J. Nash, Cashier; A.C. Anderson; E.H. Ryder; Walter S. Foster; and Bert J. Baker. During the bank's early years, the office of president was not a full time position. For example, A.M. Brown was also Secretary of the State Board of Agriculture.

The bank operated in the Chase Building on Abbott Road. Its objective was to maintain a friendly atmosphere and give financial service to businesses and individuals in East Lansing, which had a population of 2,000 residents.

Through the 1920's the bank grew rapidly and found it necessary to move to larger quarters. The East Lansing Development Corporation, which owned the 100 block of west Grand River, planned a new building — The Abbott. The building was designed by Bowd and Munson and was built by Reniger Construction Company. On November 3, 1927 the bank moved to its present location, 100 West Grand River. In 1979 the bank purchased The Abbott and extensively remodeled it.

In addition to serving East Lansing, the bank recognized further needs and opened the following branches: Okemos, August 3, 1955; Haslett, August 8, 1962; Brookfield, March 10, 1966; Trowbridge, July 8, 1970; and Lake Lansing, January 21, 1975.

East Lansing State Bank is an innovative, full service bank. In 1962 the bank joined the student loan program and in 1970 was the first bank in the nation to offer Student Aid Savings Bonds, with funds earmarked for student loans.

In 1968 the bank was the only bank of its size in the state to install a computer. In 1971 the bank started a Trust Department with one officer and one

Above: Bookkeeping Department about 1950; President A.J. Clark at the far left. Left: Bank employees about 1930.

part time employee. At the end of 1971 it had $2,166,000 in assets under administration; today it has nearly $62,000,000. In 1973 ELSB installed an automatic teller machine (Teller 24) and now has several machines located throughout the Lansing-East Lansing area. In 1980 East Lansing State Bank was the first bank in the state to offer a debit card, Super Check Visa. In 1982 the bank joined the Magic Line system, further expanding its services.

In 1983 the shareholders approved the formation of Spartan Bankcorp, Inc., a bank holding company, of which ELSB is its subsidiary. The bank's board believes the bank holding company structure is the best type of banking organization to respond to the rapid changes that are taking place in banking today.

In January 1986 a preliminary agreement was signed to join Banc One Corporation, a multi-bank holding company headquartered in Columbus, Ohio. The proposed affiliation marked the first interstate transaction between Ohio and Michigan banks under the legislation that was enacted in early January 1986 permitting regional mergers. The affiliation with Banc One will benefit the customers, community, and employees of East Lansing State Bank. In addition, all of Spartan Bankcorp's stockholders will benefit from becoming stockholders of Banc One, which is one of the most innovative and best performing banking organizations in the United States.

East Lansing State Bank believes it has a corporate responsibility to assist charitable organizations that respond to the needs of the community. In 1984 it appointed the Corporate Citizenship Committee, which directs charitable contributions. In addition to financial support, many bank employees volunteer their time to help various community and charitable events.

East Lansing State Bank is proud of its innovative history and maintains its original objective — a commitment to quality service.

Estes Furniture

A tradition of affordable excellence

One of Lansing's oldest continuing business is the Estes Furniture Company. Founded in 1917, Estes has served the Central Michigan community with quality home furnishings and excellent service. Through the years, Estes has lived up to its slogan "A tradition of affordable excellence" by offering its customers unique credit options and impeccable ethics.

In the early years the furniture and funeral businesses often went hand-in-hand. However, in the 1940's the furniture and funeral businesses separated although both retained the Estes name. Estes furniture's North store has remained on the original corner of North Washington and East Grand River. Whereas, the funeral business moved to its present location.

The Estes Furniture Company has expanded from the original 15,000 square feet of warehouse and display to today's total of 150,000 square feet encompassing four separate locations. Until Lansing became the State Capital, today's Estes location was at the hub of the City's main business district marked with streetcars and cobblestone streets. With completion of the Capitol Building the main four corners were necessarily moved one mile South to Michigan and Washington Avenues which began the building of downtown Lansing as we know it today.

In 1950 the Estes Furniture Company was purchased by Alfred Bishop who invested his energy and capital to begin building upon the company's heritage and molded the business to become recognized throughout Michigan for excellence.

Today, Estes is a landmark and a tradition. But, beyond that, it is a business dedicated to serving people and supplying the needs of the fifty families that make up its current payroll. The tomorrows in the company's future promise more of the same as the business continues to move forward with new energies and direction. It is the current management opinion that the company's potential is far from reached and present plans call for substantial increases in home furnishing services to the Lansing area. Few businesses enjoy such a reputable past from which to build a future with so much promise. Estes Furniture plays a major role in community activities and together with its pride of performance in giving back to Lansing, and its desire to further serve its community, the Company looks forward to the rewards of continuing success.

The Eyde Company (Eyde Construction Company)

Helping to build Lansing's future

The Eyde Company is a truly American success story. Its diverse holdings are a testament to the energy, the foresight and the determination to succeed of its partners Louis and George Eyde.

The partnership began some 30 years ago as Lou and George started to build residential homes together, after a childhood spent on Lansing's north side as part of a family of five brothers and two sisters. Their parents Eva and Sam, a line worker at Oldsmobile, had long instilled in them the virtues of hard work and the value of investing in real estate. George had majored in residential building at Michigan State University, while Lou had served in the U.S. Navy, then attended MSU and the Detroit College of Law.

The first Eyde-built homes were in the Whitehills and Skyline Hills area of East Lansing. From that they diversified into apartments, building Eydealvilla (now North Point Apartments) and Burcham Woods, both of which projects they have sold.

The tremendous growth of the Lansing area in the 1960's provided fertile ground for Eyde Construction Company projects: there was the elegant Northwind Farms apartment and office development just east of MSU; the ambitious Nemoke Trails Apartment complex in Haslett; and also in Haslett, the Meridian Hills Condominiums.

All during this time, Lou and George were active and eager buyers of vacant land in the Lansing metro area. Their holdings have increased to the point where today, in 1986, the Eyde Company is one of the largest single taxpayers in Meridian Township.

About 10 years ago their interest began to turn away from apartment projects and towards office buildings and office parks. Their first venture in this respect in the City of Lansing was to purchase the old Topps Department Store at the corner of Holmes and Logan, renovate it, add another building and turn the project into the successful Southwind Office Park which they still own.

They also bought the former Spartan Store at the corner of Jolly and Cedar, converting that to retail and office use, and bought the former Knapp's Department Store in downtown East Lansing. That property is now known as the University Mall and features the America's Cup Restaurant with its famous gyros, the highly-popular B'ZAR, a high energy party bar, plus other retail enterprises.

This is not to say that Lou and George Eyde have abandoned their interest in residential subdivisions — far from it! Their two current residential developments are the Shoals subdivision in Okemos, and Bennington Hills subdivision near Perry. Both communities feature custom-built homes in a pastoral setting.

The 1980's have been a time of great expansion and change for The Eyde Company. Lou and George have opened an office building in Kalamazoo, and have also developed the very successful School Haus Square in Frankenmuth. The latter is a unique selection of small shops in a converted school which now features historical murals.

In 1982 The Eyde Company became the proud owner of two Lansing landmarks: the former Knapp's Department Store, and the former Walter French Junior High School. The store has been reborn as Knapp's Office Center which is rapidly becoming Lansing's prestige professional address, if only because the classic Art-Deco building is on the National Register of Historic Places. Walter French has become an office and community center.

Lou and George Eyde are presently developing the Hannah Technology & Research Center just east of MSU, a project which will surely stand as one of their greatest contributions to the community and which is described more fully on the following page.

In addition to all their business activities, Lou and George actively participate in, and support, community and civic groups. What's the reason for their success?

As Lou says, "We're successful because we enjoy what we're doing. And we have a lot of faith in the greater Lansing area. It's a good place to live and to work."

Scott Fairmont

Builder of Neighborhoods

Communities are made up of neighborhoods and neighborhoods are comprised of homes. Fairmont Builders of East Lansing proudly and expertly builds both.

The inspiration behind Fairmont's concept of creating whole neighborhoods, not simply subdivisions, is Scott Fairmont, who graduated from Michigan State University in liberal arts in 1971.

The transplanted Floridian who is president of Fairmont Builders, 1501 North Shore Drive, East Lansing, says bringing a social attitude to designing and building homes instead of a utilitarian, business or carpenter concept is the key to the success of Fairmont's projects.

"We are neighborhood builders," he says. "We create neighborhoods, places where people enjoy themselves and where they can go out and throw a ball without disturbing anyone or anything."

This concept comes to fruition in Fairmont's construction of condominiums, which, simply put, do not look like condos. And that is on purpose, Fairmont says.

"We design our condos to look like single family homes," he says. "We concentrate on street flow so the condo appears to be in the middle of single family home neighborhoods. We do not want them to look like tenaments.

"We design and build our homes so they will have a pleasant environment 50 years from now. We concentrate on livability, the environment, open space and usable recreation amenities. I believe we have been successful."

That's an understatement. In 13 years since becoming a partner with Jim Dunn in Dunn & Fairmont, Fairmont has helped guide his firm in becoming a leader in developing neighborhoods and commercial projects in the Greater Lansing area.

Fairmont, who began working on construction sites as a carpenter helper at the age of 9, became president of Dunn & Fairmont in 1979 when Jim Dunn was elected to the U.S. House of Representatives for the 6th District.

In 1984 Fairmont Builders was formed as an employee-owned stock company. "This concept gives employees a personal stake in the company, another reason, I believe, for our continuing success," Fairmont says.

Projects Dunn & Fairmont and now Fairmont Builders have developed include:

CONDOMINIUMS — Woodstone Village, 55 units, and Stone Lake, 100 units, both in East Lansing, and Woodhill, 85 units, and Dream Lake, 150 units, both in Okemos.

APARTMENTS — Timberlake, 340 units, and Woodbrook Village, 150 units, both in East Lansing.

SINGLE FAMILY SUBDIVISIONS — Farwood, 100 units, in East Lansing, and Bear Lake, 73 units, in Okemos.

UNDER CONSTRUCTION AS OF JAN. 1, 1986 — Keystone, 103 single family homes in Okemos west of Okemos Road and northwest of the Meridian Mall; Heartwood, 47 single family homes in Okemos; and Emerald Forest, 85 luxury condominiums in Okemos.

"We have been successful in these developments because we design communities," Fairmont says. "We do it ourselves: create, build and sell.

"We communicate with our customers so they end up with personalized homes.

"I am especially proud that we are an open book builder with a strong statement of honesty and integrity. Before any major investment, we and each customer go line by line through the listing of costs, including our profit margin. This is an attempt to take voodoo out of housing. I don't want there to be guessing games."

Fairmont said he is equally proud of his firm's service department: "We don't rely on sub-contractors. We have a fulltime service department making sure things do not go wrong." Buyers get a 10-year guarantee.

Fairmont has done commercial work as well for some such customers as Frandor and Clinton Bank as well as projects for doctors and churches. Ironically, Fairmont said he is especially proud of the Kwik Kar Wash on Grand River Avenue in front of Meijers in Meridian Township. "That's because it doesn't look like a car wash; the design is attractive and enhances the area. That's what we are all about — enhancing the neighborhoods," he says.

The Fairmont firm is far from done; it plans to continue to develop and build in the East Lansing-Meridian area (where it has concentrated so far) and expand into west Lansing. "Lansing is underrated nationally as a commercial center, but the prospects are unlimited here. We plan to be a Lansing fixture for a long time," Fairmont said.

The Chateau at Heartwood

⊖ FEDERAL MOGUL

St. Johns Plant

Excellence is the Standard

The year was 1899 and the United States — with its new status as a world power — stood on the brink of the 20th Century. The mechanical age was entering another phase of its evolution and the automobile industry, although still in its infancy, was growing.

That same year, two young men — J. Howard Muzzy and Edward F. Lyon, formed a Detroit-based firm called the Muzzy Lyon Company, which specialized in the sale of mill and factory supplies.

Most bearings in those days were made of a single type of metal. Muzzy and Lyon recognized that different metals were needed for different applications and they began to produce new bearing alloys. Mogul was the brand name used to identify a metal formula developed by the two men.

Muzzy and Lyon saw the potential of casting bearings directly into shape — something entirely new to the industry. They began experimenting with this method and were so successful that the mill supply business was dropped and full time devoted to the new venture.

They expanded the business nationwide and, over the next quarter century, Muzzy-Lyon became one of the nation's leading makers of bearings and bearing alloys. In 1924, Muzzy-Lyon combined with Federal Bearing and Bushing, a manufacturer of engine bearings and bushings to form a new company called Federal-Mogul Corporation. The new company's name reflected the identities of its predecessors.

Federal-Mogul purchased the St. Johns Plant from the St. Johns Portable Building Company in 1945. The 25,000 square foot brick building with dirt floors was extensively renovated and remodeled during 1946 and 34 employees launched production of babbitt-lined, steel-backed, automotive type engine bearings in 1947. As time passed, the building was expanded five times to keep pace with increasing business demands, bringing the size of the current building to 262,000 square feet.

Initially, the plant was built to manufacture bimetal, semi-circular engine bearings. During the years that followed, processes were added for other forms of bimetal strip. In addition to full round bushings and washers, many different types of precision steel parts and assemblies were added to the product line. Engine bearings played the dominant role in plant growth until 1971, when engine bearings were moved from St. Johns to a new plant in Blacksburg, Virginia. From that time, the St. Johns Plant began to concentrate on precision bushings and washers, manufactured mainly from Copper-lead and Aluminum strip.

Today, most parts are made of steel, lined or faced with Babbitt, Copper-lead, Aluminum, or Graphite impregnated Teflon. Parts range in size from one-fourth inch to eleven inches in diameter and have a wide use of applications — automobiles; light, medium and heavy duty trucks; agricultural and construction equipment; marine and aircraft equipment; appliances and heating/air conditioning units.

All bimetal material used at St. Johns is produced on the premises. This self-sufficiency includes basic metal preparation and powder production. The plant produces more than 13 million parts each month, over 95 percent of which are sold in the original equipment market. Major customers include the Big Three automakers, Caterpillar, Cummins, and John Deere. It also manufactures and supplies bimetal strip to several Federal-Mogul plants.

Federal-Mogul is the city's largest employer with 565 employees working 3 shifts. Eighty-five to ninety percent of the work force is from the St. Johns area. The employees are what makes the St. Johns Plant special. They are interested in their work and take pride in building high quality parts for their customers.

The bushings, washers and engine bearing materials produced by the Federal-Mogul St. Johns Plant are subjected to unyielding standards and controls at every level from raw materials through material processing, forming, machining, plating and inspection.

The utilization of statistical process controls and other quality control systems allows the plant to meet Federal-Mogul's rigid standards as well as those of its customers.

Federal Mogul Headquarters, St. Johns.

Muzzy-Lyon Co.

Bushings

Fraser Trebilcock Davis & Foster, P.C.

A Tradition of Legal Excellence

Fraser Trebilcock Davis & Foster, P.C., is mid-Michigan's oldest law firm. It traces its history to 1883, when attorney Rollin H. Person re-entered private practice in Lansing after serving eight years as District Judge for Ingham and Livingston Counties. In 1913, Edmund C. Shields and Harry A. Silsbee joined him to form the firm of Person, Shields and Silsbee with offices in the Hollister Building in downtown Lansing.

Following the appointment of Justice Person to the Michigan Supreme Court in 1915, the firm he founded continued to grow and flourish, providing a solid foundation for the future. Indeed, the firm's present day representation of General Motors may be traced to the time when firm attorneys assisted R.E. Olds in obtaining the property for the first Olds Motorworks facility in Lansing.

The Fraser firm's tradition of distinguished lawyers includes Edmund C. Shields, whose leadership of the firm spanned more than four decades. Until his retirement in 1947, Mr. Shields was one of Lansing's most prominent citizens and was widely regarded as one of the finest lawyers in Michigan. His civic accomplishments were many, including a key role in the founding of St. Lawrence

Justice Rollin H. Person, whose portrait currently hangs in the Michigan Supreme Court, was the founder of the firm's legal practice in 1883.

Hospital in the early 1920's. The dedication of Mr. Shields to community and profession was matched only by his also impressive physical size. He was so imposing that the Strand Theater in Lansing constructed a double-wide seat especially for him. Mr. Shields was also one of six firm members who have served as Ingham County Bar Association president.

During World War II and the postwar period, the Fraser firm continued as the area's leading law firm. Working with former Michigan State University president John Hannah, Byron Ballard originated and implemented an innovative system of self-liquidating bonds which financed the construction of many of the University's dormitories and other buildings.

In 1958, the firm reorganized under its present name of Fraser Trebilcock Davis & Foster. The four named partners have established an impressive record of professional and community service. Among his numerous professional and civic accomplishments, Archie C. Fraser served as personal counsel to the United States Secretary of War and as president of many

civic organizations. Everett R. Trebilcock, widely considered one of the State's foremost trial lawyers, was praised by former Michigan governor Kim Sigler as the finest appellate lawyer he had ever seen. James R. Davis has also been very active in the community, including terms as president of the local United Way and the Mid-Michigan Red Cross. Joe C. Foster, Jr., has served as president of the prestigious American College of Probate Counsel and recently was named in national publications as one of the best tax and probate lawyers in America.

Edmund C. Shields was captain and centerfielder on the University of Michigan varsity baseball team in 1894 before becoming one of Michigan's most distinguished lawyers.

In recent years, the Fraser firm has grown to include 35 attorneys and a 40-person support staff in its offices on the ninth and tenth floors of the Michigan National Tower. The firm maintains a general practice of law, including most types of business and personal transactions as well as litigation at all levels of the federal and state court systems. The firm has participated in a number of cases before the United States and Michigan Supreme Courts, including a 1979 case which resulted in a landmark constitutional decision of the United States Supreme Court in favor of one of the firm's clients.

Throughout its illustrious history, the Fraser firm has maintained the same commitment to legal excellence and community service which began when Justice Person first opened the doors of his solo practice back in 1883.

The Olds Tower (now Michigan National Tower) under construction. Completed in 1931, the building contains the offices of Fraser Trebilcock Davis & Foster, P.C. on its 9th and 10th floors.

Freeman, Smith and Associates

Revivers of the historic; promoters of contemporary design

Wherever anyone looks around town, the influence of Freeman, Smith and Associates, Inc. is prominent. This highly respected Lansing-based firm of architects, planners and interior designers has left its imprint downtown, in the outlying neighborhoods and in the suburbs.

Established in 1957, Freeman, Smith and Associates has led the way with privately-based downtown rejuvenation. It has put a bright new face on buildings constructed decades ago. The firm's designs have helped downtown Lansing say: this is a modern city. Welcome to Michigan's capital!

These efforts have preceded the 1986 push by State and local officials to spruce up the downtown core. One effort was the Plaza I, II, and III project: transforming an abandoned department store, a connecting retail store and a low-slung restaurant in the block southwest of South Washington Avenue and East Kalamazoo Street into a modern, beautiful, glass-dominated office complex. The Plaza project was considered such a successful attempt to stimulate interest in a marginal downtown business district, that it became the subject of a nationwide advertising campaign.

An equally successful project by Freeman, Smith and Associates was the Union Savings & Loan Association headquarters located in an historic block that contained the State's first Capitol and just yards from the current Capitol. In order to successfully compete for attention with much larger neighbors, the Union Savings facade was approached as a two-story element instead of the traditional street-level storefront design. Massive piers emphasize the vertical component of the design and suggest stability, important to a savings and loan. Freeman, Smith and Associates also undertook a two-story addition and the remodeling of the entire interior.

Capitol Federal Savings & Loan, Bank of Lansing, and American Bank & Trust (now First of America), have also entrusted the firm created by Robert Freeman and Robert Smith with important trend-setting design projects. Among the suburban projects are the Production Credit Association in Mason and the Parkwood YMCA on the outskirts of East Lansing.

Demonstrating the versatility of Freeman, Smith and Associates are the contrasting Holy Trinity Greek Orthodox Church and the 3800 Building at Capital City Airport. The eastside church carefully blends Byzantine and contemporary details in an attempt to reflect the Greek affinity for traditional forms and liturgy combined with simplicity of style. Religious art was incorporated into the interior with painted icons and hanging lanterns. On the other hand, the 3800 Building embodies fresh design required for modern office applications such as split level, access to a hangar adjacent to an airport runway and electrically heated sidewalks for automatic snow removal.

Freeman, Smith and Associates has also enjoyed a long and close relationship with local school districts. Foremost among these are Lansing, Holt, Waverly, Haslett and the Ingham Intermediate School District. The firm's design for renovation of the Eastern-Pattengill Field House and Athletic Complex proved to be of historical importance to sports enthusiasts across the country. It was here that Earvin "Magic" Johnson and Jay Vincent displayed the athletic talents that thrust them into national prominence.

Another landmark project for the firm was the Story Oldsmobile dealership facility on East Michigan Avenue. Freeman, Smith and Associates received professional recognition for the innovative design of this 1960 complex, which still looks modern and fresh today. The recognition led to work on other similar projects in the State.

Freeman, Smith and Associates has always done more than draw sketches. The innovative firm includes interior design, planning, demographic and feasibility study, and analysis of the psychological and sociological factors of space utilization.

With sixty percent of its business in the Lansing market, Freeman, Smith and Associates are leaders in the changing face of this area. As directors and members of numerous government, civic and professional boards, they are committed to the revival of historical structures and the promotion of contemporary design.

Parkwood YMCA

Capitol Savings & Loan

General Motors

Lansing operations share pride in the past, innovation for the future

General Motors has had a close association with Lansing and mid-Michigan since before the turn of the century.

The Buick - Oldsmobile - Cadillac Group's Oldsmobile Division and Lansing Product Team were headquartered here in the mid-1980s. Facilities of the group's Powertrain Product Team and Detroit Product Team were also located here and the GM Warehousing & Distribution Division, in addition, had a major activity in the Lansing area.

Electronic Data Systems Corporation, known as EDS and a wholly-owned subsidiary of GM, provided another major presence.

More than 22,000 persons were employed by these GM units in 1985, with payrolls totaling just over $1 billion. Payments to Michigan suppliers totaled more than $1.2 billion, and Lansing-area GM facilities paid an estimated $15.5 million in real and personal property taxes to local jurisdictions.

Oldsmobile has played a significant role in the nation's automotive history. Founded here on August 21, 1897, it is the nation's oldest automobile manufacturer.

Back then it was called the Olds Motor Vehicle Company, named after Ransom E. Olds, its founder. Then, like now, the company's mission stressed quality. As Olds saw it, the goal was "to build one carriage in as nearly perfect a manner as possible."

Four complete automobiles were built by the Olds Motor Vehicle Company during its first year of existence. Two years later, it expanded to include the new Olds Motor Works in Detroit, with engine production remaining in Lansing.

Using a forerunner of today's assembly line system, employes at the Detroit Plant built the first of the famous Oldsmobile Curved Dash runabouts weighing 700 pounds and powered by a one-cylinder, seven-horsepower engine.

The Detroit plant burned in 1901 but was quickly rebuilt. The Lansing facilities moved to a new 52-acre headquarters site previously used for the state fair. Both plants continued to operate until the Detroit plant was phased out in 1905 when all Olds Motor Works operations were moved to Lansing.

Olds Motor Works became part of newly-formed General Motors in 1908. One year later, it introduced its first fully-enclosed automobile.

In 1925, Fisher Body in Lansing began producing bodies for Oldsmobiles, and 43,386 cars were built that year. Less than five years later, that number more than doubled, with 12 new buildings also added to the Oldsmobile complex.

Oldsmobile took over occupancy of the Lansing Fisher Body facility in 1935 when Fisher moved to a 21-building, 48-acre site nearby. More than 180,000 Oldsmobiles were built that year.

Auto production was suspended for the manufacture of military equipment during World War II. Three years after resuming production, the division introduced its first 135-horsepower high compression V-8 "rocket" engine. Demand for this revolutionary engine was so great that the production rate was doubled to 60 engines per hour in 1949. The engine's rocket logo remains Oldsmobile's official logo today.

During the 1950s, the division introduced its four-door hardtop automobile, along with other innovations such as two-tone color schemes, air conditioning and power brakes.

Two of Oldsmobile's most popular cars — the Cutlass and the Toronado — made their debut in the 1960s. The front-wheel-drive Toronado was hailed as "the most unique automobile in many years" during its 1966 model year premiere.

A Lansing-wide celebration of the division's 75th anniversary took place in 1972, with a vintage car rally attracting

The first Oldsmobile built by the Olds Motor Vehicle Company, organized in 1897, was this "horseless carriage" turned out that same year. It was produced in a tiny shop on River Street in Lansing.

Oldsmobile's headquarters are located in this building a few blocks south of the State Capitol.

participants from around the nation. In 1972, Oldsmobile also moved into third place in industry sales for the first time. It has retained that ranking every year since 1975.

In 1977, Oldsmobile became the third automaker in history to sell one million cars during a model year. One year later, with the opening of its new Lansing Cutlass Assembly Plant, the division became the largest passenger car assembly complex in North America.

In 1979, ground was broken for the newest of Oldsmobile's Lansing plants — a 600,000 square-foot facility known as the Delta Diesel Engine Plant in Delta Township.

The 1980s continued to bring major changes and product innovations to the division.

In the fall of 1982, plans were announced for the conversion of Oldsmobile's Lansing assembly plants to produce an all-new line of GM cars.

The multi-million-dollar project called for complete reconversion of the plants for installation of state-of-the-art assembly systems and related equipment. Innovations included an extensive use of computer-controlled Automatic Guided Vehicle Systems (AGVS) and vision-guided robotics. Thousands of employes learned to work with the new systems in the largest training effort ever undertaken by GM in Lansing.

The resulting products were the Oldsmobile Calais, Buick Somerset Regal and Pontiac Grand Am. They made their debut as coupes for the 1985 model year, with four-door sedans added in the 1986 model year.

Perhaps the most dramatic change in GM operations here occurred in early 1984, when General Motors announced the reorganization of its North American passenger car operations.

The new organization was composed of two car groups — the Chevrolet-Pontiac-GM of Canada Group and the Buick-Oldsmobile-Cadillac Group. GM's five car divisions gained a heightened emphasis on marketing and sales of their products and were no longer responsible for plant operations.

Most of Lansing's manufacturing and

This aerial view looking west shows the scope of the Lansing Product Team's manufacturing and assembly facilities along the Grand River just south of I-496 between Townsend and Logan Streets.

assembly operations came under the jurisdiction of the Lansing Product Team. The team was responsible for the Lansing-built Oldsmobile Calais and its Buick and Pontiac counterparts and for the Oldsmobile Firenza and similar cars for the other four GM passenger car divisions. The team was composed of 55,000 employes in Michigan, Ohio, Wisconsin, Missouri, and Pennsylvania assembly plants. Lansing's Plant 2 became part of the Detroit Product Team, with responsibility for the production of a new front-wheel-drive Buick sports car. Lansing's GM engine operations became a part of the Powertrain Product Team, headquartered in Flint.

GM announced several major Lansing conversion projects in the early 1980s. In addition to approving the conversion of Plant 2 for 1987 production of the new Buick, GM announced that, with the demand for diesel engines declining, the Plant 5 diesel engine facility would be converted for 1987 production of a new high-tech four-cylinder gasoline engine called the Quad 4.

In other Lansing engine production news, GM announced the conversion of major portions of engine manufacturing operations from V-8 to V-6 engine production for 1986. The project coincided with increasing demand for the V-6.

Oldsmobile sales continued to top the 1 million mark in the early 1980s, with 1984 bringing a new model year sales

record of 1,098,685 cars and 1985 a new calendar year record of 1,066,122 cars sold.

The 1986 model year was a significant one for Oldsmobile Division. A year earlier, an all-new front-wheel-drive Ninety-Eight, with a sleek new shape, high-tech electronics and improved fuel economy, had been introduced. In 1986, two more all-new front-wheel-drive cars — the redesigned Delta 88 and Toronado — made their debut, with the latest in aerodynamic styling, state-of-the-art technology and improved fuel economy.

The Lansing Parts Plant, with more than 1,000 employes, maintains its role as a key facility in GM Warehousing & Distribution Division operations nationwide.

The facility dates back to 1960 when it was operated by Oldsmobile. Following several expansions, the plant became part of the GM Parts Division in February, 1969, and in 1981 the Parts Division and AC Delco Division were consolidated into a new GM Warehousing & Distribution Division.

The 2.3 million-square-foot Lansing facility is unique in that it provides a direct link for up to 192,000 different parts required by GM dealers to satisfy the needs of their customers, the vehicle owners. There is no other plant like the Lansing facility in the division.

Hannah Technology & Research Center

A place for new ideas to grow

The Hannah Technology & Research Center began as a vision — a vision of a place where new ideas could be nurtured and grow, where new companies could lease the research space they need, where new technology could be developed to provide more jobs and a better quality of life.

But all great visions require practical implementation. And in this case, that has meant that a major developer has worked with two local governments and a worldwide bank to make the dream a reality.

The developer is The Eyde Company of Lansing, in the persons of its partners Louis and George Eyde. Their technical point man has been HTRC Executive Director Richard Baibak, who has guided the needed detail work on the Center.

The Center had its beginnings in the late 1970's when Lou and George Eyde purchased land just east of Michigan State University which had belonged to former MSU President Dr. John Hannah. At the time the land was zoned for apartments, but the Eydes thought that there could be a better use for it. So slowly, the Hannah Technology & Research Center — named for Dr. Hannah — began to take shape.

The first important step came in 1981, when the Ingham County Economic Development Corporation issued a Resolution of Inducement for the project. This set the stage for low-interest financing for the Center.

The next step was to convince the Meridian Township Board to re-zone the land, to a combination of Research Park and Community Service. After an extensive series of hearings by the Planning Commission and the Township Board, and a lot of input from the public, the land was in fact rezoned.

By that time — mid-1982 — the Project Plan for the HTRC had changed and Meridian Township had formed its own Economic Development Corporation. Scott Schultz, the Meridian EDC's Chairman and Co-founder, worked with the Eydes to make the HTRC a project of the Meridian EDC so that there would

have to be only one governmental unit involved.

In the meantime, The Eyde Company was working with the City of Lansing to secure an Urban Development Action Grant to assist with financing the project. This quest was ultimately successful and will eventually provide some $3 million in federal funds for the City of Lansing to use for local development projects.

By the time the bonds to finance the project were issued in November, 1984, the HTRC had become a $17-million project financed jointly by low-interest bonds issued through Meridian Township, by the federal UDAG, and by the developer's equity — a classic example of co-operation between business and government.

Today, in 1986, the 2-story building is open for leasing, with the 6-story building set to open later this year. Both buildings feature custom-designed laboratory and office space, always keeping in

mind the vision behind the Center: a place to develop new ideas and new technology, with the main capital investment going into research rather than into the ground.

Among the HTRC's salient features are the ability to accommodate laboratories up to the P-2 level; a state-of-the-art, computer-controlled heat-pump system; plus the latest in security devices.

The main HTRC site is 15 acres, with an additional 30 acres zoned Research Park immediately to the east. The land immediately north of the HTRC is zoned for hotel/shopping-center use, with a hotel planned to be built in the very near future.

As Director Richard Baibak has said, "The Eyde Company is very pleased to be able to take the lead in providing this type of facility in mid-Michigan. We believe the HTRC's facilities will help many new research companies get going, which in turn will help create more jobs for our community."

Hasselbring-Clark

Thirty Years of Quiet, Determined Growth

As any businessperson knows, there are at least two ways to carve a niche in the business world. Some companies do it quickly, with considerable fanfare. Others accomplish great things gradually, quietly.

For Hasselbring-Clark the trip to the top of the office equipment industry has been one of quiet, yet deliberate progress.

Reinhart Hasselbring, Seth Bidwell and James Robertson founded the firm, initially called the Hasselbring Company, in 1956, after purchasing the office machine division of the DeKleine Company. From a small office at 310 Grand Avenue, the trio sold typewriters, adding machines, addressing machines and mimeograph equipment.

Growth was modest during the Hasselbring Company's early years. But the partners had chosen an auspicious time to enter the business equipment industry. Sales surged in the late fifties when they entered the uncharted, yet growing, market of photocopiers — produced, at that time, by Kodak.

As the firm's market changed, so did its management team. Reinhart Hasselbring, long the company's driving force, became primary owner when he bought out his partners in the early sixties. At the same time, Hasselbring laid the groundwork for a future management shift by hiring deliveryman, Ellis Clark. Clark would later run the company and would lead it through the period of its most dramatic growth.

The 1960s marked a decade of stability for the Hasselbring Company, highlighted, in 1966, by a move from the Grand Avenue headquarters to roomier offices at 809 Center.

By 1970, the firm was well-established in central Michigan. Employees and services were being added and the Hasselbring marketing area widened.

The seventies also saw a deliberate, calculated move, by the company's management, toward specialization in reprographic equipment. Copiers were, and would be, the backbone of the industry — and Hasselbring, Inc. was destined to be a leader in copier sales and service.

Toward that end, the typewriter and adding machine divisions were sold to a company employee, L.E. Lighthart, in the early seventies. And, in 1976, Ellis Clark and Louis Willard purchased the company itself — changing the name to Hasselbring-Clark in the process.

Backed by a narrowed marketing strategy — encompassing exclusively, the Sharp and Canon photocopier lines — the new management team, and its growing sales/service staff witnessed an unprecedented increase in business. By mid-decade, Hasselbring-Clark was Canon's number one copier dealer, statewide. In 1977, the corporate offices moved to a spacious office/plant/showroom complex at 3942 North East Street. And, in 1979, annual sales broke the million-dollar barrier for the first time.

Instrumental in the company's rise to the top of Michigan's office equipment industry was its sales and service training program. Each staff member underwent, and still undergoes, a rigorous series of courses. The results: employees who know their products inside and out, and a service record that's second to none.

Today Hasselbring-Clark based at 5858 South Aurelius Road, continues to lead all Michigan Canon dealers in copier sales. Now, with additional branch offices serving customers in the Jackson and Mount Pleasant areas, the company records annual sales over the four-million-dollar mark. And it counts among its clients some of Michigan's largest employers, including the state of Michigan, the city of Lansing, and Michigan State University.

But Hasselbring-Clark's present officers are still committed to the simple business philosophy they consider vital to their success. It's a philosophy which dictates that each customer — whether a multi-million dollar corporation or a mom and pop retail store — be treated as a friend.

Through 30 years of quiet, yet determined growth, the Hasselbring-Clark philosophy has served the company well. And, if the firm's continuing growth through the last 10 years is any indication, it will continue to serve it well for years to come.

The future is, indeed, bright for Lansing. And for Hasselbring-Clark.

Health Central

Mid-Michigan's largest group medical practice employs a staff of 500 including more than 40 physicians and a dozen mid-level providers. It serves more than 50,000 members and more than 10,000 non-member patients in a seven-county area. This dynamic organization is Health Central. Its story is the Horatio Alger story in mid-Michigan's health care history.

Established by a group of concerned community leaders, Health Central opened in 1978 as mid-Michigan's first health maintenance organization (HMO). In September of that year, the first time membership was offered to General Motors and State of Michigan employees, the HMO grew from 4,000 to 16,000 members literally over night. The too-much-success-too-soon almost spelled catastrophe for Health Central. The phenomenal growth overwhelmed a system and medical center not prepared to care for 16,000 patients. The ensuing problems brought Health Central to the brink of financial disaster. However, Blue Cross and Blue Shield of Michigan stepped in to save and acquire the faltering HMO in mid-1979. It thus became the first of BCBSM's seven subsidiary HMOs. Since that troubled beginning, Health Central has grown to become the largest group medical practice in the area, providing both prepaid and fee-for-service medical care.

Today Health Central's comprehensive medical centers are in East Lansing, Lansing and Delta Township with a satellite office in Charlotte. Each center houses physician offices, a pharmacy, an optometry department, lab and X-ray

A satisfied Health Central family leaves Health Central West after appointments with primary care physicians at the multi-service medical center which also houses optometry, dental, x-ray and laboratory, allergy, pharmacy and child care services.

facilities and ancillary services.

Members also have the option to receive their care through more than 80 physicians affiliated through Health Central's new Community Physician Groups (CPGs) at the following locations: Holt, Mason, St. Johns, MSU Department of Family Practice, Eaton Rapids and at three locations in Jackson.

Health Central maintains strong control on the quality of care provided by its physicians and strives to maintain its reputation for quality care. Physicians maintain their own "panels" of patients. Each member is asked to select a primary care physician to provide personalized care. All care is provided on an appointment basis.

Membership plans are available for almost everyone, through employers and individual membership plans. Benefits include office visits, hospitalization, well child care, physicals, surgery, allergy

A Health Central member confers with physician assistant Mike Jones, from the Internal Medicine Department at Health Central West.

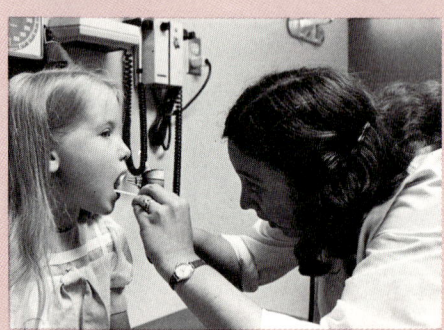

Going to the doctor is fun for young Health Central members; here pediatrician Suzanne Sorkin, MD, examines a young patient at Health Central West.

care, lab and X-ray services, and more. Under some membership plans these services are fully covered while others include copayments.

The Medicare Plus membership program provides the same comprehensive coverage to Medicare recipients with no copayments for a premium that is about 75 percent lower than most "gap filler" insurance. This is made possible through special arrangements with the Medicare Administration.

Another important component of the Health Central program is its active Health Promotion and Education Department which provides health education counseling, nutrition counseling and a registered dietitian and a wide variety of classes. The classes include Aerobics Plus, Stress Management, Weight Watchers, Smokeless, Labor and Delivery, Back School, CPR, Basic Cardiac Life Support, Infant and Toddler Safety and others.

For the future, Health Central will continue to expand membership in both the staff and CPG offices and remain flexible with the changing needs of the mid-Michigan community and the ever-changing health care industry.

Health Central's original facility on Cedar Street houses primary care physicians as well as a wide range of ancillary and specialty care services such as ophthalmology, urgent care, orthopedics, pharmacy, surgery, ob/gyn, allergy, lab and x-ray.

Impression 5 Science Museum

An explorer's playground

Where can you go to find out how cold "cold" really is, see your shadow frozen on the wall, demonstrate elementary physics on playground equipment, or actually design an automobile on sophisticated computers? These exhibits are among the over 240 "hands on" displays at Impression 5, Michigan's Science Museum, located at the Riverfront in Downtown Lansing.

The in-house design team is constantly engineering and fabricating new exhibits and improving existing ones. The motivating element behind every display is education, but somehow, this innovative team is able to design informative and amusing displays. Every exhibit demonstrates the craftiness of the design team and the visitor cannot help but to be amazed at how much genius appears when these folks brainstorm. The Impression 5 Design Team has been and continues to be a trendsetter for Science museums of this type nationwide.

Impression 5's staff is always putting on a show. Live demonstrations occur daily and include robotics, lasers, crystal shows and an energy show featuring a 250,000 volt generator.

Impression 5 offers travelling science shows as well. Their own Dr. Zap and Annie Anatomy travel state-wide to malls, parks, schools, and extra-curricular organizations. Impression 5 also offers assistance and participation in local elementary and secondary schools by developing curriculum and often by participating in instruction.

They even offer a pre-school daycare program that gives moms a chance to run errands while youngsters thrive in a learning environment.

The "behind the scenes" activity at Impression 5 is exemplary of progressive and cohesive management. This close-knit group effervesces with energy, ideas, and a quick smile or bit of information about the ever-changing exhibits and customized programs.

In short, Impression 5 has what it takes to make education amusing, enlightening and entertaining. It is no longer necessary to "burn the midnight oil" and chew on the old No. 2, just to understand scientific principles of our environment!!

Impression 5's "Playground Physics"

Family Viewing the "Geometry of Solutions"

Jackson National Life

One Man with Courage Makes a Majority

A.J. "Tony" Pasant, founder, president and chairman of Jackson National Life.

When Michigan State student A.J. "Tony" Pasant started selling life insurance part-time in 1946, he began a career that would eventually lead him to found Jackson National Life Insurance Company, one of the largest life insurance companies in America and one of her most remarkable success stories.

Pasant was one of the thousands of veterans who flocked to America's colleges and universities after World War II. Married, with a child on the way, and living in a small trailer that was then typical of Michigan State's married housing, he looked for a way to bring in some extra money that wouldn't interfere with his class schedule. Life insurance sales filled the bill. He discovered he had the necessary sales talent and persistence, and so found his calling.

After graduation in 1949 with a degree in economics, he began selling full-time. His skills and success caused him, in 1955, to be tapped by a group of prominent Chicago businessmen to help them activate the life insurance charter they had received. After finishing his administrative duties, Tony Pasant became the company's home office general agent, eventually being responsible for producing 88% of the company's new business.

But, despite his success, he wasn't happy. Pasant had always felt the urge to go out on his own, to form and lead his own company. Besides, the traditional life insurance company could not or would not offer the kinds of life insurance and annuity plans that he thought the public needed, wanted and deserved.

So on August 29, 1960, his birthday, he gave himself a present and quit his Chicago job, and came back to his native Michigan to found Jackson National Life. He named the company after Andrew Jackson, our seventh President, whose dictum "One man with courage makes a majority" remains a company motto.

It was rough going at first and Pasant had to have plenty of courage. Tony convinced some prominent Michigan businessmen to become incorporators and spent the balance of his time traveling the length and breadth of Michigan trying to persuade investors to put their money into an insurance company that had not yet sold a single policy or even opened its doors. But within only a year, the hard work and long hours paid off and, on August 30, 1961, Jackson National Life began operations with Tony Pasant as its president and chairman. It was the first life insurance company formed in Michigan in three decades. At the end of its first year, Jackson National had $23 million of insurance in force. It now writes that much business every four hours.

Exclusively through the sale of individual life insurance, and not aided by mergers or acquisitions, the Company passed the $100 million insurance-in-force milestone in 1969 and achieved its first $1 billion in 1976. At the end of 1985, after only 25 years, JNL had $26 billion in force, which ranked it among the top 2% of all U.S. life insurance companies. Revenues and profits grew in step and JNL has consistently been a favorite of Wall Street analysts. In the ten-year period from 1976-1985, the value of a share of Jackson National stock increased almost 9000%.

The company expanded geographically as well as financially. Illinois, in 1965, was the first state outside Michigan to admit JNL to business. By the end of 1985, Jackson National Life was licensed to do business in 45 states and D.C.

Recognizing that insurance buyers were becoming more informed and that rising interest and inflation rates were obsoleting the traditional whole life policy that almost all of JNL's competitors continued to market — a low-fixed-interest plan virtually unchanged since the turn of the century, Jackson National developed fresh, new and timely alternatives in both insurance and annuities.

The Company was an early and leading advocate of the advantages of term insurance and was one of the first companies to develop and market a portfolio of current era annuities. One of the Company's many innovations involved combining these two products into a unified marketing plan which anticipated, by several years, the coming revolution in interest-sensitive life insurance. Later, when the competition began rushing to develop and sell "universal" life policies, JNL had already moved beyond "universal" life with an even more innovative and attractive portfolio of life plans offering not only high current interest but such unique features as "vanishing premiums." Continuing innovations such as these have helped Jackson National to become the largest writer of individual life insurance in Michigan and one of the twenty largest writers in the country.

When Jackson National relocated to Lansing, the company's first facility, on Executive Drive, was thought sufficient to serve the firm's needs for 25 years. No one could have predicted its explosive growth in the early 1980s.

Jackson National's Home Office is located at 5901 Executive Drive in Lansing, near Pennsylvania at I-96.

In addition to individual life insurance, JNL writes annuities which are sold primarily to fund tax-qualified retirement plans such as IRA's. By specializing exclusively on individual life insurance and annuities, the Company has been able to maximize its financial and human resources and to concentrate on the fastest-growing segments of the financial services marketplace.

After headquartering in Jackson, Michigan for the first fifteen years of its existence, the Company moved its home office to Lansing over Labor Day weekend of 1976. Outgrowing in five years the facility which was to have housed it for 25 years, Jackson National now owns and occupies a modern 70,000 square-foot, 3-story building, designed and constructed entirely by local talent, at 5901 Executive Drive on Lansing's bustling southeast side, just off I-96 at South Pennsylvania. As a major national life insuror, JNL infuses much capital drawn from all over the nation into the greater Lansing area's economy through its financial activities and the more than 300 home office jobs it has created.

Jackson National Life is committed

Jackson National employees gather to break ground for the company's new World Headquarters in 1982. JNL's home office now employs over 300 Lansingites.

to the future and prosperity of the greater Lansing area. Confident in Lansing's tomorrow, JNL has developed the 252-acre Midway Park, the city's largest office park. And, for all of its wide-ranging success, Jackson National remains a Michigan company in both fact and heart with all of its board members being either current or past residents of the state.

Jackson National's portfolio of attractive products, the ability to increase its marketing efforts through geographic expansion, the growth in the personal financial planning marketplace and the Company's proven ability to profitably innovate new products augur well for its continued national success and its ongoing role as one of the major business contributors to the Lansing community.

Ingham Medical Center

Growing up with Lansing

From moderate beginnings as a 10-bed tuberculosis sanatorium, Ingham Medical Center, now a 262-bed acute care hospital south of downtown Lansing, has evolved into a sprawling 20-acre complex offering world-renown medical attention to the people of mid-Michigan and beyond.

Founded in 1911, what was then the Ingham County Tuberculosis Sanatorium opened two years later with a staff of three employees and soon expanded to meet the area's growing health needs. Six years after the construction of a 30-bed infirmary, the hospital welcomed a four-story, 100-bed main addition. By the late 1930s, the sanatorium established itself as the chest surgical center for central and northern Michigan and as a tuberculosis facility for much of the state. With the admittance of its first private patients in 1946, the sanatorium experienced previously unparalleled patient occupancy during the late 1940s.

On January 1, 1954, in response to the hospital's acceptance of many non-tuberculosis chest cases, its name was changed to Ingham Chest Hospital. During the newly named hospital's first year, a $600,000 expansion provided it with private patient rooms, a surgical suite and administration space. Tuberculosis cases decreased sharply as the decade moved on and in 1958,' with the disease finally under control, the hospital converted its beds to general usage. In 1960, the 170-bed hospital again acquired a new name, Ingham Medical Hospital. But the changes went far beyond the name.

True to its heritage as a facility specializing in chest ailments, the hospital in the mid-1960s witnessed the opening of its cardio-pulmonary laboratory and cardiac care unit and the performance of its first open-heart surgery. The operation was led by longtime medical director A.L. Stanley, MD, who would later be hailed as the "dean of chest surgery in mid-Michigan." Adding to its list of achievements, in 1966 the hospital attracted international attention as the site of the world's first heart-valve replacement.

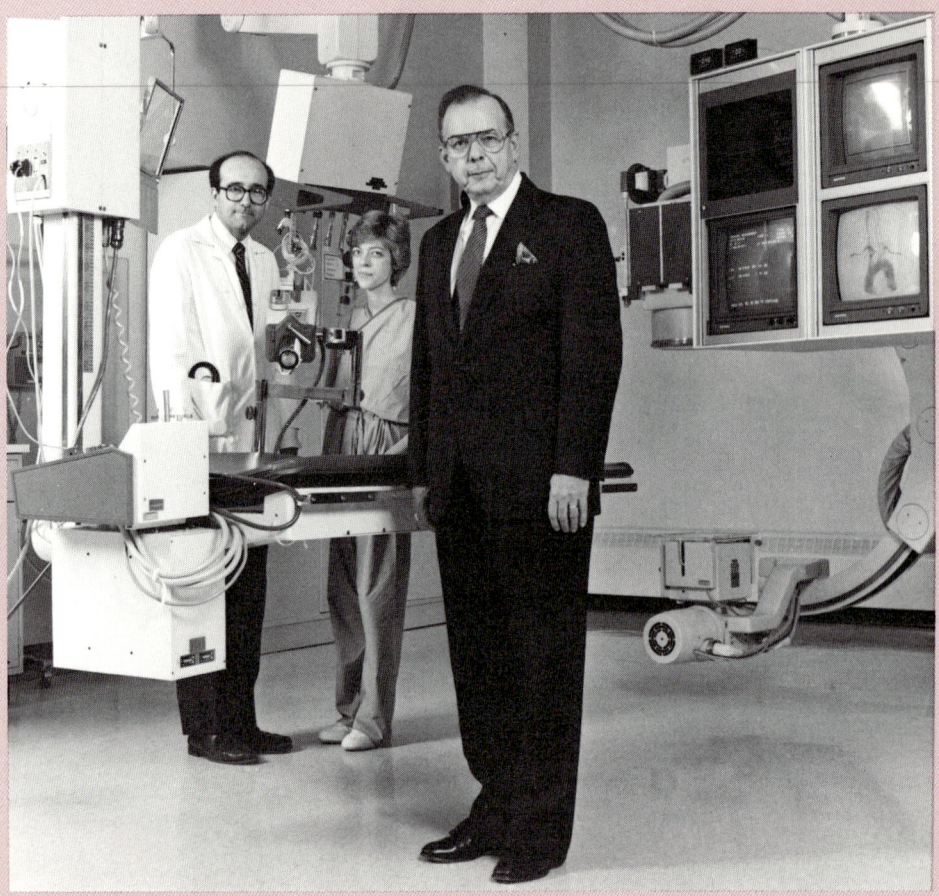

President Edward B. McRee presents Ingham Medical Center's third cardiac catheterization suite.

The hospital's most auspicious building advancement occurred in 1972 when a voter-approved $9 million new inpatient facility opened its doors. Closely following that was the extensive remodeling of many older sections and the completion of the Professional Building in 1974, the same year the hospital assumed its present name.

Another Ingham Medical Center landmark event beckoned in 1980: the opening of a first-of-its-kind arthroscopic surgery center, a prototype facility since visited by thousands of orthopedic surgeons from around the world. This and other developments in the past two and one-half decades have established the hospital as a leader in a broadening range of medical services.

Most people recognize this growth is not accidental. Its catalyst, they agree, is Edward B. McRee, hospital president and chief executive officer since 1961.

Facing at the outset a patient decline, McRee envisioned and then steadily created a medical center which today — served by 1,200 employees and another 1,000 volunteers — is widely heralded for its skilled people and the care they provide. Both are factors instilled at the top and filtered throughout the hospital ranks.

"I've always said, and believe more than ever today, the patient is the most important person at IMC," Mr. McRee says. "But there's no secret to our success. It's simply that very competent people are permitted to practice their competency, to be innovative, to be challenged and to produce. It's why we've come so far in so few years and it's why we continue to grow."

Ingham Medical Center: from a humble birth has grown a facility of which all mid-Michigan is proud.

Lansing Community College

Education and Training for the Community

Lansing Community College's 28-acre campus in the heart of downtown Lansing has contributed to the quality of life in the downtown area with its combination of modern architecture, historical buildings and scenic landscaping.

The first Lansing Community College catalog promised, "the community college will adjust its program to meet any new needs of the community."

And that has been LCC's guiding philosophy since it opened nearly three decades ago as a result of a process that began in the mid-1950's when Michigan State University was approached by Oldsmobile to consider offering a two-year program in drafting and technical education. A committee representing business, industry and state government met with university officials and concluded that the Lansing Board of Education should be approached to establish a technical institute or community college.

Dwight Rich, then-Superintendent of the Lansing Schools, hired an MSU graduate student, Philip Gannon, to conduct a feasibility study to determine the degree of community interest in a technical college, educational needs of the community and other factors. As a result of the study, LCC held its first classes in the fall of 1957, with a total enrollment of 425 and a faculty of eight including Gannon — still president today — as the first chief executive officer.

Originally established as a technical institute, the college began by offering training in mechanical, electrical and civil technologies, apprenticeship programs and licensed practical nursing. In keeping with the guiding philosophy to provide what the community wanted and needed, Gannon saw a need to institute liberal arts, business and secretarial training programs in the college's second year. Faculty tripled in size and the student body increased to 678.

As early as 1961, the college initiated a cooperative training program with local businesses, going on to offer a re-training program in industrial occupations in 1962. That same year saw the institution of seminar programs in small business management. At all times, evening classes have been a priority so that individuals could attend college part-time even though they held full-time jobs during the day.

Today, LCC continues to grow and change with the economic, educational and social trends of our community. With more than 40,000 people of all ages attending LCC each year, and with a full- and part-time faculty and staff of nearly 2,000, LCC is one of the largest and most comprehensive urban community colleges in the nation.

Programs in computer integrated manufacturing (CIM) and computer augmented design and manufacturing (CADAM), robotics and office automation prepare individuals for the demands of today's workplace. Seminars and classes in management, marketing and employee relations further sharpen the skills of area workers.

Besides offering programs at the downtown campus, LCC classes are held at more than 20 learning centers in areas surrounding Lansing. And LCC's "community" has expanded beyond Lansing and Michigan. LCC maintains sister-college relationships with institutions in Belize, the Republic of Korea, Japan, the Republic of China (Taiwan) and the People's Republic of China. The college's president, staff and faculty have taught and participated in educational exchange with people in other parts of the world, and LCC's Japan Adventure academic work-study program is a one-of-a-kind experience for LCC students who have the opportunity to work and study in Japan for nine months.

LCC President Gannon was asked by the World Bank to serve as a consultant working with poly-technical institutions in China. In addition, Gannon has served as a consultant to the Ministry of Education in the Republic of Korea and he is a member of the U.S. Department of Education National Advisory Board on International Education Programs.

Over the years, the LCC Board of Trustees has set the policy and upheld the philosophy that has guided the college through periods of change and growth. And LCC remains dedicated to excellence in educational offerings, and to anticipatory action and responsible reaction to community needs.

In 1981, the Lansing Community College Foundation was established to provide a vehicle for private financial support of college programs, equipment and scholarships. In addition, more than 500 people representing business, industry, labor, government and education serve on advisory committees that help set the direction and update the curriculum of college programs.

The college has also contributed to the quality of life in the downtown Lansing area by developing a 28-acre campus that links the beauty of the past with modern architectural design and scenic landscaping. Two nineteenth-century homes on campus have been preserved and used as office space. A third, known as the Herrmann Conference Center, has been carefully restored and decorated with assistance from community contributions, and is used by the community as well as the college for meetings and other official functions.

As a community college, LCC has lived up to its name. Almost every family in Lansing and surrounding areas has been touched by LCC. Lansing Community College is truly a college for the community — local, state, national and international. That's what it set out to be, and that's what it will continue to be, for years to come.

Lansing General Hospital

When doctors Lawrence and Harriet Jarrett opened McLaughlin Osteopathic Hospital in April of 1942, they probably never envisioned the house with eight hospital beds being the forerunner of today's 243-bed Lansing General Hospital. With the help of the hospital's first administrator, Jeannette Brown; and first chief of staff, Dr. R.C. Shaft, they coordinated the care of 297 Lansing-area residents during their first full year of operation. That's just a little more than the number of patients Lansing General currently cares for in a single week.

McLaughlin continued to serve the needs of Lansing residents, but over the years the demand for care finally outgrew its original facility. By the mid-1950s the rapid increase in the hospital's number of patients prompted the Board of Trustees to begin planning a move to a 20-acre site south of the city. In late 1958 the hospital began operating at its present location in a new 86-bed facility, Lansing General Hospital, Osteopathic.

By 1962 the first of several expansions was necessary, nearly doubling the hospital's bed capacity to 165 beds in addition to expanding X-ray, laboratory, central supply and surgery. In early 1972 a $2.7 million construction project was completed which contributed another 75 beds for patient care. It was in that same year that Lansing General Hospital and Michigan State University arranged for an affiliation with their college of osteopathic medicine.

1942

The construction phase was not yet complete, however. Need for Lansing General services continued to grow, and in the fall of 1973 ground was broken for a one million dollar project. An $18.9 million expansion was unveiled in September, 1976, which brought Lansing General to its present size.

A residential drug and alcohol treatment facility which accommodates 25 clients for stays up to 28 days was opened in 1984. Horizon Center also offers extensive outpatient services and a day treatment program.

In the more recent past, Lansing General Hospital has expanded in different ways. Medical/surgical care remains an integral part of its total program of care, but it has proven itself a leader in the community through programs and services which promote health and wellness.

Lansing General Hospital offers a unique Alternative Birthing Suite, which permits entire families to take part in the birthing process in a room furnished like an efficiency apartment.

Services such as the Sleep Disorders Center, Breast Cancer Detection Center and, most recently, the Medical Rehabilitation Center, offer valuable, unique services to Lansing area residents.

Lansing General Hospital continues to grow and change, planning for the future healthcare needs of the people of greater Lansing.

1986

Lansing School District

Serving the community's educational needs since 1861

The first public school in what was then known as the City of Michigan was organized in 1847 under the direction of Miss Eliza Powell who taught in a small, one-room schoolhouse on the north side of town. Two additional schools were opened in the next 14 years, each of which was governed by an independent board of directors.

The charter granted to the City of Lansing in March of 1861 provided for the consolidation of the separate schools within the new city limits. Thus, the Lansing School District became a legal entity on March 13, 1861 under the supervision of a newly elected, 12-member Board of Education.

In 1861, the city's population was slightly under 3,100 and the number of students being served by the consolidated district totaled 700. The system's operating budget that year was $1,700 and its physical plant was valued at $12,000.

From its humble beginnings as a small rural district, the Lansing School District has emerged in the mid-1980's as an outstanding urban system which serves a diverse, multi-ethnic population of more than 23,000 students in the K-12 program and an additional 2,500 adults who have returned to school to earn their diplomas or equivalency certificates.

Since 1882, the school system has also been responsible for providing the community with public library services which are currently available at the main downtown library, two branch libraries, and the Bookmobile which makes regularly scheduled stops in neighborhoods and shopping centers throughout the area.

As of 1986, the Lansing School District encompassed 64 square miles and was operating 33 elementary schools (K-5), 4 middle schools (6-8), and 3 high schools (9-12), along with the Beekman Center for the severely handicapped and the Hill Academic and Vocational Center. Its annual operating budget was in excess of $90 million and the physical plant was valued at more than $240 million.

Educational services are currently being provided by a dedicated staff of 1,100 classroom teachers and another 2,000 employees who provide a variety of support services.

The Lansing school system prides itself on offering a multitude of educational programs that are aimed at addressing the needs of not only the low-achieving students, but also the gifted and talented.

The vocational programs initiated in 1912 have continually been modified and upgraded to meeting emerging technological and employment trends. In addition to the traditional business classes available in each high school, the Hill Academic and Vocational Center offers training in 22 different areas, ranging from architectural drafting and auto mechanics to TV-radio production and word processing.

Lansing is also well-known as a national leader in the education of handicapped students and provides a wide range of services to those who are severely retarded, mentally impaired, physically handicapped, and learning disabled. The district's programs at Beekman Center and Henry H. North Elementary School continue to attract visitors from across the nation.

In 1977, the system opened the Vernon D. Ebersole Environmental Education and Conference Center in Wayland about 60 miles west of Lansing. One of the most unique educational facilities in the state, it serves as an outdoor laboratory for teachers and students in grades K-12 and is also available for use by other school districts and outside adult groups.

In addition to programs available to adults who have less than a high school diploma, the district offers adult enrichment classes in arts and crafts, business, foods and nutrition, and recreation/leisure-time activities.

The Lansing schools also attempt to meet the needs of senior citizens with a variety of special programs and services, including the food co-op operated by Gardner Middle School and the Gold Card Club which entitles retirees to free admission to enrichment classes, athletic events, musicals, plays, and concerts.

In recent years, the 9-member Board of Education and the administrative staff have responded to the growing educational reform movement by improving curricular areas and strengthening graduation requirements which, in part, have been responsible for dramatically increased student test scores on both state and national exams.

Though its size and structure have changed considerably in the past 125 years, the Lansing School District continues to focus on excellence as it strives to provide the best possible education for the children and adults of this community.

North elementary classroom setting.

LEE GMC INC.

Trucks Are What We're All About

R. William Lee, president of Lee GMC Trucks Inc., is an image shatterer. At 44, the married father of three children operates a truck sales and service agency that is second to none in the country.

Better known as Bill to his friends and customers (and often they are one in the same), the 1964 graduate of Western Michigan University and the holder of a BA in finance has opened a truck dealership that explodes all public myths of what a truck facility looks like.

In 1970, Bill purchased the Jackson GMC agency, making him then one of the youngest dealers in the country at 28. In 1983, Bill purchased an existing GMC dealership that had been in business for 40 years in Lansing from Vic Rhynard, located at 200 North Larch Street. Twice he has been nominated for national awards as a top truck dealer.

The dealership, consisting of 40,000 square feet on 22 acres of land, at 6333 Lansing Road at the corner of Creyts Road west of Lansing, greets customers with a white floor; the walls are white and the cushions on the dark wicker furniture are white. Computers are being used by receptionists as well as by most departments. Attentive sales personnel wear shirts with "Lee GMC, Inc." emblazoned on them. A husband and wife stroll through the bright showroom inspecting the vehicles, including a classy van; a father and son look at sporty 4×4 pickup trucks.

Where is the tough, greasy image of the trucking industry? Long gone, says Bill Lee in his modern, comfortable corporate office.

Small trucks are now family transportation, prompting modern truck dealers to appeal to this portion of the market. But Lee GMC does not cater to this segment at

the sake of the rest of the trucking industry. Lee GMC is a corporation with six divisions boasting nearly 100 employees working in a "State of the Art" facility.

Lee GMC has a complete new look with the most modern equipment in the country to service the truck industry. The Black-Hawk frame machine and the 54' Binks Paint Booth can accommodate the largest of the trucks and off-road equipment along with 50' trailers. The computerized front-end alignment machine is second to none. The Dynomometer and Cummins Compucheck will satisfy all the requirements when it comes to proper diagnosis. The radiator shop and degreasing tank complements and puts the finishing touches on the engine rebuild shop to give the customer a one-stop service facility.

The service department is also second to none in the country. It is self-contained. "We don't have to wait for parts; we probably have it in our $750,000 inventory."

This first class operation is appropriate for Lansing which is known as the home of Oldsmobile and REO trucks, the now defunct-manufacturer of what many truckers considered the best built truck in the country. Bill Lee agrees that he has better facilities for building trucks than REO had in its last years of assembling trucks near downtown Lansing. Of course, both Oldsmobile and REO were the inspiration of Lansing's R.E. Olds.

As indicated by the corporate name, Lee is a General Motors agency. But it is much more, selling two other lines of trucks: Western Star, heavy duty long distance hauling trucks hand made in Canada; and Nissan Motor Trucks of North America. They are also a dealer for Detroit Diesel Allison, Cummins Engine and

Caterpiller Engine.

In addition, they are the area agency for the Dollar Rent A Car, the world's second largest car rental company and the fourth largest in the U.S., also leasing trucks under the corporation's name.

Each department is supervised by its own manager and the salesmen in the heavy- and medium-duty truck sales are usually on the road, creating a statewide territory for Lee, including Detroit.

Word on the new facility has ranged far and wide. It is not unusual to have truckers pull off the expressway and drive their long rigs past the showroom and service department before resuming their journey.

It is this access to the expressways, both I-96 between Detroit and Grand Rapids, and I-69 between Indianapolis and Canada, that led Bill Lee to build in Delta Township. Not only was his former facility on Larch Street inaccessible to most major truckers, there was little room for expanding the rapidly growing company Bill Lee purchased in 1983. The new facility gives better access for his local customers, such as Meijer Thrifty Acres, the Buick-Oldsmobile-Cadillac assembly group, Anchor Motor Freight which hauls automobiles out of Lansing, and Keena truck leasing.

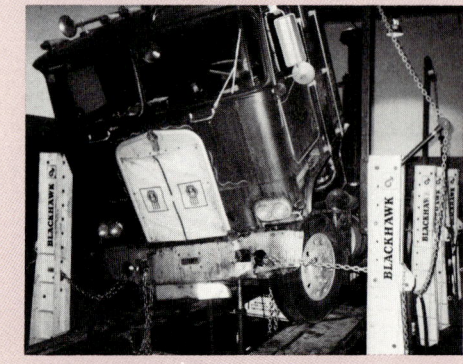

Maner, Costerisan & Ellis

New Dimensions Rooted in Tradition

Maner, Costerisan & Ellis, one of Michigan's leading accounting firms, is rooted in tradition dating back to 1906. The firm's original founder, John J. Jerome, was the 14th accountant in Michigan to be certified when the state first began the requirement back in 1906.

Max D. Harris, the 240th Michigan CPA, joined him in partnership in 1918, and the team moved to the Michigan National Tower upon its opening. It's interesting to note that, while the current M,C&E staff is housed in 10,000 square feet, the company had its beginnings in a 400 square foot space. Of course the staff has also grown considerably — from eight in 1951 to more than 50 employees today.

Floyd Costerisan (Seated at the computer) is the firm's president, while Leon Ellis is the firm's secretary.

Growth has not only come in size, but in the expansion of services offered. The firm's current range of expertise offers clients accounting services in auditing, tax planning, management consulting, and small business accounting.

The firm's auditing experience includes clients in finance, manufacturing, commercial, retail, government, and nonprofit organizations. Additional expertise gives them an edge in individual estate planning, business tax planning, and governmental audits of tax returns. The staff keeps current with changes through a comprehensive program of continuing education and a complete library that is updated weekly. The firm's tax specialists, with backgrounds in the IRS and years of solid experience in taxpayer representation, further enhance their wealth of accounting knowledge.

Maner, Costerisan & Ellis management advisory clients are served by full time professional consultants. Typical assignments include accounting system design and installation, cost accounting systems, feasibility studies, personnel recommendations, cost-reduction programs, financing, data-processing studies, and acquisition programs.

The small business department provides monthly services to businesses not large enough to warrant the cost of a full accounting department. Services include computerized ledgers, financial statements, employee earnings records, payroll tax reports, and bank reconciliations.

Equipped with state-of-the-art computer capabilities, the Lansing offices offer the additional advantages of state capitol contacts and proximity to many governmental agencies.

The firm's stated philosophy is "to contribute to the community in which we live and the profession to which we belong," and further, "to grow, but never to lose the identity and personal relationship with clients which is the foundation of our practice."

Goals like these blended with traditional, yet innovative attitudes, are the primary ingredients in Maner, Costerisan & Ellis' continued growth and expansion throughout its 80-year history.

Mayhood/Mertz Realtors, Inc.

Devoted to Personal Attention and Careful Research

Martha Mertz

Mayhood/Mertz Realtors, Inc. was founded in 1978 by Martha Mayhood Mertz with offices at 4868 Grandview, Okemos. The company is involved with both residential and commercial real estate sales and has always been devoted to the careful research and personal attention that a small company can provide. Creating and sustaining a warm and harmonious working environment for members of the company and its clients has been as much a goal and a satisfaction as a high volume of sales. In addition, there has been a strong history of community appreciation, participation and support within the company.

Gloria Stulz, who has a Masters Degree in Business from Michigan State University joined the company shortly after its inception and as Administrative Assistant set a standard of excellence in business management that built a solid foundation for the firm. Gloria has since departed and this Administrative work is now deftly managed by Diane Lyon.

Onalee Elliott was the first Realtor Associate to join Martha and the company roster has included, Deborah Staudt, Robin Teichert, Lil Schirmer, Jackie Horuczi, Valerie Lafferty, Margie Nolta, Betty Markham and Marlene Skehan.

The charming blue-grey Cape Cod style home of Mayhood/Mertz offices, on a quiet street in Okemos, now serves primarily as a corporate base for commercial real estate endeavors.

Meridian Center Investments commercial land development is a partnership of Martha Mertz and Roger Drobney who purchased approximately 55 acres of land in Okemos in 1978. The construction of a cluster of restaurants and Newman Road is the present cornerstone of this partnership's efforts.

Central Park Group, a commercial development partnership of Martha Mertz, Marlene Skehan and Robert Phipps, has created the exquisite Central Park Place convenience shopping and office center on Marsh Road in Okemos, officially opening in September of 1986.

Central Park Place

Michigan Millers
Mutual Insurance Company

Company service spans a century

Founded by mill owners from various communities in the heartland of Michigan, Michigan Millers Mutual Fire Insurance Company was incorporated in 1881 as one of the first Millers' Cooperative insurance companies in America.

By the turn of the century, Michigan Millers was playing a major role in the growth of mutual insurance. The company expanded into other states and began writing general insurance business. In 1954, the company shortened its name to Michigan Millers Mutual Insurance Company to reflect more truly the multiple line risks it was writing.

Today, Michigan Millers offers a full range of personal and commercial lines insurance. The company issues policies from its home office in Lansing and through its Western Department in Glendale, Calif. There are also service and branch claim offices strategically located in each operating state.

The first home office was built in 1890 at 120 W. Ottawa St. at a total cost of $6,000 including land. This building, which was placed in the National Register of Historic Places in 1980, served the company for nearly 40 years.

Arthur D. Baker (standing), who served Michigan Millers as president and chairman of the board from 1928 until 1941, oversees operations of the original home office on West Ottawa Street in this 1918 photo.

Charles B. McGill
President

By the late 1920s, Michigan Millers had outgrown the building. With an eye to the future, the Mutual Building was designed and constructed at 208 N. Capitol Ave. Hundred-year-old millstones were imbedded in the adjacent concrete walk as a reminder of the mills to which the company owed its early success. Subsequently, the building became the home of the Michigan Historical Museum.

The current home office at 2425 E. Grand River is a 60,000-square-foot facility settled on an eight-acre site. Despite its growth, the company has never lost sight of its origins — the early mill owners and their battle with fire. Encased in glass on the front lawn of the home office is a 1895-vintage steam pumper fire engine. It has become a local landmark and a symbol of company heritage.

In 1966, Michigan Millers instituted a companywide "quiet hour" which made headlines around the world. In an effort to promote good work habits, the company designated the first hour of every day as time for all employees to plan their day's work and to handle important matters without disruption. This has remained a corporate policy.

Although not a "family" operation per se, the company has always maintained an overall corporate "family feeling." Each employee automatically becomes a member of the Mutuality Association which plans company social activities.

Both the company and its employees are community-minded as well. Each year during the holiday season, employees make donations to the Lansing Food Bank. The company also participates in an annual Career Day held by the Ingham County Intermediate School District. And, on the last Friday of each month since 1953, employees have trekked to the American Red Cross to donate blood.

Throughout its existence, the company has been committed to serving the mutual needs of its policyholders. The company's financial strength and integrity are reflected in its consistent A+ (excellent) rating from A.M. Best Co., analysts for the insurance industry since 1899.

After more than 100 years of success, the Michigan Millers Mutual Insurance Company faces the future with confidence. The company has a long-term strategic plan for growth, which includes moving into agency-company automation.

Michigan National Bank

Lansing's Tower of Strength

Michigan National Tower; The early years.

When it was completed in 1931, after almost two years of construction, "the Tower" was hailed as Lansing's monumental high-rise masterpiece. Rising 300 feet above the street, the 25-story Art Deco landmark structure still looms high above the city as Lansing's tallest and most imposing architectural statement.

For most of the past half century, the Tower has been synonymous with Michigan National Bank. Commissioned by auto pioneer Ransom E. Olds, the building was originally known as the "Olds Tower."

Because it was completed at the height of the Great Depression, the Tower's first decade recalls a time of great challenge for the people of Michigan and its institutions — not the least of which was a national banking crisis. Fortunately, there were a few who responded to the economic catastrophe with new ideas. One such man was Michigan National founder, Howard J. Stoddard.

In 1932, Stoddard joined the Reconstruction Finance Corporation, a commission set up by the President to help banks through the crisis. When he arrived in Michigan to help unsnarl the financial mess that had already engulfed most of the state's banks, Stoddard began to earn the reputation as a master banker. By the end of the decade, he unveiled a plan that was to revolutionize Michigan banking.

The plan was simple, combine the money and know-how of several strategically situated Michigan banks and then organize them into a branch-banking operation. Each bank would have to have access to important financial markets — places like Battle Creek, Flint, Grand Rapids, Saginaw, Port Huron and, of course, Lansing.

Lansing National was one of six banks that formed the nucleus for Michigan National. Its predecessor, Capital National, had been taken over by City National Bank in 1931. Over the next decade, Lansing gradually emerged as the logical center for the bold new bank made up of smaller banks. On January 1, 1941, Michigan National Bank was founded by Howard J. Stoddard and

Lansing became its home base. Stoddard had long been an advocate of branch banking as a method of combining the loaning advantages of a large bank, with the consumer orientation, community roots, autonomy and friendliness of a local bank. This clearly was the direction that banking in Michigan would follow.

Over the years, Michigan National has continued to bring new and better ideas to Michigan banking. When "auto-age" banking began in earnest for the very first time, it happened in Lansing. That was when the world's first drive-in bank opened its doors in 1948. Naturally, the bank was a Michigan National branch office.

Today, the Michigan National tradition of service continues with savings, checking and investment accounts, Individual Retirement Accounts (IRAs), trust and brokerage services, Mutual Funds, personal, business and auto loans and with Michigan Bankard™, the state's largest credit card system.

Michigan National's tradition of innovative banking continues with Michigan Money™, the state's smartest and most convenient system of banking — and Michigan's largest network of 24-hour automatic teller machines (ATMs). Michigan Money is also compatible across Michigan with Magic Line® and all across America with the Plus System®.

Across the country and around the corner, Michigan National Bank continues to serve the people of Lansing with a true "tower" of strength in hometown banking.

Customers at the main office of Michigan National Bank see FasTeller ATMs even before they reach the teller line.

Michigan State University

It was a daring experiment

On Feb. 12, 1855, Governor Kinsley S. Bingham signed the law that founded the Agricultural College of the State of Michigan (today Michigan State University) — the nation's first agricultural college.

When those first 63 students gathered with five faculty members under the leadership of President Joseph R. Williams, they inscribed a new page in higher education history.

Formerly, higher education had been provided only for the favored few, but, with its birth, Michigan State University created a new citadel of democracy, bringing scientific, liberal and practical training within the reach of all who hungered for it. Nowhere else in the nation was such an education available, simply because the existing colleges and universities were devoted to the nurturing of doctors, lawyers, clergymen and gentlemen.

Michigan State set the standard for the nation's 72 land-grant colleges and universities established under the Morrill Act of 1862. In urging his fellow Congressmen to endow these land-grant institutions, Justin S. Morrill pointed to schools "like that of Michigan, liberally supported by the State, in the full tide of successful experiment."

In the years since its founding, Michigan State University has continued that experiment in education, dedicating its resources to the land-grant mission of teaching, research and public service.

The early curriculum emphasized agricultural science and rural leadership. Today undergraduates may choose from more than 200 programs of instruction, and graduate study is offered through more than 75 departments and schools in 14 colleges — all taught by a faculty and staff of more than 3,000.

From its earliest enrollments of 100-plus to its present enrollment of more than 41,000, MSU has striven to remain accessible. Today's students come from every county in Michigan, every state in the nation, and some 100 foreign countries. They represent in microcosm the nation's ethnic, racial, religious, and socioeconomic diversity. And they're high-achievers: MSU can claim 10

Aerial View of Michigan State University Campus
At upper right is stadium. Right center is Beaumont Tower. About one-fourth of the way down on the left is Agriculture Hall.

Rhodes Scholars in the past 14 years, a mark unmatched by any other public institution. MSU is also a leader in attracting Merit Scholars and in the number of students who win National Science Foundation fellowships and Churchill, Marshall, and Truman Scholarships.

The quality of MSU's programs is evidenced by its membership in the nation's leading organization of academically superior institutions — the 56-member Association of American Universities.

Beginning with the basic agricultural research of a century ago, the MSU research program, with grants of $68 million this year, has expanded to some 2,800 projects that utilize such on-campus facilities as the world's first superconducting cyclotron laboratory, the Pesticide Research Center, the Mass Spectrometry Laboratory and the National Institute for Research on Teaching. Long known for its programs in botany, plant pathology, horticulture, and field crop science, the University has become a national center for plant research, with its selection by the Atomic Energy Commission (now the Department of Energy) as the base for its efforts in that field.

MSU research has led to such distinctions as the discovery of cisplatin, the widest-selling anti-cancer drug in the United States today; the exploratory use of a white-rot fungus to degrade toxic chemicals; the introduction of more than 100 varieties of grains, vegetables and fruits, tailored for optimal production in Michigan; the development of the first superconducting cyclotron for medical use; and the use of computer technology to give speech to those without voice.

Under the leadership of its 17th president, Dr. John A. DiBiaggio, MSU continues to pursue an innovative approach to education. The nation's only university with three medical colleges (veterinary medicine, osteopathic medicine, and human medicine), Michigan State is also at the forefront in international programs and studies and offers the nation's most extensive array of opportunities for study overseas.

The outstate winter institutes of more than a century ago have grown into the many dimensions of the Cooperative Extension Service and Lifelong Education Programs, offering educational opportunity and stimulating thought for a lifetime.

It may have been a daring experiment in 1855. But in hindsight, it was a sure bet.

Motor Wheel Corporation

Motor Wheel keeps pace as a Lansing leader

From the nation's leading producer of wood-spoked wheels in the 1920's, Motor Wheel Corporation has maintained its leadership and is now the world's largest manufacturer of styled wheels.

The company is also a top supplier of brake parts for automobiles and trucks, and a major producer of rims and wheels for earthmoving equipment.

In addition to its Lansing headquarters, Motor Wheel has five other plants in the United States and Canada.

Motor Wheel was organized in Lansing in 1920 by founders Harry F. Harper, D.L. Porter and B.S. Gier. At that time, 90 percent of all vehicles used wood-spoked wheels.

Back in the 1920s at Motor Wheel, assembling wood wheels involved ramming down the spoke into the rim.

Though the company soon became the nation's largest producer of wooden wheels, its leaders foresaw the time when steel would rule the market. By 1924, Motor Wheel had become the world's top manufacturer of both wood *and* steel wheels.

The remainder of the '20s and the '30s was a period of diversification for the company as it expanded its product line into Duo-Therm oil-fired water heaters, furnaces and space heaters.

Motor Wheel achieved a major milestone in 1931 with its production of Centrifuse brake drums for passenger cars.

Between 1933 and 1938, the company devoted a vast amount of research and money to the development of wheels

for agricultural equipment, including steel wheels with pneumatic tires for farm tractors and implements.

Motor Wheel also pioneered the installation of steel wheels with pneumatic tires on earthmoving equipment, mining and logging machinery, concrete mixers, power shovels and road rollers.

As the house trailer increased in popularity, the firm sold thousands of wheels to trailer builders. Wrapping up a decade of change, Motor Wheel started production of railroad equipment.

In the 1940s, Motor Wheel became an important business force in the American war effort. The company produced cartridge cases, rocket bodies and motors, aluminum propeller domes and various armament components. It also became the country's leading producer of military tank wheels.

After the war, Motor Wheel pursued an expansion program, purchasing the Nash-Kelvinator Propeller Plant in Lansing for production of Duo-Therm products, adding gas space heaters and water heaters to its Duo-Therm line, and pioneering the production of power adjustable wheels for farm tractors.

Motor Wheel continued expansion in the '50s, building a wheel manufacturing plant in Delaware to serve car assembly plants on the East Coast. The firm also kept pace with the accelerated automobile era when it developed the Electrofuse welding process for use with tubeless-tire wheels — a process now used by virtually all automobile wheel manufacturers.

Innovation was the hallmark in the '60s. In 1962, Motor Wheel introduced the Centrue/Light wheel, the lightest and truest-running steel truck wheel on the market at that time.

One year later, the firm announced the Unistyle passenger car custom wheel, the first new concept in wheel design since the steel disc wheel replaced the spoke wheel. Motor Wheel became a subsidiary of The Goodyear Tire & Rubber Company in 1964.

Through the years, the company has been a leader in community and environmental improvements. Many of

One of Motor Wheel's many employee activities is the Women's Club. Here, club members "toast" in the new year with new company coffee mugs.

Motor Wheel's employees hold positions in the United Way, Chamber of Commerce, Boys and Girls Club, Junior Achievement, YMCA, Little League and many other worthwhile civic groups. And the company has spent more than $60 million in the past few years on modernization programs.

Innovations and new products are the hallmark of Motor Wheel. Examining an industry-first composite styled wheel is engineer Jim Woelfel.

In Motor Wheel's 65-year industrial journey, the firm has created innovative technological processes and new products, and in so doing has become a leader in the industry and a solid force in the Lansing area.

McElmurry Service Transport

Lansing Trucking Company Stresses Efficiency and Service

For approximately 12 years Scott McElmurry trucked milk through the Michigan countryside, pulled loads of cattle through the Midwest and hauled freight for Mason's Dart Container Corp.

During the many hours "on the road," McElmurry had lots of time to think about and plan what he wanted to do with the rest of his life. One of the things he thought about was starting his own trucking company.

A determined man who had confidence in his own ability to succeed, McElmurry decided to put his ideas into motion. The 1980 deregulation of the trucking industry was the opportunity for McElmurry and, in June of 1981, he purchased his first truck. Soon more equipment was added, a corporation was formed and an office was opened in Portland. In February of 1983, MST was granted 48 state authority (the right to operate in the continental United States) as a carrier.

McElmurry gave up driving in 1983 to concentrate on running his new company. He readily admits, however, that he misses the "road," and still feels that driving the trucks is the best job in the trucking industry. Consequently, he takes great pride in the quality of drivers he has been able to hire. Drivers with the ability to deal effectively with the public and are conscientious about their work and themselves fit the mold on the MST team.

Today, MST (McElmurry Service Transport) has 35 employees and operates 24 tractors and 35 trailers. To provide maximum service to its customers, MST is officially associated with Keena Truck Leasing, a full-lease maintenance company with nation-wide coverage.

MST is the only common-contract carrier firm to be headquartered in the Lansing area. Its current headquarters at 6025 Aurelius Rd. is an up-to-date office complex, featuring the latest in equipment needed to efficiently run a modern trucking firm.

MST, being a small business, depends on high efficiency from all of their employees for the company's ultimate success. In McElmurry's efforts to succeed, he surrounds himself with highly motivated people who strive as a team to see that MST's customers receive continuous satisfaction.

McElmurry believes that people first, along with high tech equipment and computerization, is what is going to make MST a leader in the transportation industry. To keep his people growing, he provides college tuition assistance as well as providing support to employees with outside interests such as community service. This support along with profit sharing keep MST employees striving to be innovative and solve business and customers' problems before they arise.

MST covers virtually the entire country and it is common to see McElmurry's trucks carrying such food-related items as potatoes and onions grown in Michigan or styrofoam cups made by Mason's Dart Container Corp. to distant states. Because MST believes in using its trucks as efficiently as possible, return trips to Michigan will frequently bring furniture from Mississippi or Alabama, building products from Iowa and medical supplies from the Carolinas.

Even though MST cannot compete with the nation's largest trucking firms in terms of size, McElmurry believes that smaller firms can be industry leaders in efficiency and innovation. MST's computer system, for example, provides clients with economical routing and efficient scheduling. Drivers benefit from the company's driver training program and are offered special incentives for reduced fuel consumption and safe driving habits. And, in the future, McElmurry is considering putting computers in each one of his trucks.

MST customers can expect regular inspection of MST equipment, a country-wide maintenance network for emergency repairs, or if needed, substitute trucks. MST's 48-foot trailers can haul a wide range of goods and, because they operate an average 90% loaded, can provide competitive rates. Its drivers personally supervise all loading and unloading operations at the docks.

McElmurry, a native of nearby Mason, is continually striving for efficiency, maximizing his profits and, most important, providing superior service to his customers. He is also fiercely proud of the Lansing area, impressed by the quality people he has been able to hire and feels good that he is contributing to the community by bringing jobs to Michigan.

"I really am proud of Lansing," he says. "When I have customers come here, I take them around showing the latest developments in the area. I located my business here because it is my home."

"Across America and to your door"
MST equipment enroute

MST corporate headquarters
Lansing, MI.

Physicians Health Plan

...emerging from its cocoon — this HMO soars into the future

Physicians Health Plan's unprecedented success as Lansing's largest HMO exemplifies the increasing involvement of business in today's health care industry. Physicians Health Plan provides a cost-effective alternative to traditional medical coverage, and by applying leadership principles that dictate success in other industries, Physicians Health Plan has aggressively become *the* pacesetter for Lansing's HMOs.

Since 1981, Physicians Health Plan has been serving the medical benefit needs of the Lansing community. This commitment to Lansing has led to several customized programs for our business people, our medical care facilities, and the individual consumer. With Physicians Health Plan coverage, subscribers enjoy an exceptional degree of personal choice in their physicians, their pharmacies and their hospitals. At this writing, 98% of Greater Lansing's doctors and all of the hospitals in the Greater Lansing Area are members.

This year, Physicians Health Plan is introducing several customized programs, including a Medicare benefit package and individualized plans and programs for the self-employed and small business person. These programs reflect the innovation that exists throughout Physicians Health Plan, and are *only* the beginning of greater programs to come.

Physicians Health Plan has created a balance within its nonprofit organization that enhances its subscriber services.

The balance begins at the top, where the board involvement is an equal balance of physicians, business people, and hospitals. This equilibrium creates the ideal environment for ideas and input from all directions, and insures proper controls for all concerned.

Physicians Health Plan is an action-oriented organization. Their ongoing attention to the needs and problems of their people, their members and their users requires flexibility, innovation, customization and most importantly, *action*. Physicians Health Plan is equipped with highly trained professionals with diverse backgrounds and abilities *committed* to creating the *best medical benefit programs available* to its subscribers. Its project management approach enables members and subscribers alike to utilize their options with the education and experience of the Physicians Health Plan professionals to assist

in developing the most progressive, "made to order," cost effective programs required.

Behind the scenes at Physicians Health Plan lies one of the many secrets to its success. The Physicians Health Plan professional has necessary and timely information available at its fingertips. Sophisticated computerized data information centers bring every request to light immediately.

The data management team is alert and responsive to all ingoing and outgoing information, and is exemplary of the entire Physicians Health Plan staff.

Constant forecasting and troubleshooting has brought Greater Lansing the *best* in HMO coverage. The service-oriented and cost-conscious attitude that originated this organization continues to thrive at Physicians Health Plan. While other HMOs strive to outrun competition, Physicians Health Plan is concentrating on cultivating themselves by improving their management style, improving their benefit programs and remaining in tune and one step ahead in meeting needs of the medical profession.

Physicians Health Plan is on the move ... and will continue to be a major benefactor and asset to the Lansing Community as an attractive drawing card to new business and a friend to the medical profession.

"...When you have to call a doctor, it's nice to call your own..."

Roberts Corporation – A Cross & Trecker Company

Hi-Tech Firm Part of World's Leading Machine Tool Company

In the southwest outskirts of Lansing, on the hills overlooking the Grand River, the headquarters of Roberts Corporation is one of Michigan's prime examples that big industry can be an aesthetic mesh of sophisticated technology and unspoiled surroundings.

Inside the Roberts' headquarters, modern art, soft carpeting and well-designed offices create an atmosphere that seems quite distant from the machinery and the manufacturing plants that make up such a large part of America's industrial complex. Outside, the grounds are more reminiscent of the New England countryside than the edges of a Midwestern city. Within this tranquil-appearing atmosphere, however, Roberts' engineers, computer specialists and other technicians are busy at work with the challenges of engineering foundry systems and equipment, designing robot installations and creating automatic guided vehicle systems.

Founded in 1965 by Robert E. French, Robert E. Place and Joseph M. Post, Roberts was initially located in Southpointe Plaza on Cedar Street. Originally created to be manufacturer's representatives with the capability of custom-designing material handling systems, the firm began manufacturing its own products in a converted Grand Ledge welding shop in 1966.

In 1973, Roberts merged with one of the nation's leading machine tool concerns, the Cross Company of Fraser, Michigan. Six years later, Cross joined with Kearney and Trecker Corporation, Milwaukee, Wisconsin to form Cross & Trecker Corporation, the nation's largest and broadest-based machine tool company and Roberts emerged as the material-handling wing of its parent company.

Today, Roberts' president, Joseph Post, directs 250 employees in five facilities, including a plant in Homberg, West Germany. The company recently celebrated its 20th year at its Grand Ledge manufacturing facility (greatly expanded since 1966). Other Michigan facilities are located in Clarkston and Warren, where its Sys-T-Mation and Shalco Systems divisions are headquartered, respectively. Sys-T-Mation markets a broad range of handling equipment and automation machin-

Roberts Headquarters

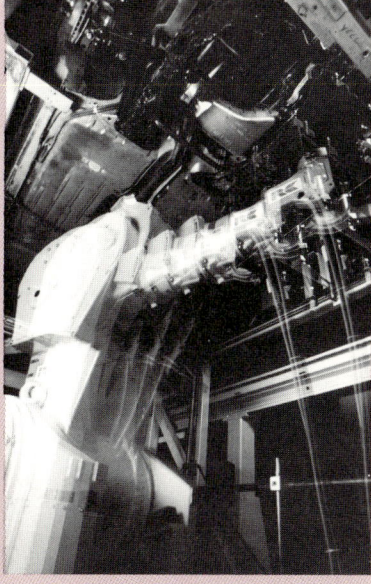

A Roberts robot tightening bolts on automobile undercarriage.

ery geared principally to the automotive industry, while Shalco markets a line of foundry core and mold making machines which utilize both thermal and chemical bonding processes.

Roberts specializes in solving the specific material handling problems for a wide variety of industries. Computer-aided design, modeling and simulation techniques are all used to produce these unique systems. Additional services provided by Roberts feature installation, project management and financing. Among its customers are aerospace companies, foundries, power generation stations and a wide variety of manufacturing and assembly plants serving automotive and general industries.

The high-technology firm can produce systems for handling parts weighing less than an ounce to systems handling parts and pallets weighing over 50 tons. Its Roberts/Motoman robots are high-speed, high-accuracy devices with capacities up to 262 pounds and are ideal for machine tending, assembly and material handling applications. Every day in the United States a greater tonnage of castings are produced by using Roberts' Roto Pours than by any other automatic iron pouring system.

The basic strategy of Roberts is to stay out in front in its fast-changing indus-

try and to continue to broaden its ability to equip the emerging factory of the future. That means having the right products, the right strengths and the right organization. To meet these goals, the company's recent investments have been focused on enhancing the quality and value of its products and by intensifying its research and development efforts. Roberts expects to complete its best year ever in 1986 and anticipates continued growth throughout the next decade.

Being a part of Cross & Trecker Corporation allows Roberts to utilize the skills of its parent company's other technology-oriented subdivisions (The Cross Company, Kearney & Trecker Corporation and the Warner & Swasey Company), in providing the latest in high-tech services to its clients. The Cross & Trecker Credit Corporation, C&T Technical Services, and the Machine Remarketing Corporation, all serve to broaden the range of services available to Roberts' customers.

With the recent integration of Shalco Systems into Roberts, the Lansing-based company has entered the international market and is currently doing business in such far away places as Australia, India, Poland and Yugoslavia, as well as several countries in Western Europe and the Near East.

St. Lawrence

Excellence in Healthcare

From the moment the Sisters of Mercy opened what was to become St. Lawrence Hospital in 1920 during an influenza epidemic, the institution has set a standard of excellence in healthcare.

During the next 66 years, St. Lawrence grew from its humble 28-bed beginning to a leader in meeting the healthcare needs of the community. As a member of the Sisters of Mercy Health Corporation, St. Lawrence has been able to combine that local focus with the advantages of group purchasing, insurance risk pooling, consultative expertise and a network of skills and resources in developing new programs.

Today, St. Lawrence serves the greater Lansing area with 200 medical/surgical beds, 59 mental health beds, 100 substance abuse beds and 164 nursing center beds. Our medical staff numbers over 600, with 1,400 other healthcare professionals and 700 volunteers.

Family Centered Care

All of the programs of St. Lawrence, whether at the familiar West Saginaw Street location or at the institution's Dimondale campus, are guided by the concept of family-centered care. This practice, which we pioneered in 1971, emphasizes the role of family members in the caring of a patient. We are committed to serving the community — including the needy and the disabled — by providing those health services which help individuals realize their fullest potential.

A multi-million dollar renovation several years ago turned a former nursing home into much more. Our Dimondale campus now provides not only nursing center care, but also houses highly successful inpatient substance abuse and psychiatric care programs for adolescents and adults. Outpatient substance abuse and psychiatric programs are available at the West Saginaw Street site, in addition to a short-term inpatient psychiatric program operated in conjunction with the Community Mental Health Board.

Programs for the Aging

St. Lawrence's concern for the aged goes beyond the nursing center care offered at our Dimondale location. Geriatric healthcare programs, operated in coopera-

St. Lawrence's convenient location has made it possible for our Emergency Department to care for over 30,000 patients each year with health problems ranging from minor illness to major trauma. We are the first hospital in Lansing to provide special trauma care to patients who require this high level of treatment.

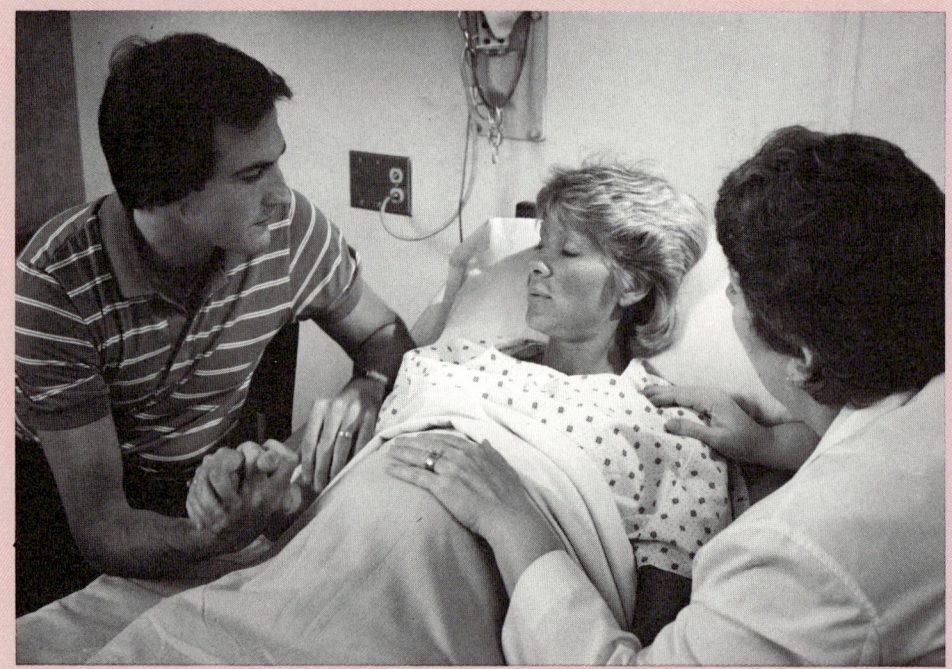

Having a baby at St. Lawrence provides the "Special Beginning" that so many families treasure today.

tion with Michigan State University, focus on helping older adults over the age of 60 maintain a high quality of life. The inpatient and outpatient programs help older adults remain as independent as possible and avoid premature placement in nursing homes.

Our Geriatric Assessment Center is an outpatient program aimed at helping older adults and their families identify and adjust to changes in function, thinking, mood and behavior due to changing life circumstances or medical problems.

A short-term inpatient program for older adults, known as the Geriatric Psychiatry Service, helps older adults ex-

St. Lawrence doesn't forget the special human touch that is sometimes lost in the high-tech world of critical care.

periencing emotional problems. An interdisciplinary team provides assessment, management and coordination with a goal of restoring function and independence.

Education a Major Focus

Through its commitment to education, St. Lawrence uses current information to help manage and avoid future health problems. The hospital sponsors training opportunities for medical technologists, radiology technicians, and pharmacists (one of only three such residency programs in the country), in addition to residency programs for physicians in a number of specialties. We also help provide education for the community through health education programs (including a 32-foot mobile unit) and a recently installed teleconferencing system. In addition to the expected healthcare-related topics, teleconferences are also available on a wide range of non-healthcare topics and professional and civic groups are welcome to use the various education rooms at the hospital.

Full Range of Services — Emergency to Obstetrics

Our Emergency Department is staffed by board-certified emergency physicians, working with RNs with advanced training in trauma and life support. A special emergency department fee schedule ensures that patients' bills are related only to the level of care they receive.

For acutely ill patients, St. Lawrence also has a 16-bed critical/cardiac unit, with each bed linked to a technically advanced computer monitoring system.

"Special Beginnings" continues a tradition of family-centered maternity options. Other inpatient services include a Cardiopulmonary Department that offers respiratory therapy, cardiology and electrocardiography for the critically ill and/or recovering patient. Patients can also take advantage of services offered by the Physical Medicine and Rehabilitation Department, which include a wide range of diagnostic and therapy services.

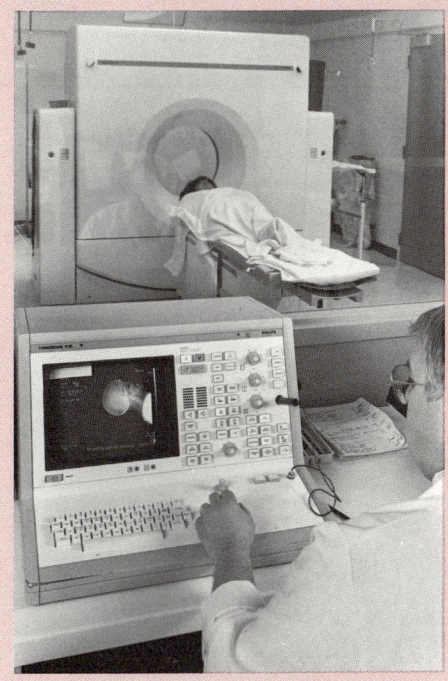

The St. Lawrence Radiology Department consists of several specialized fields. The area's most modern Computerized Tomography (CT) Scanner allows radiologists to learn more about the problems of the brain, lung, chest, spine and abdomen.

Maintaining the Sisters of Mercy focus on the needs of the whole person, all patients have access to assistance from the Social Services Department and Pastoral Care to help them and their families adjust to the demands of changing economic and spiritual conditions.

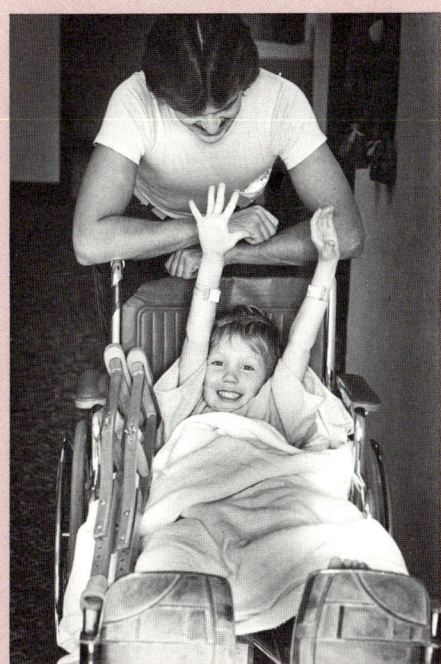

In physical therapy, patients learn how to restore, prevent or minimize disabilities from diseases, trauma or illness — no matter what their age!

Whether persons are receiving inpatient or outpatient care, we offer a full range of ancillary services, including a Pharmacy, Radiology Department and Pathology Department. And a newly developed program offers special services just to women.

Unique Focus on Women's Health

The Marjorie J. Gardner Wellness Center for Women, located near the Meridian Mall in Okemos, represents a new focus on the health of women. The Center's programs recognize that area women want to make choices and seek care that combines traditional healthcare services with information and education, presented in a setting that says: "We are your *partners* in healthcare."

A "Tradition of Mercy"

St. Lawrence's many specialized services and programs for women and men (of all ages), children and adolescents all focus on the patient and patient's family, continuing a 66-year-old "Tradition of Mercy" unique to the mid-Michigan area.

For more information about the healthcare programs and services at St. Lawrence, call 517/377-0460.

SEALED POWER

A Tradition of Achievement

On December 20, 1911, mechanical expert Charles E. Johnson and sales administrator Paul R. Beardsley each deposited $1,000 in the National Lumberman's Bank of Muskegon, Michigan, as the initial working capital for their new firm, the Piston Ring Company.

Original Sealed Power Plant, Muskegon, Michigan.

In a simple schoolbook ledger, first entries included such items as "postage stamps, $.50; entertainment, Fowl and Kimball, $3.00; stenographers' notebooks, $.10; office expense, $1.55.

From their rented 1,800 square foot factory headquarters, they personally delivered the first piston rings of their own manufacture to the firm's first customer, Continental Motors Corporation.

At the end of another December, 73 years later, the Piston Ring Company, its name changed to Sealed Power Corporation, had some 3,900 shareholders instead of two, showed sales for the year 1984 of $500.1 million and operating income of $35.8 million. In place of the 30-by-60 foot factory of the beginning, Sealed Power now operates manufacturing and distribution facilities totaling over four million square feet. From a one product company, Sealed Power has evolved into a worldwide manufacturer and supplier of a wide variety of precision metal parts, components, service tools and equipment primarily for the transportation industry.

Behind this story of growth lies the company's policy of no compromise with superior quality, creative research, skillful engineering and product design, sound planning, and aggressive salesmanship, plus the maintenance of a knowledgeable engineering staff that is always available to transportation equipment manufacturers.

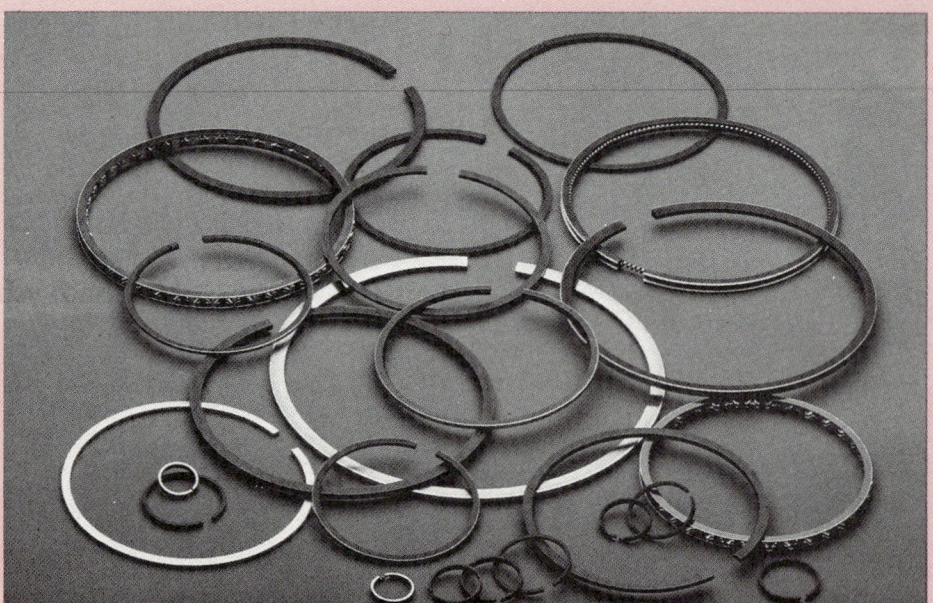

Sealed Power makes more than 14,000 sizes and types of piston and transmission rings to meet the requirements of the marketplace.

In its first years, Sealed Power devoted itself entirely to the production of piston rings for leading engine builders. In 1912, the company moved to its present location in Muskegon. Its first plant expansion was undertaken in 1916 to meet World War I production requirements. In 1920, it entered the replacement market. It acquired the No-Leak-O Piston Ring Company in 1923, and began export sales two years later. In 1931, the year of the name change to Sealed Power, it expanded its product line by acquiring Accuralite Company, a manufacturer of pistons and cylinder sleeves. In 1946, the company began to expand outside Muskegon with construction of a ring machining facility at St. Johns, Michigan, close to the Detroit vehicle manufacturers who are among Sealed Power's primary customers. Two years later, in 1948, a cylinder sleeve machining facility was built in Rochester, Indiana.

In 1952, the company began to market replacement rings through the American Hammered automotive replacement division. The year 1955 was noteworthy for the first public offering of Sealed Power common stock.

Sealed Power made a major product breakthrough in 1956 with the introduction of the first stainless steel piston oil ring. The ring quickly achieved 100 percent car factory and replacement market acceptance. It is a three-piece ring, consisting of two circular outer rails with a stainless steel expander spaced between them. The spacer has 16 to 50 spring tension points, which act to keep the rails in contact with the cylinder bore around the entire circumference. Combining the tension-retaining quality of stainless steel with the greatest flexibility and ease of installation ever built into an oil ring, it was a vast improvement over the older carbon steel rings, which lost tension and efficiency under engine heat.

The St. Johns, Michigan plant, now in its 40th year, continues to make the stainless steel expander as well as other compression rings for original equipment engines at Ford, Chrysler and General Motors.

Sealed Power Plant, St. Johns, Michigan.

Smith Floral

80 Years Old and Still Growing

This article has been dedicated in loving memory to Larry Smith, a loving husband and a fine businessman, by his wife, Gertrude.

The seeds were sown over eighty years ago, and Smith Floral has been a growing concern ever since. The founders, brothers Gurdon and Charles Smith, were reared on a farm in Eagle Township. They carefully cultivated a flourishing business that is now three generations old, and one of the area's leaders in floral design and delivery.

In 1903, Gurdon and his wife, Antionette, made plans to build a greenhouse in the backyard of their home on Sycamore Street, but before construction began, located an existing greenhouse on the corner of Kalamazoo and River Street, adjacent to the Grand River. Gurdon soon discovered that this purchase was not practical, due to seasonal river flooding at Easter (one of the best seasons in the industry) for three to four months.

Gurdon then sought the advice of Charles, the businessman in the family. The result was the purchase of five acres of land on Mount Hope Avenue, in what was then Lansing Township. The two brothers bought the land with Angel Priggooris, a well-known landowner and financier of the day, and constructed the greenhouse there.

The business was later taken over by the Smith brothers alone, with Charles holding two thirds of the investment.

Although the greenhouse was on Mt. Hope Avenue, the flower shop stayed downtown, opening at 105 West Michigan Avenue (the present Paramount Newscenter) in 1912. Nine years later a fire wiped the store out.

According to Lawrence Smith (Charles' son) in a 1983 article in the *State Journal*, "It burned down on the coldest night of the year. The fire started at 2 or 3 in the morning, and the only things that survived were the safe and a burnedup refrigerator."

The fire forced Gurdon and Charles into temporary quarters at the Hotel Kern, which sat on the northeast corner of Michigan and Grand Avenues. They remained there until a new shop was opened on Washington Avenue at what is now The Peanut Shop.

"The white tile floor is still there now," Smith said. "I swear it's the same floor."

In 1935 the shop moved two blocks south to a store now occupied by Barnes Floral. Smith Floral remained downtown until 1950, when it relocated to 1124 East Mount Hope Avenue.

Lawrence Smith joined the business in 1950, following a stint with the Army and several years in government service retraining veterans. His uncle, Gurdon, died in 1943 and his father in 1953.

Larry was faced with immediate financial problems when he took control. Smith Floral was $55,000 in debt.

"When my dad put this up, he borrowed practically every nickel he had," Larry confessed. "The business cost an estimated $22,000 in 1949. When he got her up and got her going, he invested $25,000, and was heavily in debt. I said, 'by God, if he can do all of that I can turn it around.'"

The business is worth much more now. "It's beyond comprehension," Smith said. "It'd cost just a half million for the greenhouse!" Lawrence Smith died in December of 1985.

Larry's son, Charles, is the third generation to join the business. "I'm very proud of Smith Floral," said Charlie. "We are the oldest family owned floral shop in Lansing, 80 years old and still growing!"

Smith Floral continues to blossom under the direction of the third generation. What was once a seedling, is now a flourishing and healthy growing concern reaping benefits for Lansing and its residents with its flower shop and over an acre of greenhouse under glass.

Sparrow Hospital:

A Healthy Tradition

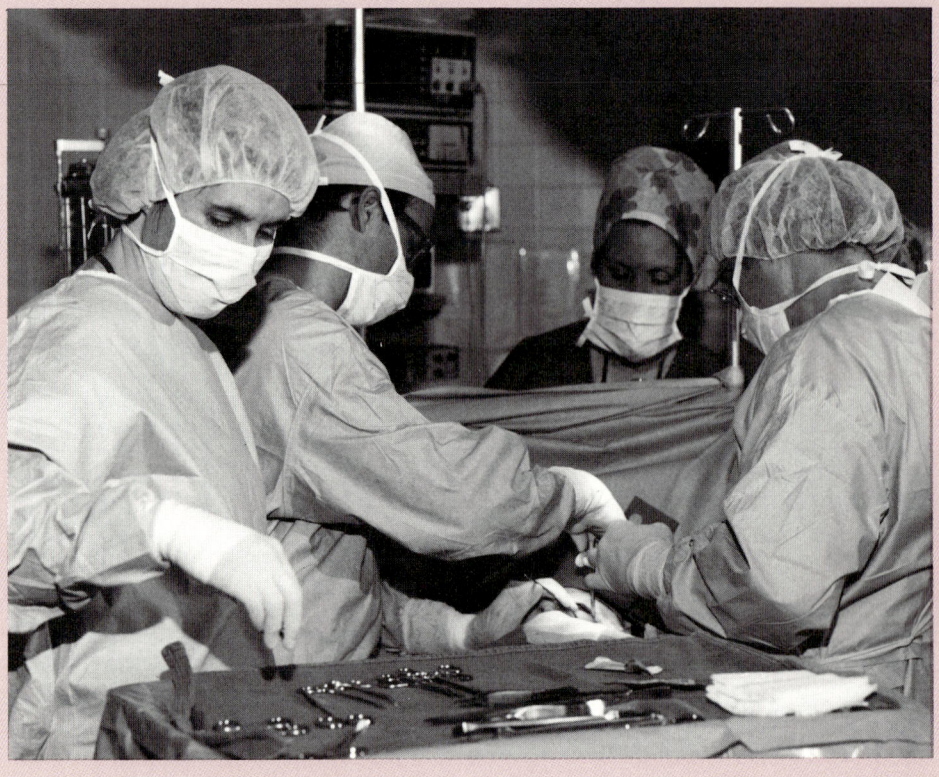

On the first floor of Lansing's Sparrow Hospital is an example of modern medical technology at its finest. Here, in the Regional Oncology Center, medicine and technology combine to deliver state-of-the-art care to cancer patients.

From behind a glassed-in station, doctors and technologists, utilizing computer-controlled equipment, guide a $900,000 linear accelerator to administer radiation therapy with pin-point accuracy. Prolonging and improving the quality of life has been Sparrow Hospital's reason for being since its beginning 90 years ago.

On March 5, 1896, a group of enterprising young women met at Lansing's Downey Hotel to discuss the growing need for a hospital and form the Women's Hospital Association. Armed with sheer determination, this group of the 114 charter members, many of them wives of local businessmen, set about to raise funds to buy the DeViney House on West Ottawa Street. Having just $400, they settled for renting. Not easily discouraged, these women opened and operated an 11-bed hospital, hired a doctor and a nurse, and used their own linens when the hospital supply ran low.

The first surgery at the DeViney House was a leg amputation with water sterilized in a teakettle on the stove. The women would proudly boast of no surgical infections during their first two and one-half years.

A brief move to the Moffett House on Grand Avenue followed, after which the women's dream of hospital ownership was realized with the purchase of the James Mead House on Cedar Street in 1899 at a cost of $65 a month.

In 1899, the women also began a nurse training program which later became the Sparrow Hospital School of Nursing. The school closed in 1961, but not before graduating 1,017 nurses, many of whom chose careers at Sparrow.

Raising money was a constant challenge and prompted the start of the Auxiliary, the first volunteer group. The Auxiliary is one of 22 volunteer groups in existence at Sparrow. In 1902, the Auxiliary's 12 members started what has become the annual Charity Ball, an event

which in 1985 raised over $7,000 for Sparrow's Pediatrics Department.

It was the presence of Margaret Sparrow on the Women's Board of Managers, however, which would prove crucial to the future of health care in the Lansing area. Married to Edward W. Sparrow, an Irish immigrant and locally prominent citizen, her influence became obvious. Mr. Sparrow realized that a larger health care facility was sorely needed to meet the needs of the growing Lansing area.

In 1910, Mr. Sparrow donated the land at 1215 East Michigan Avenue, along with a generous gift of $100,000, for the purpose of building a hospital. And the Women's Hospital Association, with its 14 years of experience in running a hospital, became a crucial part of this plan.

On November 6, 1912, Edward W. Sparrow Hospital admitted the first patient to the 44-bed facility. The new hospital opened under a dual Board system, the Women's Board of Managers to handle day-to-day operations and an all male Board of Trustees to handle financial affairs. This dual board structure still exists. However, the Board of Trustees long ago

recognized and accepted women as Trustees. Today women play many key roles, including operation of one of America's largest volunteer service organizations with over 1200 members.

Sparrow Hospital has changed dramatically since the early years in the original three-story brick building where mattresses were aired on the roof and patients placed in sun rooms to kill germs. The constant addition of major medical services and new technology have made Sparrow Hospital the health care leader that it is today.

Ninety-five percent of the current structure is less than 25 years old. Completed in 1983 as part of a $36,000,000 West Wing addition, the new entrance greets visitors with skylights, lush plants and modular furniture. Modern art decorates the walls to the right of a futuristic reception desk where volunteers greet tens of thousands of visitors each year.

On the Hospital's lower concourse is the Surgical Unit which is an essential part of the new 170,000 square-foot West Wing. As recently as 1973, ambulatory-surgery programs' first year, just 100 outpatient surgeries were performed out of more than 12,000 cases. By 1985, over one-half of the more than 14,000 surgeries were completed on an outpatient basis. And the length of stay for inpatient care has been drastically reduced. In 1985, the average length of stay for inpatient care was just 5.18 days, a number which includes inpatient treatment of more seriously-ill patients.

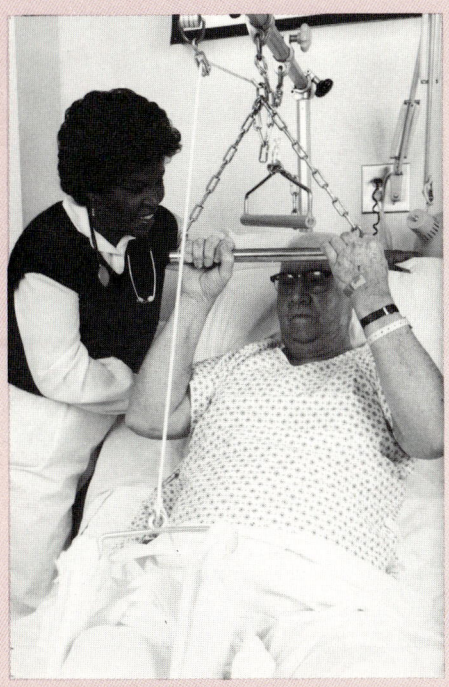

Sparrow is equipped to handle a wide range of medical needs, ranging from removing a patient's appendix or delivering a healthy baby, to conducting neuro surgical procedures on comprehensive rehabilitation services.

Some of the major treatment programs added at Sparrow over recent years include: a Regional Burn Center, the Hemodialysis Unit and a federally-approved Rehabilitation Center. Sparrow takes special pride in its reputation as a forerunner in neonatal intensive care. The Regional Neonatal Intensive Care Unit (RNICU) has skillfully provided care allowing babies as tiny as only one and one-half pounds to survive. Serving 10 counties in the mid-Michigan area, the RNICU treated over 600 infants in 1985.

Heading the unit are two neonatologists, who are pediatricians specifically trained to work with high-risk infants. The unit also offers a Developmental Assessment Clinic which follows the first 7 years of the babies' lives.

Sparrow Hospital has constantly sought to ready itself for the future. The formation of a holding company in 1984 called Sparrow, Inc., provides the corporate flexibility required to rapidly develop and efficiently provide patients with a wide-range of vital services.

Home Health Care of Sparrow, Inc., provides at-home services for patients once they leave the hospital. Sparrow Health Care Supply, is a medical supply and equipment business designed with an eye on meeting the future needs of outpatients.

Sparrow was also the first hospital to start an independent-practice Health Maintenance Organization (HMO). Physician's Health Plan (PHP) founded in 1981, now provides subscribers the opportunity to choose from over 600 private-practice physicians in the Greater Lansing Area.

The Women's Health Center of Sparrow, established in 1986, provides essential assistance to the women of the mid-Michigan area. The main purpose of the center is to provide women with information regarding available resources and referrals to area physicians.

Some of the services offered by the center include: a free Breast Self-Examination Clinic, diagnostic services such as ultrasound and mammography, a Diet-Instruction Clinic, as well as community education programs on important topics such as PMS (pre-menstrual syndrome), osteoporosis and breast cancer.

During 90 years of growth, from an 11-bed hospital on West Ottawa Street to a 502-bed major teaching institution which offers the most modern health care services available today, the goal of Sparrow Hospital remains the same — to provide high quality patient care in the most economical way possible.

Spartan Paper and Office Supply Company

From One-Man Operation to Small Businessman of the Year

Just 10 years ago Dave Buxton was an unknown entrepreneur who was hoping to make his mark in the Lansing business world. Today, he runs one of the nation's fastest growing companies and has been officially recognized as one of his community's outstanding business leaders.

It was on April Fools Day in 1975 that Buxton established Spartan Paper and Office Supply Company in the extra bedroom of his East Lansing apartment. Buxton was the new firm's only employee and had to perform the duties of salesman, warehouse worker, clerk and customer service representative all by himself. He even had to use a friend's truck to make deliveries.

Buxton quickly proved, however, that he was a talented businessman and soon hired a full-time delivery driver, moved to a larger warehouse and began recruiting salesmen. With the advice of Arnold Robinson, who had accrued more than 40 years' experience in the office supply business before joining Spartan, Buxton steadily increased both his staff and his delivery service. Within five years his warehouse space had expanded from just 480 feet to a sprawling 15,000 feet, and his staff had jumped from two to 31 employees. The increase gave him a unique competitive edge when landing large commercial contracts

in the Lansing area and the demand for Buxton's office supplies and paper products kept growing.

Now, in the mid-1980's, Spartan Paper and Office Supply is a leading mid-Michigan business and twice has been recognized by Inc. 500 as one of the 500 fastest growing companies in the United States. Buxton, who currently serves as the firm's president and sales manager, doesn't have to do all the work by himself anymore. He employs 70 people with a payroll of more than $1.5 million, and the extra bedroom where he began back in 1975 could fit into a small corner of the thousands of feet of warehouse space that now houses the firm's huge inventory.

Buxton is especially proud of the abilities and professionalism of his staff and has a reputation for rewarding employees for their good work. Many of Spartan's officers and top salesmen were originally hired as delivery drivers and advanced through the company because of their hard work and dedication to providing high-quality services to the firm's clients.

Located on Commerce Drive in South Lansing, Spartan has been a long-time leader in supplying local businesses with everything from Scotch tape to office furniture. The company has gained considerable expertise in advising major Fortune 500 clients on

office design systems which improve the work flow and productivity of employees. Its dozen delivery trucks guarantee prompt and dependable service for clients and the enormous Spartan inventory can accommodate "rush" orders within hours.

During the past five years, Buxton has supplemented his already comprehensive services with sales in institutional and modular furniture. To support its tremendous growth in the furniture market, Spartan now has a full-time design department comprised of Michigan State University graduates.

As Spartan Paper and Office Supply has grown and prospered, Dave Buxton has been increasingly recognized for his business ability and his commitment to civic activities. In 1982, for example, he was honored by the Greater Lansing Chamber of Commerce as Small Businessman of the Year. He has also been recognized by President Reagan, the Wall Street Journal and Time for his work with an educational charity, Assistance, Inc.

While Buxton is interested in markets outside the Lansing area, he still believes that the unusual blend of state government, numerous law firms, a major university and the many area business offices make Lansing an ideal location for Spartan Paper and Office Supply.

Dave Buxton

Story Incorporated

Automotive story creates an impact on community

The story of Story Incorporated is an American success story; it is a story with strong ties to Lansing history; it is a true story; and, it is a continuing story.

This story is about how Karl D. Story took a keen interest in cars and turned it into one of Lansing's strongest businesses with two major Oldsmobile dealerships in the birthplace and headquarters of Oldsmobile.

His ability to successfully sell Oldsmobiles did not go unnoticed by General Motors executives. In just six years after his first association with Fincher Olds of Miami, he was able to purchase in 1954 an Oldsmobile dealership virtually in the shadows of the Olds assembly line and within three blocks of where Ransom E. Olds tinkered on his first horseless carriage.

The dealership was located in the heart of downtown Lansing, just two blocks from where the first Capitol was constructed a century earlier and three blocks from the current Capitol.

Faced with limited space and high overhead in operating an auto dealership in a downtown area, Mr. Story demonstrated the foresight and leadership that made him and his business operations a success. He reasoned that since most of his customers have headed for the suburbs, he would locate his showrooms and service area where they would have easy access. And he would have room to build spacious facilities.

The result was a move in 1960 to its present location at 3165 East Michigan Ave., the historically important artery between the campus of Michigan State University and the Capitol. The dealership was built in what has become the retailing heart of the Lansing-East Lansing area. However, it was kept close to its Lansing roots: from the front of the dealership, the Capitol Dome can be spotted several blocks west and the fringe of the beautiful campus can be seen two blocks east.

The dealership itself is just as modern and attractive today as it was when it was built a quarter of a century ago. The prize-winning design that Mr. Story commissioned and approved was copied by many other dealerships around the country.

The wisdom of locating at a site adjacent to the area's first suburban shopping complex bore fruit when an expressway was constructed just two blocks away, giving loyal Story customers and potential Oldsmobile buyers easy access to one of the nation's leading Oldsmobile dealerships.

The importance of easier access for the customer was not lost. Soon, Story wrote another chapter by moving the University Oldsmobile dealership from the outskirts of downtown across from Sparrow Hospital to the southside of Lansing, near the southern suburban area. Perhaps more importantly, the dealership is adjacent to an expressway giving Oldsmobile buyers and owners easy access from as far away as Howell and Detroit to the southeast and to Portland and Ionia to the northwest.

These judicial moves have brought the Story Oldsmobile operation to the forefront of Oldsmobile sales: the two outlets have helped Story become one of the largest dealerships in retail sales in the country. Offering the complete line of Oldsmobiles, recreational vehicles, GMC trucks, Nissan cars and trucks and Isuzu cars and trucks, both locations employ more than 250 people.

But Karl Story was not one to be satisfied with these accomplishments. Foreseeing the growing demand for foreign made automobiles, Mr. Story wisely added to his product line. He now handles Nissan and Isuzu cars and trucks. His three Nissan franchises in Michigan made him the largest volume Nissan dealer east of the Mississippi River. Besides expanding to dealerships around Michigan, New York, and in Florida, Story Incorporated has established two insurance companies, a large leasing company and a real estate investment firm as well as a diesel engine distributorship.

Although Mr. Story moved his dealerships to the outskirts of Lansing, he did not forget downtown and its importance to a thriving city. While many firms were abandoning the area, Story Incorporated purchased the 400 block of South Washington, which contained the former Arbaugh Department store, a downtown landmark since 1906. It is a short block away from the Story's former downtown dealership. This effort brought a fresh face to a previously decaying portion of the business district. So successful was Mr. Story in rejuvenating three buildings in the block, it became the subject of a nationwide advertising campaign. Story Incorporated, Michigan Manufacturers Association, and the Michigan AFL-CIO offices are among many tenants proud to be based in the Plaza I-II-III complex.

The leadership shown in rejuvenating the 400 block is typical of Mr. Story's commitment to Lansing and Michigan. Mr. Karl Story has served on numerous boards, including Sparrow Hospital, First of America and Northwood Institute. He received the Distinguished Citizen Award from the Michigan State University Board of Trustees. This was an addition to the numerous Dealer of the Year and service awards he has earned from Oldsmobile.

A firm which has the former president of two major universities helping operate it can't help but be public spirited. So it is no surprise that Dr. Edgar L. Harden, Vice Chairman of Story Incorporated and one-time president of Northern Michigan University and later Michigan State University, is proud to point out that the corporation follows the philosophy expressed by Abraham Lincoln: "so live that (the) community is proud of you."

Karl and his wife, Kay, have two daughters. Older daughter, Eleanor Jean, is married to Leo Jerome, President, Key Oldsmobile, Inc. in Warren, Michigan. Nancy, the younger daughter, is married to Douglas Milbury who is President of Story Incorporated. The Milbury's and their three children, Mark, Todd, and Christyna, live in East Lansing.

Not content just to sit back and enjoy their successes, under the direction of Mr. Doug Milbury the Story organization is always searching for additional challenges and new areas of diversification. Mr. Milbury continues the tradition of community-mindedness, returning personal service to his community as well as financial aid. In 1984, Mr. Milbury was President of the Capital Area United Way when the campaign far exceeded its goals. He serves on the Board of Directors of the Chief Okemos Boy Scout Council and the First of America Bank.

And the third generation of this dynasty is yet to come, carrying surely that same dedication. The "Story" is certain to proudly continue through the Story generations.

WKAR-TV, Channel 23

Partners with Lansing

WKAR-TV has been partners with Lansing since 1954. Now, more than three decades later, the Michigan State University public television station brings to the community's residents an enticing mix of entertainment and information.

We're the place for the performing arts, bringing "Great Performances" by the world's most renowned musicians, opera presented "Live From the Met," and drama from England and America into viewer's homes.

"Great Performances" brings dance, drama, and music.

We're a sports arena, too, with broadcasts of MSU football, basketball and hockey games and championship skating. Programs like "Michigan Outdoors" expand that arena to the lakes and woods of our state.

WKAR-TV is a classroom. Parents find that "Sesame Street" and "Mister Rogers Neighborhood" provide their children with the benefits of a nursery school, teaching them basic learning skills and values. The adult classroom features programs like "Vietnam," "The Brain," and "The Constitution: That Delicate Balance," available for credit at Michigan State University and Lansing Community College. Others learn more informally by watching "How-To" shows

"Sesame Street" helps educate pre-school children.

on cooking, painting, home renovation and other subjects.

WKAR-TV is a science and nature center. Programs like "Nova" and "The Brain" make life's most complicated and abstract ideas easier to understand, while "Nature" and "National Geographic Specials" bring into focus the lives and living patterns of the world's great animals.

"Off the Record" is one of several programs produced by WKAR-TV and aired statewide.

We're a town hall, providing news and information on contemporary issues with programs like "The MacNeil/Lehrer NewsHour," "Washington Week In Review," "Off the Record" and Michigan government specials, which help make our state's government more accessible.

WKAR-TV is an investment center, with "Wall Street Week" and "Nightly Business Report" providing sound advice. We're an armchair travel agency, a movie theatre, a museum filled with great art and treasures.

WKAR-TV is not only a part of Lansing, but Lansing is a part of us as well. Many take an active role in the station itself, volunteering for the Auction, membership drives, and in the station offices. The Community Advisory Board and Corporate Development Council provide valuable input to station management. And, the partnership with the community provides the station with two-thirds of its annual budget.

Community volunteers answer phones during membership drives.

Businesses find WKAR-TV's desirable audience a useful target for their marketing strategy. Whether they participate by underwriting programs or donating items to Auction, businesses realize their partnership with WKAR-TV is a mutually beneficial and valuable one.

Gallery. Theatre. Town Hall. Science and Nature Center. Travel Agency. Sports Arena. Concert Hall. Volunteer Center.

WKAR-TV is, indeed, "Partners With Lansing."

WLNS-TV

WLNS Feels "Lansing is Special"

WLNS-TV, Channel 6, has the unique distinction of not only being Lansing and Mid-Michigan's oldest television station, but also the youngest! For over 34 years, WLNS-TV was known to Lansing as WJIM-TV. The transition took place in 1984, when Backe Communications purchased WJIM-TV and sister station WDKY-TV of LaCrosse, Wisconsin. On July 15, 1984, Channel 6 started their broadcast day with the new call letters WLNS-TV.

In 1950, Gross Telecasting, which then owned Lansing's pioneer radio station, introduced the strange new concept known as television to the area. For founder Harold Gross, this was a serious gamble. Television, which demanded a major financial commitment, was thought by many people to be a fad and a risky investment. Ignoring the warnings, Gross broadcast the first black and white pictures across Mid-Michigan from a cramped studio atop the Bank of Lansing building. WJIM-TV had become part of the first one hundred stations in the United States to go on the air.

During the 1950's, only a limited number of stations were granted a license to broadcast. WJIM-TV was one of those stations and was allowed to select programming from any of the national networks. Local viewers saw on Channel 6 a variety of programming from CBS, NBC, ABC and the no longer operating Dumont Network. It was the "Golden Age of Television" and WJIM-TV broadcast the very best the networks had to offer.

Programing during the early years of television was actually an extension of many popular radio shows. Lansing viewers were delighted to see their favorite radio personalities come to life on a flickering black and white screen. Jack Benny, Bob Hope, Fred Allen and Amos and Andy were a few who captured the hearts of those who tuned in to watch each week.

This was a time of innovation for the industry. Unlike radio, television programming had no precedent to work from. National and local stations had to experiment to develop quality programs from scratch. WJIM-TV made a commitment to innovative programming in 1950 and WLNS-TV continues that commitment to quality programming today.

In 1953, WJIM-TV moved to the station's current location. Once considered the edge of town, the station sits on what has become the busy corner of East Saginaw and Howard Street. From the spectacular new studios, WJIM-TV began extensive production of a number of locally produced programs. Many who grew up in Lansing will remember, "Ranger Jim," and later, "Alley Cat and the Mayor." Many learned to cook with Martha Dixon and "Copper Kettle," or fondly recall the "Country House Matinee," a local variety program. Channel 6 became a part of the lives of Lansing area residents.

WLNS-TV continues that heritage today. Channel 6 remains the dominant figure in Lansing television from morning to night. During an average week, over 90% of Lansing area residents will tune in to Channel 6 for locally produced or network television programming. WLNS-TV takes great pride in offering local news, special presentations and entertainment to the city. The station has made the strongest commitment to serving the people of the Lansing area.

Part of that commitment is in keeping Lansing in touch with the events affecting our city. "NewsCenter 6" has become a trusted news source. Utilizing the area's only mobile live unit, "NewsCenter 6" brings the latest information from Lan-

Live election night coverage at Channel 6, 1960.

WLNS-TV Studios today.

sing and the world to viewers seven times a day. The team of skilled reporters, producers, and technicians are dedicated to delivering the latest news in a clear, accurate, and fair manner.

Channel 6 is also proud of its commitment to public affairs programming. WLNS-TV has five programs which allow a closer, more personal look at issues affecting our area. "People Ask," takes today's issue to the community. A roving camera allows local residents to ask questions or express their views. "Minority Viewpoint" examines the issues affecting Lansing's minority community and "Michigan Focus" puts the state's problems and successes into a local perspective. These are a few of the many shows which attempt to look at not only the big problems, but the rarely discussed problems as well.

Direct contact with our viewers is also an important concern of WLNS-TV. Channel 6 has helped develop programs which combat hunger, and teenage drunk driving. We have encouraged strides towards better education with our "Best of the Class" and station internship programs. Each year we are proud to join the fight against Muscular Dystrophy with the Labor Day Telethon.

WLNS-TV, Channel 6, believes that it is important for a station to not only provide quality entertaining programming, but to use the airways to serve the many needs of a community. Channel 6 will continue to grow with Lansing and promote the strides our community makes. WLNS-TV feels the same about our city as the founders of Channel 6 did some 35 years ago that, "Lansing is Special!".

Courtesy University Publications

Photo Credits

Arts Council Center of Greater Lansing
BoarsHead Theatre
Bob Bouck
Gary Boynton
Boynton Photography
Buick-Oldsmobile-Cadillac Group
Matt Burton
K. R. Cranson
Coral Gables Restaurant
Diocese of Lansing
East Lansing Public Library
Doug Elbinger Studios
Jeff Fish
GayMarie Granger
Vaughn Gurganian
Robert Killips
Balthazar Korab
Lansing Community College
Lansing State Journal
LCC Lookout

Leavenworth Photographics Inc.
Michigan State Archives
MSU Archives and Historical Collections
MSU Information Services
MSU Museum
MSU Sports Information
William Mitcham
Randall Nolin
Donald Norris
David Olds
W. Spencer Parshall*
Henry Reniger
REOlds Museum
Dianne Schwartz
David A. Thomas
Marc Thomas
University Club
University Publications
Bonnie Zell

*All contemporary photos not credited or supplied by source or authors

Adams, Mrs. Frank L. *Pioneer History of Ingham County*, WynKoop, Hollenbeck and Crawford, Lansing, 1923.

"After 50 Years, 1881-1931," a publication by the Michigan Millers Mutual Insurance Company, Lansing, 1931.

Aldinger, Frederick C. *The History and Growth of the Lansing Public Schools*, Vol. I, Lansing: Lansing School District, 1847-1944.

Alumni Catalogue, Michigan State College Bulletin, June 1931, Vol. 25, No. 11.

Annual Meeting, Pioneer Society of Michigan, Lansing, 1895.

Bald, F. Clever, *Michigan in Four Centuries*, New York: Harper & Brothers, 1954.

Beal, W.J. *History of the Michigan Agricultural College* published by the Agricultural College, East Lansing, 1915.

Berg, Peter Iversen. "Welfare Capitalism at the Reo Motor Car Company, " *Michigan History*, November/December 1985, Vol. 69, No. 6.

Blair, Lyle and Kuhn, Madison. *A Short History of Michigan State*, Michigan State College Press, East Lansing, 1955.

Blaisdell, Thomas C., ed. *Semi-Centennial Celebration of Michigan State Agricultural College*, published by the College, 1907.

Board of Water & Light, 100 Years, 1885-1985, 1984 Annual Report, Lansing.

Borbas, Hope. "How Come Lake Lansing," Friends of Historic Meridian, Okemos, 1975.

Brown, C. Exera (cq). *History of Lansing*, Brown's Directory, 1873.

Carver, Carlisle, *Lansing's Biggest Fire*, Lansing, Mich., February 8, 1951.

Catalogue of the Agricultural College of the State of Michigan, 1860.

Catalogues of the Michigan Agricultural College, 1909-1924.

Catalogues of the State Agricultural College, 1861-1908.

Ceasar, Ford S. *The Bicentennial History of Ingham County, Michigan*. Braun-Brumfield, 1976.

Centennial Edition, 1855-1955. *State Journal*, Lansing, Mich., April 23, 1955.

Cycle and Auto Journal, "Lockwood-Ash 2-Cycle Motors," Motor Boat Department, December 1, 1906.

Darling, Birt. *City in the Forest – The Story of Lansing*. New York: Stratford House, 1950.

Dash, M. *A History of Lansing*, Lansing: W.S. George and Co., 1870.

"Diamond Jubilee," East Lansing, Mich., May 21-22, 1982 (Booklet honoring the City of East Lansing's 75th Anniversary).

"Directory of Computer Related Firms in the Lansing Metropolitan Area," Greater Lansing Chamber of Commerce, July 1984.

Druse, Joseph. *Pulpit and Prayer in Earliest Lansing*. Lansing: The Historical Society of Greater Lansing, 1959.

Durant, Samuel W. *History of Ingham and Eaton Counties*, Philadelphia: D.W. Ensign & Co., 1880.

Early Lansing, Michigan Pioneer and Historical Collections, Vol. 28, State Printers and Binders, Lansing, 1900.

Edmonds, J.P. *Early Lansing History*, Lansing: Franklin DeKleine Company, 1944.

Edmonds, James Pelton, *Gasoline Age*, Lansing: Franklin DeKleine Company, 1942.

Elliott, Frank N. "When the Railroad was King," Michigan History Division, Michigan Department of State, Lansing, 1977.

Grainger, Helen F. *Pictorial Lansing: Great City on the Grand*, Lansing: Wellman Press, 1976.

"Governor Blanchard's Report on the Revitalization of Downtown Lansing," Lansing, February, 1986.

Hayek, John. "A Pictorial History of Lake Lansing Park," *Merry-Go-Round-Up*, National Carousel Association, Vol. 11, No. 1, Spring 1984.

"Headlight Flashes," Michigan Central Railroad Magazine, 1895.

Hendry, Fay L. *Outdoor Sculpture in Lansing*, Okemos: Iota Press, 1980.

The History of Clinton County, published by the Clinton County Historical Society, St. Johns, Michigan, 1980.

History of Olds Motor Works. General Motors Corporation, Lansing, 1936.

"History of Lansing Community College," A self-survey report by the college staff. *The Lookout*, April 22, 1964.

"Industrial Directory of Metropolitan Lansing," Greater Lansing Chamber of Commerce, Lansing, Mich., 1955.

Jacobson, Helen and Wilson, Jane. *Lansing – A Look to the Past*, St. Paul's Episcopal Church, October 1975.

Letters written home by Mr. Charlie Jewell while a student at Michigan Agricultural College, 1860-1865. Part of archival collection at Michigan State University.

Kestenbaum, Justin L., editor. *At the Campus Gate: A History of East Lansing*. East Lansing: East Lansing Bicentennial Commission, 1976.

Kestenbaum, Justin L., *Out of a Wilderness*. Windsor Publishing, 1980.

Kimes, Beverly Rae, ed. *Oldsmobile: Its 75th Year*, Automobile Quarterly Publications, New York, New York, 1972.

Kooistra, George, ed. "A Profile of Michigan State University," Published September 1985 by the Division of University Relations.

Kuhn, Madison. *Michigan State: The First Hundred Years, 1855-1955*. East Lansing: Michigan State University Press, 1955.

"Lansing: A Progressive American City," Lansing Chamber of Commerce, 1926.

Lansing/East Lansing. Published by the Lansing Regional Chamber of Commerce and the Greater Lansing Board of Realtors.

Lansing, Michigan – A City of Stable Industry, Satisfied Workers and Civic Soundness. Lansing: Dick Short and Company for the Lansing Chamber of Commerce, 1926.

Lansing Centennial Souvenir Historical Program. Lansing: City of Lansing, 1959.

Summary of History of Lansing Community College, 1956-1985. Unpublished manuscript by Lansing Community College Office of Community Relations.

"Lansing and Its Yesterdays." A compilation of a portion of the Historical Material published in the 75th Anniversary Edition of the *Lansing State Journal*,, January 1, 1930.

"Lansing – This Week," The Lansing City Guide Publishing Company, 119 E. Ottawa Street, Lansing, 1925-1929.

Long, John C. *Roy Chapin*. Bethlehem, PA, privately printed, 1945.

Mason, Phillip P. "The Plank Road Craze," Great Lake Informant, Michigan History Division, Michigan Department of State, Series 2, Number 1 (date missing).

May, George S. *A Most Unique Machine: The Michigan Origins of the American Automobile Industry*. Grand Rapids, Eerdmanns, 1975.

May, George S. *R.E. Olds: Auto Industry Pioneer*. Grand Rapids: William B. Eerdmanns Publishing Company, 1977.

Memorandum '76 – Historic Lansing, Lansing Historic District Study Committee, Lansing, 1972.

Michigan Manufacturer and Financial Record, Detroit: Manufacturer Publishing Company (various volumes between 1920 and 1952).

"From Fireside and Lumbercamp." The Collection of the Michigan Historical Museum, The Michigan History Division, Michigan Department of State, 1976.

Michigan State University 1985 Facts Book, compiled by the Division of University Relations.

Metropolitan Profile, Lansing Regional Chamber of Commerce, Lansing, Michigan, 1984.

Mevis, Daniel S. *Pioneer Recollection*, Lansing: Robert Smith Printing Company, 1911.

National Grange in Michigan, Souvenir Program, Lansing, November 12-22, 1902.

Niemeyer, Glenn A. *The Automotive Career of Ransom E. Olds*. East Lansing: MSU Business Studies, 1963.

Official Guide of the Railways, New York: National Railway Publication Co., 1919.

Olds, Fred C. Mackinaw Division, *Railroad Magazine*, Vol. 59, 1952.

Olds, Fred C. "Michigan's Iron Cobweb," The Railway and Locomotive Historical Society, Railroad History, No. 129, Harvard Business School, Boston, Mass, 1973.

Olds, Fred C. "Michigan's Lumber Pikes," *Railroad Magazine*, Vol. 61, 1953.

Olds, Ransom E. "The Horseless Carriage." Michigan Engineers' Annual, 1898, pp. 92-96.

The Oracle, published annually by the Senior Class of the Lansing High School, 1892-

Perkins, James, coordinator. Lansing Area Congregations Together in Service. Directory of Churches, Religious Headquarter, Clergy and Staff, 1983-84.

Peters, Scott. "A New Home." *Michigan History*, Vol. 69, No. 5, September/October 1985.

Peterson, Eugene T. "Hunters' Heritage," Michigan United Conservation Clubs, Lansing, 1979.

History of the Agricultural College. Presented to the library of the State Agricultural College in April 1896 by A. N. Prentiss, B.S., '61. (A bound collection of documents arranged by Mr. Prentiss.)

Proctor, Hazel. *Old Lansing Town*, Great Lakes Federal Savings, Battle Creek, 1980.

Raphael, Evelyn Huber. *A History of the Haslett – Lake Lansing Area, Meridian Township, Ingham County, Michigan*. Ann Arbor: Edwards Brothers, Inc., 1985.

Reutter, J. Gottlieb. *Memories of J. Gottlieb Reutter*. Lansing, Michigan 1947.

Scientific American. "A Gasoline Steam Carriage," May 32, 1892.

"75th Anniversary, American Bank and Trust," Lansing, 1967.

The Story of the City of East Lansing on its Golden Anniversary, 1959.

Summers, Virginia. A History of the Lansing Public Library.

Towar, James D. *History of the City of East Lansing*, East Lansing: East Lansing Public Library, 1933.

"25th Anniversary, Bank of Lansing," Lansing, 1953.

"25th Anniversary Year Issue," Jackson National Life, Lansing, Michigan, 1985.

Wright, Karle T., ed. *The First 50 Years. A History of the University Club of Michigan State University, 1929-1982*. Lansing: University Club of Michigan State University, 1982.

Yarnell, Duane. *Auto Pioneering: A Remarkable Story of Ransom E. Olds, father of Oldsmobile and Reo*. Franklin DeKleine Company, Lansing, Michigan 1949.

Bank of Lansing Art Fair

Children's Ward Sparrow Hospital

ACKNOWLEDGMENTS

*T*he authors wish to thank the many Lansingites – artists, copywriters, typographers, and photographic support people – who have contributed to the production of this book. And most especially the authors who preceded them and provided the foundations on which they built: Birt Darling, Ford Ceasar, the State Journal, and Justin Kestenbaum. Equally vital, the reporters, writers and photographers, whose files provided the records of the past for our research.

Certain individuals are the well-springs of Lansing heritage that we all rely on: Jane McClary of the Lansing Public Library, John Curry and Dave Johnson of the State of Michigan Archives, the staff of the State of Michigan Library, and Dr. Fred Honhart of the Michigan State University Archives and Historical Collections. Professionally, George Kooistra's excellent mastery of books, print, and publishing were invaluable; Diana Grinwis' artistry and knowledge of the mechanicals; as were John Kroone's support and advice on computers and finances. Our thanks to America by Rail for the use of the computer and expertise of its staff, especially Bill Greenleaf. And personally, Terri Brantley's daily, patient, practical advice; Kimberly Masters who was ever pleasant and can handle anything; and the patient, supportive nurturing of Geneva Wiskemann. An added thanks to our families: the Manassahs, Thomases, Wallingtons, and Moffetts, for letting mom or dad give so much time for so little under so much pressure.

If you have enjoyed this book as much as we have in lovingly putting it together, please give thanks to our sponsors – The Partners in Progress – who made it possible.

Joyce Moffett

Photo D. Norris

Our appreciation to the City Hall staff, Jo Ellen Flaherty, Mayor Terry McKane, the publisher, and Pamela K. Fowler (pictured) as well as Rosemarie Kazenko, Lois Bennett, and Kacia Coats.